Phantom Dream™

VOLUME 1

NATSUKI TAKAYA

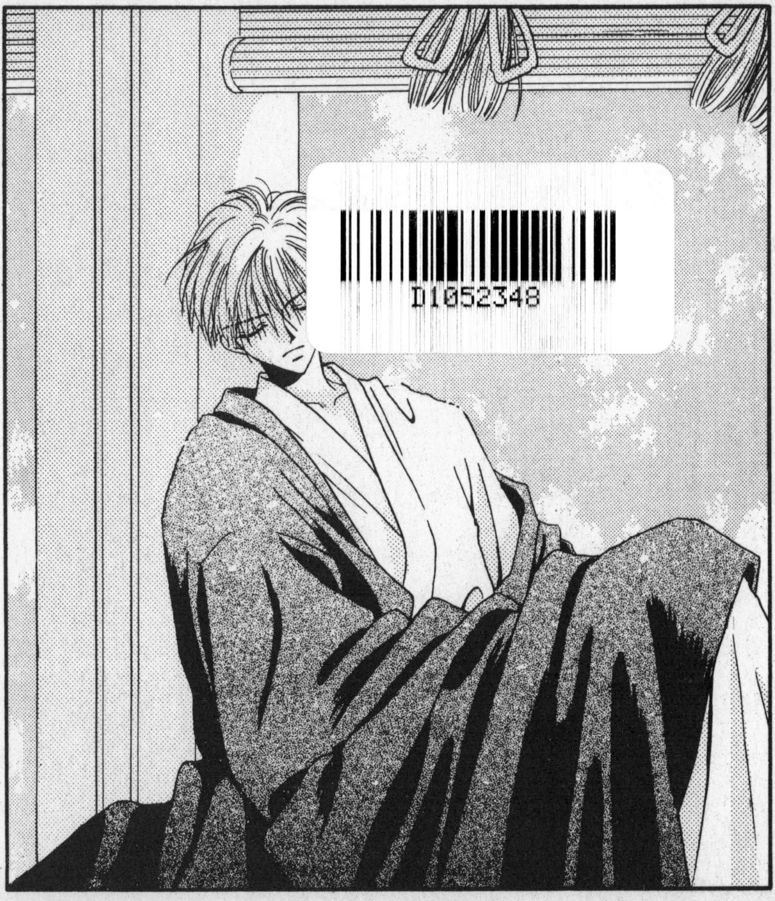

Phantom Dream Volume 1
Written by Natsuki Takaya

Translation - Beni Axia Conrad
English Adaptation - Ysabet Reinhardt MacFarlane
Retouch and Lettering - Star Print Brokers
Production Artist - Vicente Rivera, Jr.
Graphic Designer - Jose Macasocol, Jr.

Editor - Hyun Joo Kim
Pre-Production Supervisor - Vicente Rivera, Jr.
Pre-Production Specialist - Lucas Rivera
Managing Editor - Vy Nguyen
Senior Designer - Louis Csontos
Senior Designer - James Lee
Senior Editor - Bryce P. Coleman
Senior Editor - Jenna Winterberg
Associate Publisher - Marco F. Pavia
President and C.O.O. - John Parker
C.E.O. and Chief Creative Officer - Stu Levy

A  Manga

TOKYOPOP Inc.
5900 Wilshire Blvd. Suite 2000
Los Angeles, CA 90036

E-mail: info@TOKYOPOP.com
Come visit us online at www.TOKYOPOP.com

GENEIMUSOU by Natsuki Takaya © Natsuki Takaya 1994 All rights reserved. First published in Japan in 1996 by HAKUSENSHA, INC., Tokyo English language translation rights in the United States of America and Canada arranged with HAKUSENSHA, INC., Tokyo through Tuttle-Mori Agency Inc., Tokyo English text copyright © 2008 TOKYOPOP Inc.

ISBN: 978-1-4278-1089-2

First TOKYOPOP printing: December 2008
10 9 8 7 6 5 4 3 2 1
Printed in the USA

Phantom Dream

Volume 1

By Natsuki Takaya

HAMBURG // LONDON // LOS ANGELES // TOKYO

Table of Contents

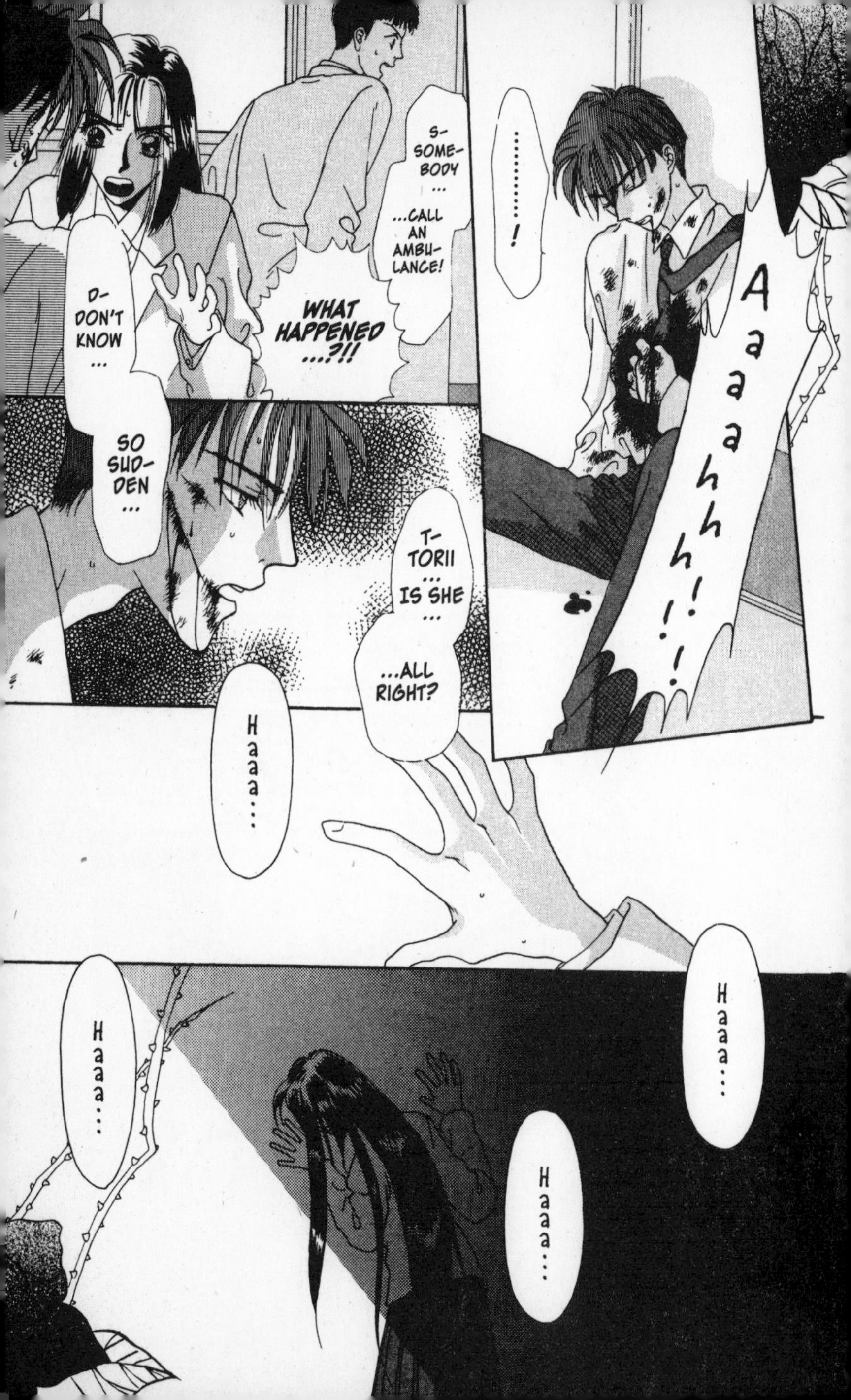

........!
Aaaahhh!!!
S-SOMEBODY ... ...CALL AN AMBULANCE!
WHAT HAPPENED ....?!!
D-DON'T KNOW ...
SO SUDDEN ...
T-TORII ... IS SHE ... ...ALL RIGHT?
Haaa...
Haaa...
Haaa...
Haaa...

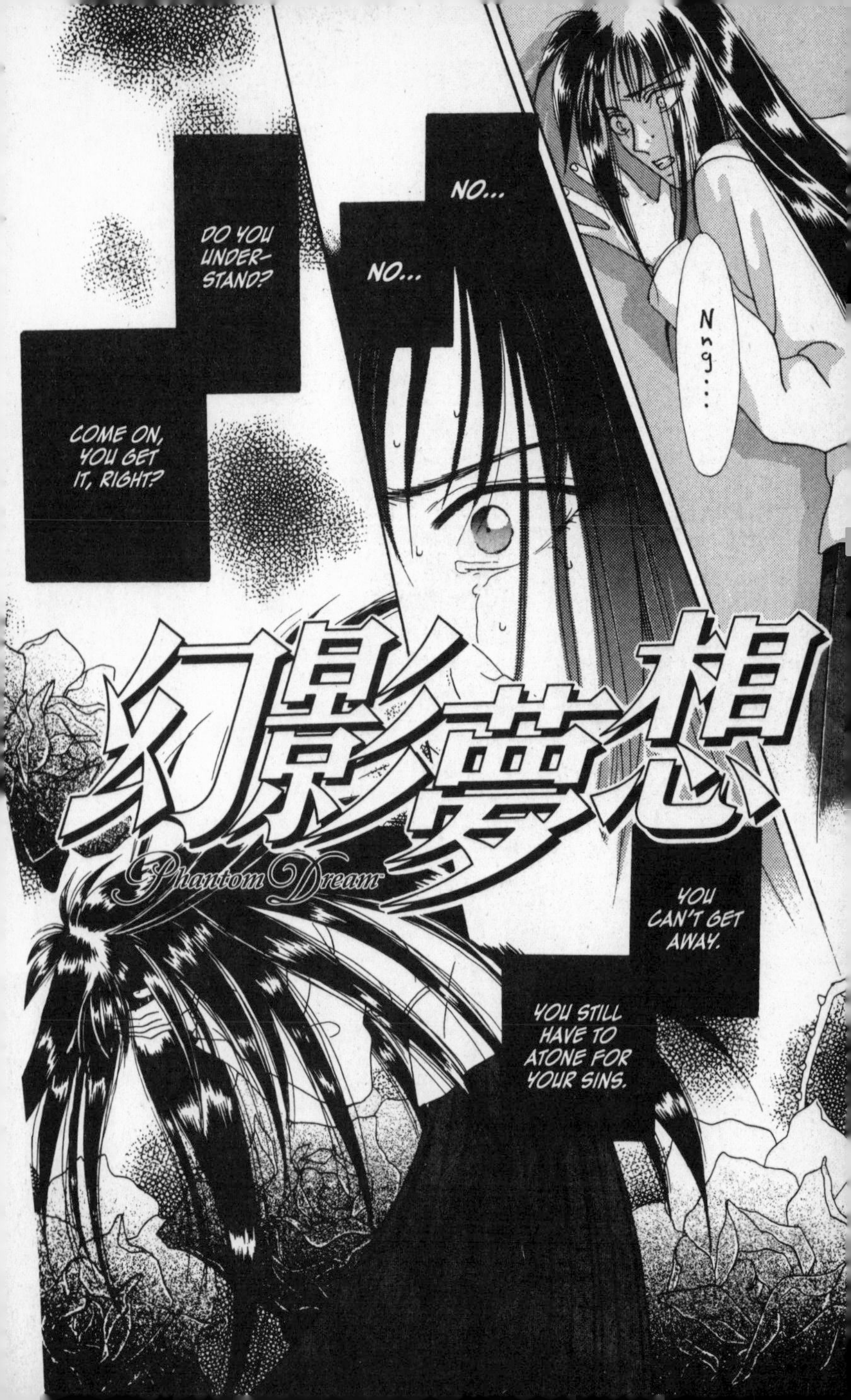
Nng...
NO...
NO...
DO YOU UNDER-STAND?
COME ON, YOU GET IT, RIGHT?
幻影夢想
Phantom Dream
YOU CAN'T GET AWAY.
YOU STILL HAVE TO ATONE FOR YOUR SINS.

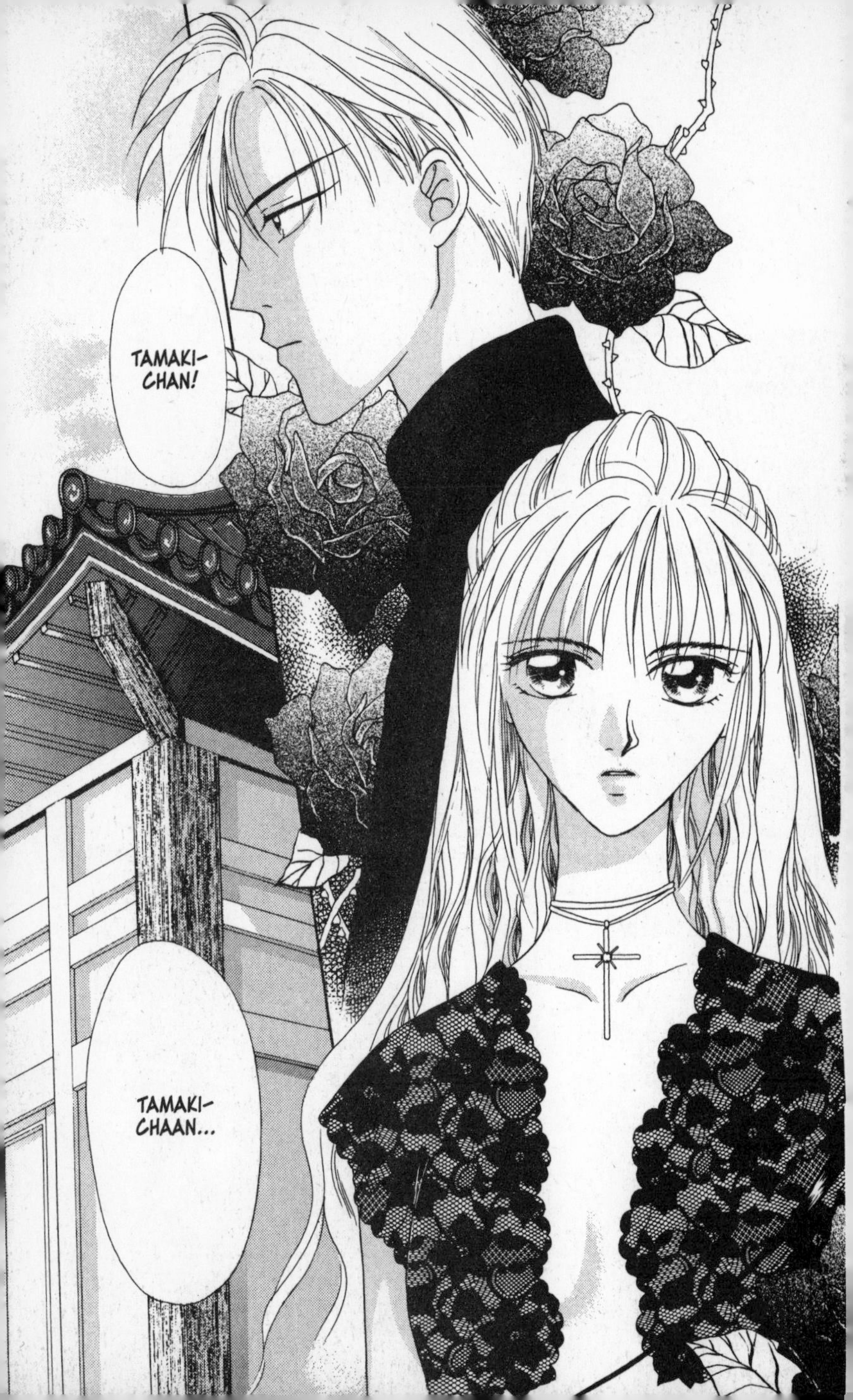
TAMAKI-CHAN!
TAMAKI-CHAAN...

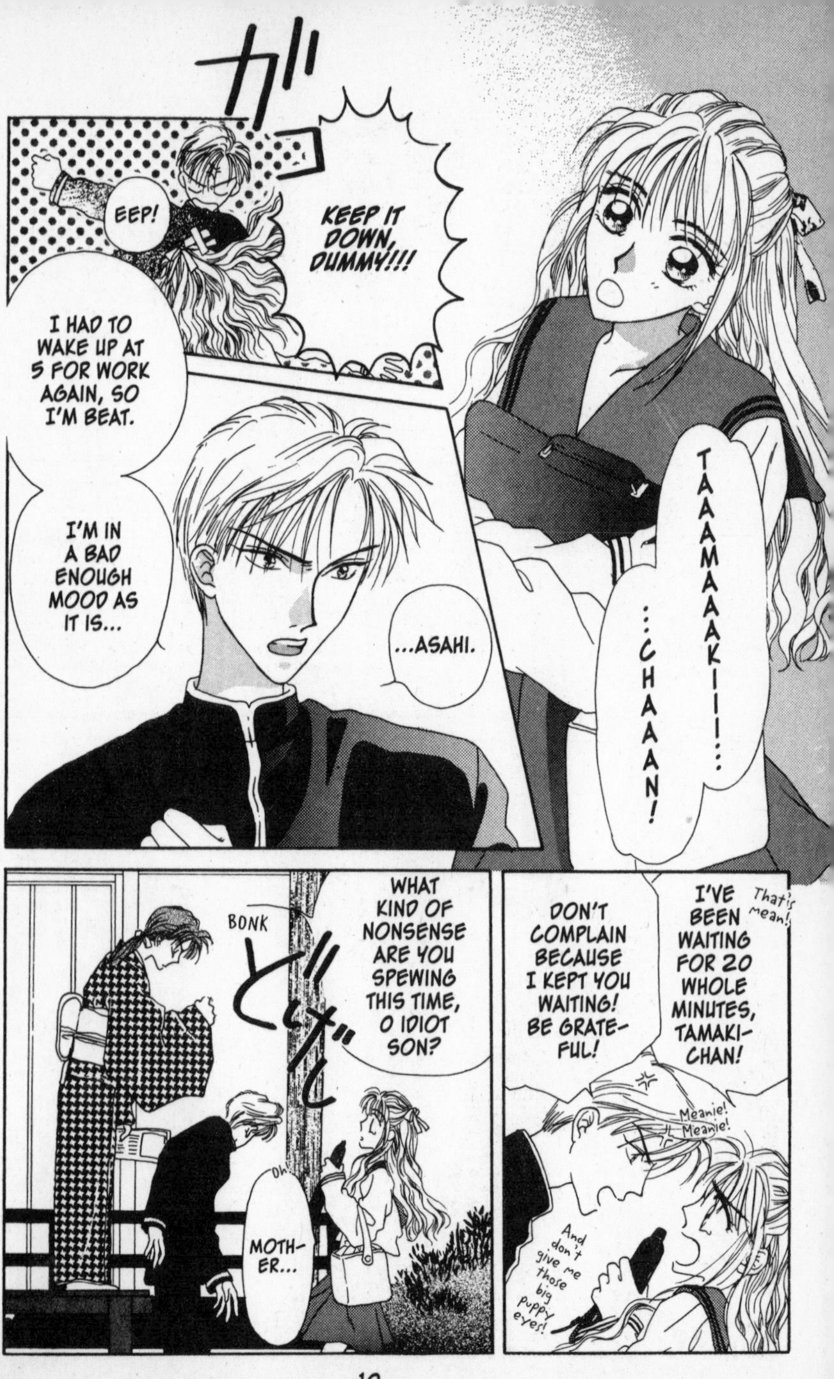
TAAAMAAAKIIII...
...CHAAAAN!
KEEP IT DOWN, DUMMY!!!
EEP!
...ASAHI.
I HAD TO WAKE UP AT 5 FOR WORK AGAIN, SO I'M BEAT.
I'M IN A BAD ENOUGH MOOD AS IT IS...
I'VE BEEN WAITING FOR 20 WHOLE MINUTES, TAMAKI-CHAN!
That's mean!
DON'T COMPLAIN BECAUSE I KEPT YOU WAITING! BE GRATE-FUL!
Meanie! Meanie!
And don't give me those big puppy eyes!
WHAT KIND OF NONSENSE ARE YOU SPEWING THIS TIME, O IDIOT SON?
BONK
Oh
MOTH-ER...

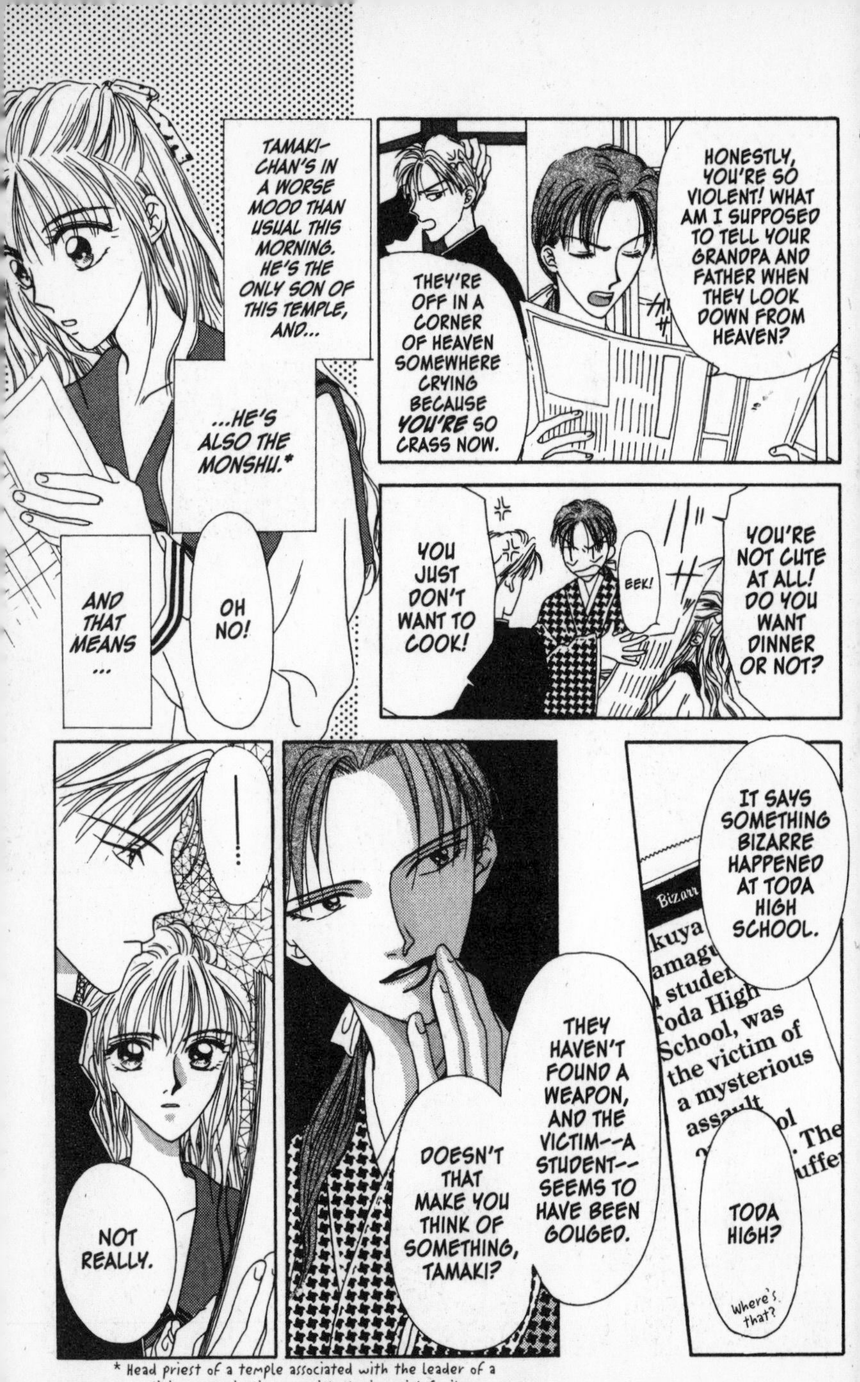
HONESTLY, YOU'RE SO VIOLENT! WHAT AM I SUPPOSED TO TELL YOUR GRANDPA AND FATHER WHEN THEY LOOK DOWN FROM HEAVEN?
THEY'RE OFF IN A CORNER OF HEAVEN SOMEWHERE CRYING BECAUSE *YOU'RE* SO CRASS NOW.
YOU'RE NOT CUTE AT ALL! DO YOU WANT DINNER OR NOT?
EEK!
YOU JUST DON'T WANT TO COOK!
TAMAKI-CHAN'S IN A WORSE MOOD THAN USUAL THIS MORNING. HE'S THE ONLY SON OF THIS TEMPLE, AND...
...HE'S ALSO THE MONSHU.*
OH NO!
AND THAT MEANS...
IT SAYS SOMETHING BIZARRE HAPPENED AT TODA HIGH SCHOOL.
TODA HIGH?
Where's that?
THEY HAVEN'T FOUND A WEAPON, AND THE VICTIM--A STUDENT--SEEMS TO HAVE BEEN GOUGED.
DOESN'T THAT MAKE YOU THINK OF SOMETHING, TAMAKI?
!
NOT REALLY.

* Head priest of a temple associated with the leader of a religious organization, or with the imperial family.

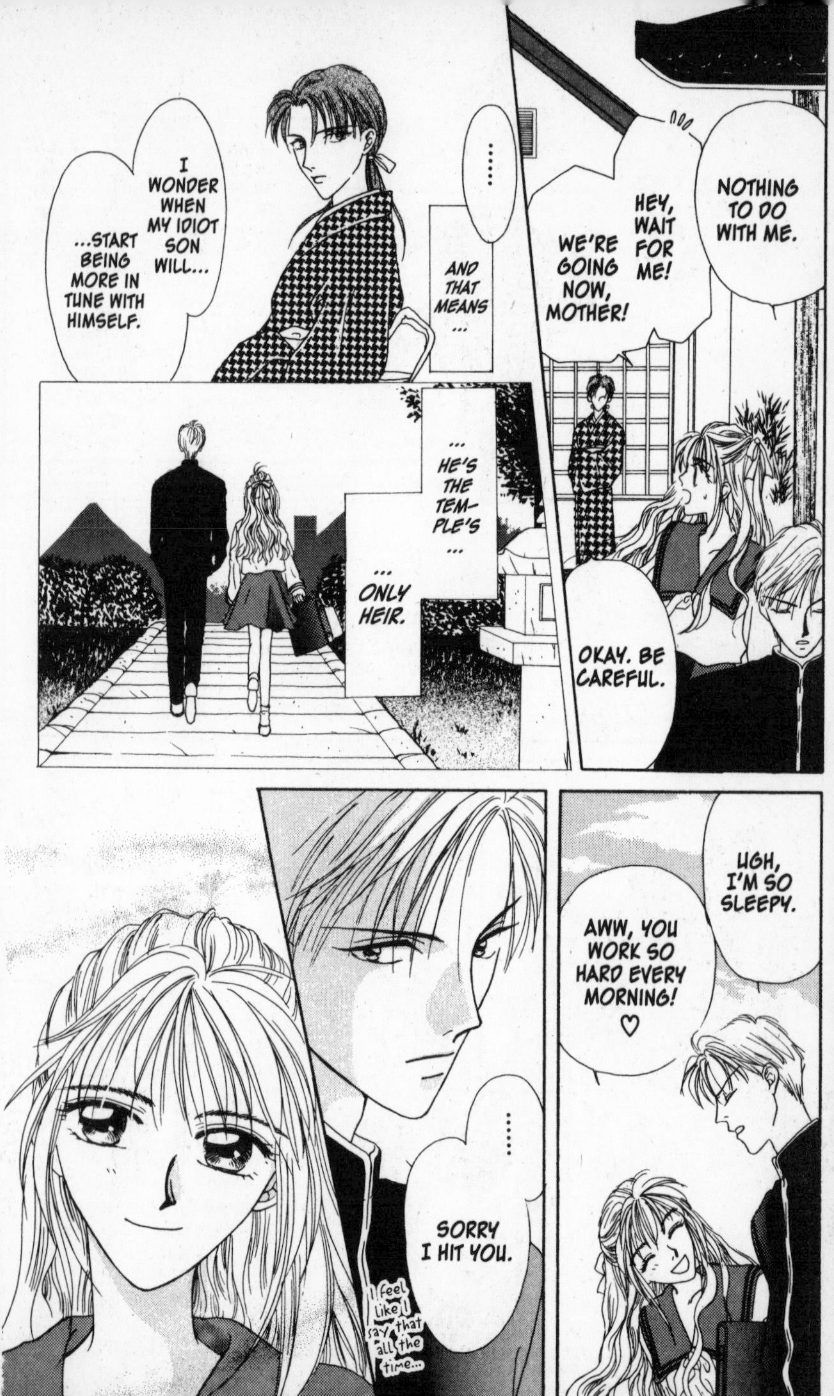
NOTHING TO DO WITH ME.
HEY, WAIT FOR ME!
WE'RE GOING NOW, MOTHER!
OKAY. BE CAREFUL.
......
AND THAT MEANS...
I WONDER WHEN MY IDIOT SON WILL...
...START BEING MORE IN TUNE WITH HIMSELF.
...HE'S THE TEMPLE'S...
...ONLY HEIR.
UGH, I'M SO SLEEPY.
AWW, YOU WORK SO HARD EVERY MORNING! ♡
......
SORRY I HIT YOU.
I feel like I say that all the time...

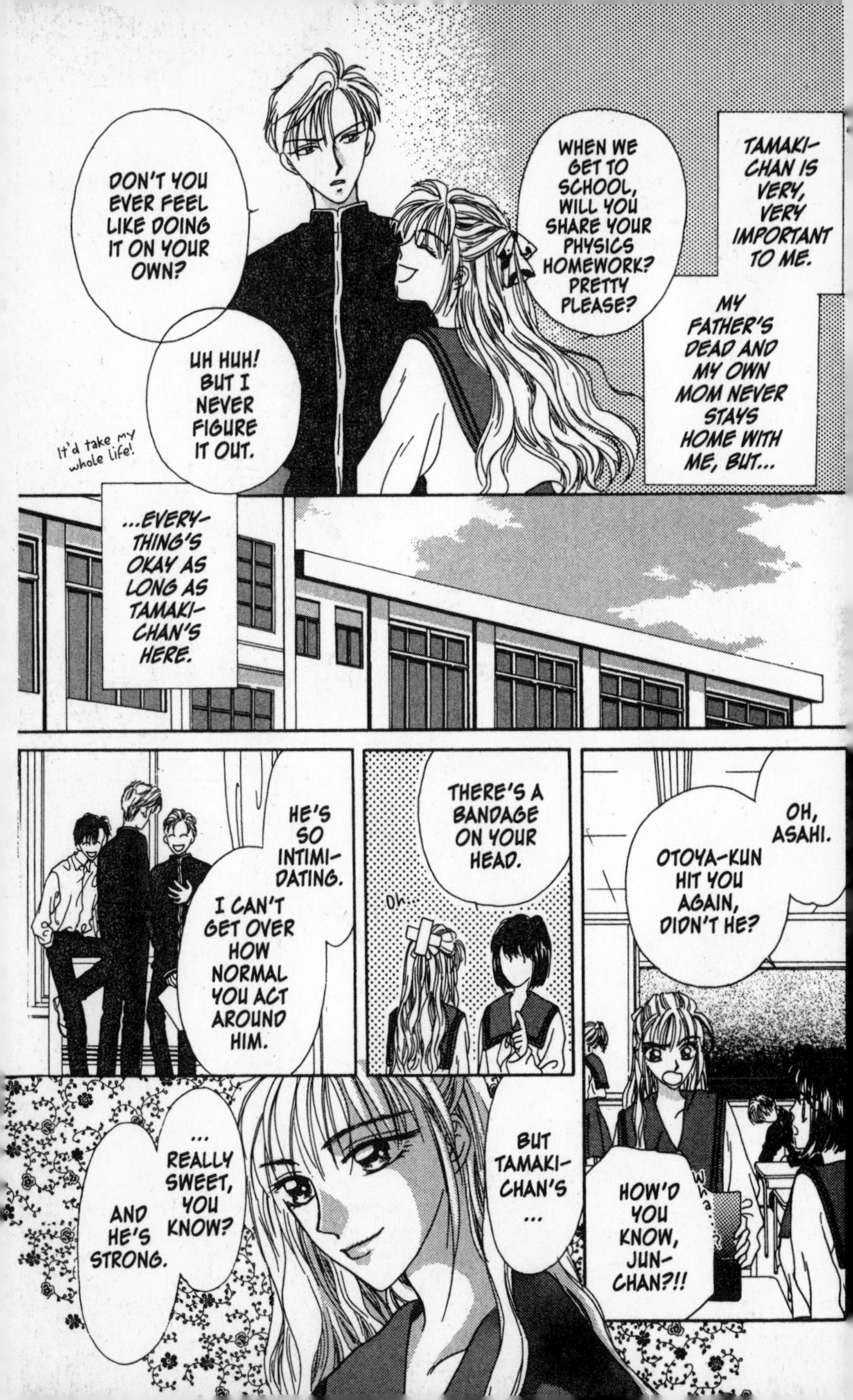
TAMAKI-CHAN IS VERY, VERY IMPORTANT TO ME.
MY FATHER'S DEAD AND MY OWN MOM NEVER STAYS HOME WITH ME, BUT...
WHEN WE GET TO SCHOOL, WILL YOU SHARE YOUR PHYSICS HOMEWORK? PRETTY PLEASE?
DON'T YOU EVER FEEL LIKE DOING IT ON YOUR OWN?
UH HUH! BUT I NEVER FIGURE IT OUT.
It'd take my whole life!
...EVERY-THING'S OKAY AS LONG AS TAMAKI-CHAN'S HERE.
OH, ASAHI.
OTOYA-KUN HIT YOU AGAIN, DIDN'T HE?
Wha...
HOW'D YOU KNOW, JUN-CHAN?!!
THERE'S A BANDAGE ON YOUR HEAD.
Oh...
HE'S SO INTIMI-DATING.
I CAN'T GET OVER HOW NORMAL YOU ACT AROUND HIM.
BUT TAMAKI-CHAN'S ...
... REALLY SWEET, YOU KNOW?
AND HE'S STRONG.

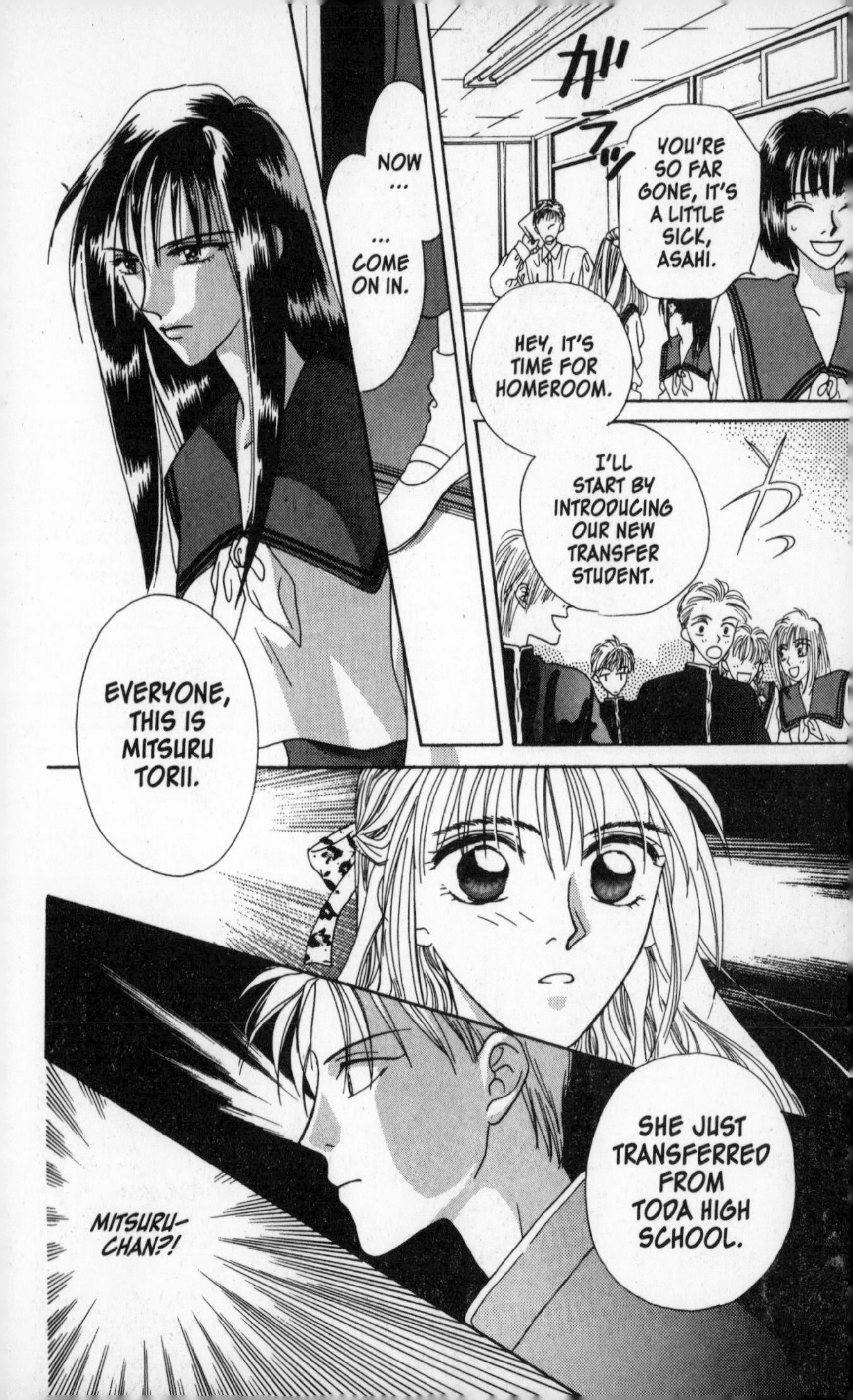
ガラッ
YOU'RE SO FAR GONE, IT'S A LITTLE SICK, ASAHI.
HEY, IT'S TIME FOR HOMEROOM.
I'LL START BY INTRODUCING OUR NEW TRANSFER STUDENT.
NOW ...
... COME ON IN.
EVERYONE, THIS IS MITSURU TORII.
SHE JUST TRANSFERRED FROM TODA HIGH SCHOOL.
MITSURU-CHAN?!

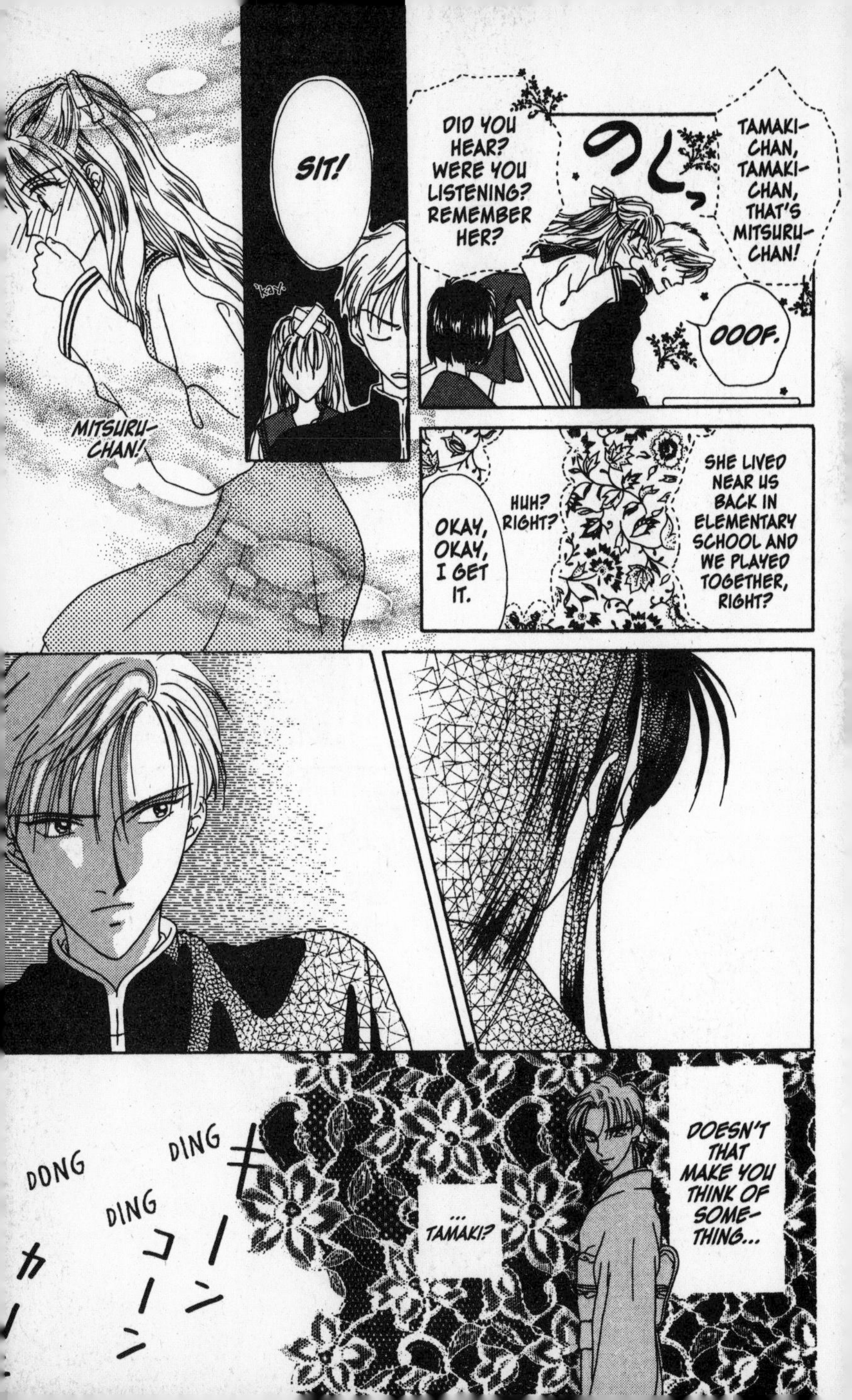
TAMAKI-CHAN, TAMAKI-CHAN, THAT'S MITSURU-CHAN!
のし
DID YOU HEAR? WERE YOU LISTENING? REMEMBER HER?
OOOF.
SHE LIVED NEAR US BACK IN ELEMENTARY SCHOOL AND WE PLAYED TOGETHER, RIGHT?
HUH? RIGHT?
OKAY, OKAY, I GET IT.
SIT!
MITSURU-CHAN!
DOESN'T THAT MAKE YOU THINK OF SOMETHING...
...TAMAKI?
DING
キーン
DING
コーン
DONG
カーン

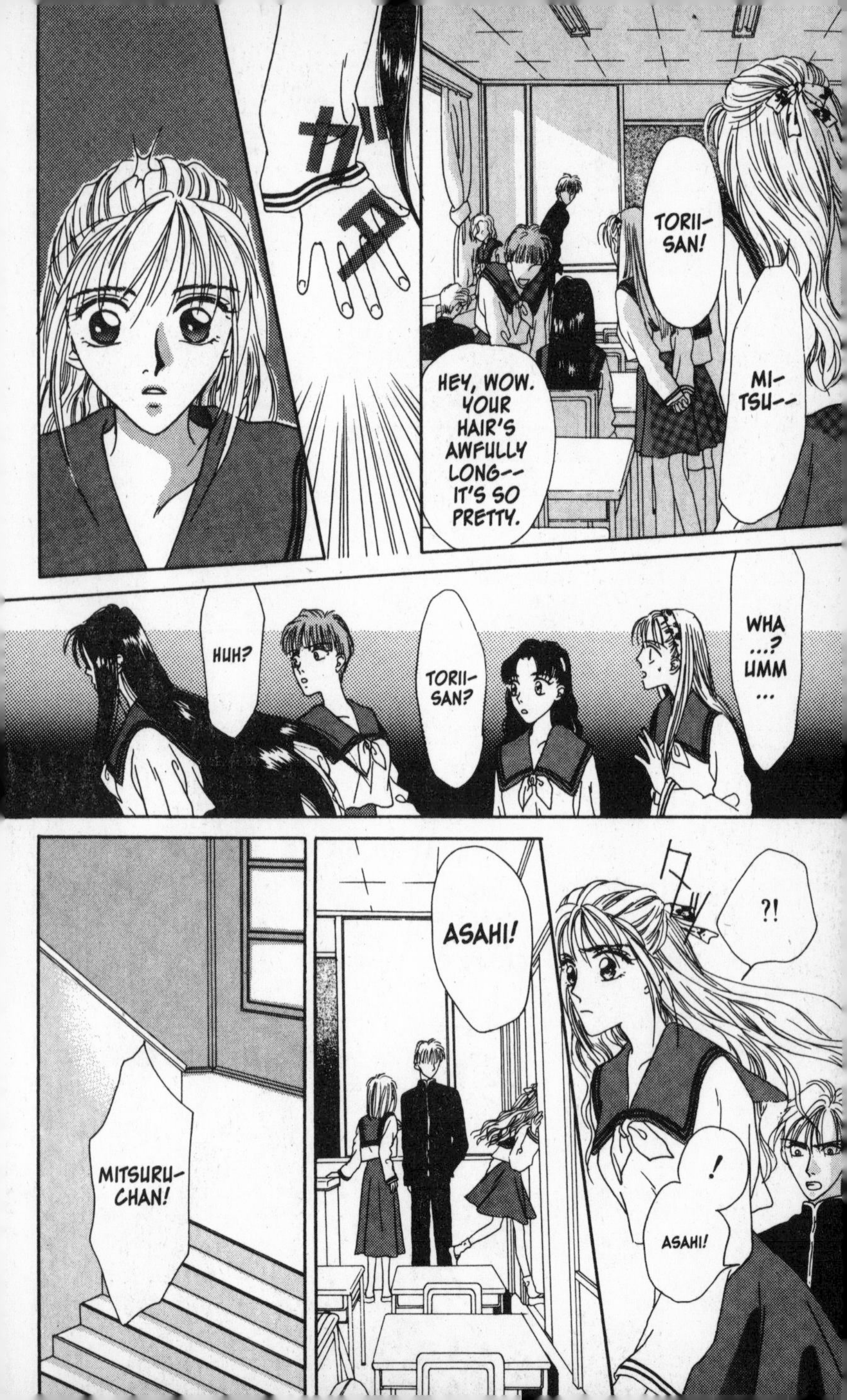

TORII-SAN!
MI-TSU--
HEY, WOW. YOUR HAIR'S AWFULLY LONG-- IT'S SO PRETTY.
ガタ
WHA ...? UMM ...
TORII-SAN?
HUH?
タッ
?!
ASAHI!
!
ASAHI!
MITSURU-CHAN!

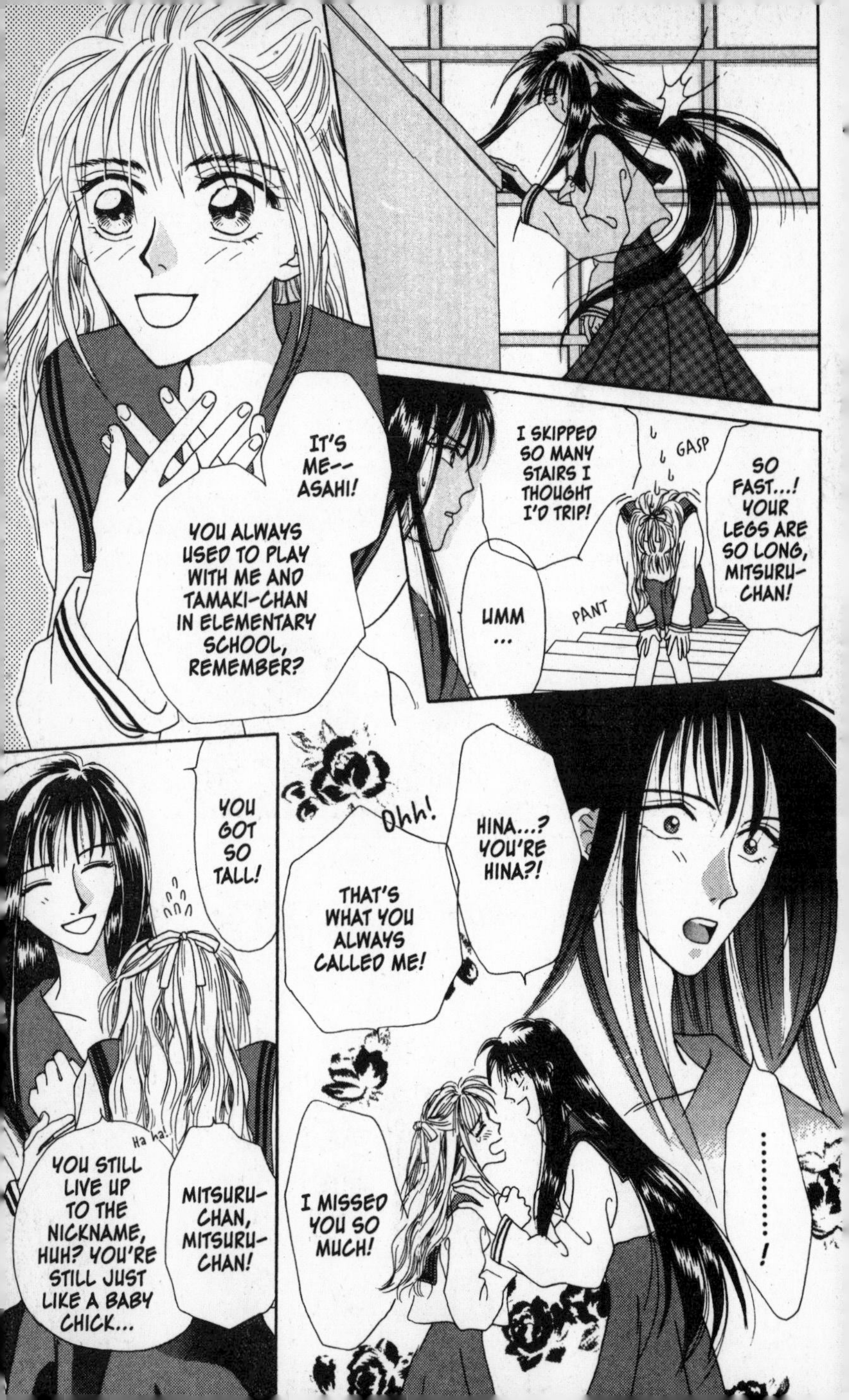
SO FAST...! YOUR LEGS ARE SO LONG, MITSURU-CHAN!
GASP
I SKIPPED SO MANY STAIRS I THOUGHT I'D TRIP!
PANT
UMM ...
IT'S ME-- ASAHI!
YOU ALWAYS USED TO PLAY WITH ME AND TAMAKI-CHAN IN ELEMENTARY SCHOOL, REMEMBER?
........!
HINA...? YOU'RE HINA?!
Ohh!
THAT'S WHAT YOU ALWAYS CALLED ME!
I MISSED YOU SO MUCH!
YOU GOT SO TALL!
MITSURU-CHAN, MITSURU-CHAN!
Ha ha!
YOU STILL LIVE UP TO THE NICKNAME, HUH? YOU'RE STILL JUST LIKE A BABY CHICK...

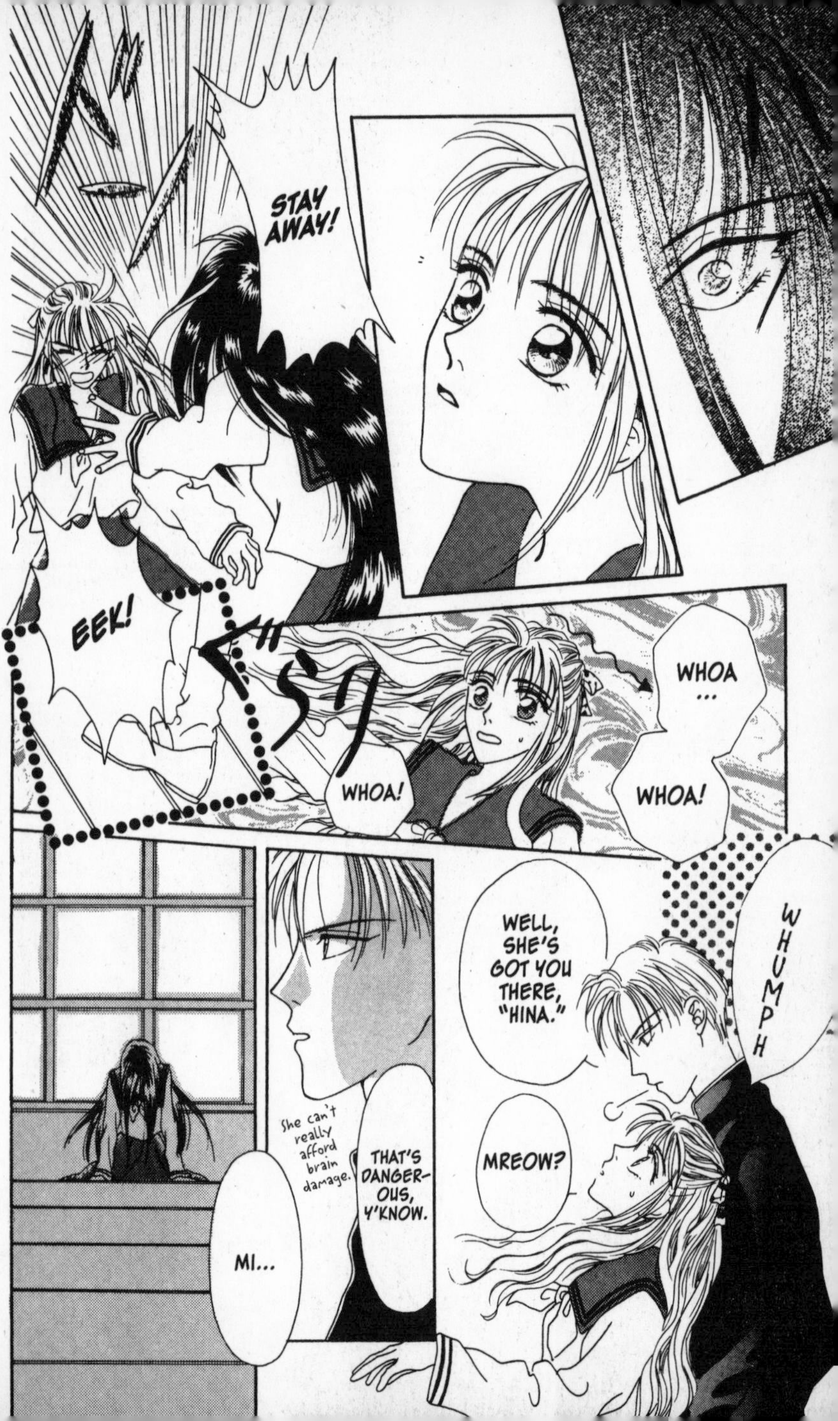
STAY AWAY!
EEK!
WHOA ...
WHOA!
WHOA!
WHUMPH
WELL, SHE'S GOT YOU THERE, "HINA."
MREOW?
THAT'S DANGER-OUS, Y'KNOW.
She can't really afford brain damage.
MI...

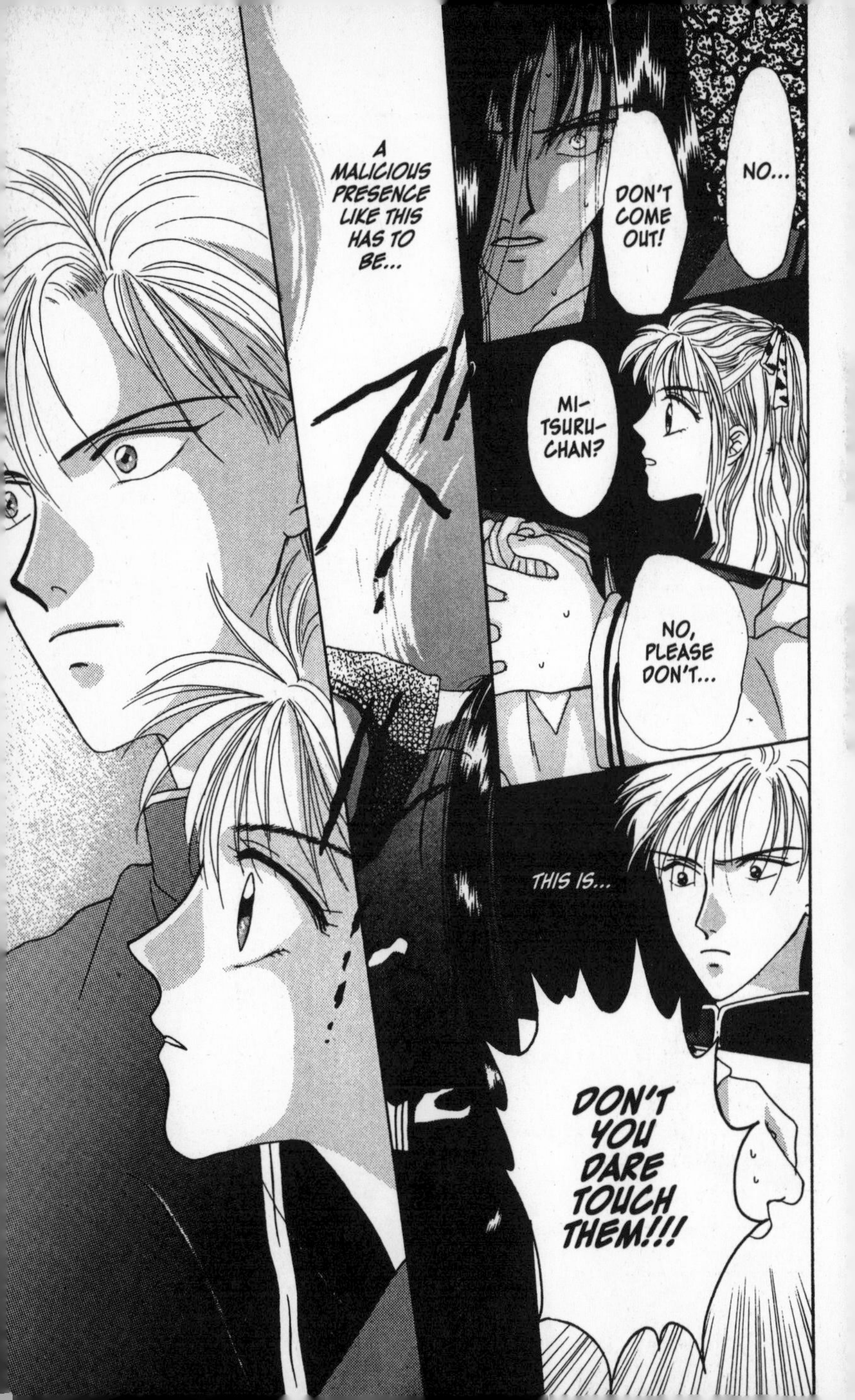
NO...
DON'T COME OUT!
MI-TSURU-CHAN?
NO, PLEASE DON'T...
THIS IS...
DON'T YOU DARE TOUCH THEM!!!
A MALICIOUS PRESENCE LIKE THIS HAS TO BE...

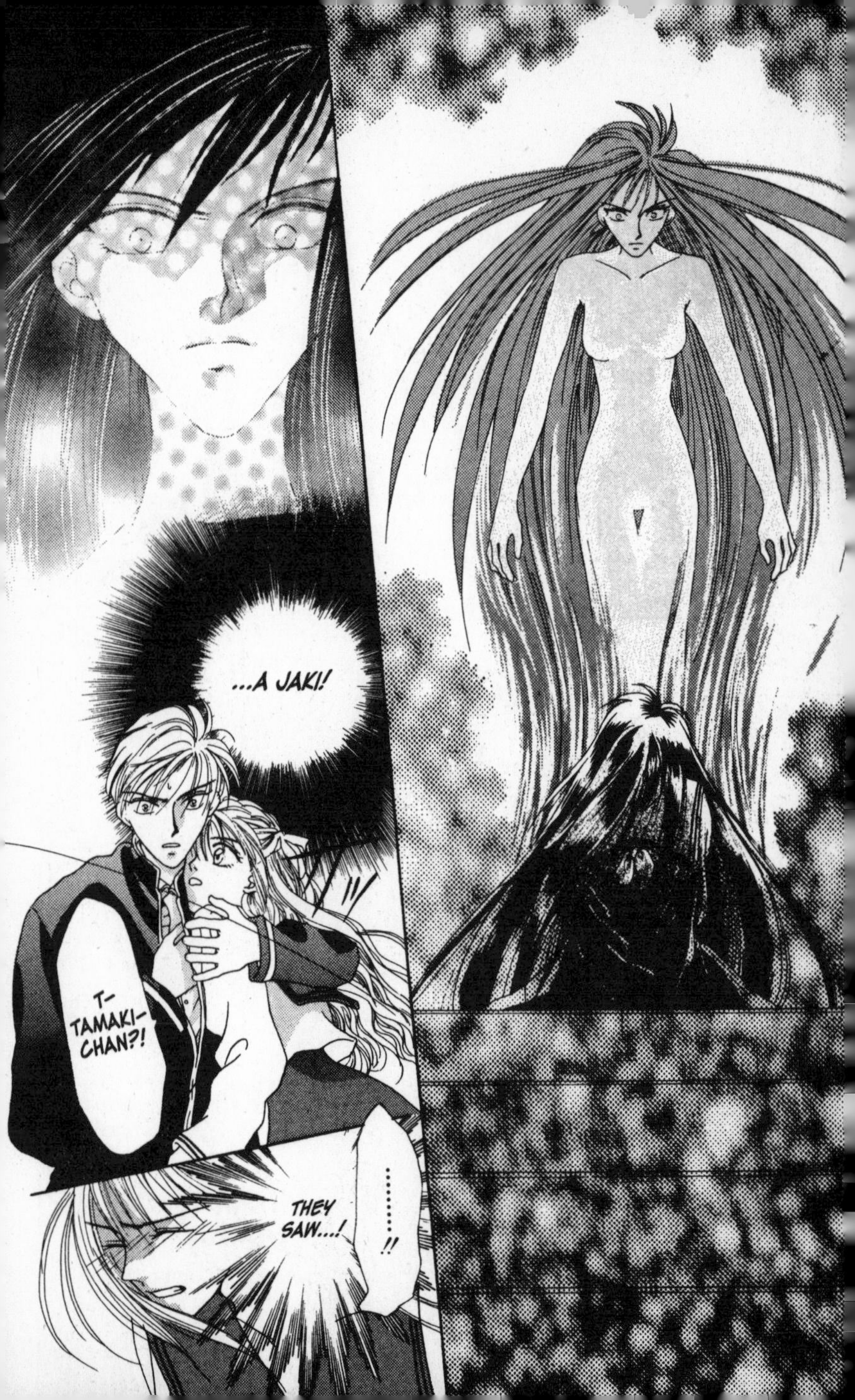
...A JAKI!
!!
T-TAMAKI-CHAN?!
......!!
THEY SAW...!

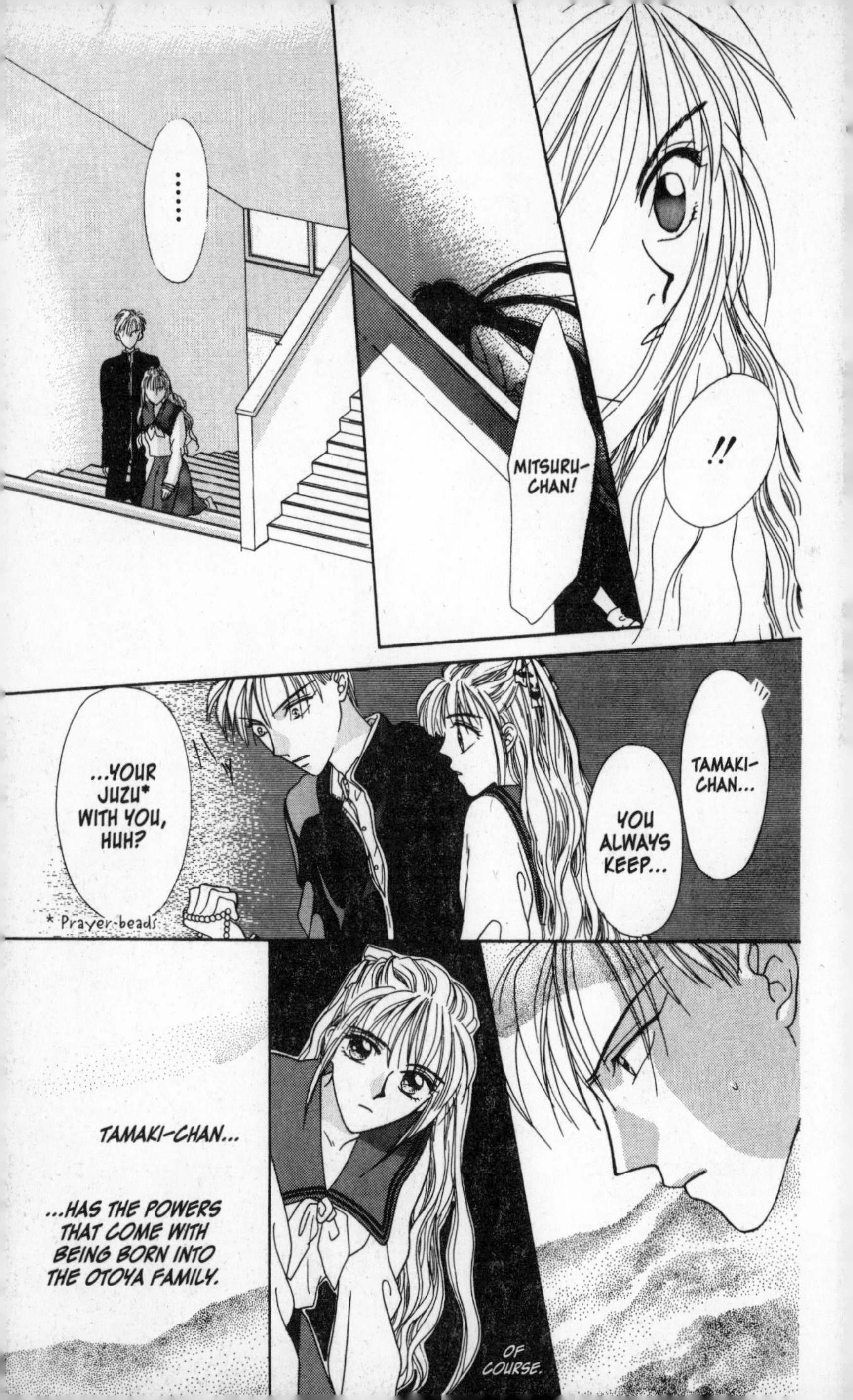
!!
MITSURU-CHAN!
......
TAMAKI-CHAN...
YOU ALWAYS KEEP...
...YOUR JUZU* WITH YOU, HUH?
* Prayer-beads
OF COURSE.
TAMAKI-CHAN...
...HAS THE POWERS THAT COME WITH BEING BORN INTO THE OTOYA FAMILY.

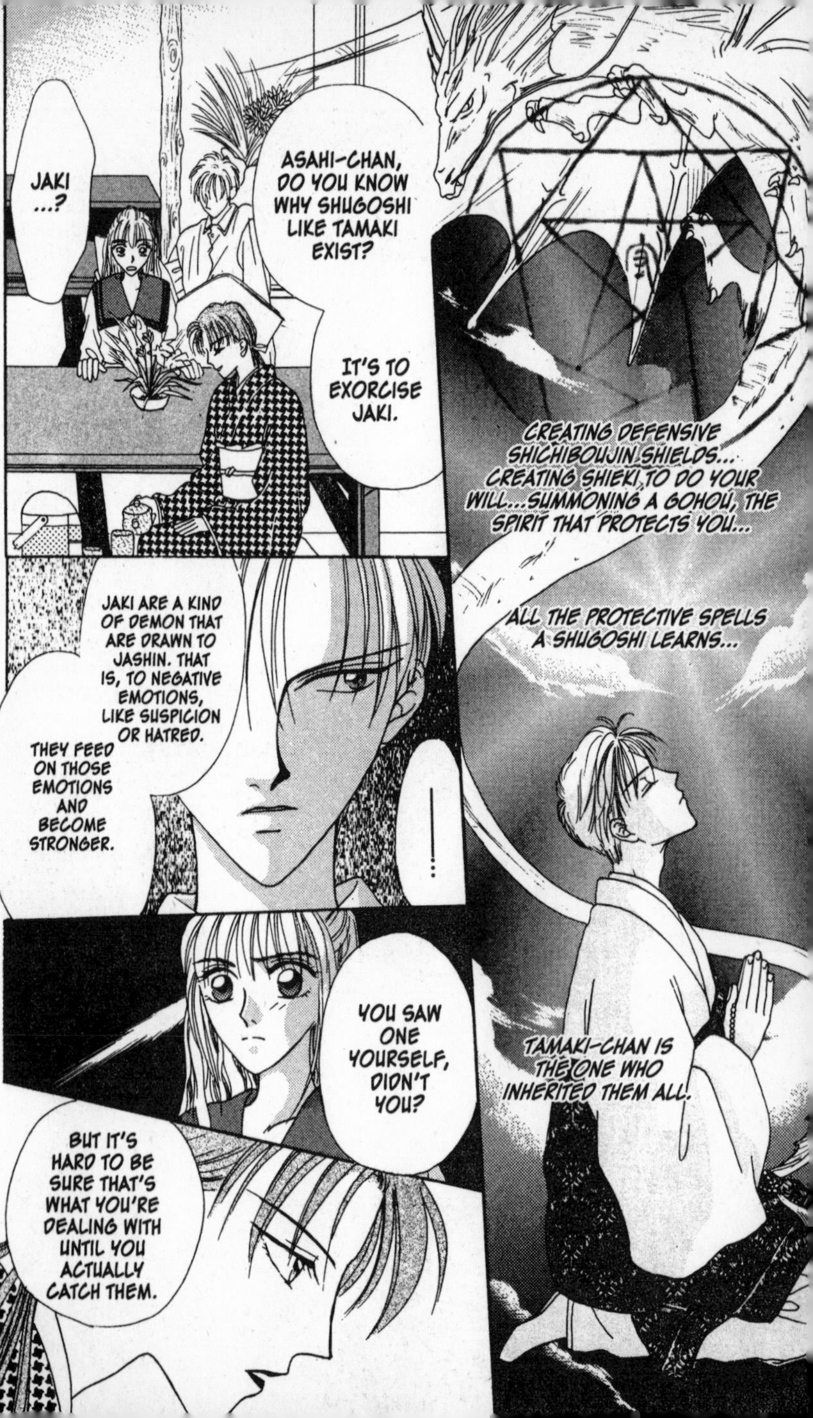
CREATING DEFENSIVE SHICHIBOUJIN SHIELDS... CREATING SHIEKI TO DO YOUR WILL...SUMMONING A GOHOU, THE SPIRIT THAT PROTECTS YOU...
ALL THE PROTECTIVE SPELLS A SHUGOSHI LEARNS...
TAMAKI-CHAN IS THE ONE WHO INHERITED THEM ALL.
ASAHI-CHAN, DO YOU KNOW WHY SHUGOSHI LIKE TAMAKI EXIST?
JAKI ...?
IT'S TO EXORCISE JAKI.
JAKI ARE A KIND OF DEMON THAT ARE DRAWN TO JASHIN. THAT IS, TO NEGATIVE EMOTIONS, LIKE SUSPICION OR HATRED.
THEY FEED ON THOSE EMOTIONS AND BECOME STRONGER.
......
YOU SAW ONE YOURSELF, DIDN'T YOU?
BUT IT'S HARD TO BE SURE THAT'S WHAT YOU'RE DEALING WITH UNTIL YOU ACTUALLY CATCH THEM.

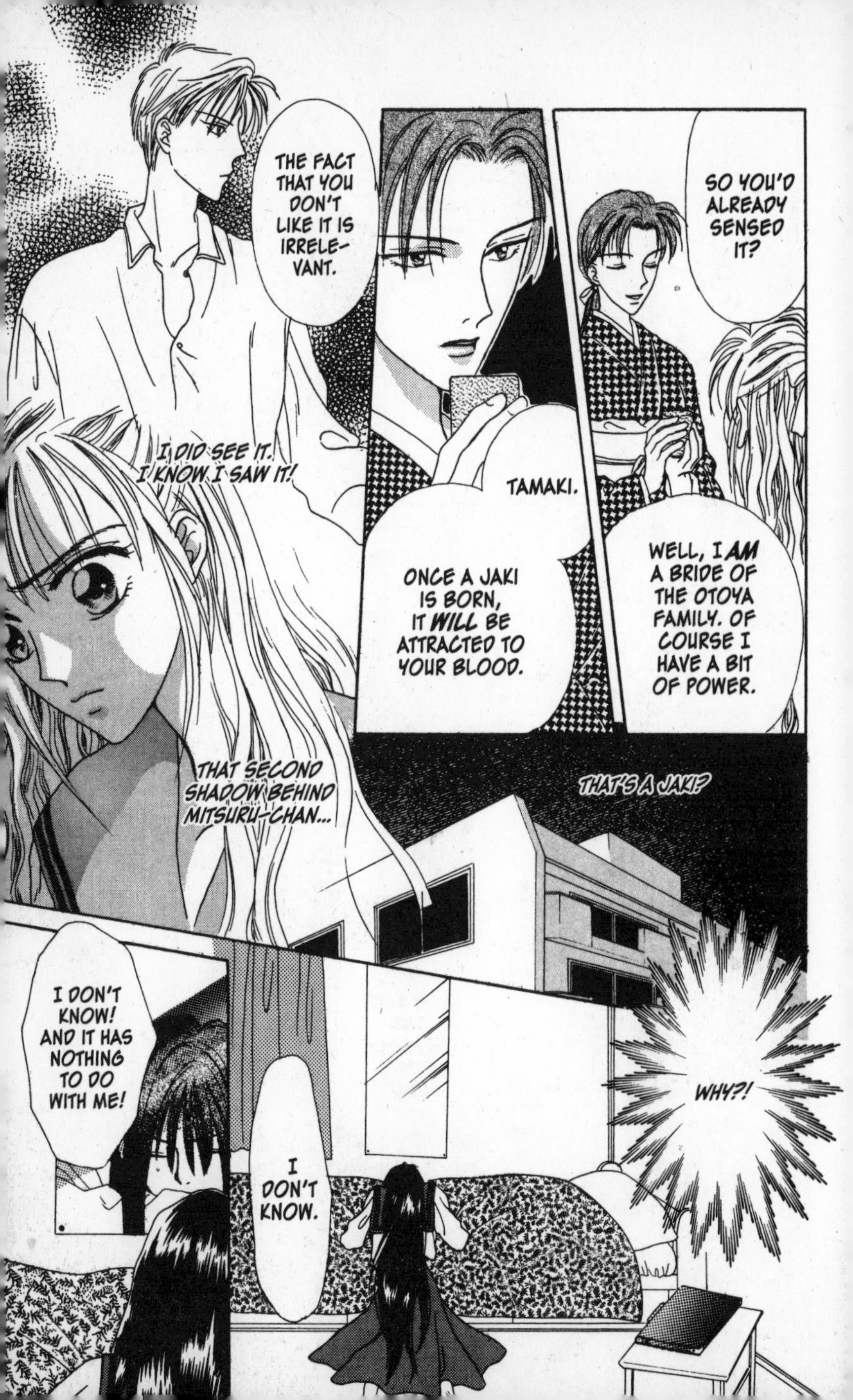

SO YOU'D ALREADY SENSED IT?
WELL, I AM A BRIDE OF THE OTOYA FAMILY. OF COURSE I HAVE A BIT OF POWER.
TAMAKI.
ONCE A JAKI IS BORN, IT WILL BE ATTRACTED TO YOUR BLOOD.
THE FACT THAT YOU DON'T LIKE IT IS IRRELEVANT.
I DID SEE IT. I KNOW I SAW IT!
THAT SECOND SHADOW BEHIND MITSURU-CHAN...
THAT'S A JAKI?
WHY?!
I DON'T KNOW.
I DON'T KNOW! AND IT HAS NOTHING TO DO WITH ME!

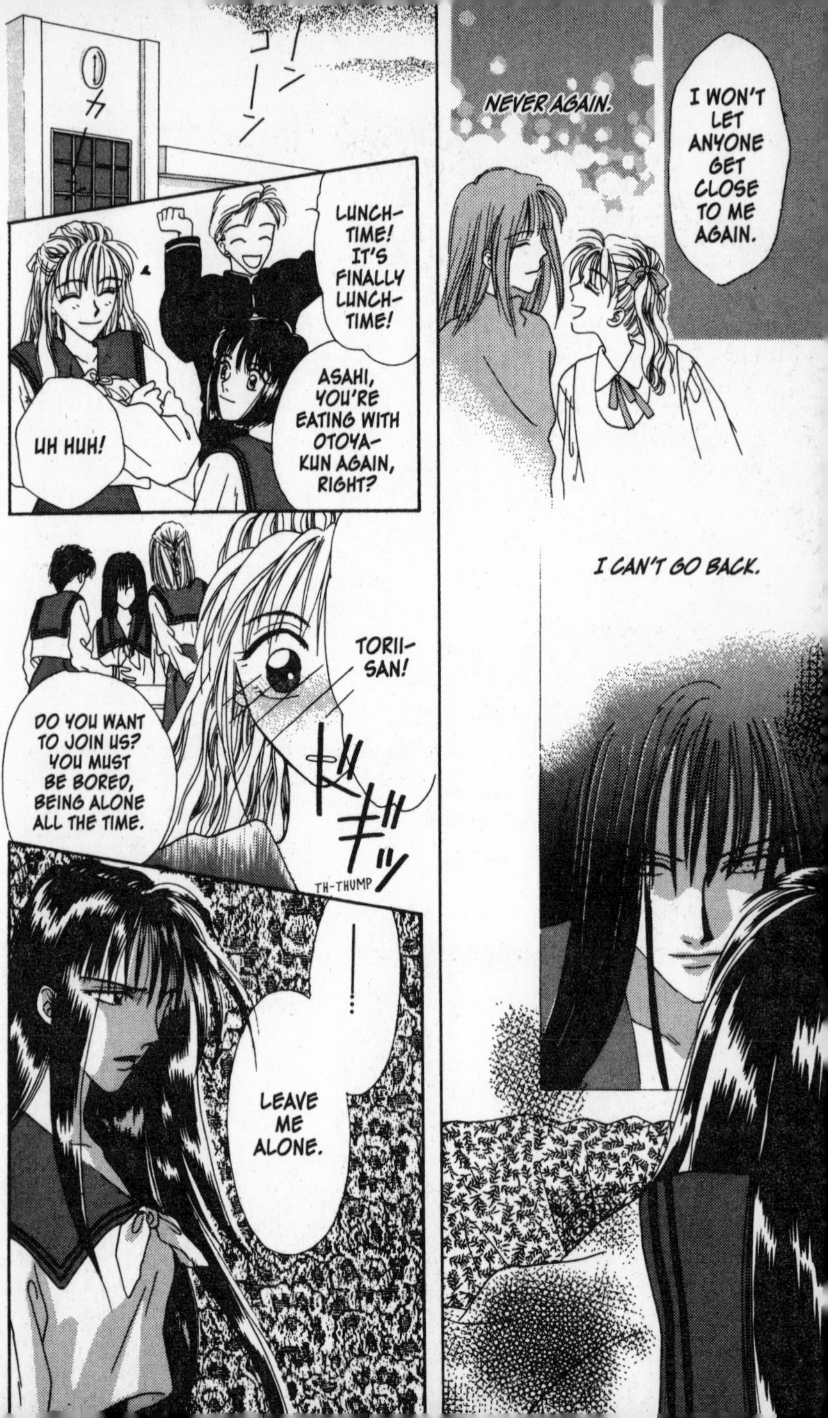
I WON'T LET ANYONE GET CLOSE TO ME AGAIN.
NEVER AGAIN.
I CAN'T GO BACK.
LUNCH-TIME! IT'S FINALLY LUNCH-TIME!
ASAHI, YOU'RE EATING WITH OTOYA-KUN AGAIN, RIGHT?
UH HUH!
TORII-SAN!
DO YOU WANT TO JOIN US? YOU MUST BE BORED, BEING ALONE ALL THE TIME.
TH-THUMP
LEAVE ME ALONE.

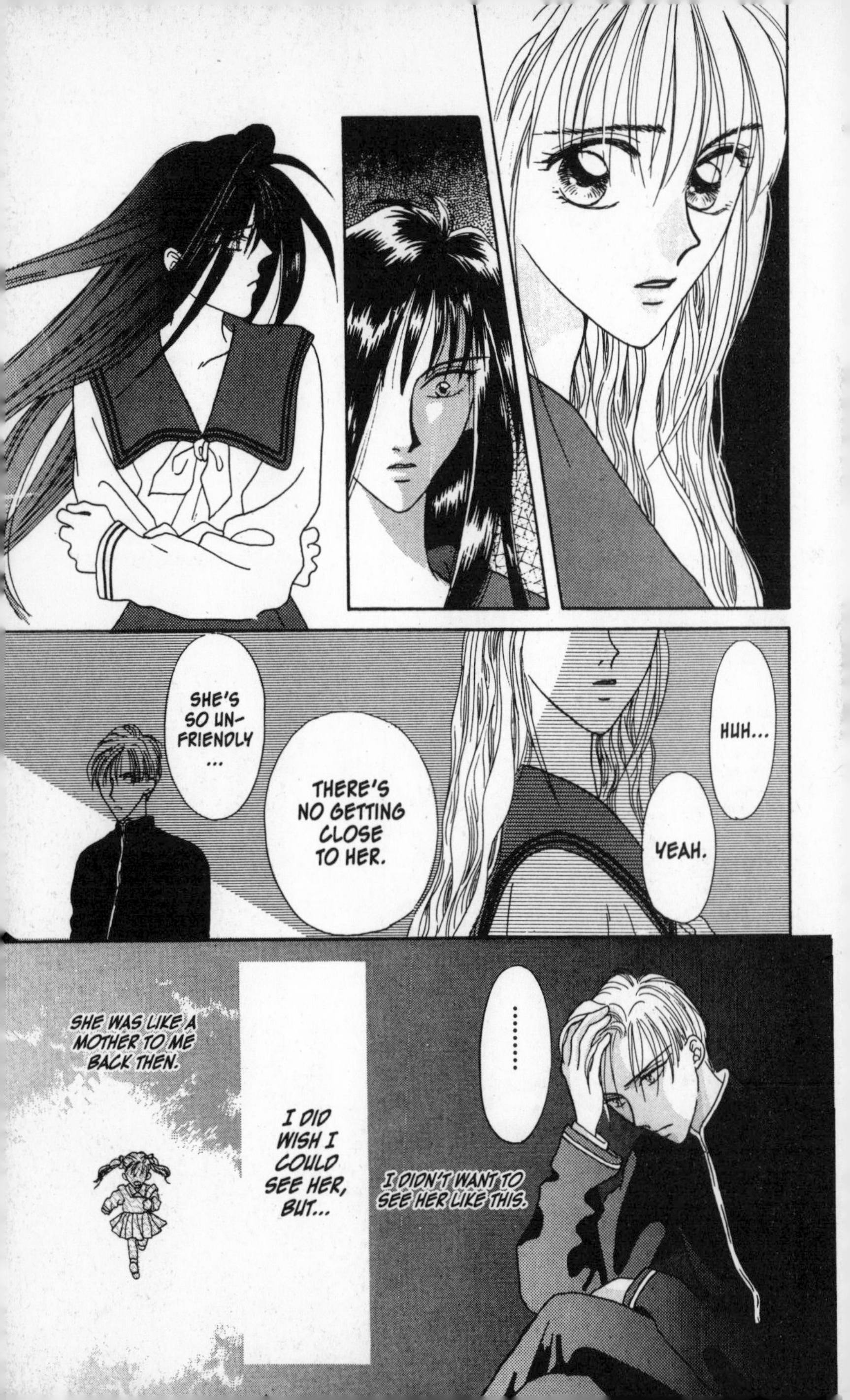
HUH...
SHE'S SO UN-FRIENDLY ...
THERE'S NO GETTING CLOSE TO HER.
YEAH.
......
SHE WAS LIKE A MOTHER TO ME BACK THEN.
I DID WISH I COULD SEE HER, BUT...
I DIDN'T WANT TO SEE HER LIKE THIS.

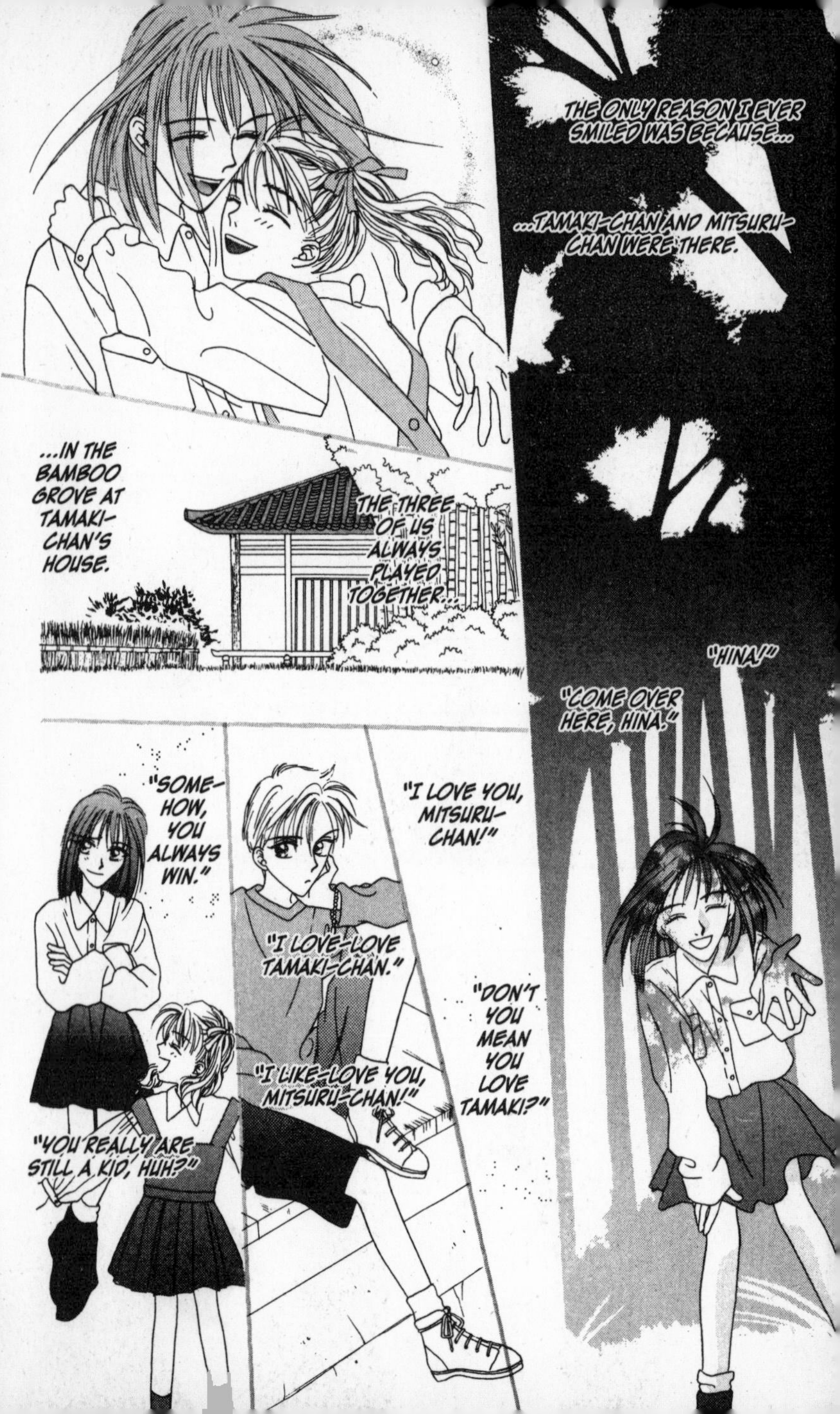
THE ONLY REASON I EVER SMILED WAS BECAUSE...
...TAMAKI-CHAN AND MITSURU-CHAN WERE THERE.
THE THREE OF US ALWAYS PLAYED TOGETHER...
...IN THE BAMBOO GROVE AT TAMAKI-CHAN'S HOUSE.
"HINA!"
"COME OVER HERE, HINA."
"I LOVE YOU, MITSURU-CHAN!"
"DON'T YOU MEAN YOU LOVE TAMAKI?"
"I LOVE-LOVE TAMAKI-CHAN."
"I LIKE-LOVE YOU, MITSURU-CHAN!"
"SOME-HOW, YOU ALWAYS WIN."
"YOU REALLY ARE STILL A KID, HUH?"

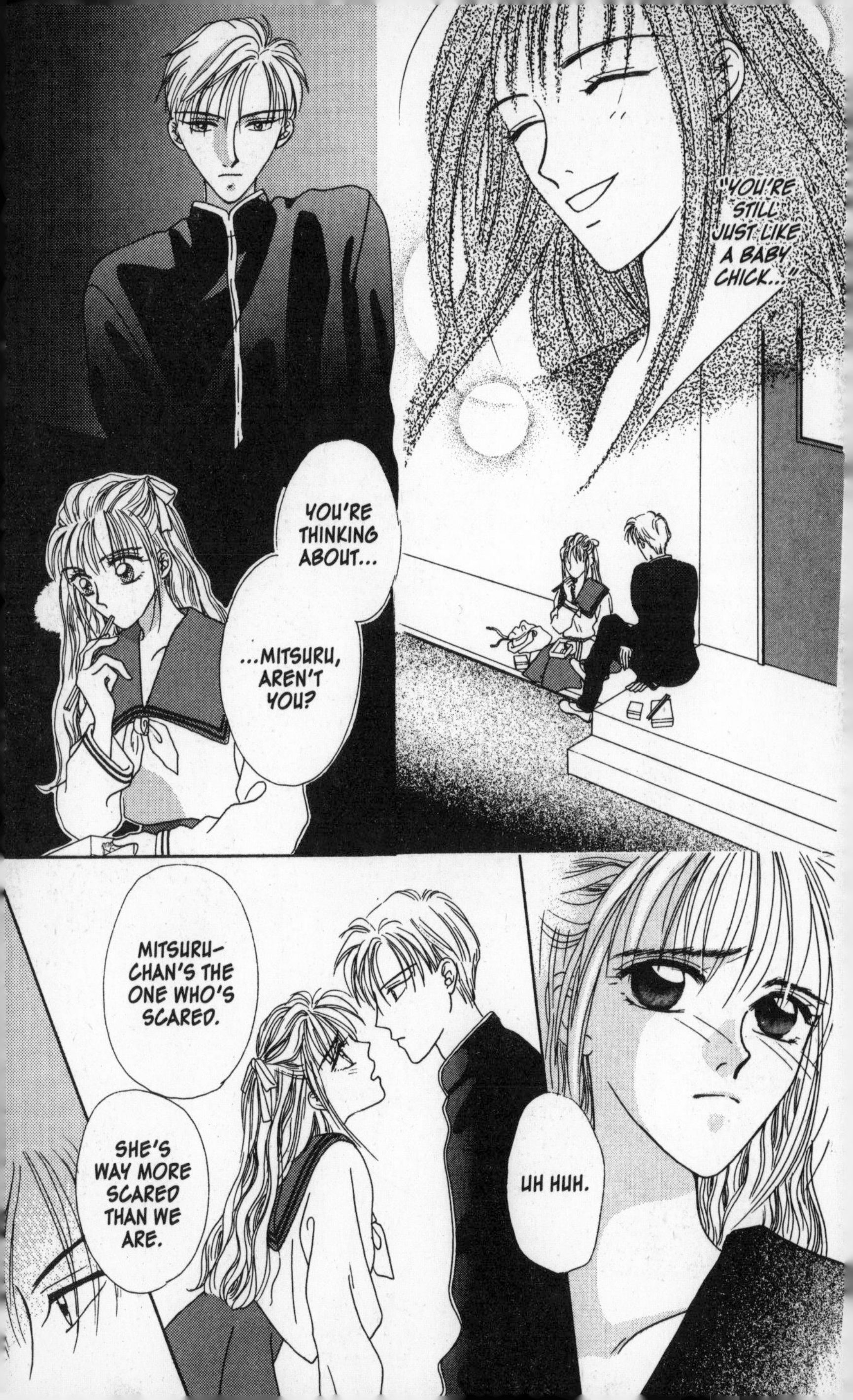
"YOU'RE STILL JUST LIKE A BABY CHICK..."
YOU'RE THINKING ABOUT...
...MITSURU, AREN'T YOU?
UH HUH.
MITSURU-CHAN'S THE ONE WHO'S SCARED.
SHE'S WAY MORE SCARED THAN WE ARE.

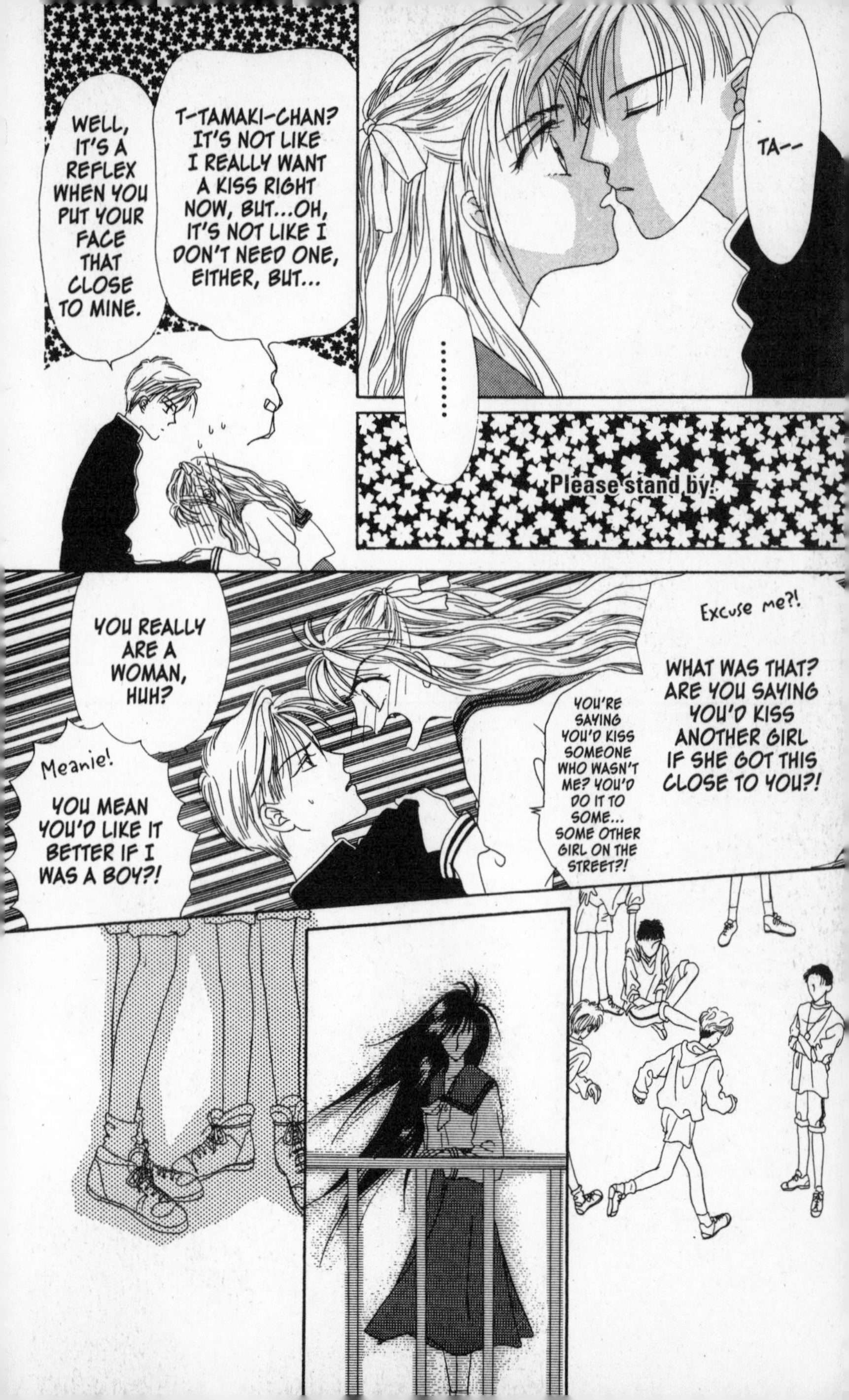
TA--
......
Please stand by!
T-TAMAKI-CHAN? IT'S NOT LIKE I REALLY WANT A KISS RIGHT NOW, BUT...OH, IT'S NOT LIKE I DON'T NEED ONE, EITHER, BUT...
WELL, IT'S A REFLEX WHEN YOU PUT YOUR FACE THAT CLOSE TO MINE.
Excuse me?!
WHAT WAS THAT? ARE YOU SAYING YOU'D KISS ANOTHER GIRL IF SHE GOT THIS CLOSE TO YOU?!
YOU'RE SAYING YOU'D KISS SOMEONE WHO WASN'T ME? YOU'D DO IT TO SOME... SOME OTHER GIRL ON THE STREET?!
YOU REALLY ARE A WOMAN, HUH?
Meanie!
YOU MEAN YOU'D LIKE IT BETTER IF I WAS A BOY?!

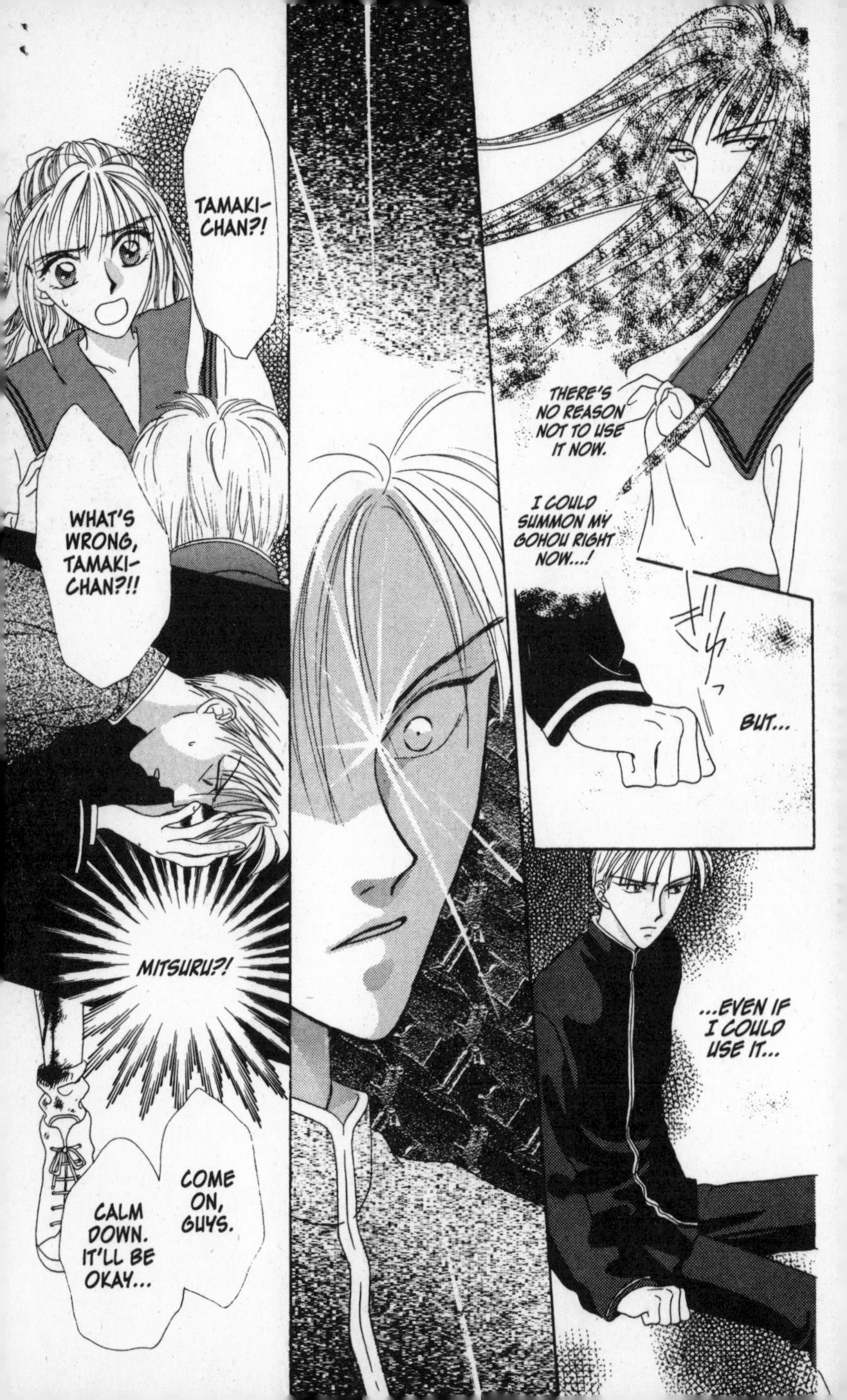
THERE'S NO REASON NOT TO USE IT NOW.
I COULD SUMMON MY GOHOU RIGHT NOW...!
ぎゅっ
BUT...
...EVEN IF I COULD USE IT...
TAMAKI-CHAN?!
WHAT'S WRONG, TAMAKI-CHAN?!!
MITSURU?!
COME ON, GUYS.
CALM DOWN. IT'LL BE OKAY...

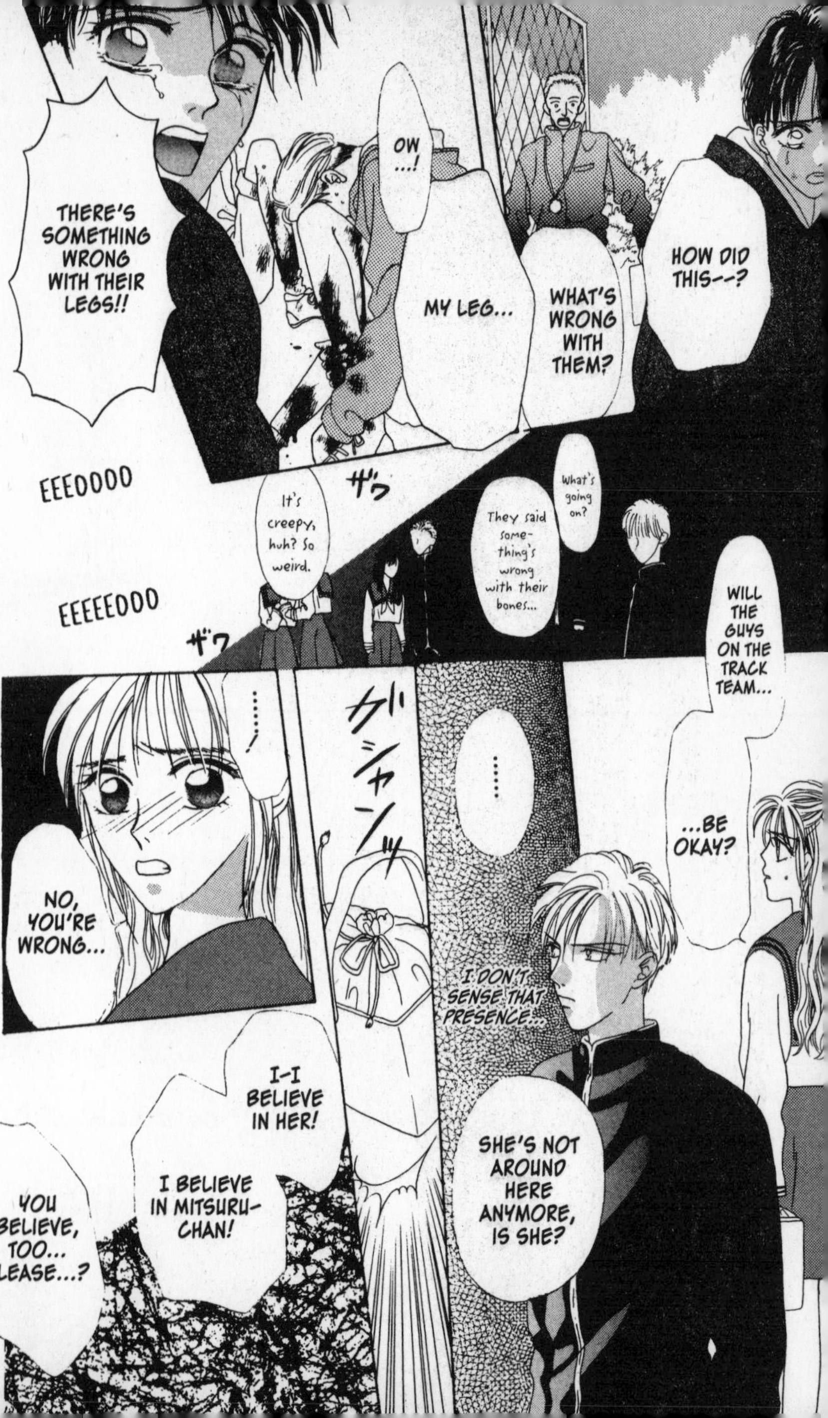
HOW DID THIS--?
WHAT'S WRONG WITH THEM?
MY LEG...
OW...!
THERE'S SOMETHING WRONG WITH THEIR LEGS!!
What's going on?
They said something's wrong with their bones...
ザワ
It's creepy, huh? So weird.
EEEOOOO
EEEEEOOO
ザワ
WILL THE GUYS ON THE TRACK TEAM...
...BE OKAY?
......
I DON'T SENSE THAT PRESENCE...
SHE'S NOT AROUND HERE ANYMORE, IS SHE?
ガシャーンッ
......!
NO, YOU'RE WRONG...
I-I BELIEVE IN HER!
I BELIEVE IN MITSURU-CHAN!
YOU BELIEVE, TOO... PLEASE...?

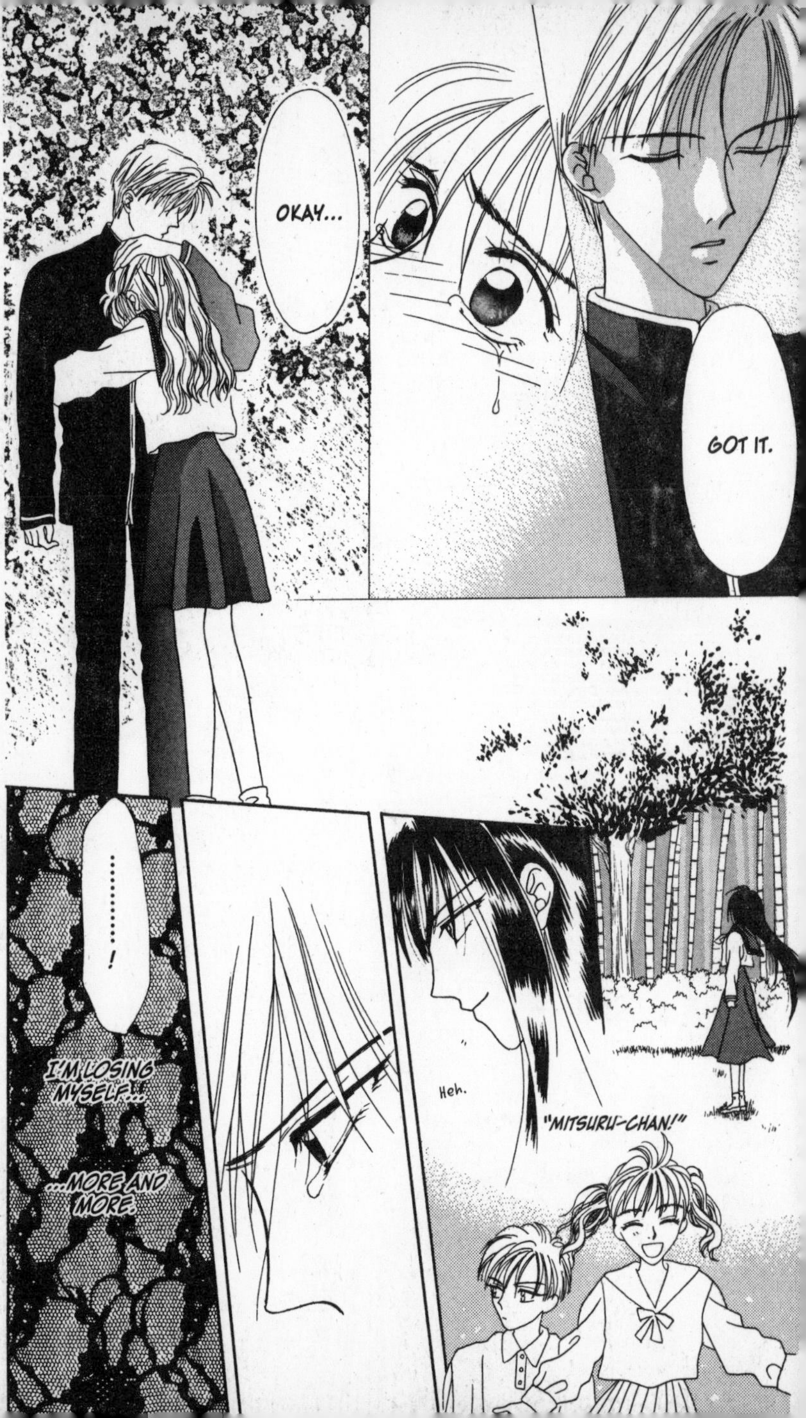
GOT IT.
OKAY...
Heh.
"MITSURU-CHAN!"
......!
I'M LOSING MYSELF...
...MORE AND MORE.

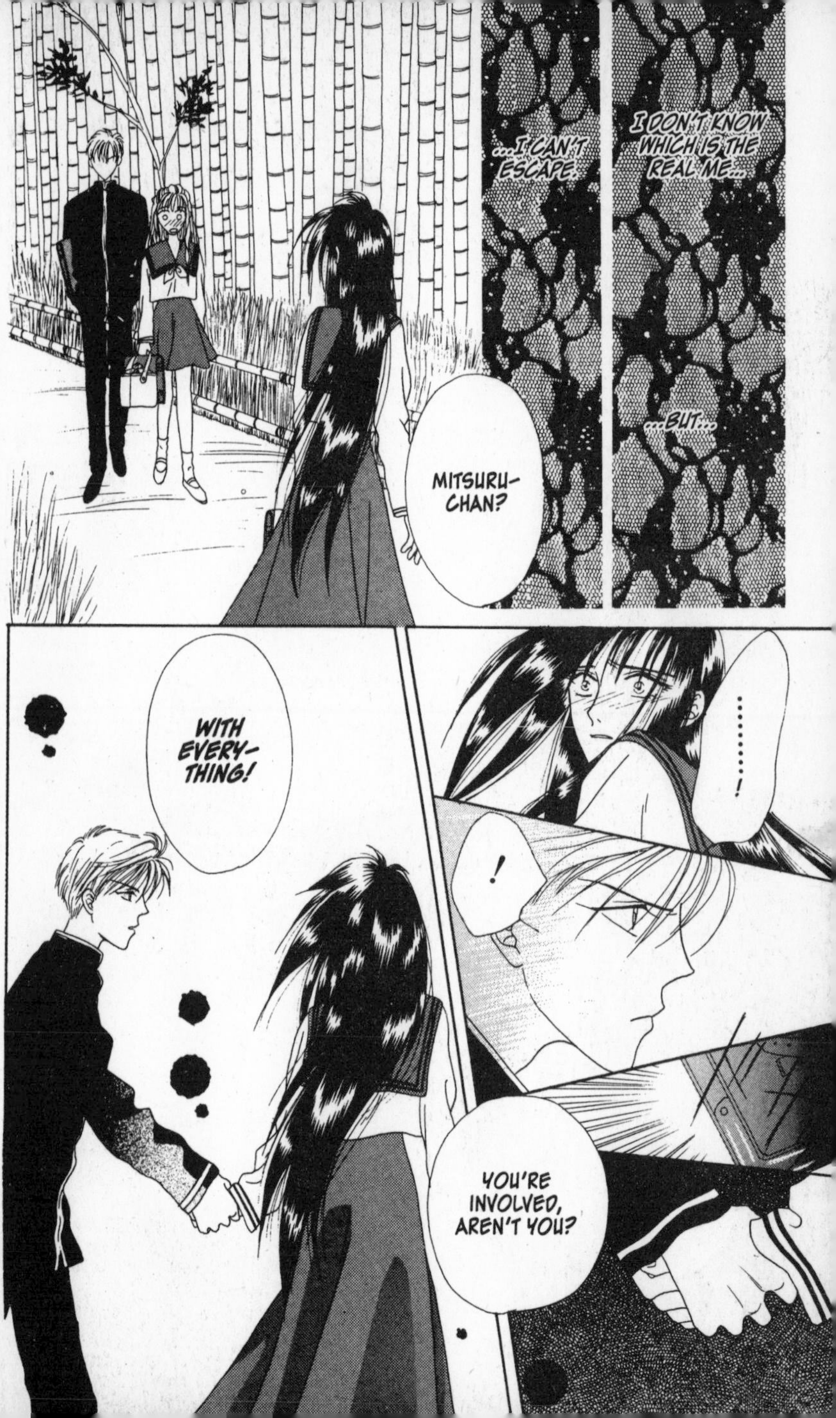
I DON'T KNOW WHICH IS THE REAL ME...
...BUT...
...I CAN'T ESCAPE.
MITSURU-CHAN?
......!
!
YOU'RE INVOLVED, AREN'T YOU?
WITH EVERY-THING!

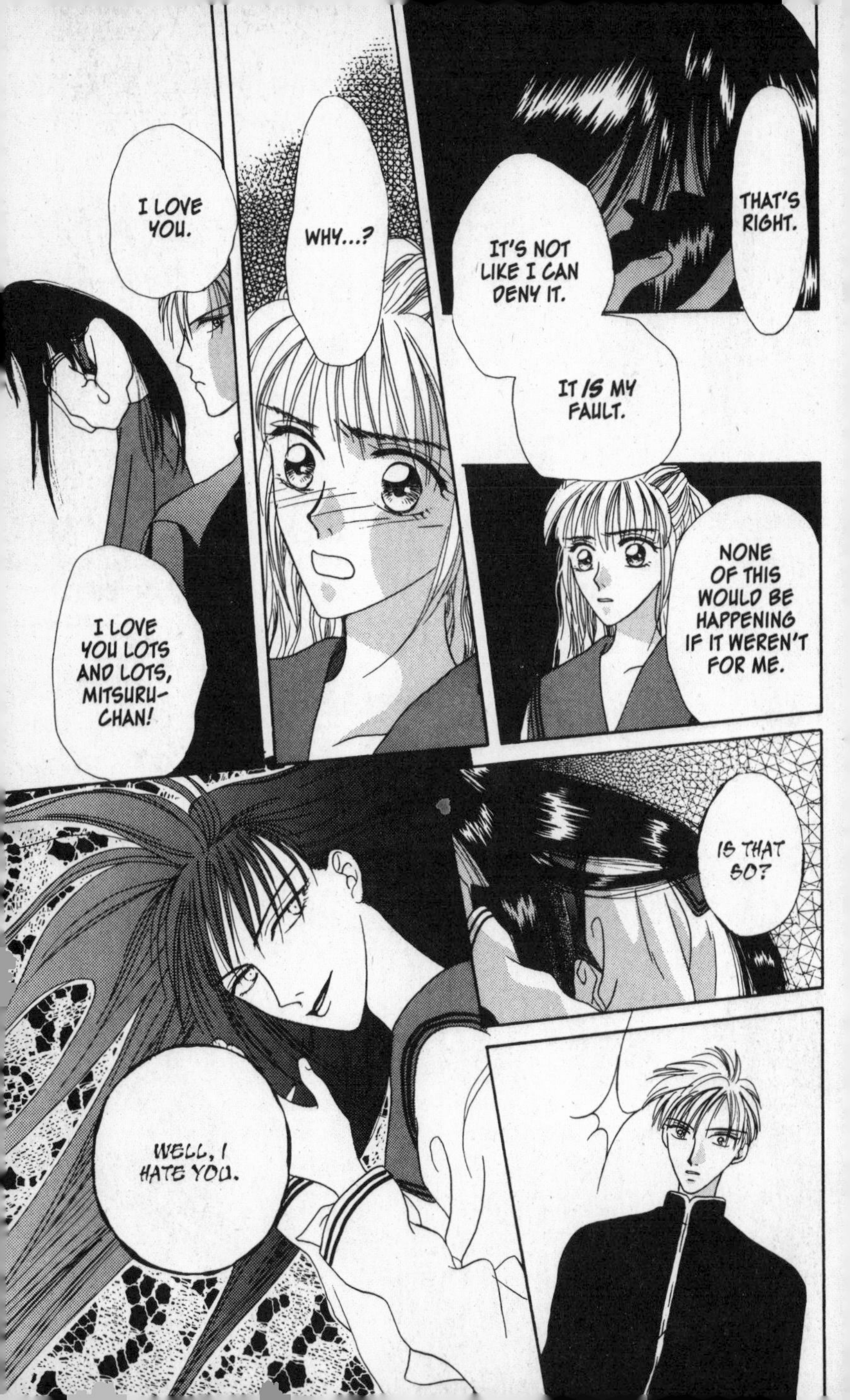
THAT'S RIGHT.
IT'S NOT LIKE I CAN DENY IT.
IT *IS* MY FAULT.
NONE OF THIS WOULD BE HAPPENING IF IT WEREN'T FOR ME.
WHY...?
I LOVE YOU.
I LOVE YOU LOTS AND LOTS, MITSURU-CHAN!
IS THAT SO?
WELL, I HATE YOU.

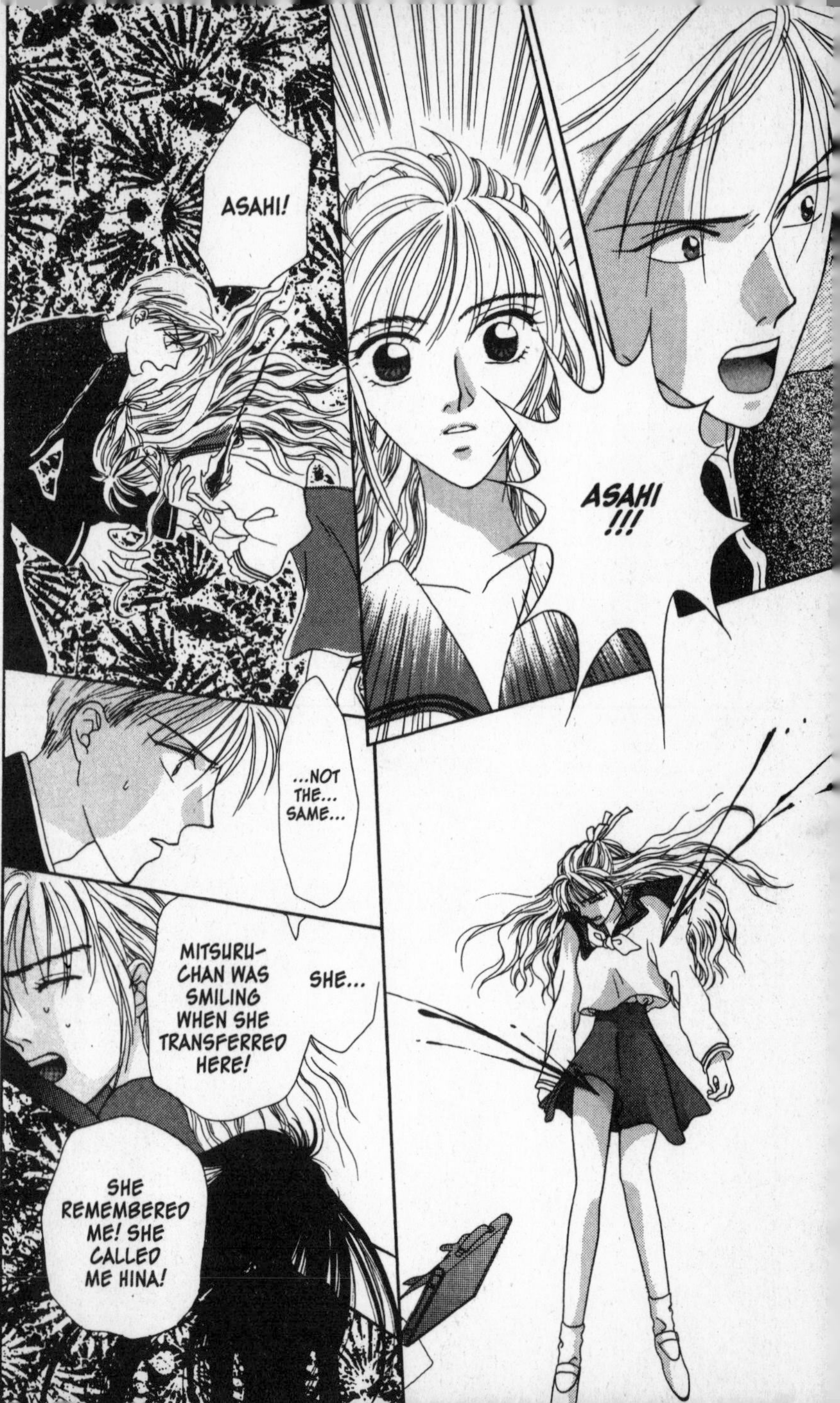
ASAHI!!!
ASAHI!
...NOT THE... SAME...
SHE...
MITSURU-CHAN WAS SMILING WHEN SHE TRANSFERRED HERE!
SHE REMEMBERED ME! SHE CALLED ME HINA!

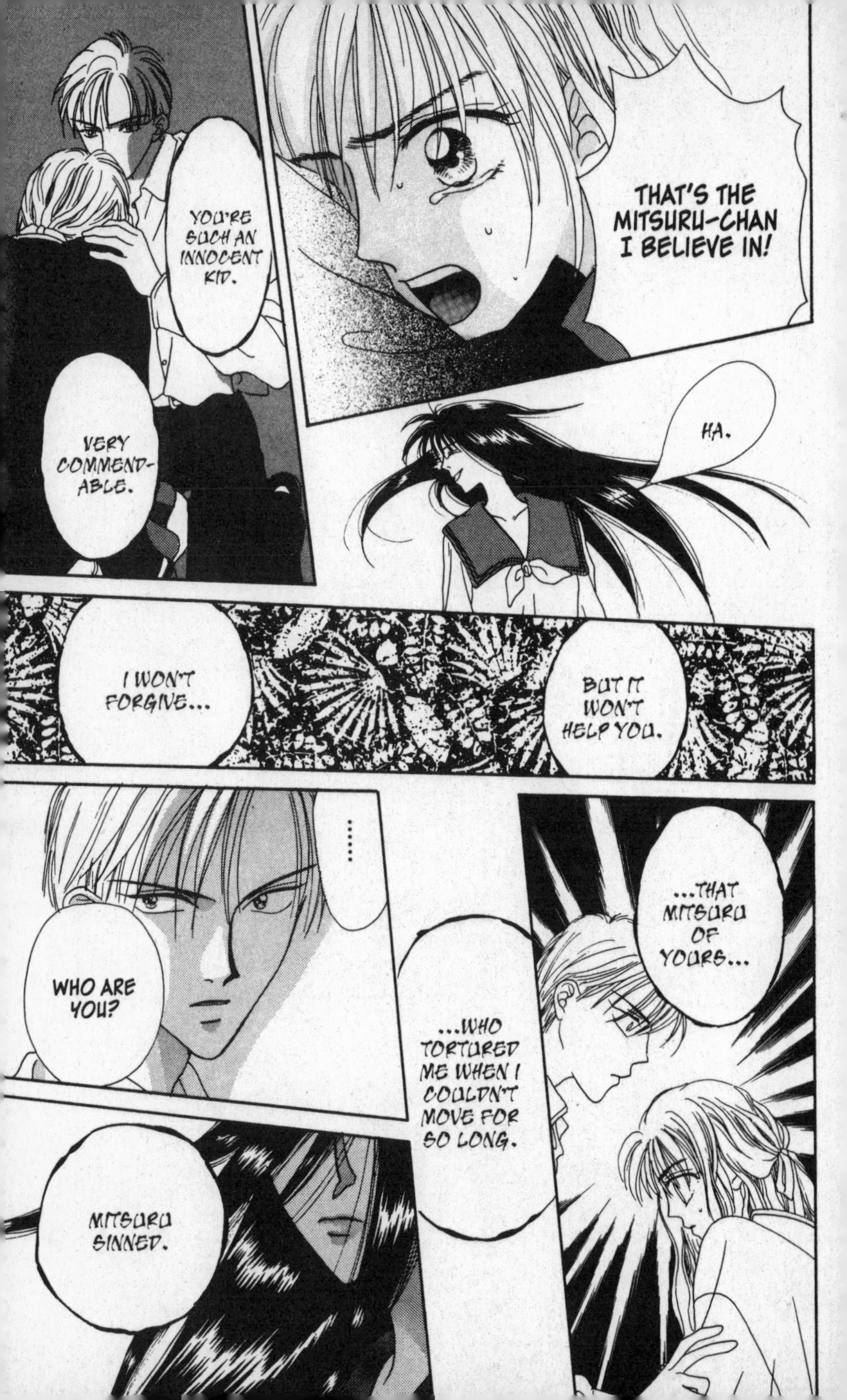
THAT'S THE MITSURU-CHAN I BELIEVE IN!
HA.
YOU'RE SUCH AN INNOCENT KID.
VERY COMMEND-ABLE.
BUT IT WON'T HELP YOU.
I WON'T FORGIVE...
...THAT MITSURU OF YOURS...
...WHO TORTURED ME WHEN I COULDN'T MOVE FOR SO LONG.
......
WHO ARE YOU?
MITSURU SINNED.

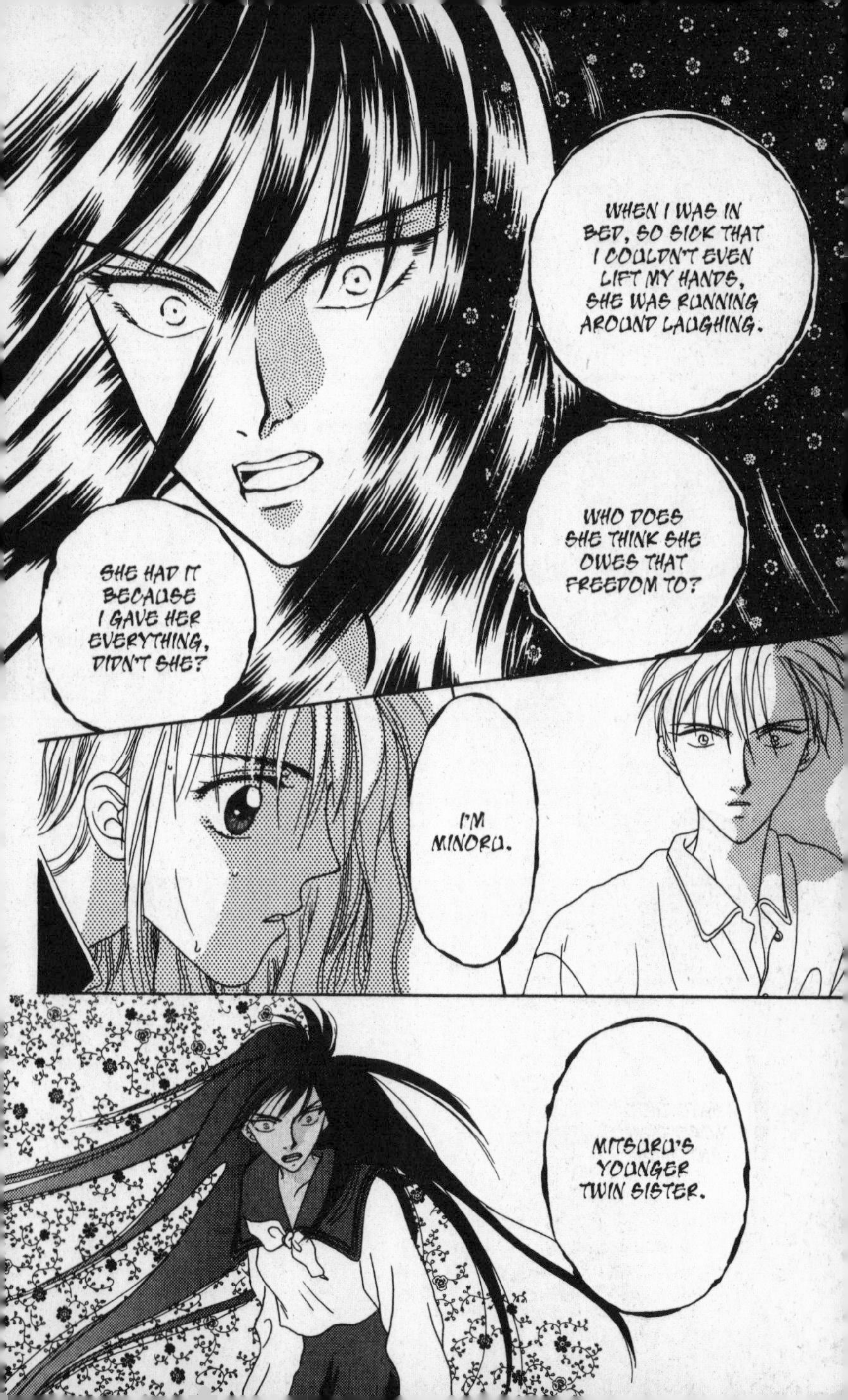
WHEN I WAS IN BED, SO SICK THAT I COULDN'T EVEN LIFT MY HANDS, SHE WAS RUNNING AROUND LAUGHING.
WHO DOES SHE THINK SHE OWES THAT FREEDOM TO?
SHE HAD IT BECAUSE I GAVE HER EVERYTHING, DIDN'T SHE?
I'M MINORU.
MITSURU'S YOUNGER TWIN SISTER.

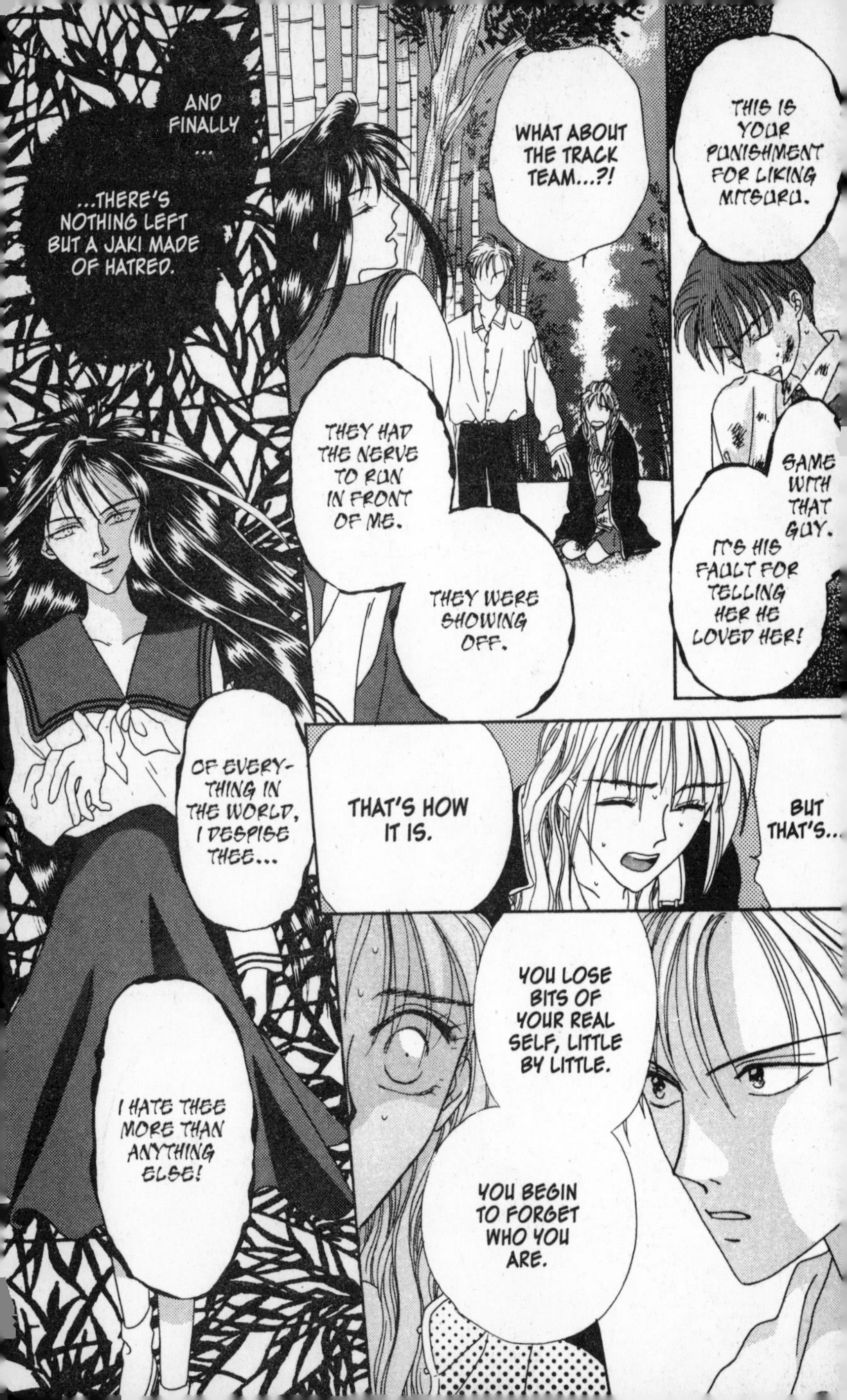
THIS IS YOUR PUNISHMENT FOR LIKING MITSURU.
SAME WITH THAT GUY.
IT'S HIS FAULT FOR TELLING HER HE LOVED HER!
WHAT ABOUT THE TRACK TEAM...?!
THEY HAD THE NERVE TO RUN IN FRONT OF ME.
THEY WERE SHOWING OFF.
BUT THAT'S...
THAT'S HOW IT IS.
YOU LOSE BITS OF YOUR REAL SELF, LITTLE BY LITTLE.
YOU BEGIN TO FORGET WHO YOU ARE.
AND FINALLY...
...THERE'S NOTHING LEFT BUT A JAKI MADE OF HATRED.
OF EVERY-THING IN THE WORLD, I DESPISE THEE...
I HATE THEE MORE THAN ANYTHING ELSE!

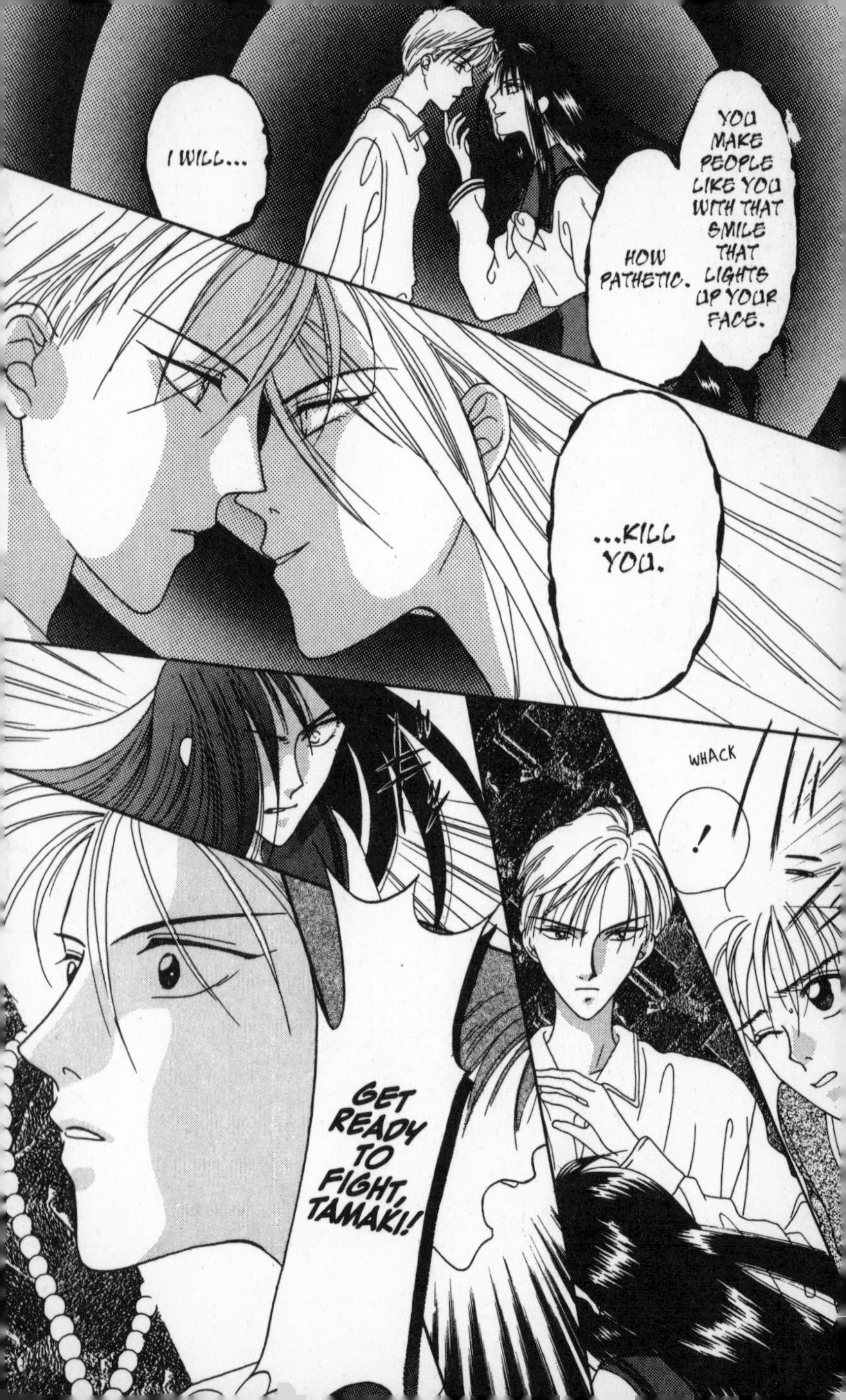
YOU MAKE PEOPLE LIKE YOU WITH THAT SMILE THAT LIGHTS UP YOUR FACE.
HOW PATHETIC.
I WILL...
...KILL YOU.
WHACK
!
GET READY TO FIGHT, TAMAKI!

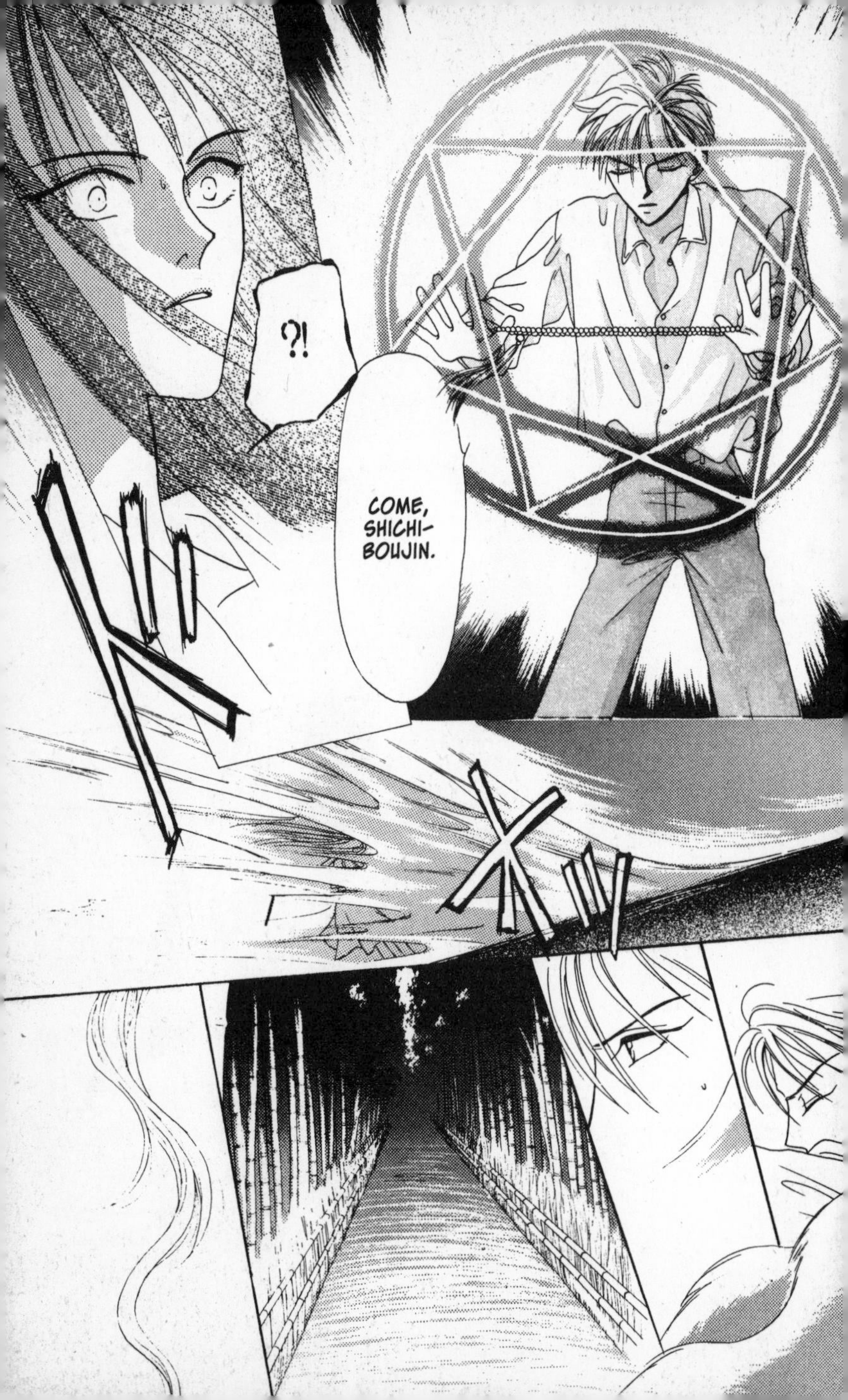
?!
COME, SHICHI-BOUJIN.

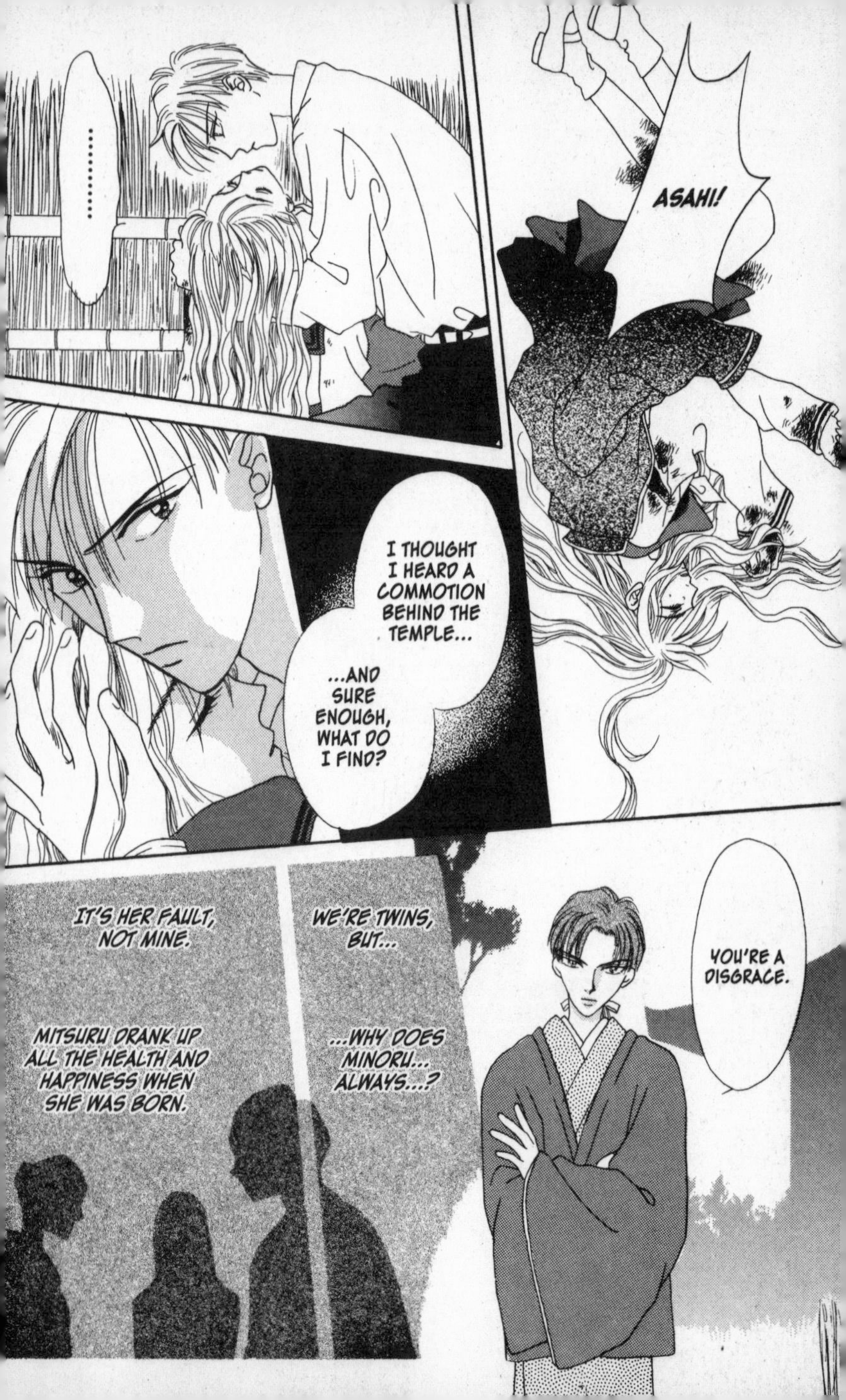
ASAHI!
......
I THOUGHT I HEARD A COMMOTION BEHIND THE TEMPLE...
...AND SURE ENOUGH, WHAT DO I FIND?
YOU'RE A DISGRACE.
WE'RE TWINS, BUT...
...WHY DOES MINORU... ALWAYS...?
IT'S HER FAULT, NOT MINE.
MITSURU DRANK UP ALL THE HEALTH AND HAPPINESS WHEN SHE WAS BORN.

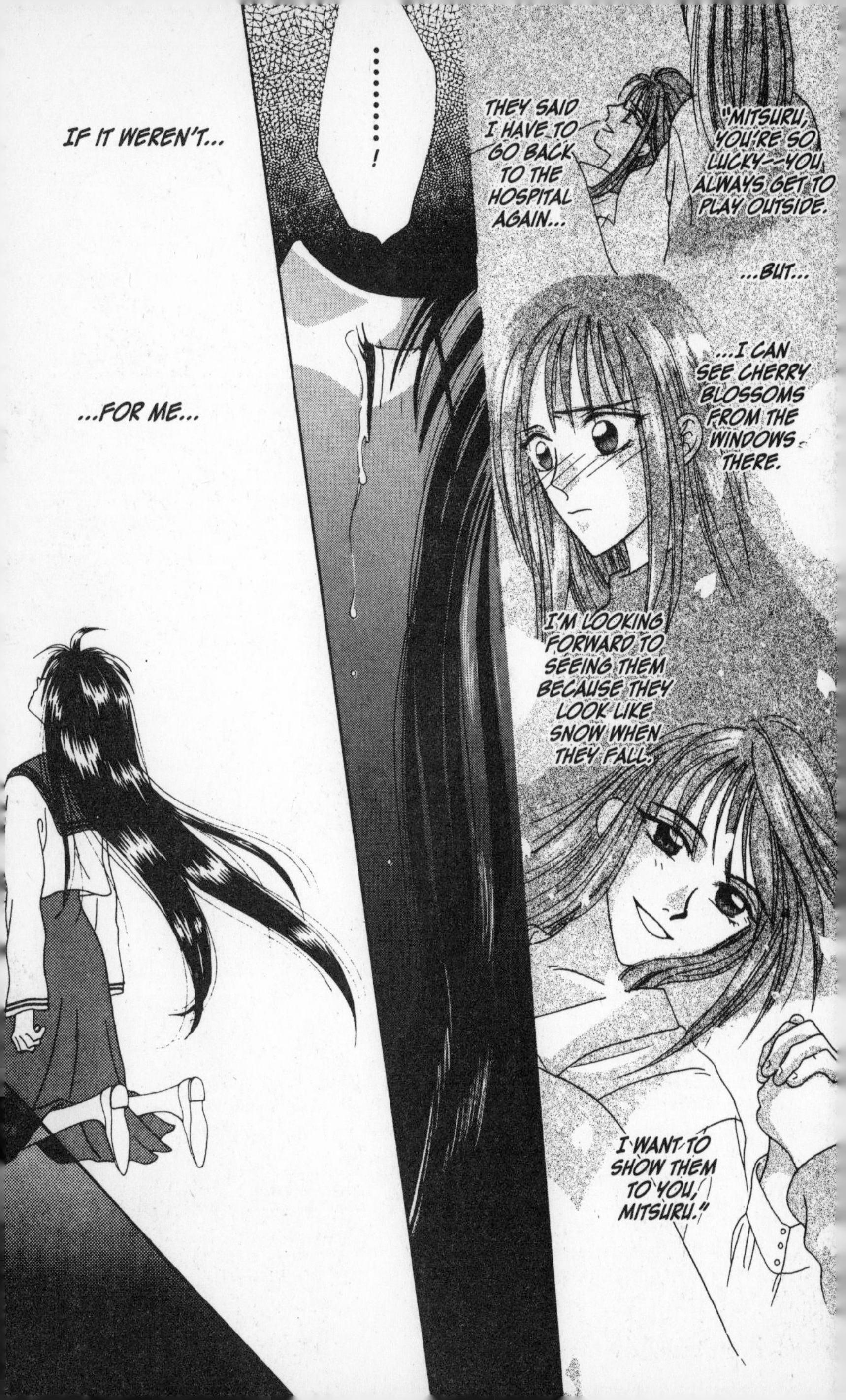
"MITSURU, YOU'RE SO LUCKY--YOU ALWAYS GET TO PLAY OUTSIDE.
THEY SAID I HAVE TO GO BACK TO THE HOSPITAL AGAIN...
...BUT...
...I CAN SEE CHERRY BLOSSOMS FROM THE WINDOWS THERE.
I'M LOOKING FORWARD TO SEEING THEM BECAUSE THEY LOOK LIKE SNOW WHEN THEY FALL.
I WANT TO SHOW THEM TO YOU, MITSURU."
......!
IF IT WEREN'T...
...FOR ME...

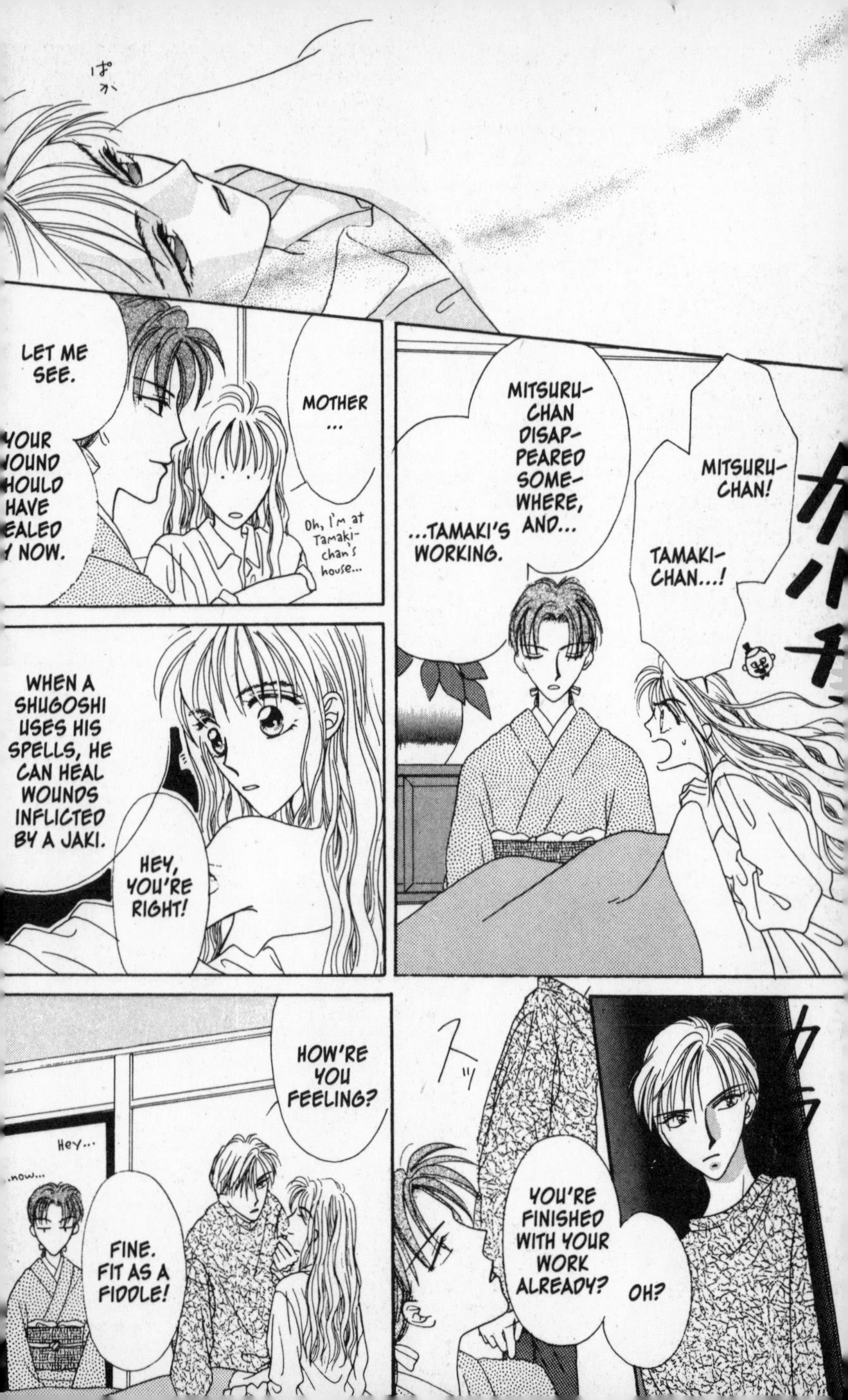
ぱか
MITSURU-CHAN!
TAMAKI-CHAN...!
MITSURU-CHAN DISAPPEARED SOMEWHERE, AND...
...TAMAKI'S WORKING.
MOTHER...
Oh, I'm at Tamaki-chan's house...
LET ME SEE.
YOUR OUND HOULD HAVE EALED NOW.
HEY, YOU'RE RIGHT!
WHEN A SHUGOSHI USES HIS SPELLS, HE CAN HEAL WOUNDS INFLICTED BY A JAKI.
OH?
YOU'RE FINISHED WITH YOUR WORK ALREADY?
HOW'RE YOU FEELING?
FINE. FIT AS A FIDDLE!
Hey...
...now...

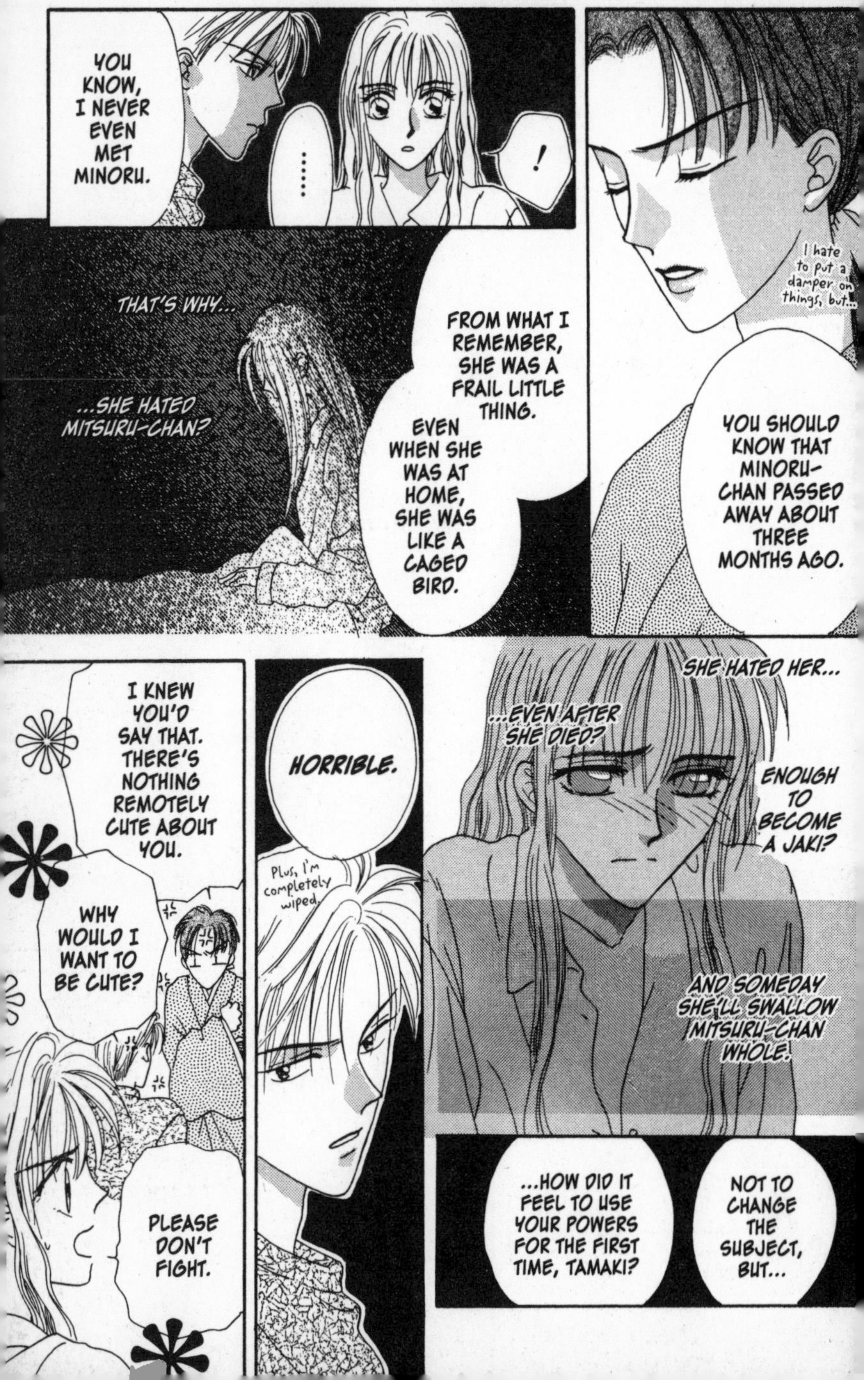
I hate to put a damper on things, but...
YOU SHOULD KNOW THAT MINORU-CHAN PASSED AWAY ABOUT THREE MONTHS AGO.
!
......
YOU KNOW, I NEVER EVEN MET MINORU.
FROM WHAT I REMEMBER, SHE WAS A FRAIL LITTLE THING.
EVEN WHEN SHE WAS AT HOME, SHE WAS LIKE A CAGED BIRD.
THAT'S WHY...
...SHE HATED MITSURU-CHAN?
SHE HATED HER...
...EVEN AFTER SHE DIED?
ENOUGH TO BECOME A JAKI?
AND SOMEDAY SHE'LL SWALLOW MITSURU-CHAN WHOLE.
NOT TO CHANGE THE SUBJECT, BUT...
...HOW DID IT FEEL TO USE YOUR POWERS FOR THE FIRST TIME, TAMAKI?
HORRIBLE.
Plus, I'm completely wiped.
I KNEW YOU'D SAY THAT. THERE'S NOTHING REMOTELY CUTE ABOUT YOU.
WHY WOULD I WANT TO BE CUTE?
PLEASE DON'T FIGHT.

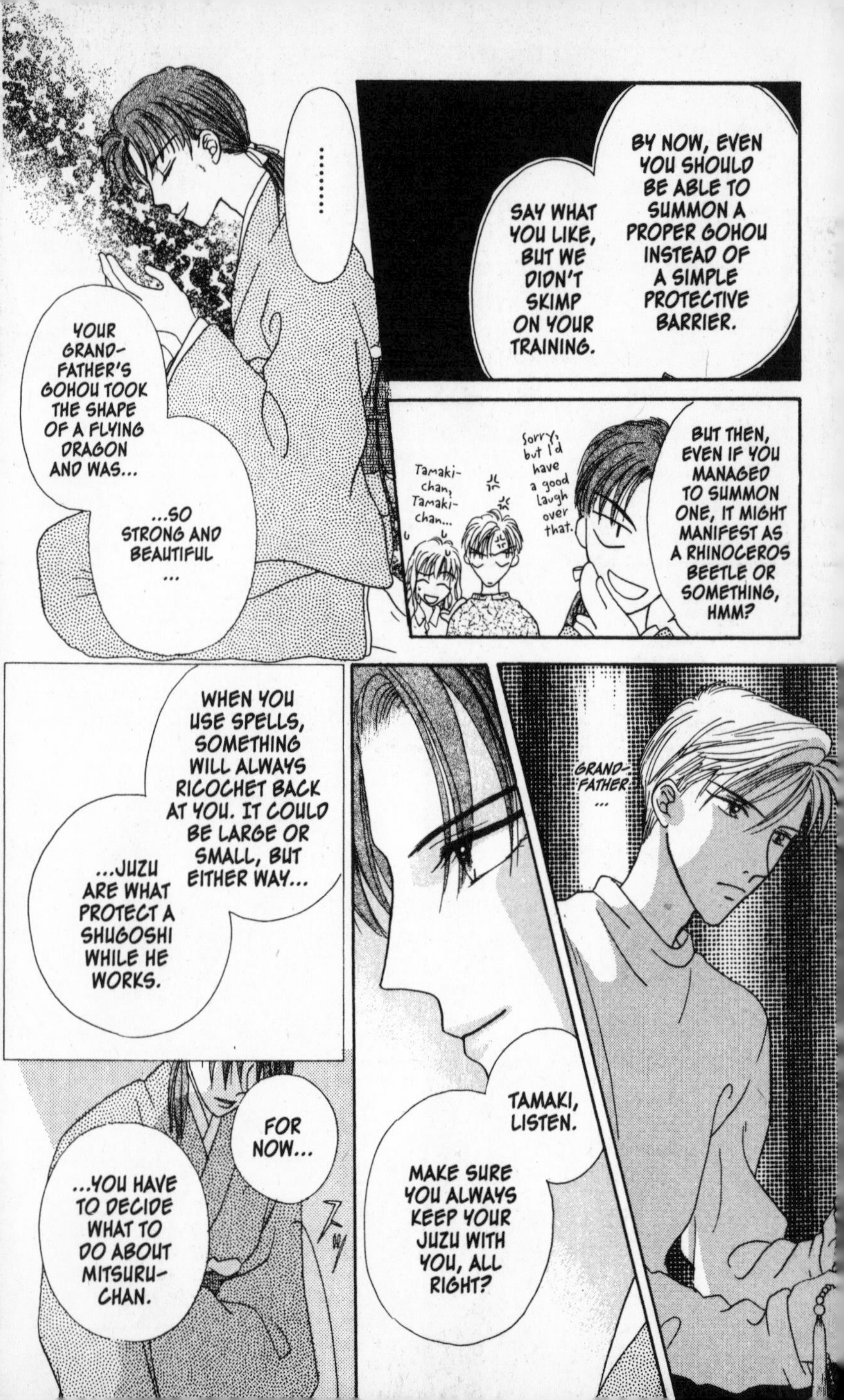
SAY WHAT YOU LIKE, BUT WE DIDN'T SKIMP ON YOUR TRAINING.
BY NOW, EVEN YOU SHOULD BE ABLE TO SUMMON A PROPER GOHOU INSTEAD OF A SIMPLE PROTECTIVE BARRIER.
BUT THEN, EVEN IF YOU MANAGED TO SUMMON ONE, IT MIGHT MANIFEST AS A RHINOCEROS BEETLE OR SOMETHING, HMM?
Sorry, but I'd have a good laugh over that.
Tamaki-chan, Tamaki-chan...
......
YOUR GRAND-FATHER'S GOHOU TOOK THE SHAPE OF A FLYING DRAGON AND WAS...
...SO STRONG AND BEAUTIFUL...
GRAND-FATHER...
TAMAKI, LISTEN.
MAKE SURE YOU ALWAYS KEEP YOUR JUZU WITH YOU, ALL RIGHT?
WHEN YOU USE SPELLS, SOMETHING WILL ALWAYS RICOCHET BACK AT YOU. IT COULD BE LARGE OR SMALL, BUT EITHER WAY...
...JUZU ARE WHAT PROTECT A SHUGOSHI WHILE HE WORKS.
FOR NOW...
...YOU HAVE TO DECIDE WHAT TO DO ABOUT MITSURU-CHAN.

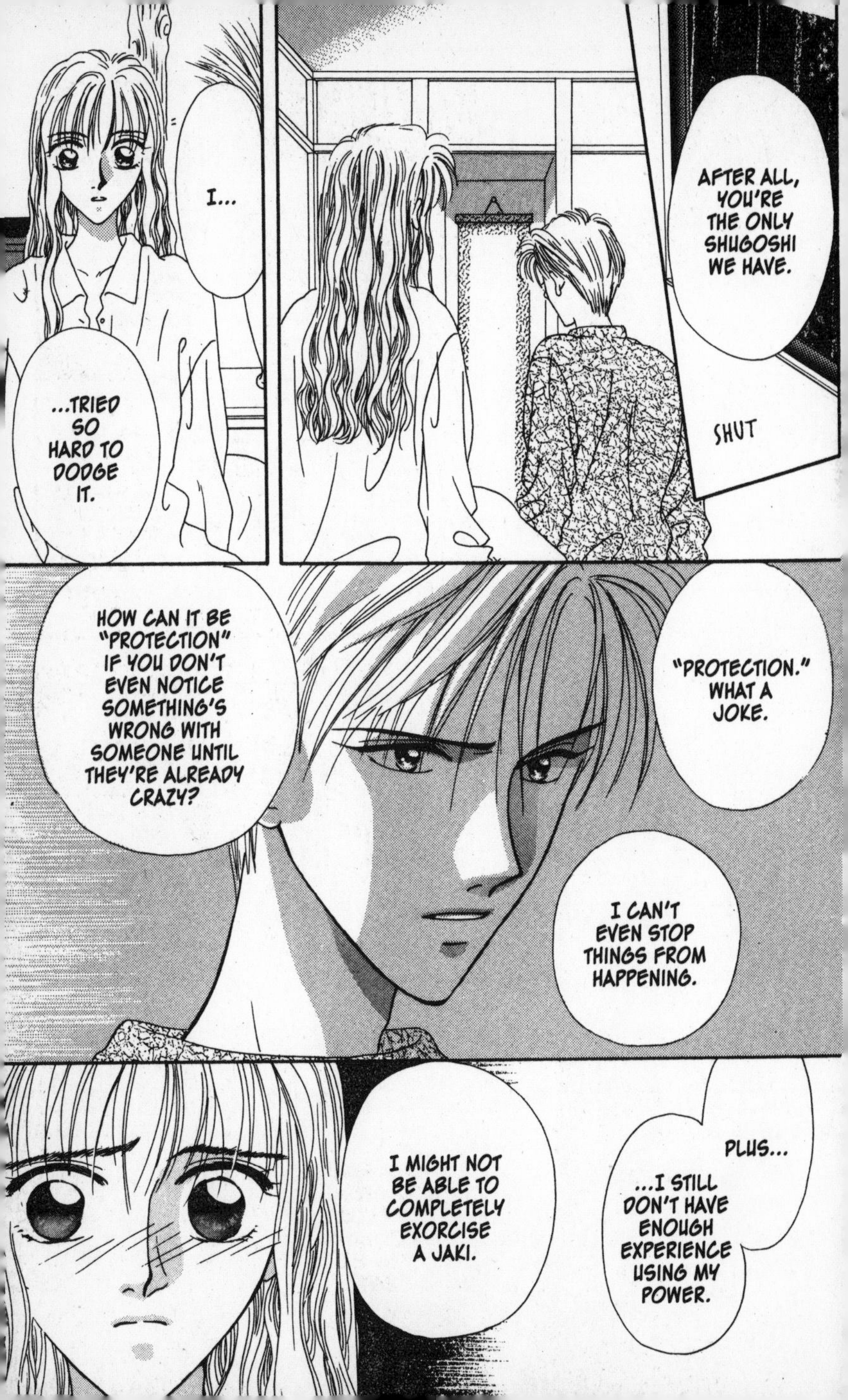
AFTER ALL, YOU'RE THE ONLY SHUGOSHI WE HAVE.
SHUT
I...
...TRIED SO HARD TO DODGE IT.
"PROTECTION." WHAT A JOKE.
HOW CAN IT BE "PROTECTION" IF YOU DON'T EVEN NOTICE SOMETHING'S WRONG WITH SOMEONE UNTIL THEY'RE ALREADY CRAZY?
I CAN'T EVEN STOP THINGS FROM HAPPENING.
PLUS...
...I STILL DON'T HAVE ENOUGH EXPERIENCE USING MY POWER.
I MIGHT NOT BE ABLE TO COMPLETELY EXORCISE A JAKI.

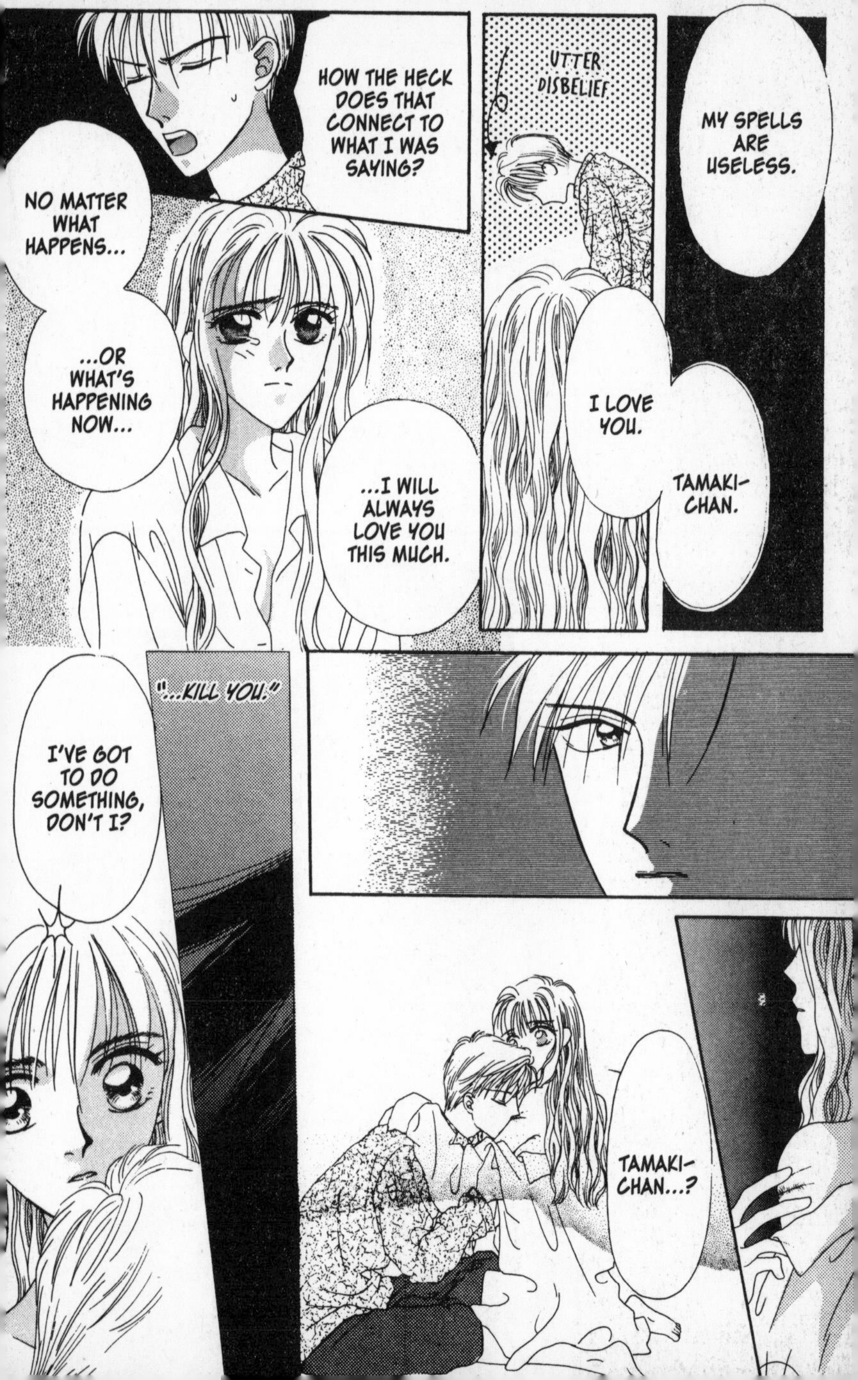
MY SPELLS ARE USELESS.
I LOVE YOU.
TAMAKI-CHAN.
UTTER DISBELIEF
HOW THE HECK DOES THAT CONNECT TO WHAT I WAS SAYING?
NO MATTER WHAT HAPPENS...
...OR WHAT'S HAPPENING NOW...
...I WILL ALWAYS LOVE YOU THIS MUCH.
"...KILL YOU."
I'VE GOT TO DO SOMETHING, DON'T I?
TAMAKI-CHAN...?

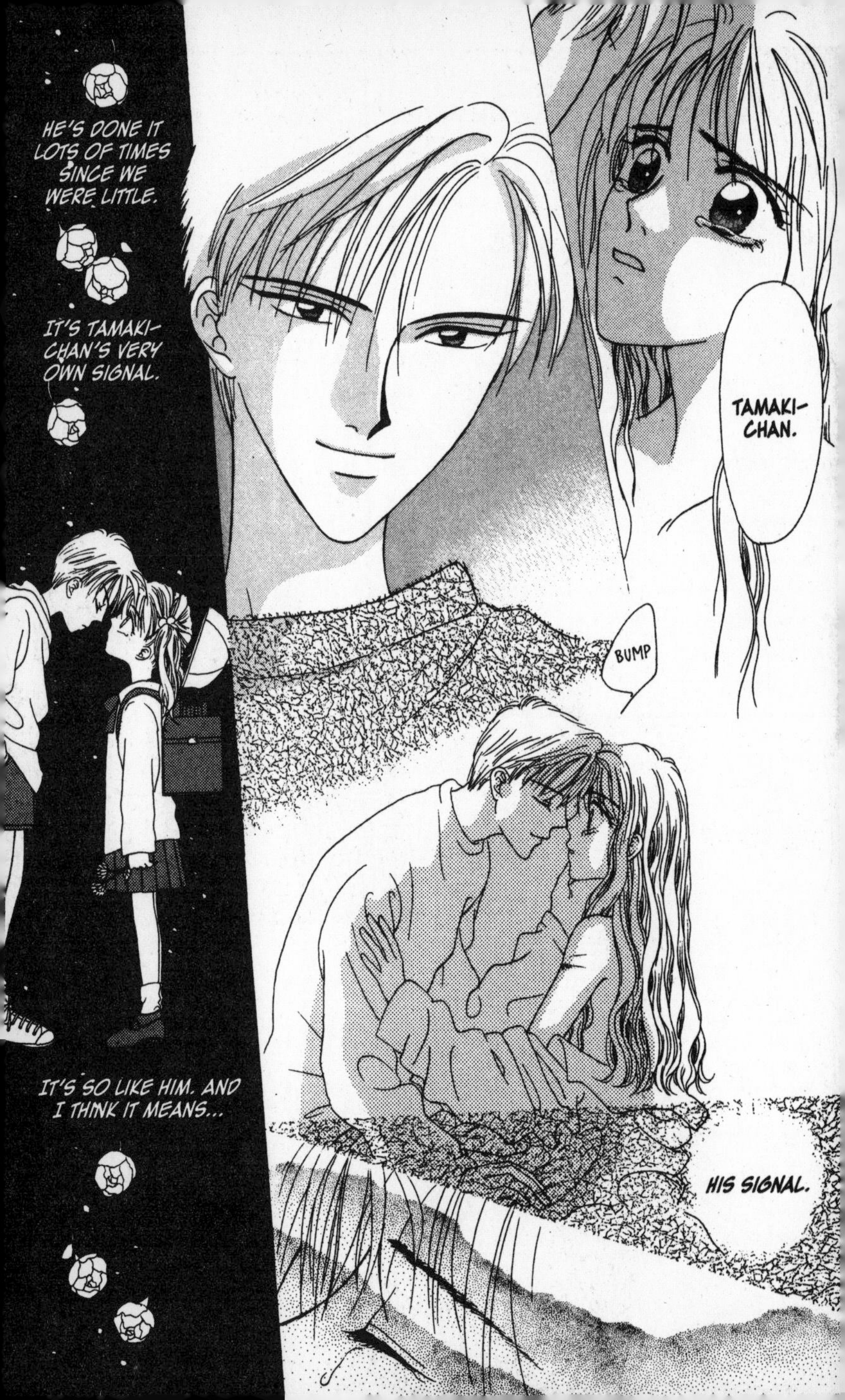
TAMAKI-CHAN.
BUMP
HIS SIGNAL.
HE'S DONE IT LOTS OF TIMES SINCE WE WERE LITTLE.
IT'S TAMAKI-CHAN'S VERY OWN SIGNAL.
IT'S SO LIKE HIM. AND I THINK IT MEANS...

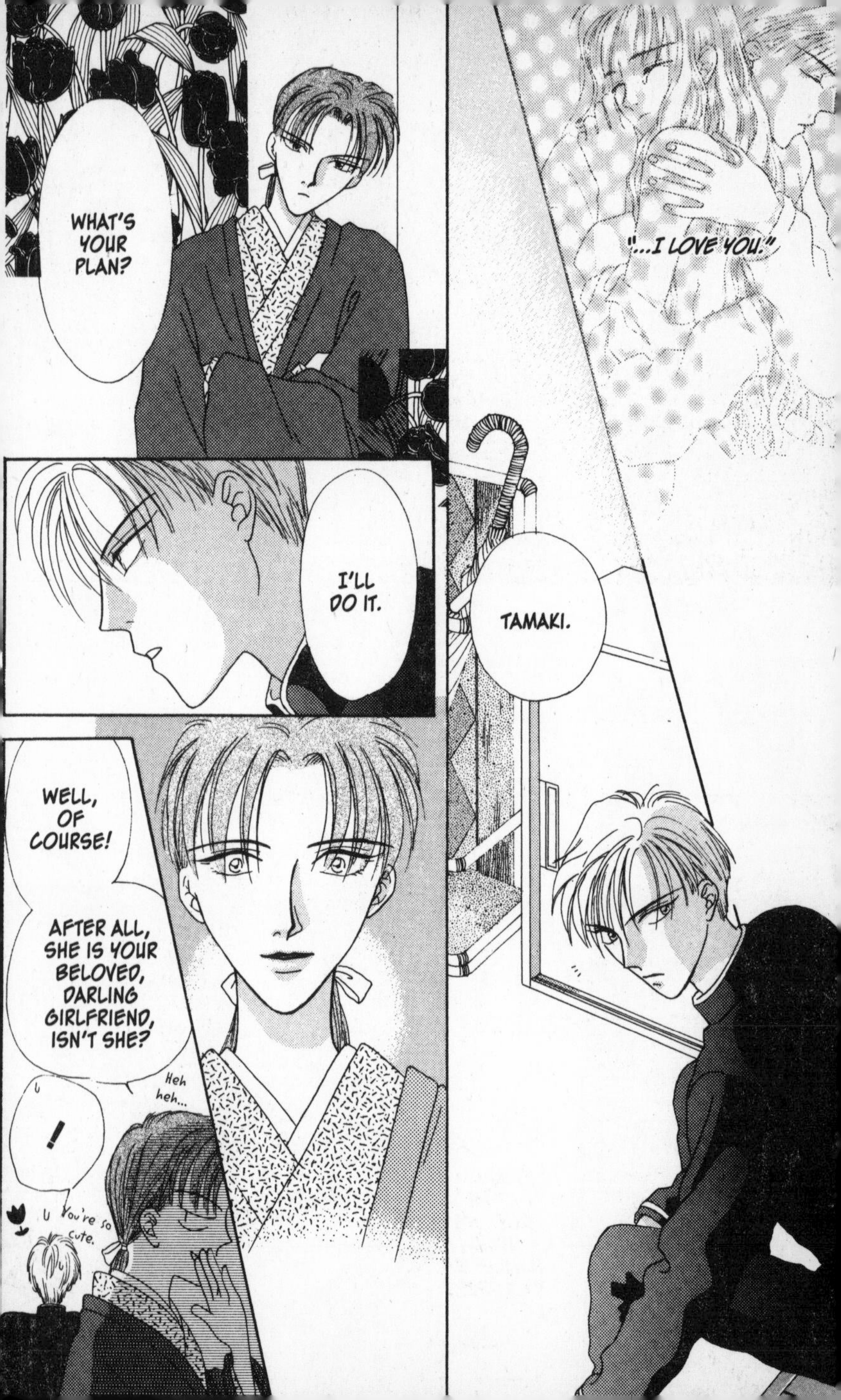
"...I LOVE YOU."
TAMAKI.
WHAT'S YOUR PLAN?
I'LL DO IT.
WELL, OF COURSE!
AFTER ALL, SHE IS YOUR BELOVED, DARLING GIRLFRIEND, ISN'T SHE?
Heh heh...
!
You're so cute.

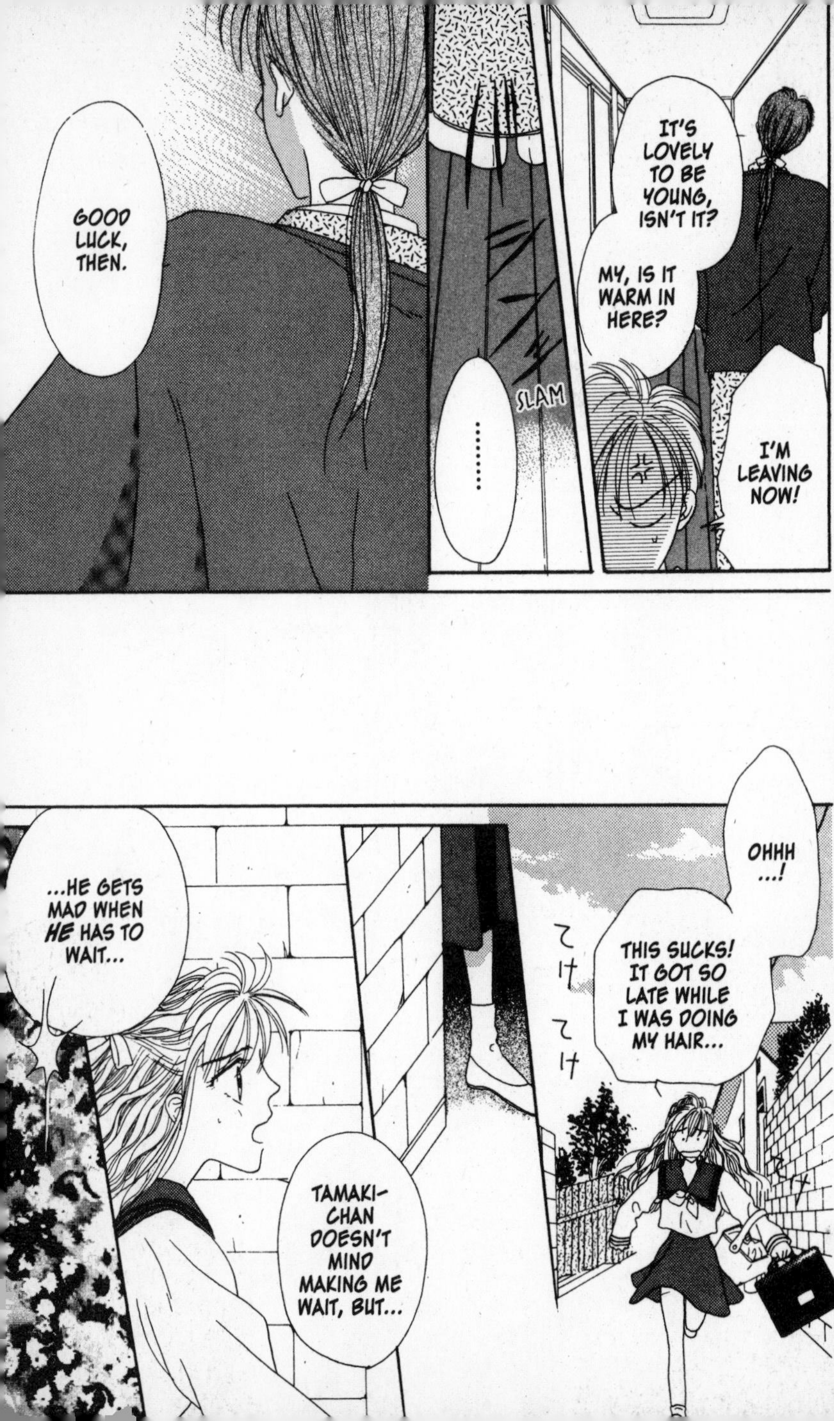

IT'S LOVELY TO BE YOUNG, ISN'T IT?
MY, IS IT WARM IN HERE?
I'M LEAVING NOW!
SLAM
......
GOOD LUCK, THEN.
OHHH ...!
THIS SUCKS! IT GOT SO LATE WHILE I WAS DOING MY HAIR...
てけ てけ
TAMAKI-CHAN DOESN'T MIND MAKING ME WAIT, BUT...
...HE GETS MAD WHEN *HE* HAS TO WAIT...

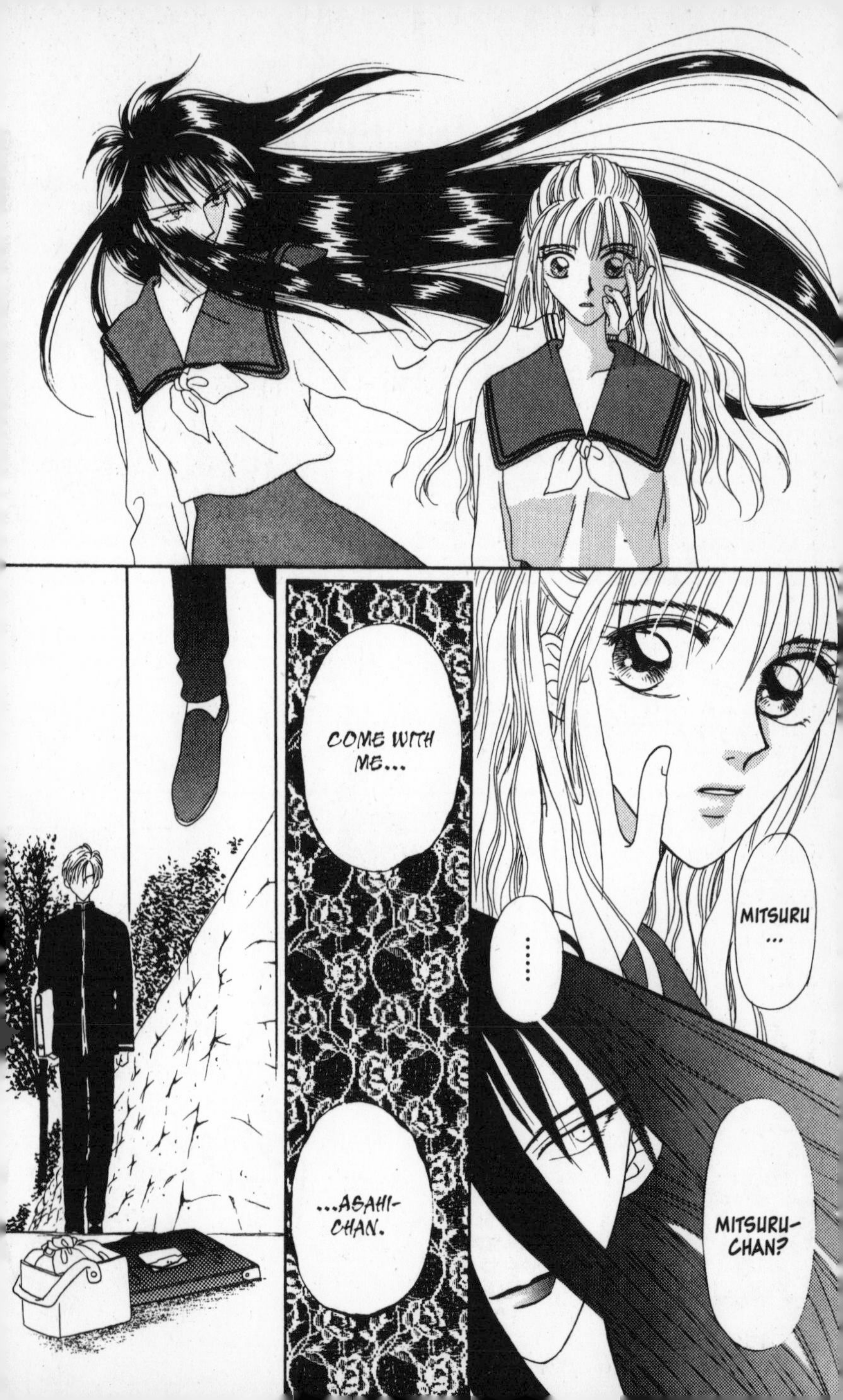
MITSURU...
......
MITSURU-CHAN?
COME WITH ME...
...ASAHI-CHAN.

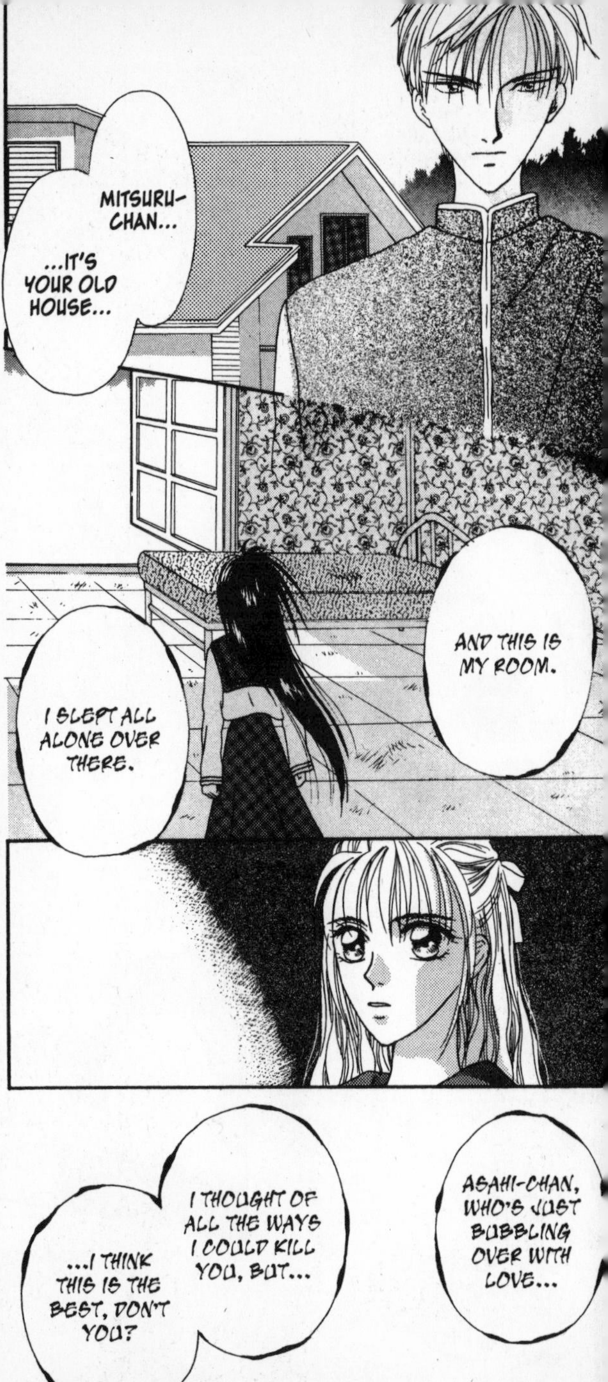
MITSURU-CHAN...
...IT'S YOUR OLD HOUSE...
AND THIS IS MY ROOM.
I SLEPT ALL ALONE OVER THERE.
ASAHI-CHAN, WHO'S JUST BUBBLING OVER WITH LOVE...
I THOUGHT OF ALL THE WAYS I COULD KILL YOU, BUT...
...I THINK THIS IS THE BEST, DON'T YOU?

Phantom Dream

One

Pleased to meet you! Or maybe I should say, hello, this is Takaya. And this is my first comic. It's amazing, isn't it? Is it really okay for me to be writing this? I feel like I've walked into someone's house with my muddy shoes on a rainy day. (Even newbies get to wear clothes, don't they?) Anyway, this was my first work, which first appeared in...the April '94 issue of *Planet*. You've got to be kidding! Has it really been two years since then? Meow... Well, that explains why the art looks like this. But if I were ever to draw it over, it wouldn't end so quickly--I'm sorry! It's history now, so please overlook that... Aaaahhhh!!! What am I going to do, if I'm already making excuses in the margins of the first book? That's not right, is it? Can I start over and say something more impressive? And this margin's almost full already...!

Ohh...

wait...!

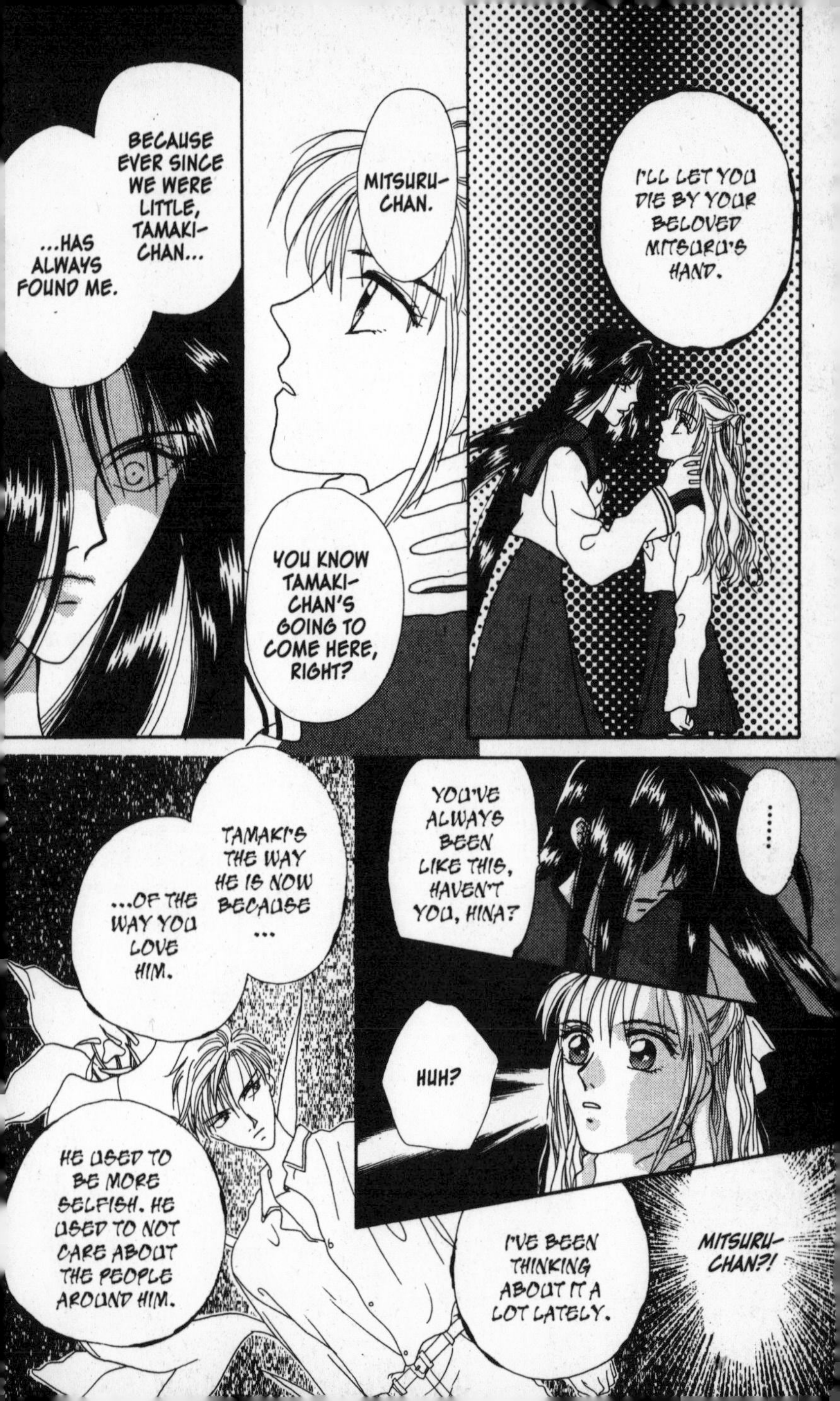
I'LL LET YOU DIE BY YOUR BELOVED MITSURU'S HAND.
MITSURU-CHAN.
YOU KNOW TAMAKI-CHAN'S GOING TO COME HERE, RIGHT?
BECAUSE EVER SINCE WE WERE LITTLE, TAMAKI-CHAN...
...HAS ALWAYS FOUND ME.
......
YOU'VE ALWAYS BEEN LIKE THIS, HAVEN'T YOU, HINA?
HUH?
MITSURU-CHAN?!
I'VE BEEN THINKING ABOUT IT A LOT LATELY.
TAMAKI'S THE WAY HE IS NOW BECAUSE...
...OF THE WAY YOU LOVE HIM.
HE USED TO BE MORE SELFISH. HE USED TO NOT CARE ABOUT THE PEOPLE AROUND HIM.

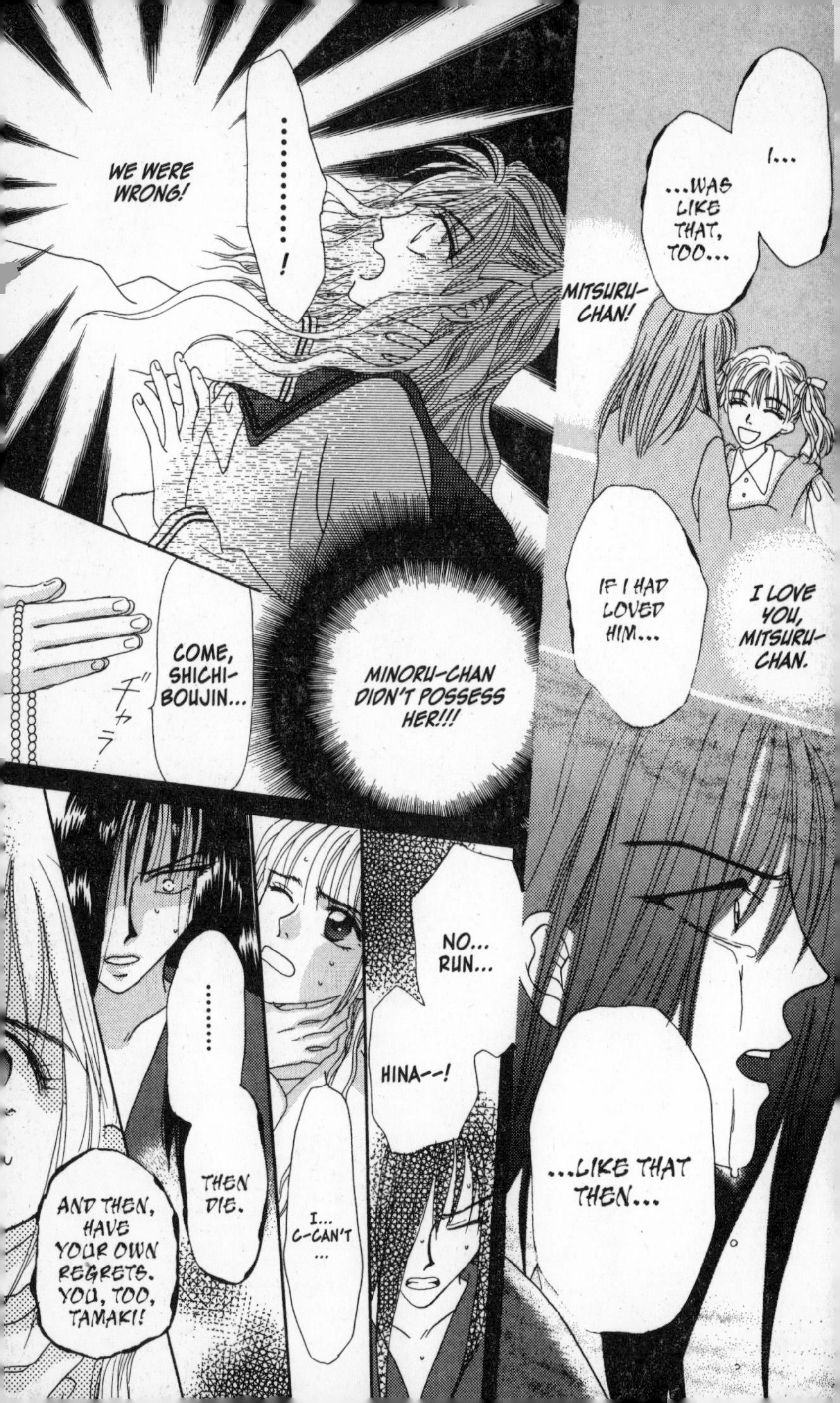
I...
...WAS LIKE THAT, TOO...
MITSURU-CHAN!
I LOVE YOU, MITSURU-CHAN.
IF I HAD LOVED HIM...
...LIKE THAT THEN...
......!
WE WERE WRONG!
MINORU-CHAN DIDN'T POSSESS HER!!!
COME, SHICHI-BOUJIN...
ヂャラ
NO... RUN...
HINA--!
I... C-CAN'T ...
......
THEN DIE.
AND THEN, HAVE YOUR OWN REGRETS. YOU, TOO, TAMAKI!

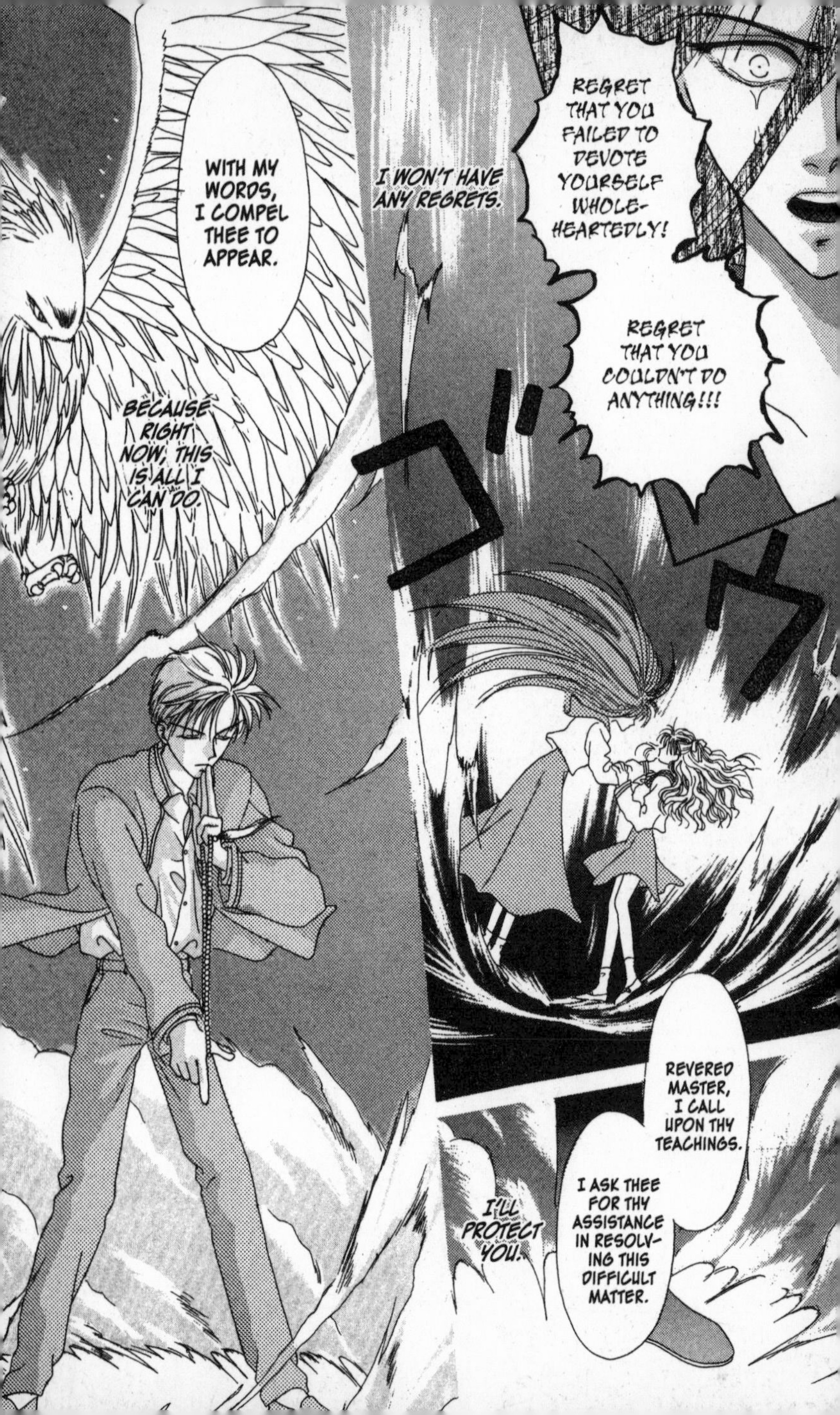
REGRET THAT YOU FAILED TO DEVOTE YOURSELF WHOLE-HEARTEDLY!
REGRET THAT YOU COULDN'T DO ANYTHING!!!
I WON'T HAVE ANY REGRETS.
ゴウ
REVERED MASTER, I CALL UPON THY TEACHINGS.
I ASK THEE FOR THY ASSISTANCE IN RESOLV-ING THIS DIFFICULT MATTER.
I'LL PROTECT YOU.
WITH MY WORDS, I COMPEL THEE TO APPEAR.
BECAUSE RIGHT NOW, THIS IS ALL I CAN DO.

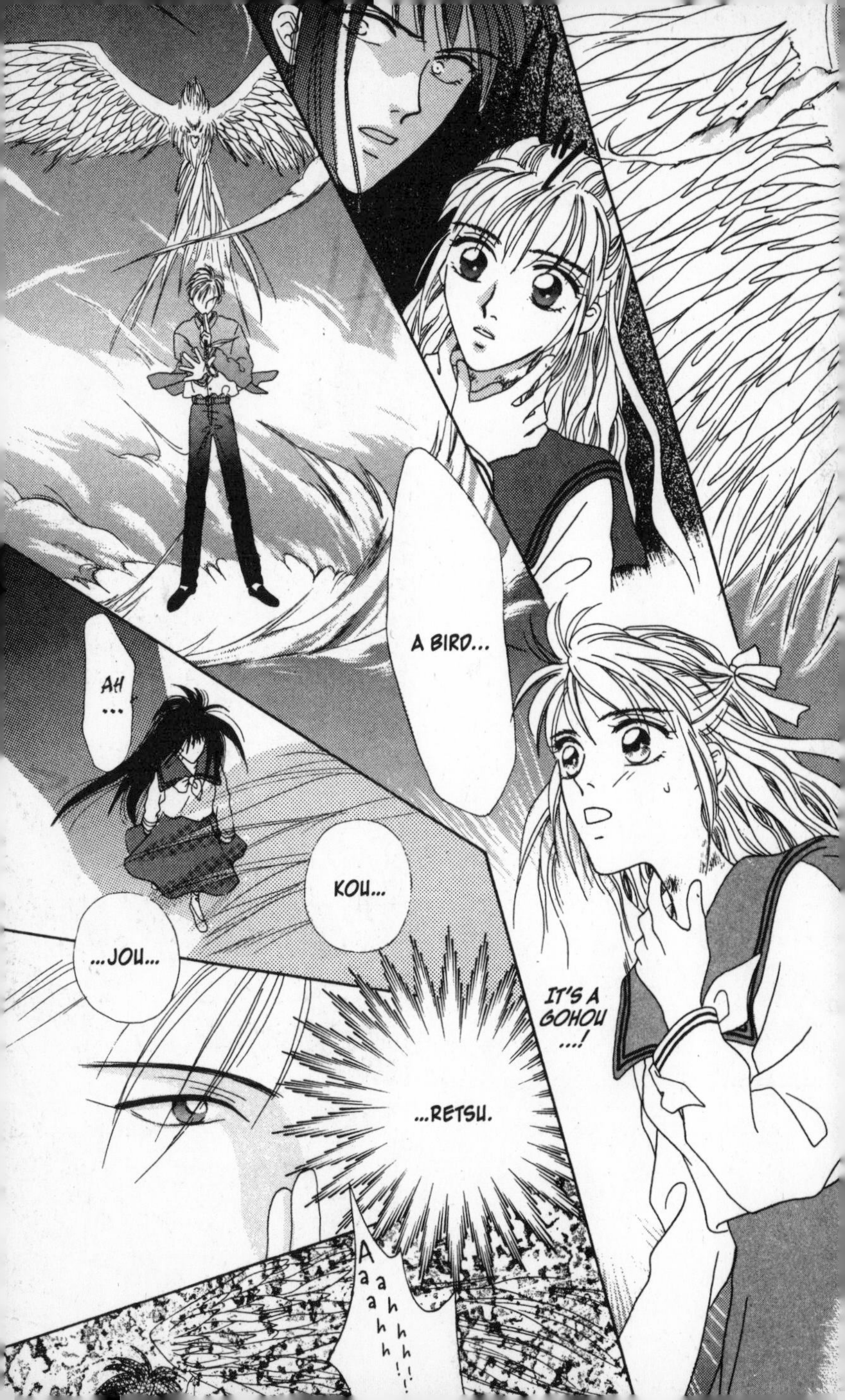
A BIRD...
IT'S A GOHOU ...!
AH ...
KOU...
...JOU...
...RETSU.
Aaaahhhh!!

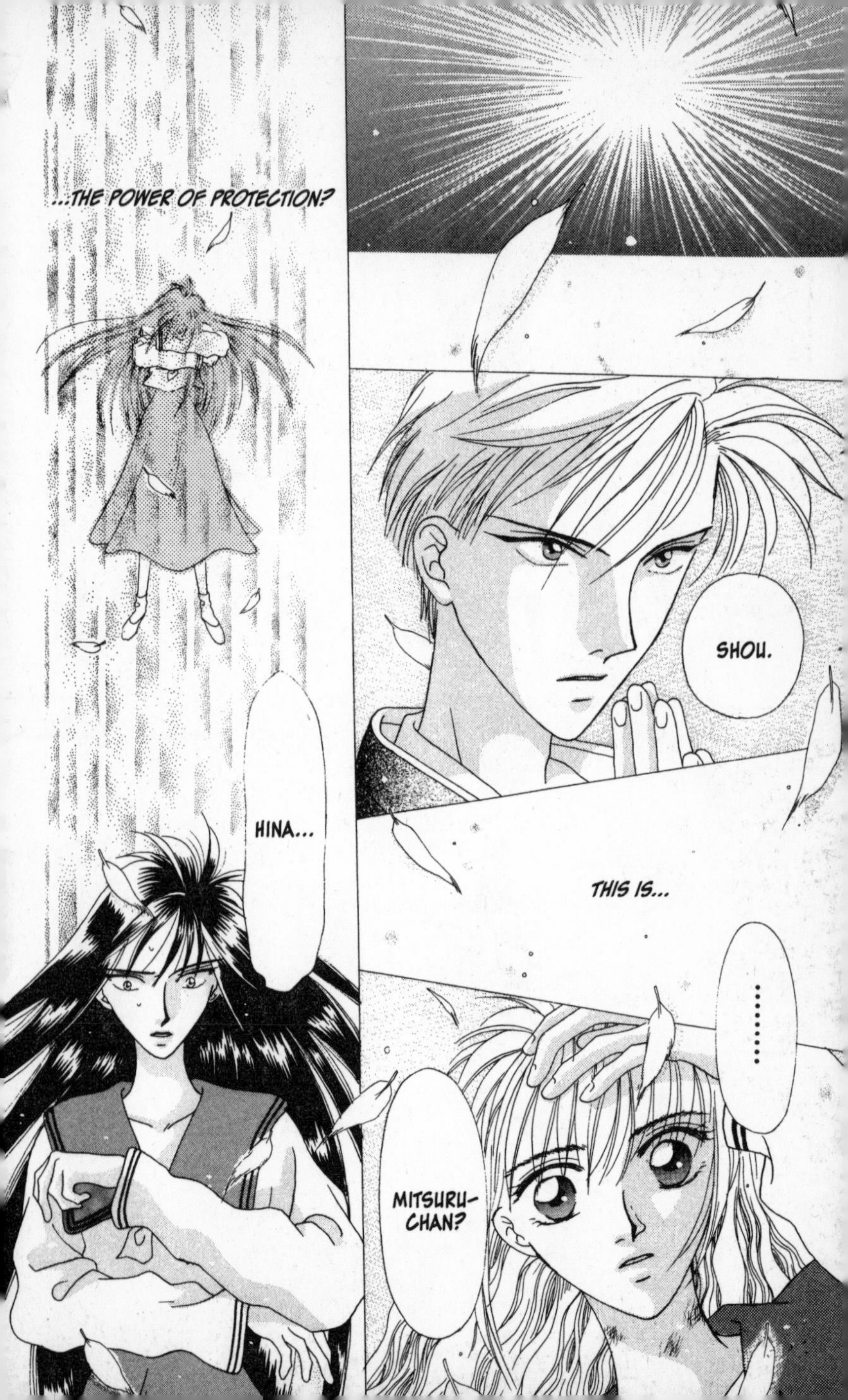
SHOU.
THIS IS...
......
MITSURU-CHAN?
...THE POWER OF PROTECTION?
HINA...

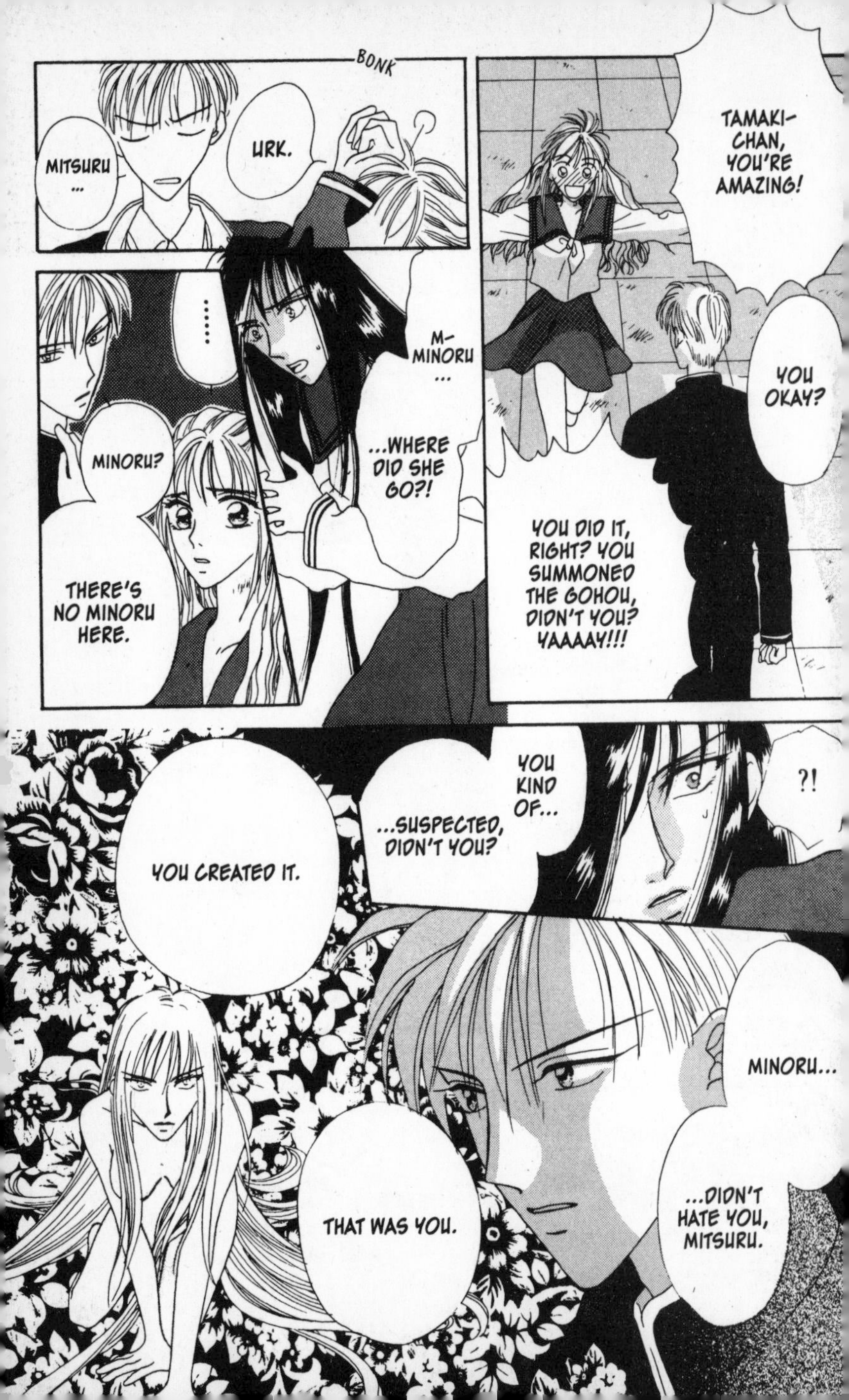
TAMAKI-CHAN, YOU'RE AMAZING!
YOU OKAY?
YOU DID IT, RIGHT? YOU SUMMONED THE GOHOU, DIDN'T YOU? YAAAAY!!!
BONK
URK.
MITSURU ...
M-MINORU ...
......
...WHERE DID SHE GO?!
MINORU?
THERE'S NO MINORU HERE.
?!
YOU KIND OF...
...SUSPECTED, DIDN'T YOU?
YOU CREATED IT.
MINORU...
...DIDN'T HATE YOU, MITSURU.
THAT WAS YOU.

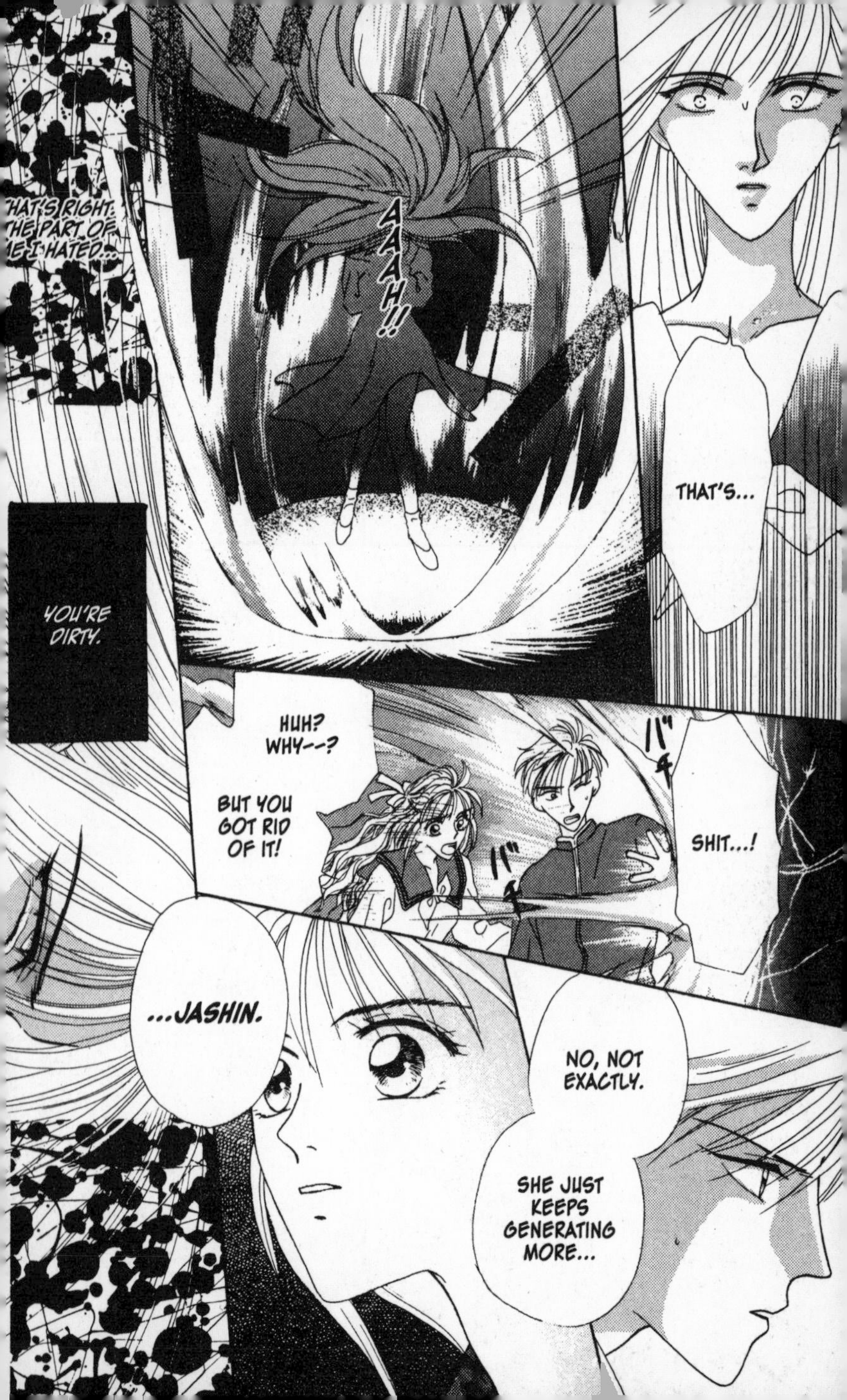
THAT'S...
AAAAH!!
THAT'S RIGHT. THE PART OF ME I HATED...
YOU'RE DIRTY.
バチ
SHIT...!
HUH? WHY--?
BUT YOU GOT RID OF IT!
バ
NO, NOT EXACTLY.
SHE JUST KEEPS GENERATING MORE...
...JASHIN.

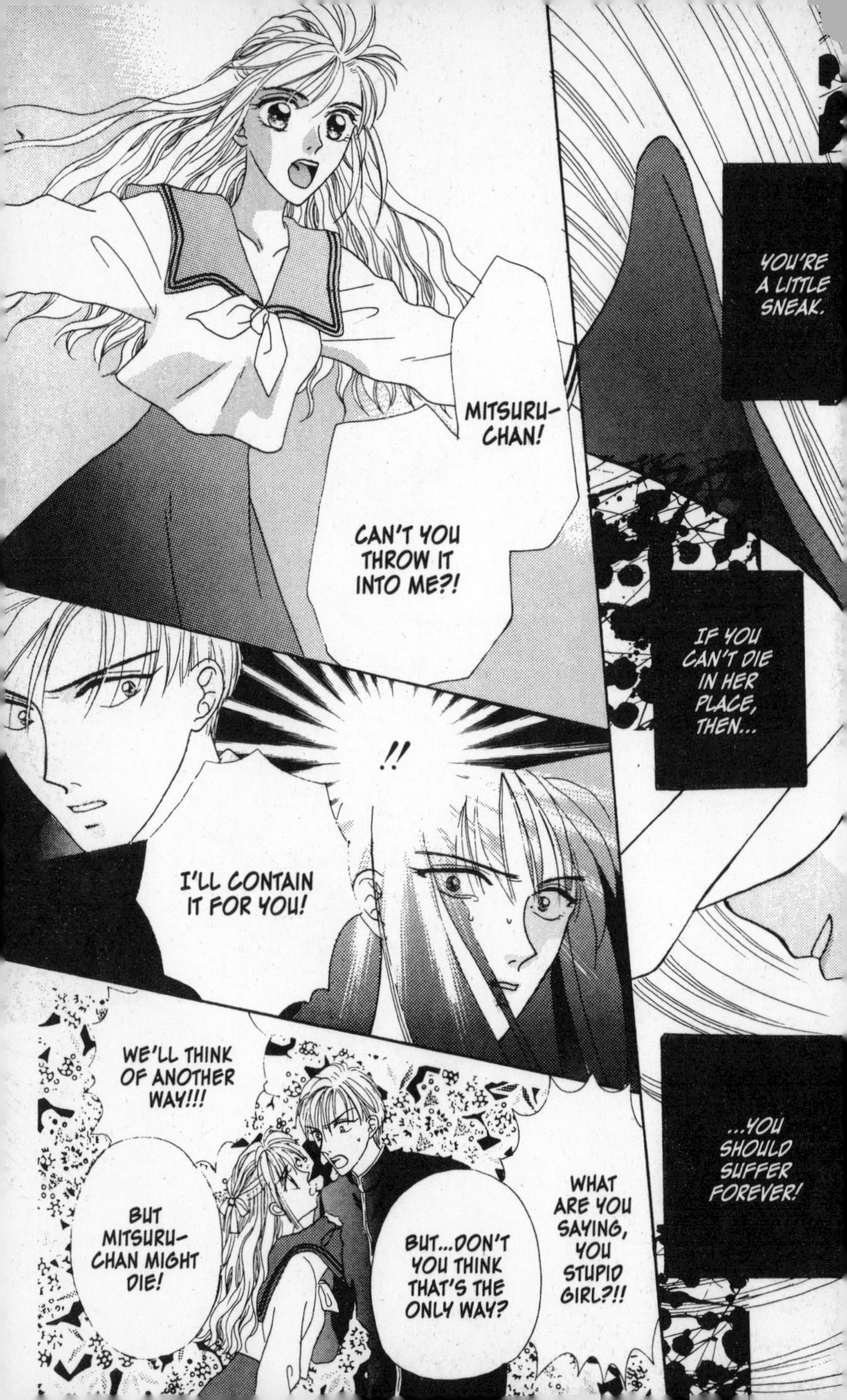
YOU'RE A LITTLE SNEAK.
IF YOU CAN'T DIE IN HER PLACE, THEN...
...YOU SHOULD SUFFER FOREVER!
MITSURU-CHAN!
CAN'T YOU THROW IT INTO ME?!
!!
I'LL CONTAIN IT FOR YOU!
WHAT ARE YOU SAYING, YOU STUPID GIRL?!!
BUT...DON'T YOU THINK THAT'S THE ONLY WAY?
WE'LL THINK OF ANOTHER WAY!!!
BUT MITSURU-CHAN MIGHT DIE!

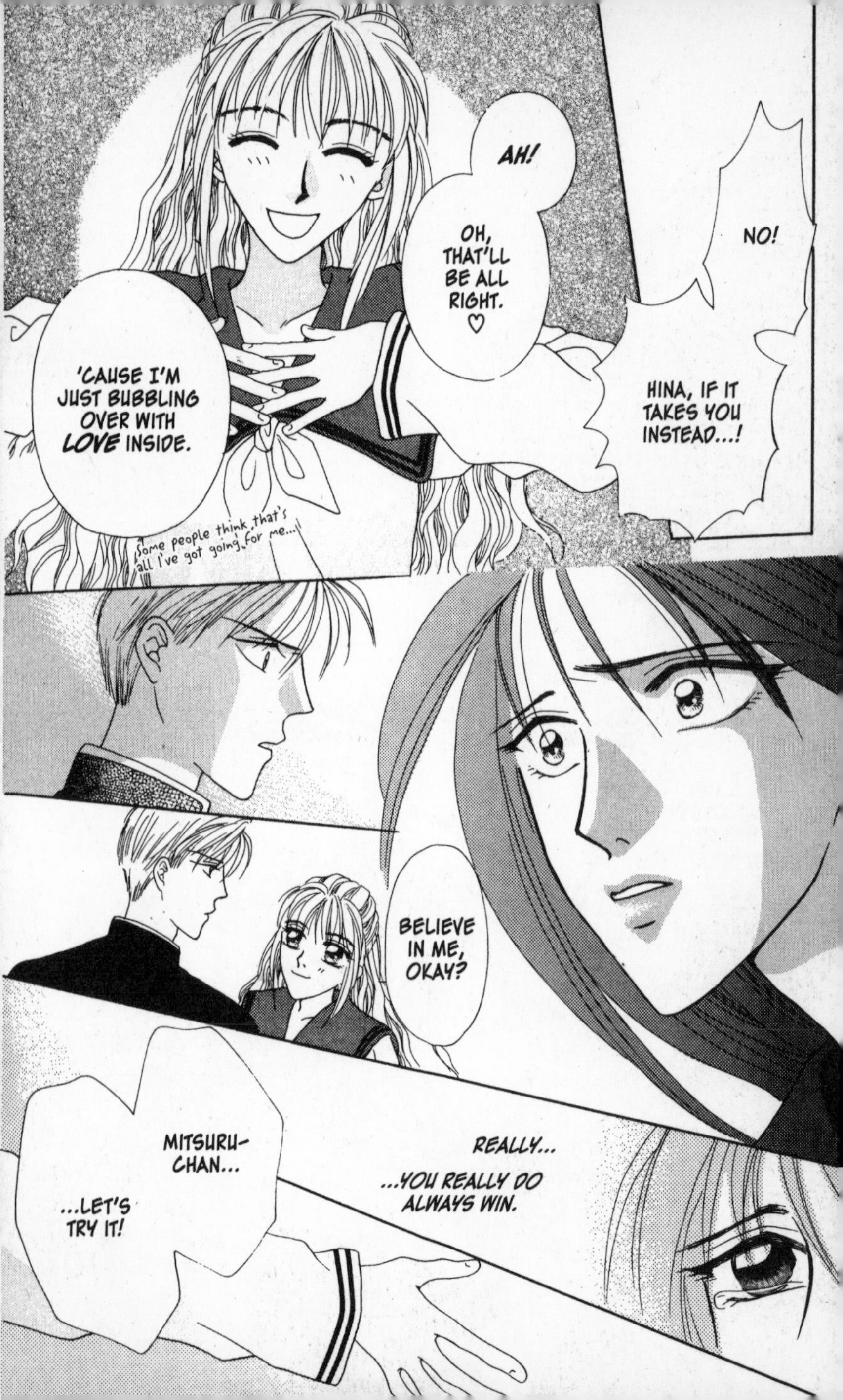
NO!
HINA, IF IT TAKES YOU INSTEAD...!
AH!
OH, THAT'LL BE ALL RIGHT. ♡
'CAUSE I'M JUST BUBBLING OVER WITH LOVE INSIDE.
Some people think that's all I've got going for me...
BELIEVE IN ME, OKAY?
REALLY...
...YOU REALLY DO ALWAYS WIN.
MITSURU-CHAN...
...LET'S TRY IT!

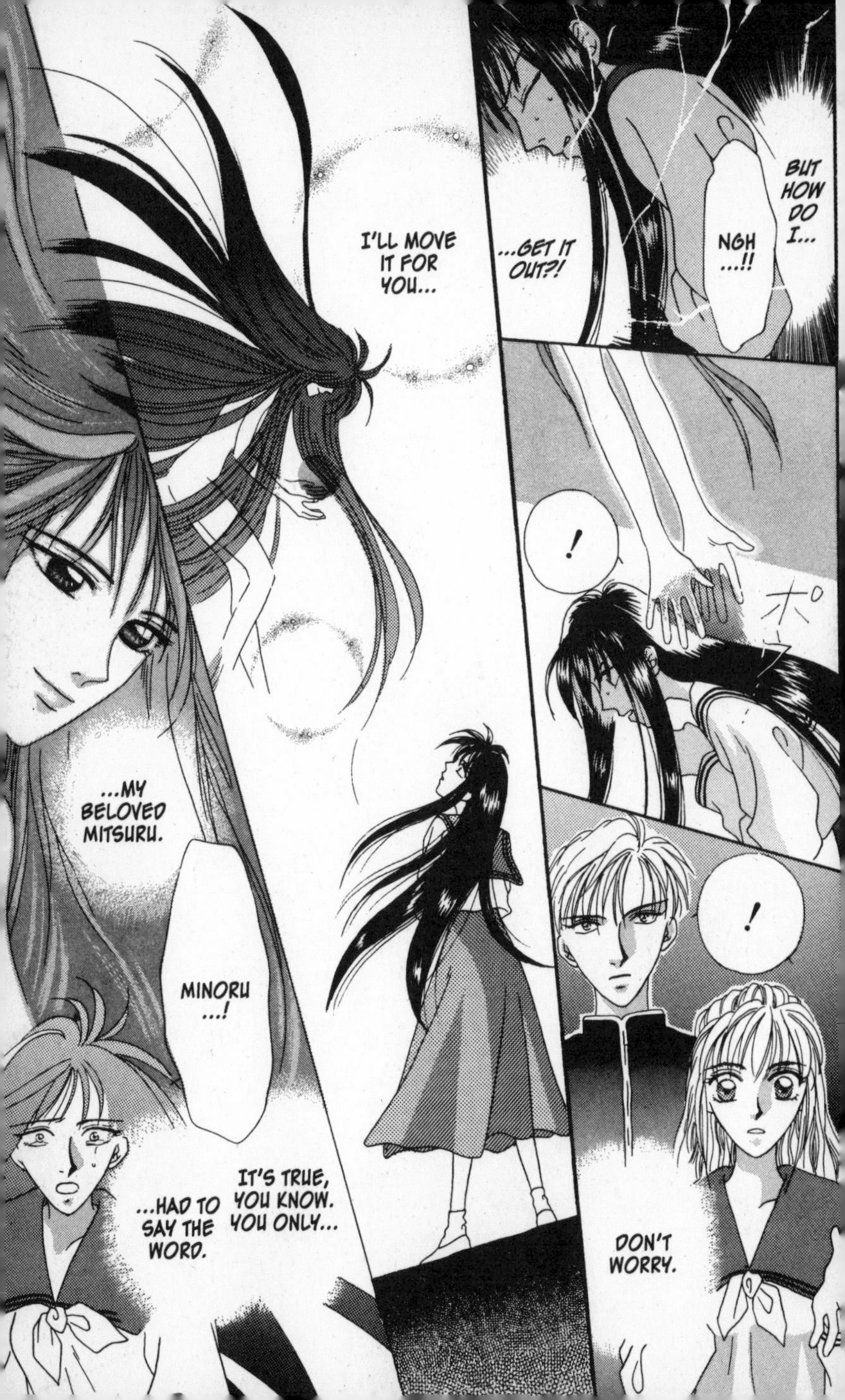
BUT HOW DO I...
NGH ...!!
...GET IT OUT?!
!
ポ
!
DON'T WORRY.
I'LL MOVE IT FOR YOU...
...MY BELOVED MITSURU.
MINORU ...!
IT'S TRUE, YOU KNOW. YOU ONLY...
...HAD TO SAY THE WORD.

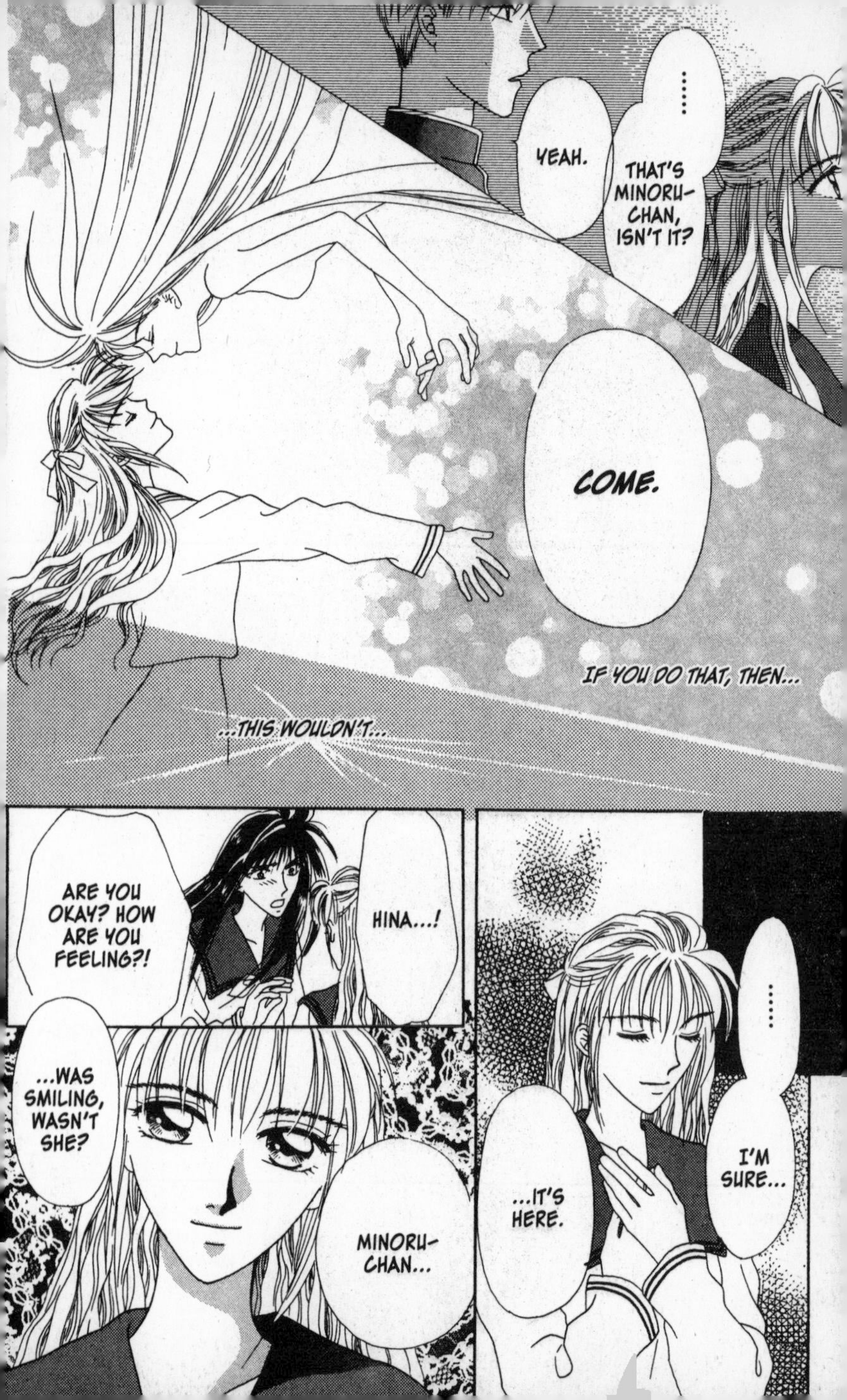
......
THAT'S MINORU-CHAN, ISN'T IT?
YEAH.
COME.
IF YOU DO THAT, THEN...
...THIS WOULDN'T...
......
I'M SURE...
...IT'S HERE.
HINA...!
ARE YOU OKAY? HOW ARE YOU FEELING?!
MINORU-CHAN...
...WAS SMILING, WASN'T SHE?

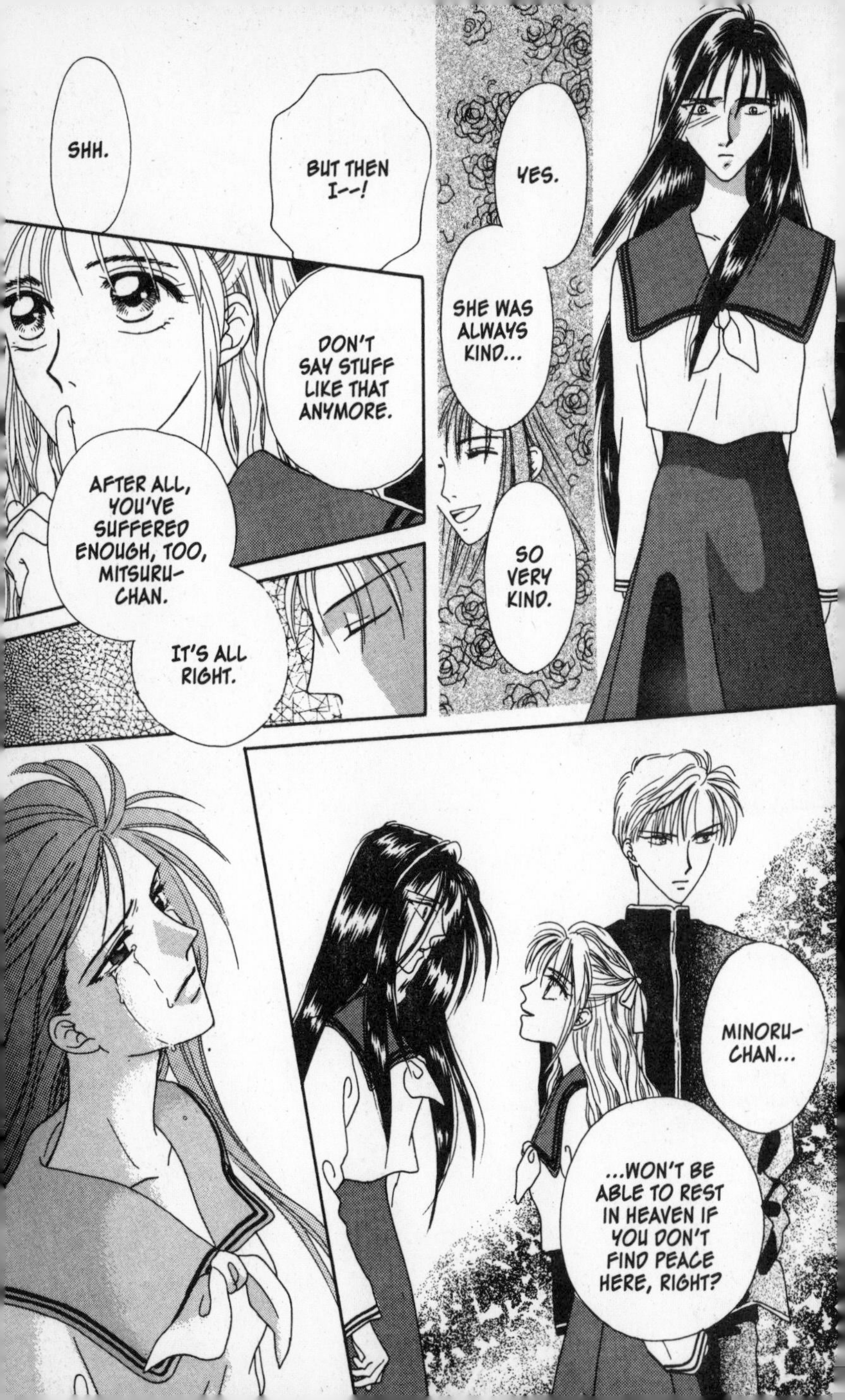
YES.
SHE WAS ALWAYS KIND...
SO VERY KIND.
BUT THEN I--!
SHH.
DON'T SAY STUFF LIKE THAT ANYMORE.
AFTER ALL, YOU'VE SUFFERED ENOUGH, TOO, MITSURU-CHAN.
IT'S ALL RIGHT.
MINORU-CHAN...
...WON'T BE ABLE TO REST IN HEAVEN IF YOU DON'T FIND PEACE HERE, RIGHT?

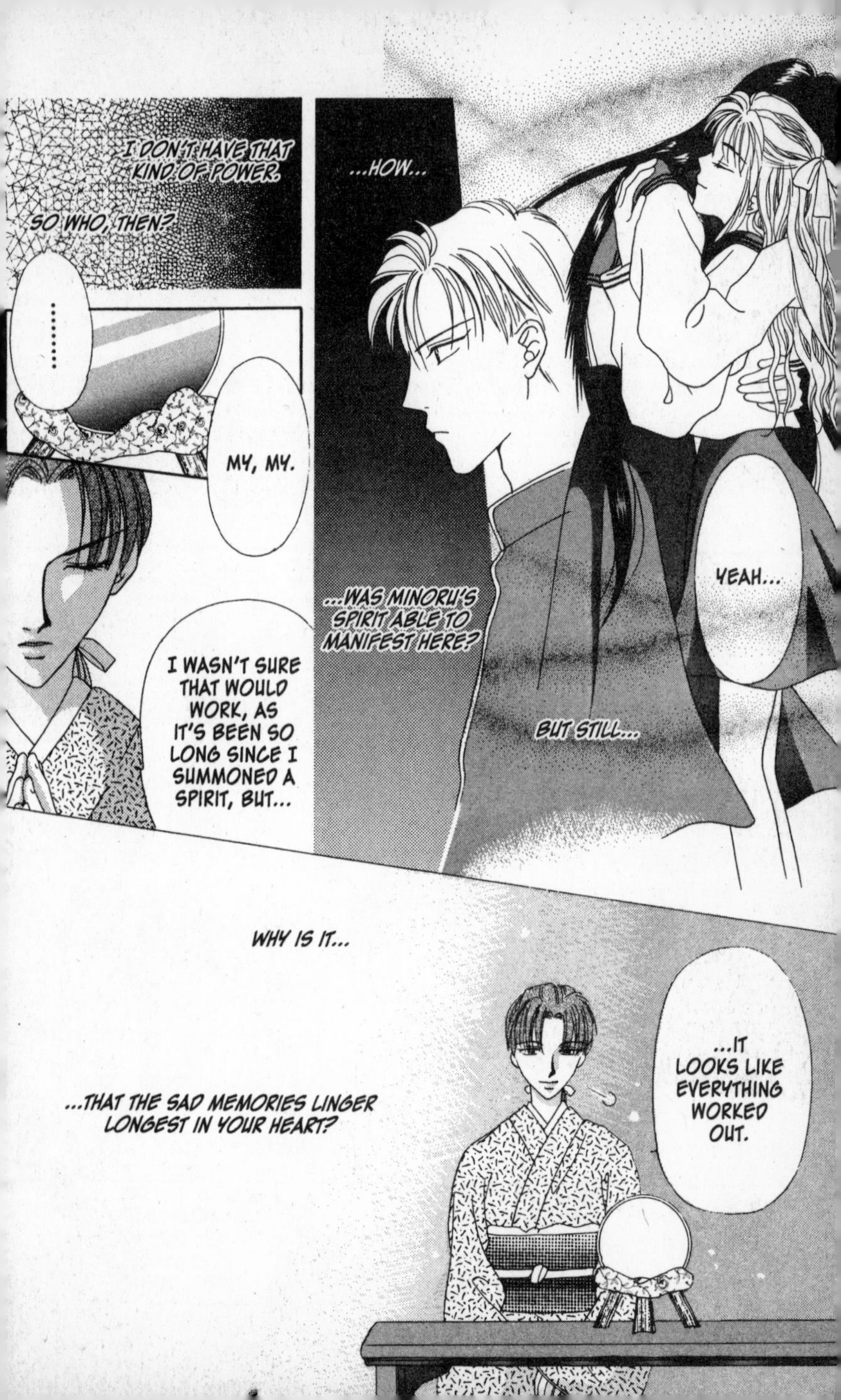
...HOW...
...WAS MINORU'S SPIRIT ABLE TO MANIFEST HERE?
YEAH...
BUT STILL...
I DON'T HAVE THAT KIND OF POWER.
SO WHO, THEN?
......
MY, MY.
I WASN'T SURE THAT WOULD WORK, AS IT'S BEEN SO LONG SINCE I SUMMONED A SPIRIT, BUT...
...IT LOOKS LIKE EVERYTHING WORKED OUT.
WHY IS IT...
...THAT THE SAD MEMORIES LINGER LONGEST IN YOUR HEART?

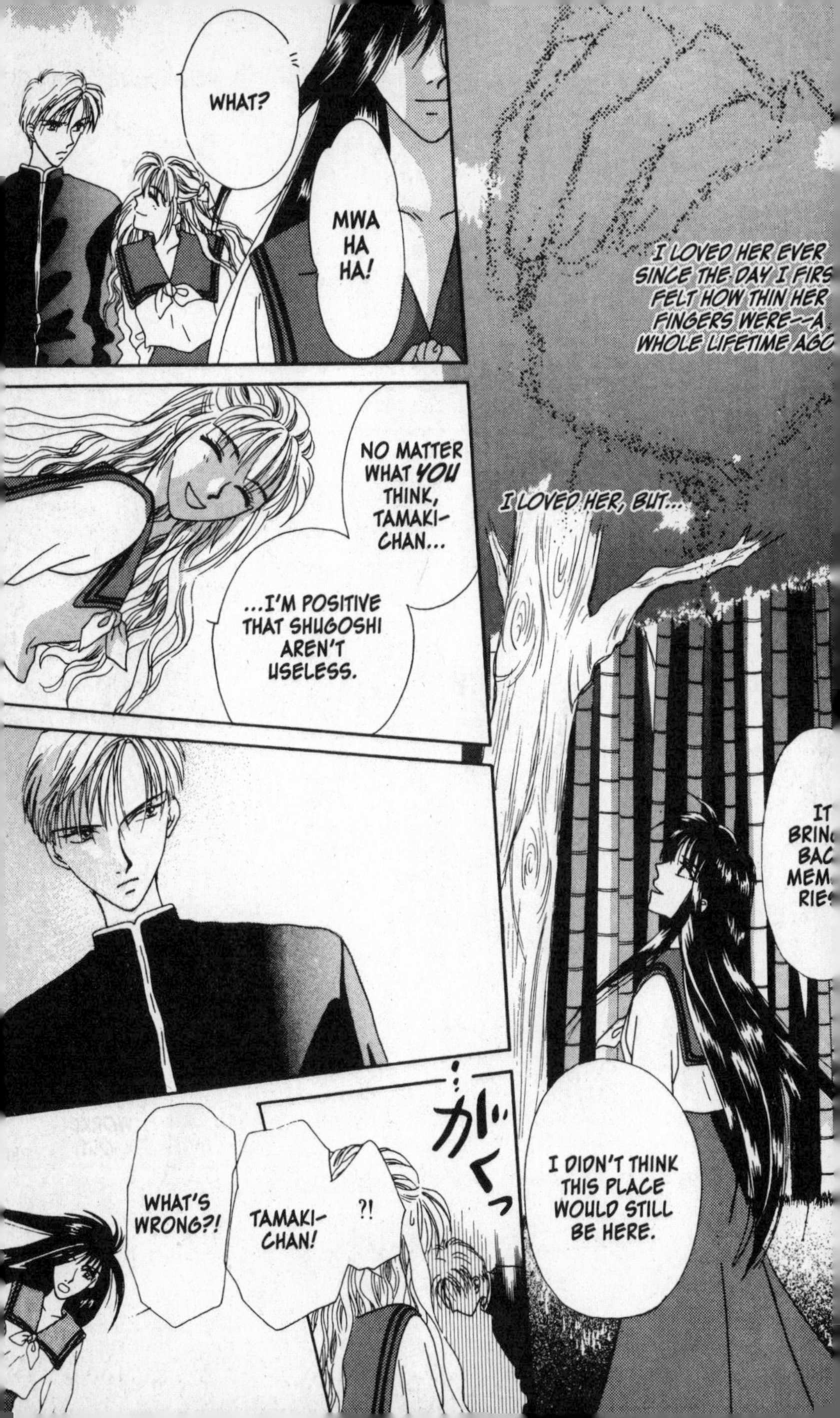
I LOVED HER EVER SINCE THE DAY I FIRS FELT HOW THIN HER FINGERS WERE--A WHOLE LIFETIME AGO
I LOVED HER, BUT...
IT BRIN BAC MEM RIES
I DIDN'T THINK THIS PLACE WOULD STILL BE HERE.
WHAT?
MWA HA HA!
NO MATTER WHAT *YOU* THINK, TAMAKI-CHAN...
...I'M POSITIVE THAT SHUGOSHI AREN'T USELESS.
がくっ
?!
TAMAKI-CHAN!
WHAT'S WRONG?!

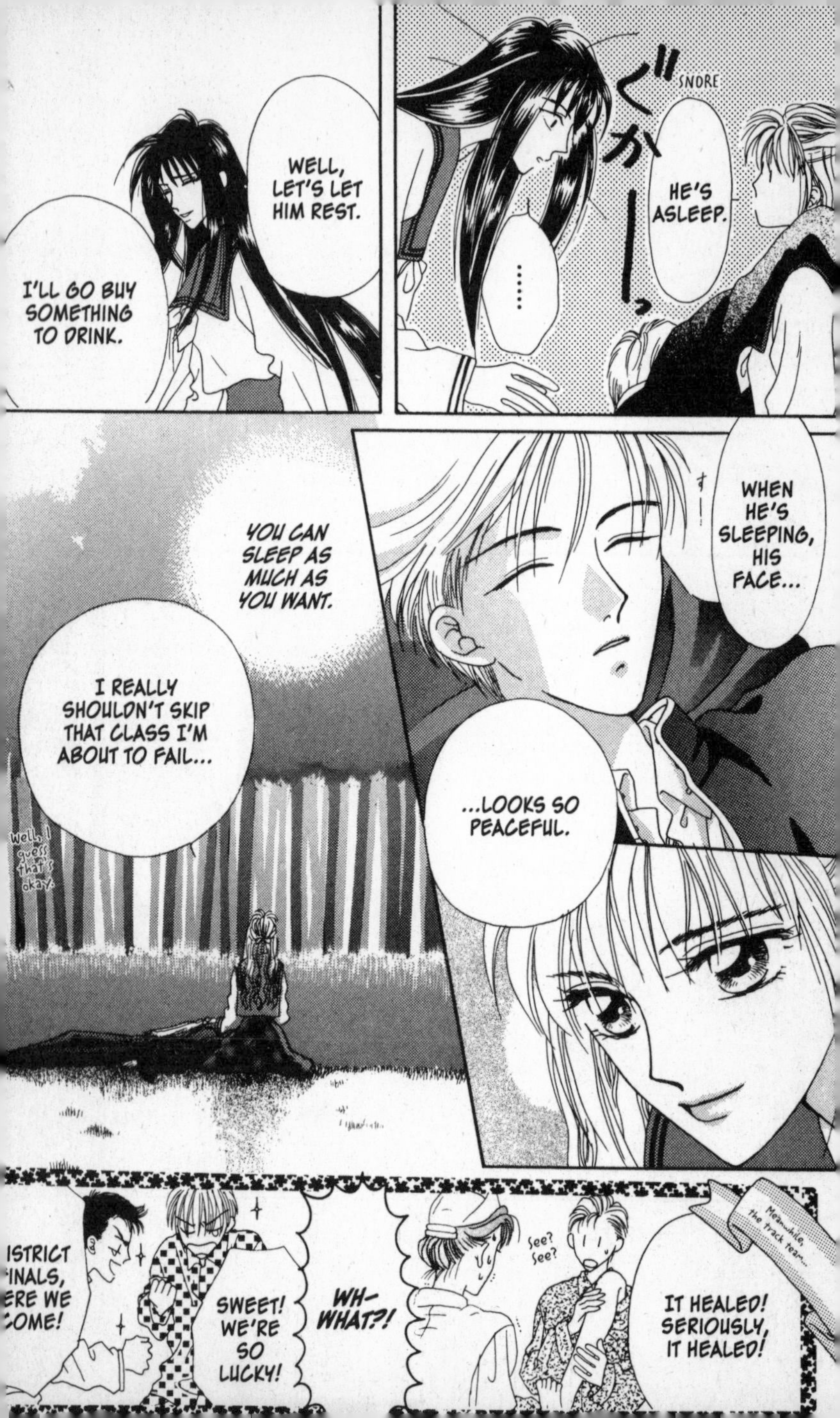
SNORE
HE'S ASLEEP.
......
WELL, LET'S LET HIM REST.
I'LL GO BUY SOMETHING TO DRINK.
WHEN HE'S SLEEPING, HIS FACE...
...LOOKS SO PEACEFUL.
YOU CAN SLEEP AS MUCH AS YOU WANT.
I REALLY SHOULDN'T SKIP THAT CLASS I'M ABOUT TO FAIL...
Well, I guess that's okay.
Meanwhile, the track team...
IT HEALED! SERIOUSLY, IT HEALED!
See? See?
WH- WHAT?!
SWEET! WE'RE SO LUCKY!
ISTRICT FINALS, ERE WE COME!

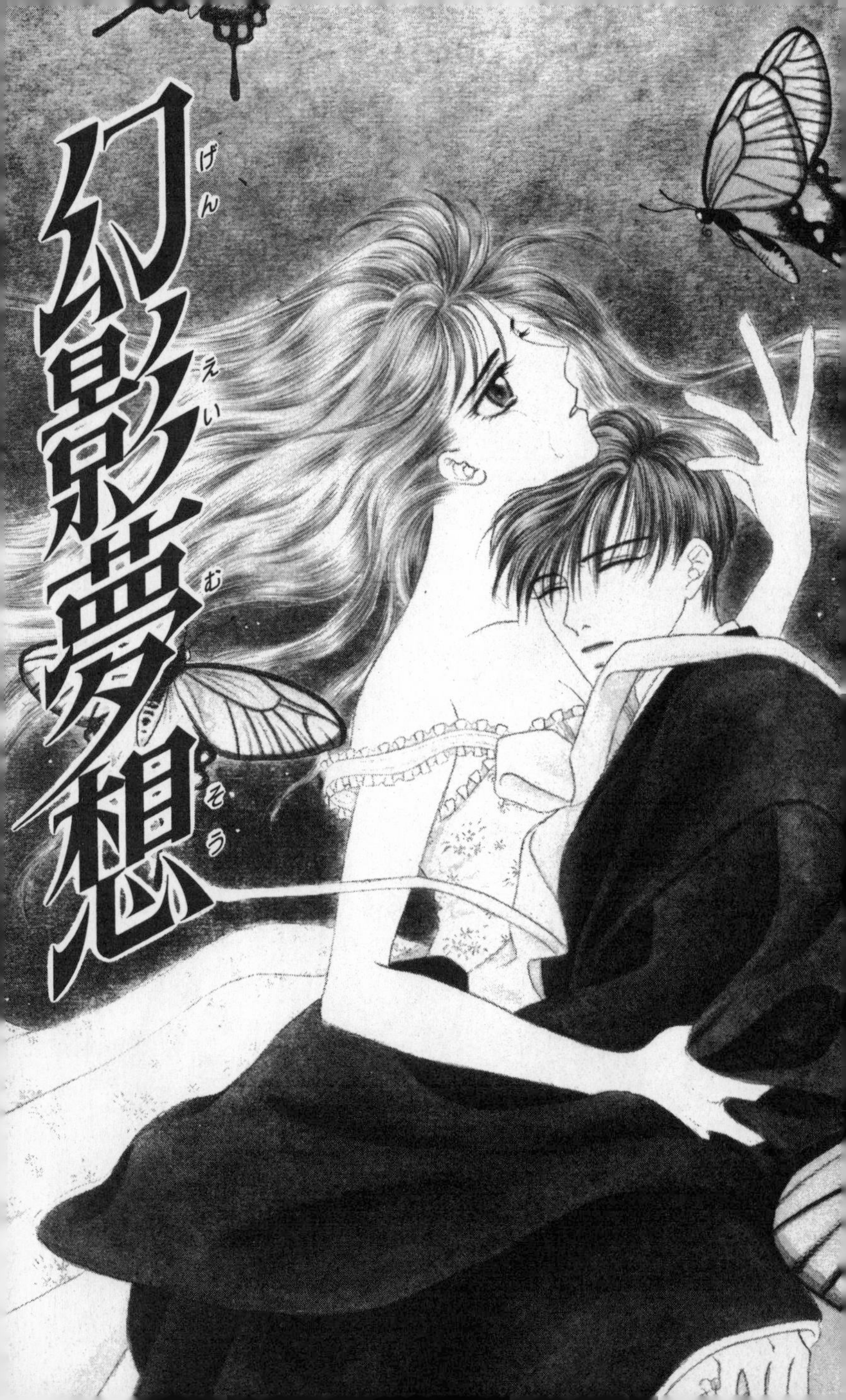
幻影夢想(げんえいむそう)

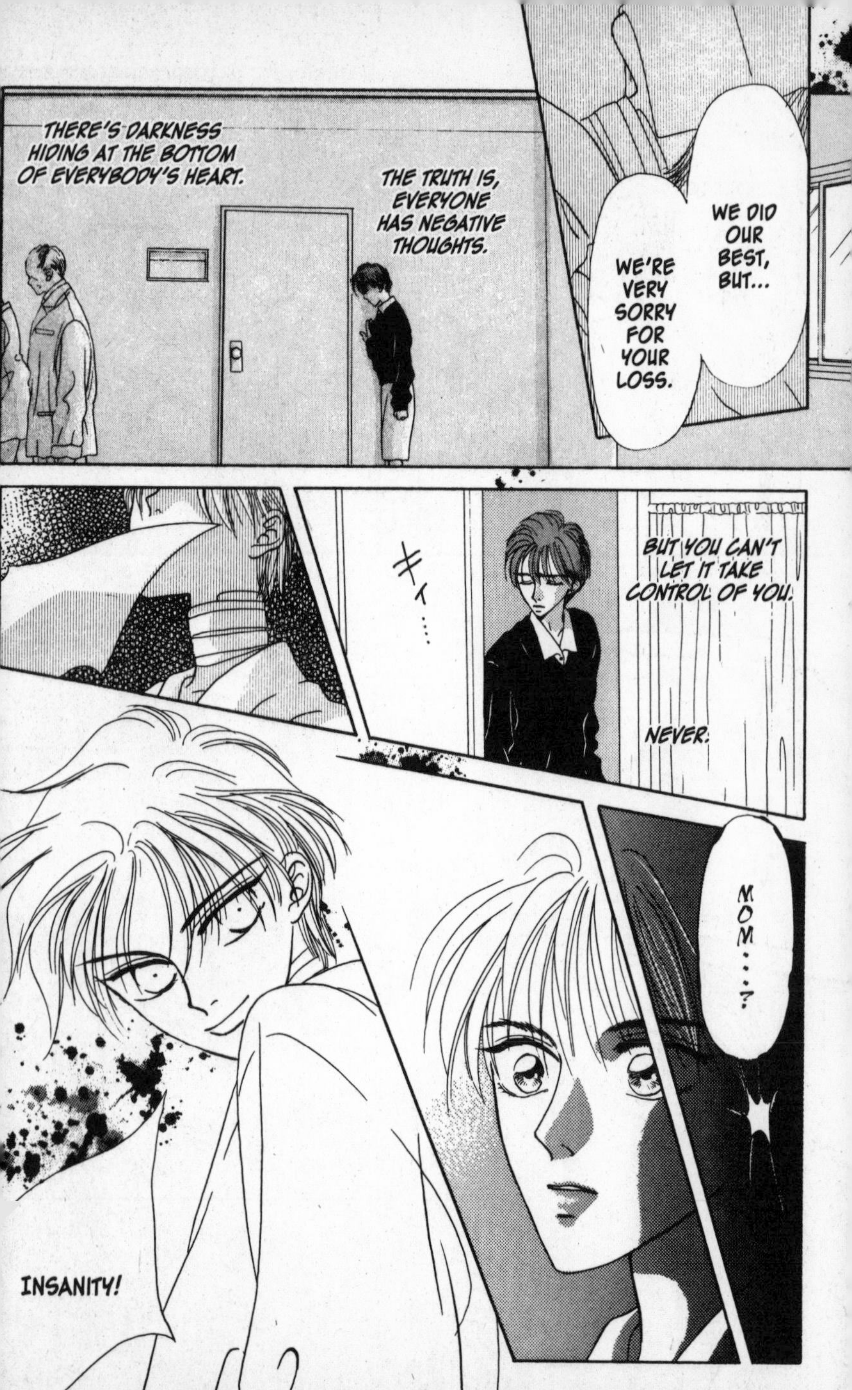
WE DID OUR BEST, BUT...
WE'RE VERY SORRY FOR YOUR LOSS.
THERE'S DARKNESS HIDING AT THE BOTTOM OF EVERYBODY'S HEART.
THE TRUTH IS, EVERYONE HAS NEGATIVE THOUGHTS.
BUT YOU CAN'T LET IT TAKE CONTROL OF YOU.
キィ…
NEVER.
MOM...?
INSANITY!

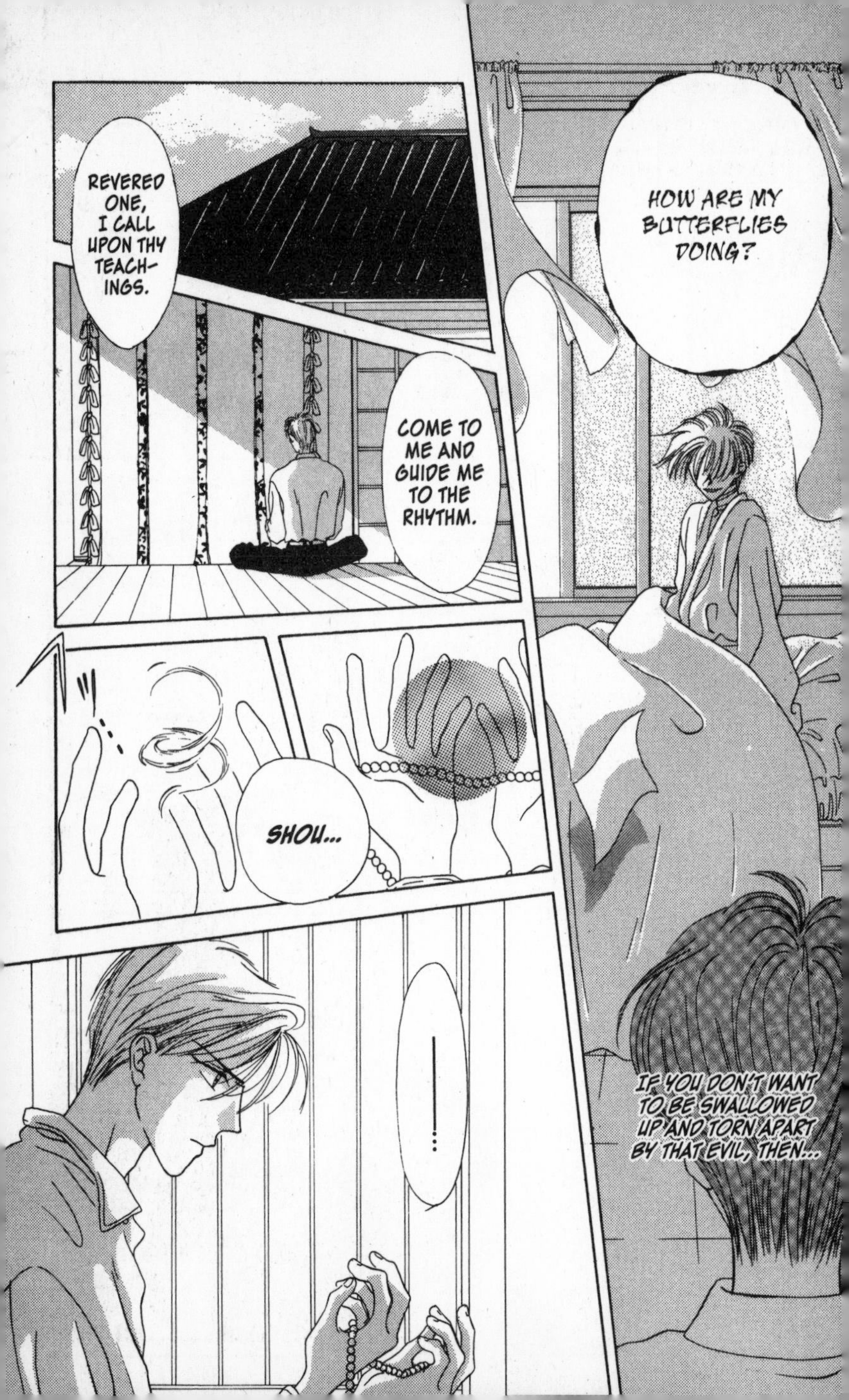
HOW ARE MY BUTTERFLIES DOING?
IF YOU DON'T WANT TO BE SWALLOWED UP AND TORN APART BY THAT EVIL, THEN...
REVERED ONE, I CALL UPON THY TEACHINGS.
COME TO ME AND GUIDE ME TO THE RHYTHM.
SHOU...

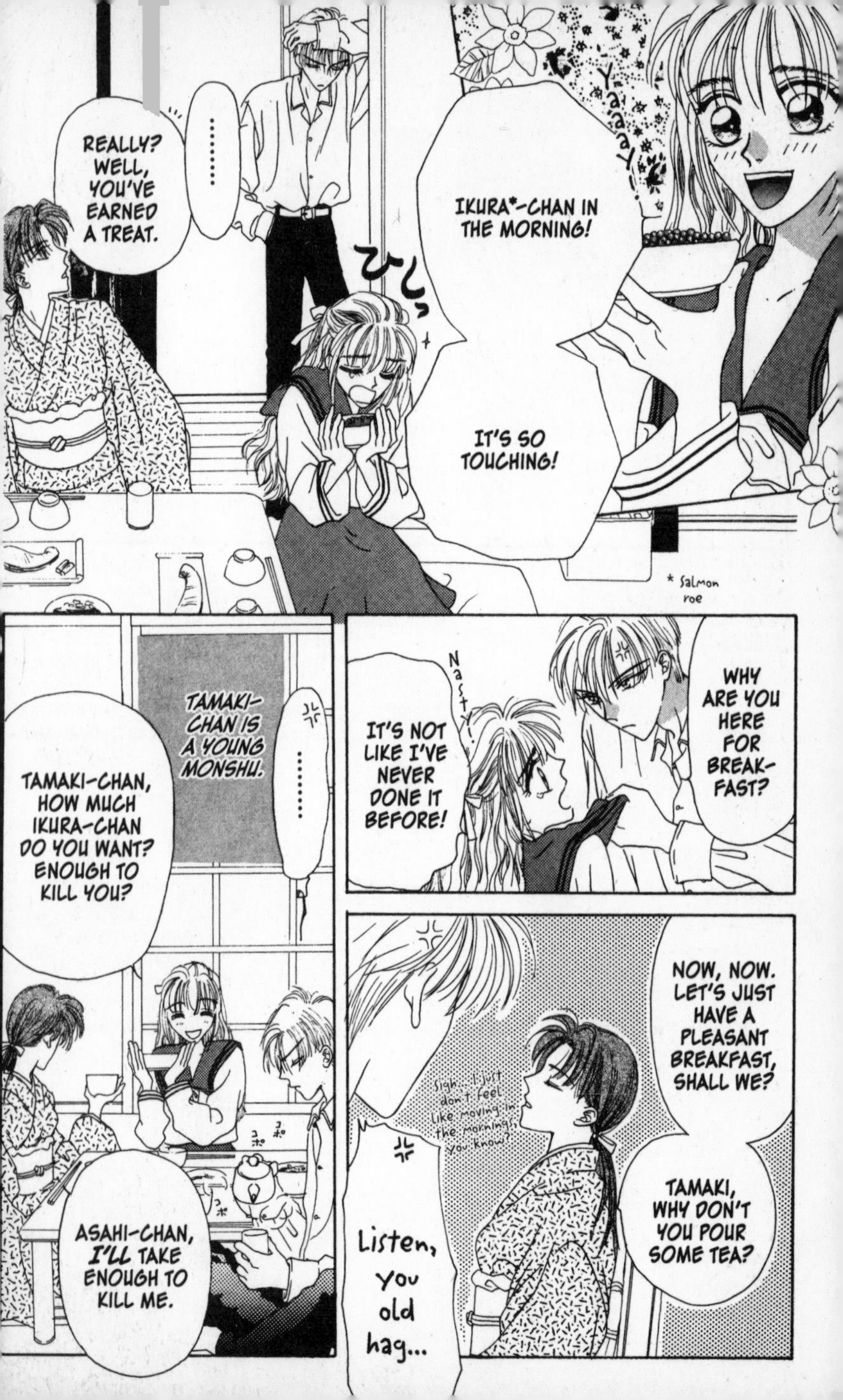
Yaaaay!
IKURA*-CHAN IN THE MORNING!
IT'S SO TOUCHING!
ひしっ
......
REALLY? WELL, YOU'VE EARNED A TREAT.
WHY ARE YOU HERE FOR BREAKFAST?
Nasty!
IT'S NOT LIKE I'VE NEVER DONE IT BEFORE!
NOW, NOW. LET'S JUST HAVE A PLEASANT BREAKFAST, SHALL WE?
TAMAKI, WHY DON'T YOU POUR SOME TEA?
Sigh... I just don't feel like moving in the mornings, you know?
Listen, you old hag...
......
TAMAKI-CHAN IS A YOUNG MONSHU.
TAMAKI-CHAN, HOW MUCH IKURA-CHAN DO YOU WANT? ENOUGH TO KILL YOU?
コポ
コポ
ASAHI-CHAN, I'LL TAKE ENOUGH TO KILL ME.
* Salmon roe

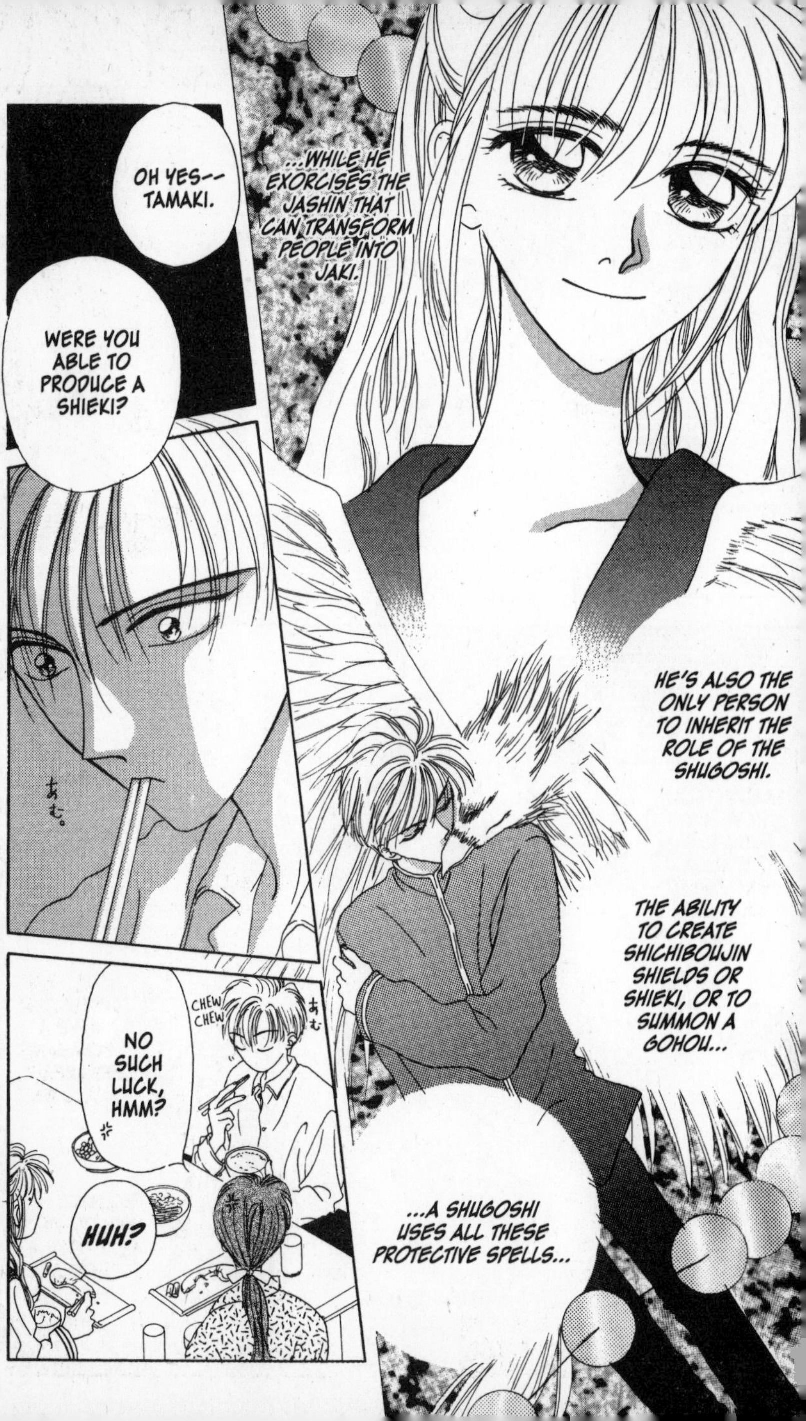
...WHILE HE EXORCISES THE JASHIN THAT CAN TRANSFORM PEOPLE INTO JAKI.
HE'S ALSO THE ONLY PERSON TO INHERIT THE ROLE OF THE SHUGOSHI.
THE ABILITY TO CREATE SHICHIBOUJIN SHIELDS OR SHIEKI, OR TO SUMMON A GOHOU...
...A SHUGOSHI USES ALL THESE PROTECTIVE SPELLS...
OH YES--TAMAKI.
WERE YOU ABLE TO PRODUCE A SHIEKI?
あむ。
あむ
CHEW CHEW
NO SUCH LUCK, HMM?
HUH?

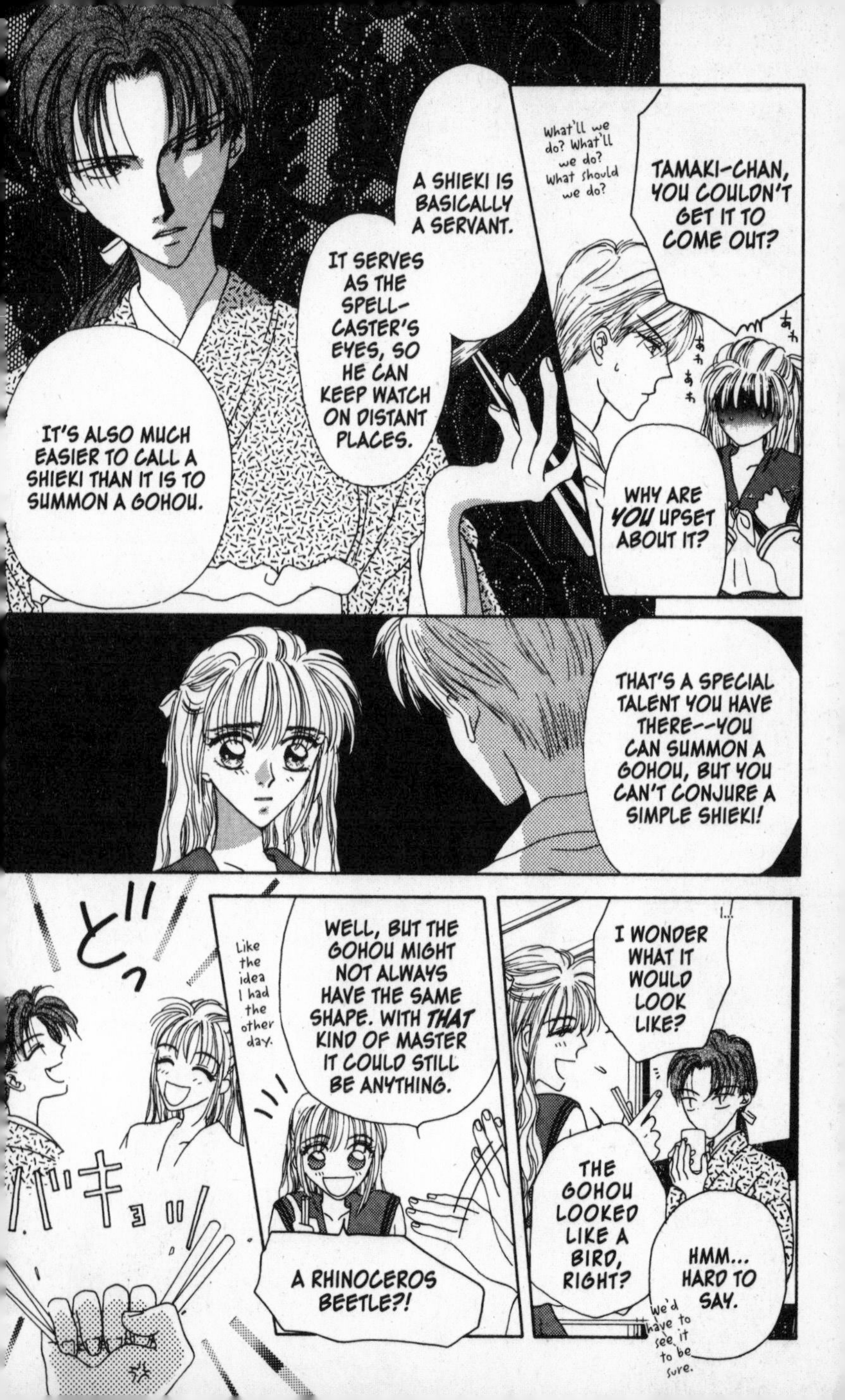

TAMAKI-CHAN, YOU COULDN'T GET IT TO COME OUT?
What'll we do? What'll we do? What should we do?
あわ あわ あわ あわ
WHY ARE *YOU* UPSET ABOUT IT?
A SHIEKI IS BASICALLY A SERVANT.
IT SERVES AS THE SPELL-CASTER'S EYES, SO HE CAN KEEP WATCH ON DISTANT PLACES.
IT'S ALSO MUCH EASIER TO CALL A SHIEKI THAN IT IS TO SUMMON A GOHOU.
THAT'S A SPECIAL TALENT YOU HAVE THERE--YOU CAN SUMMON A GOHOU, BUT YOU CAN'T CONJURE A SIMPLE SHIEKI!
I...
I WONDER WHAT IT WOULD LOOK LIKE?
THE GOHOU LOOKED LIKE A BIRD, RIGHT?
HMM... HARD TO SAY.
We'd have to see it to be sure.
WELL, BUT THE GOHOU MIGHT NOT ALWAYS HAVE THE SAME SHAPE. WITH *THAT* KIND OF MASTER IT COULD STILL BE ANYTHING.
Like the idea I had the other day.
A RHINOCEROS BEETLE?!
どっ
バキョッ

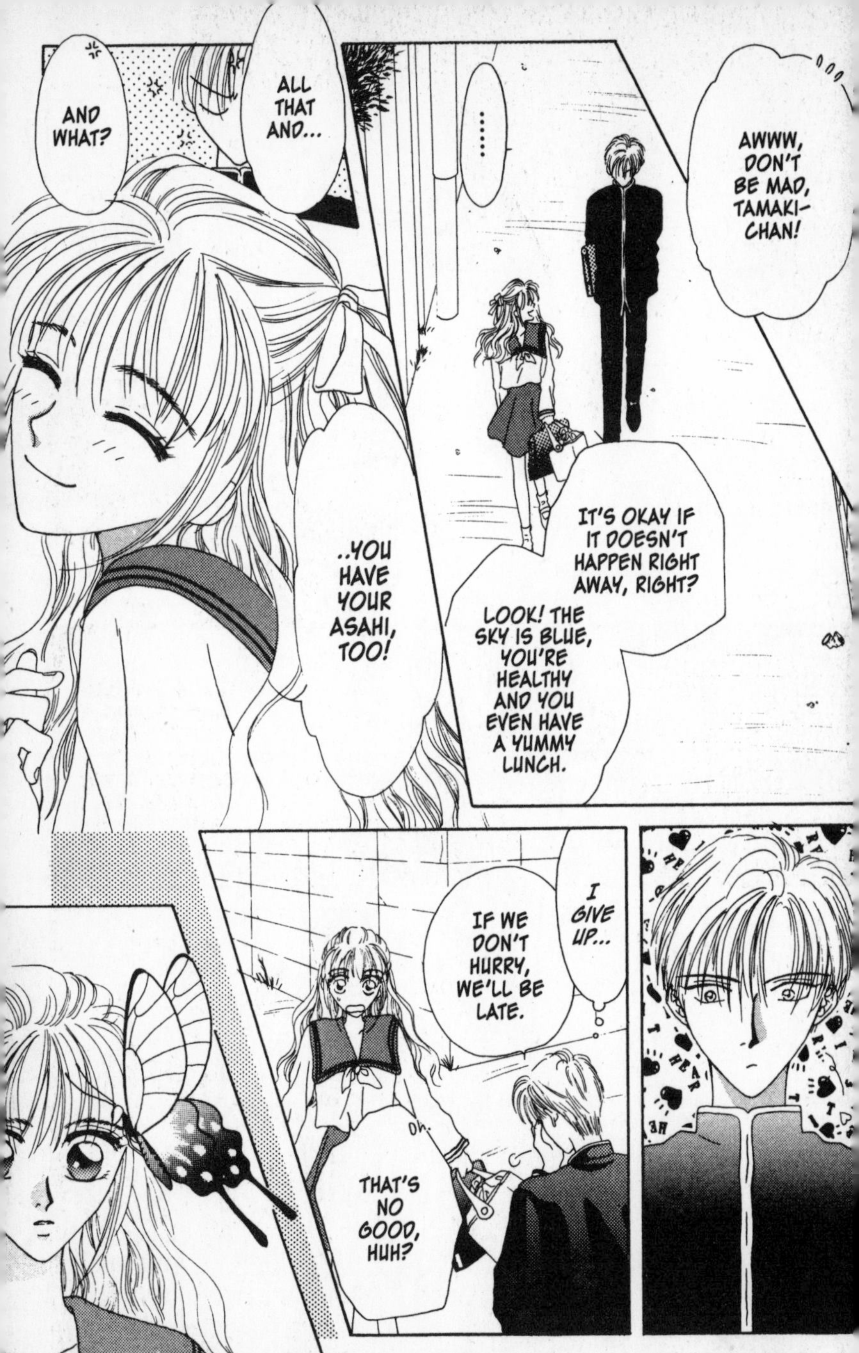

AWWW, DON'T BE MAD, TAMAKI-CHAN!
......
IT'S OKAY IF IT DOESN'T HAPPEN RIGHT AWAY, RIGHT?
LOOK! THE SKY IS BLUE, YOU'RE HEALTHY AND YOU EVEN HAVE A YUMMY LUNCH.
ALL THAT AND...
AND WHAT?
..YOU HAVE YOUR ASAHI, TOO!
I GIVE UP...
IF WE DON'T HURRY, WE'LL BE LATE.
OH.
THAT'S NO GOOD, HUH?

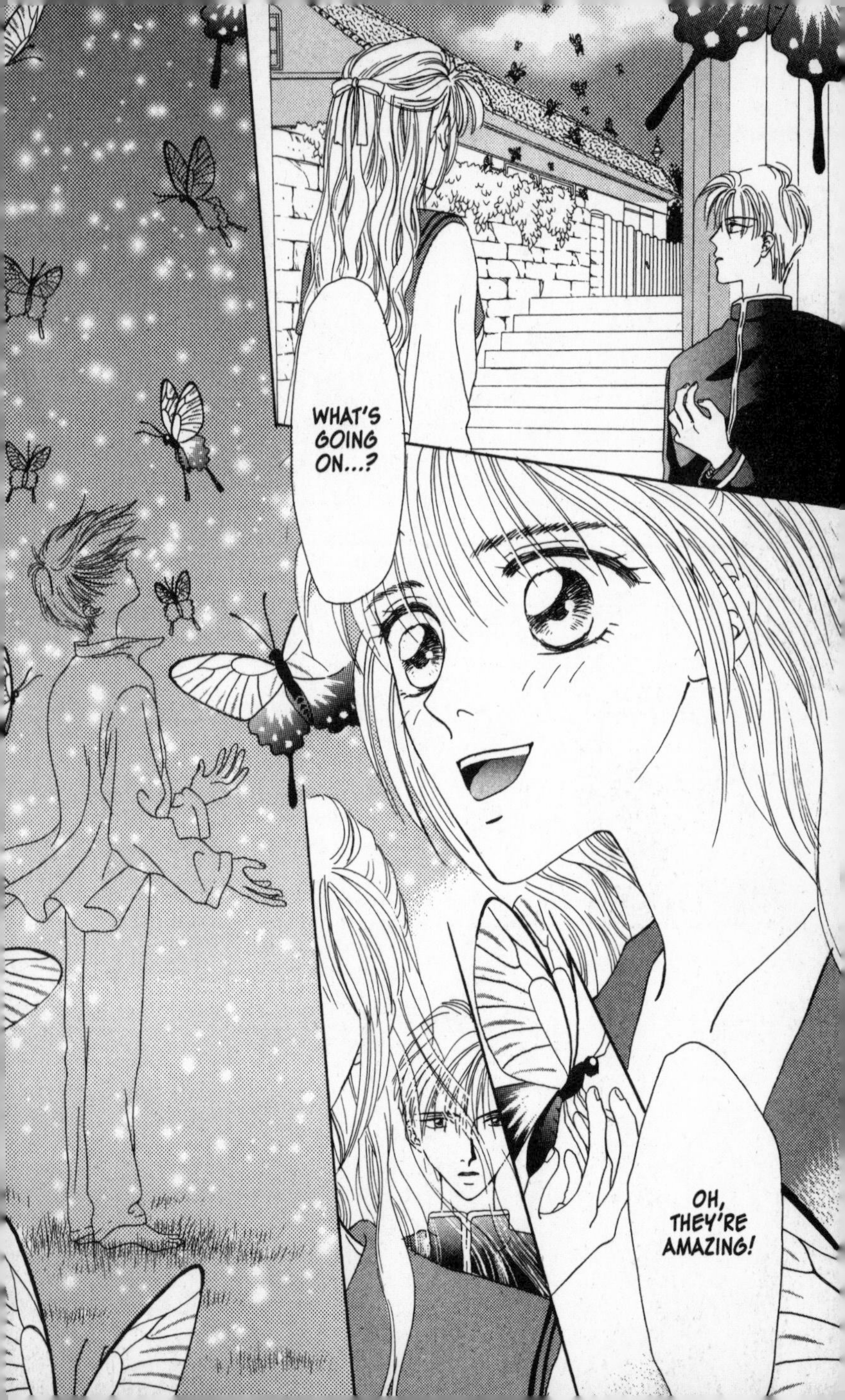
WHAT'S GOING ON...?
OH, THEY'RE AMAZING!

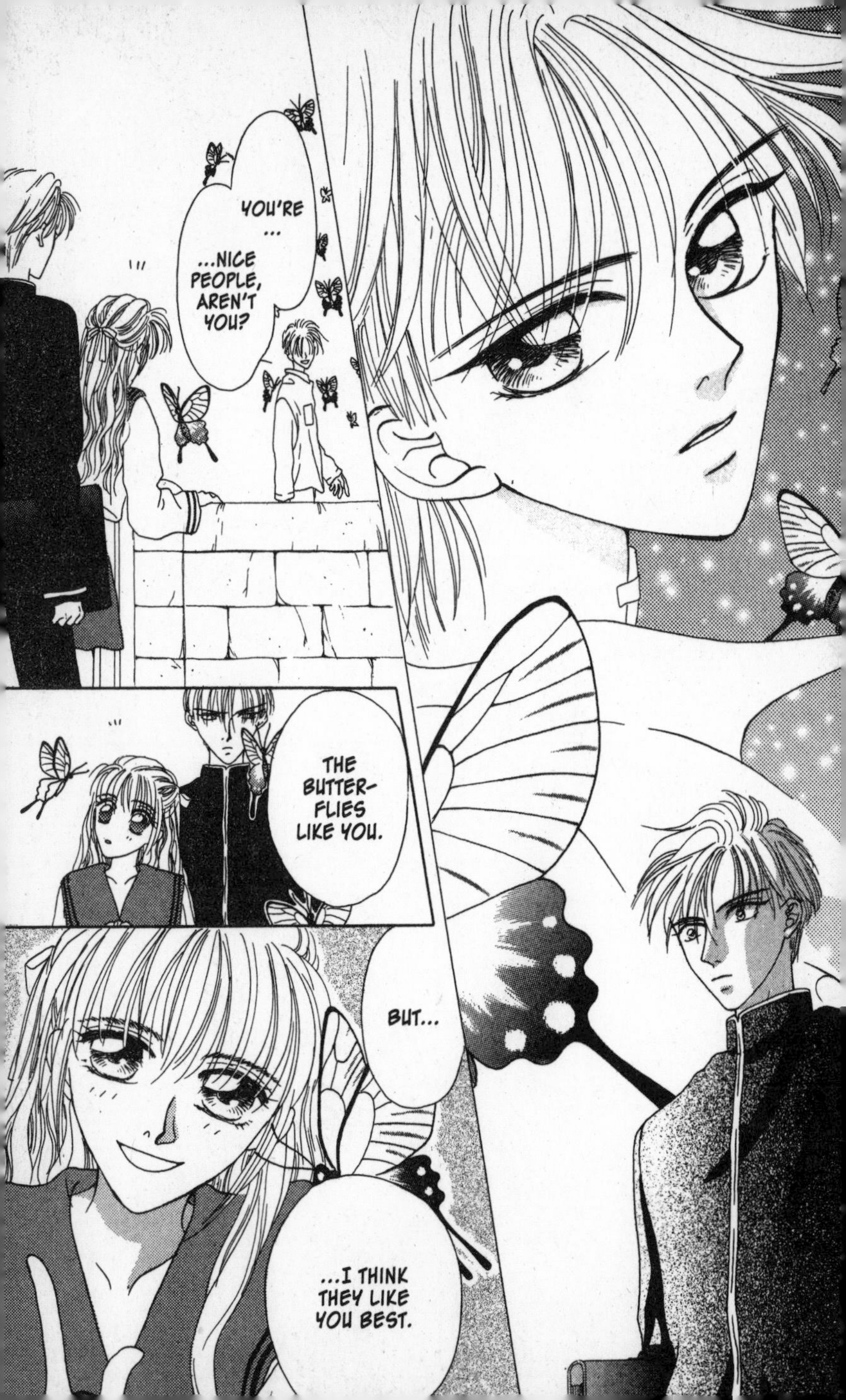
YOU'RE ...
...NICE PEOPLE, AREN'T YOU?
THE BUTTER-FLIES LIKE YOU.
BUT...
...I THINK THEY LIKE YOU BEST.

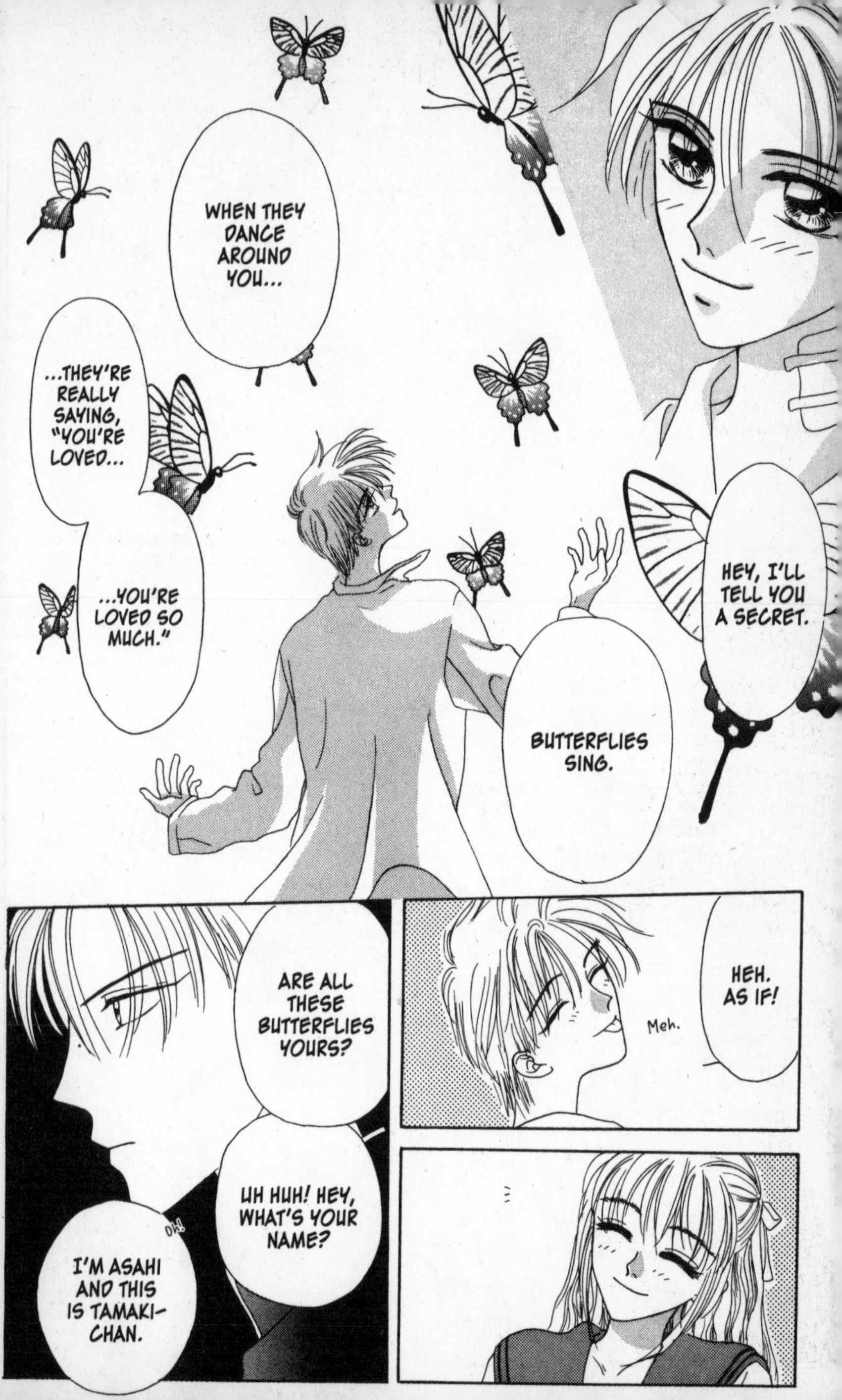
HEY, I'LL TELL YOU A SECRET.
BUTTERFLIES SING.
WHEN THEY DANCE AROUND YOU...
...THEY'RE REALLY SAYING, "YOU'RE LOVED...
...YOU'RE LOVED SO MUCH."
HEH. AS IF!
Meh.
ARE ALL THESE BUTTERFLIES YOURS?
UH HUH! HEY, WHAT'S YOUR NAME?
OH!
I'M ASAHI AND THIS IS TAMAKI-CHAN.

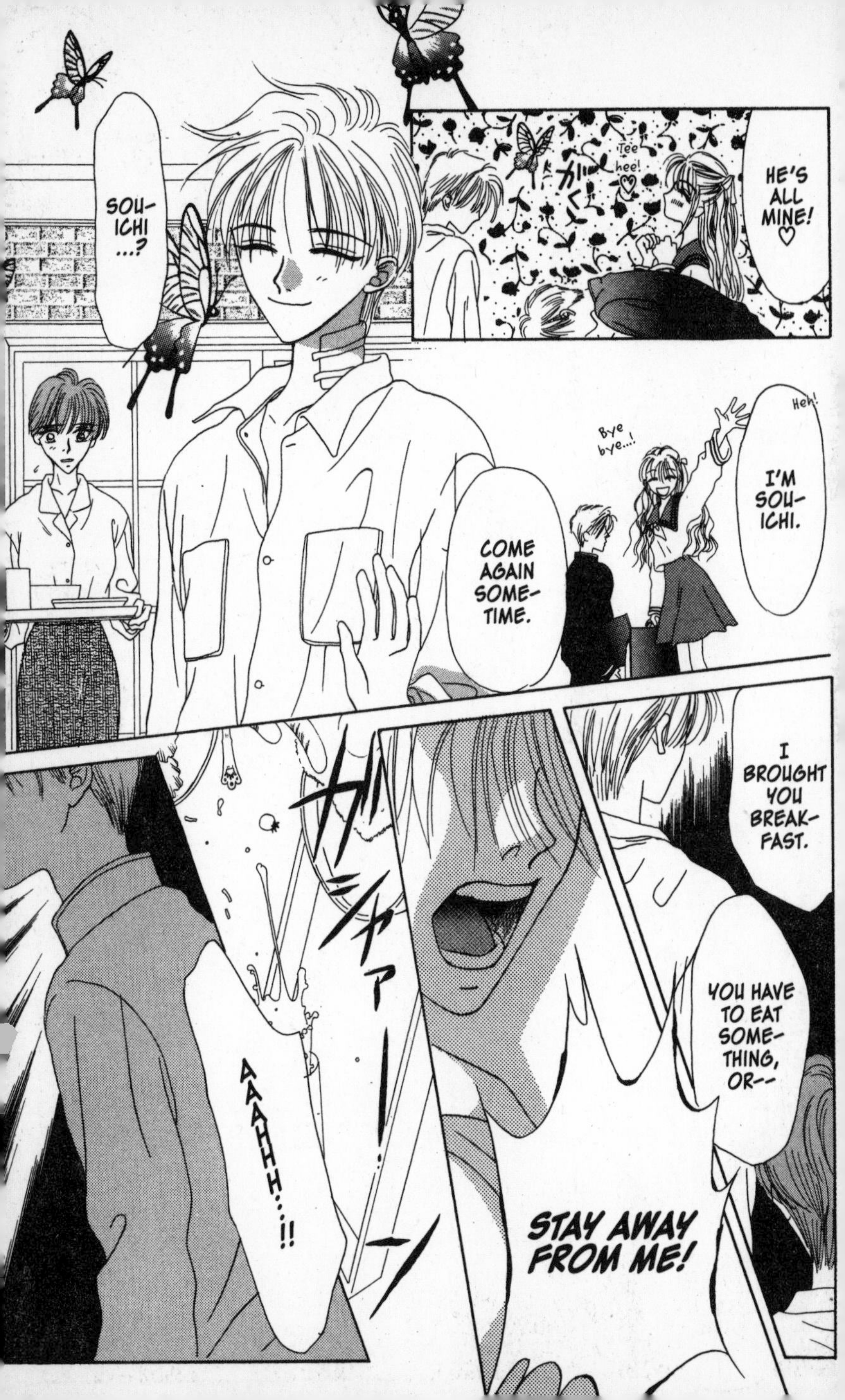

Tee hee! ♡
HE'S ALL MINE! ♡
Heh!
I'M SOU-ICHI.
Bye bye...!
COME AGAIN SOME-TIME.
SOU-ICHI ...?
I BROUGHT YOU BREAK-FAST.
YOU HAVE TO EAT SOME-THING, OR--
STAY AWAY FROM ME!
ガシャアーー
AAAHHH...!!

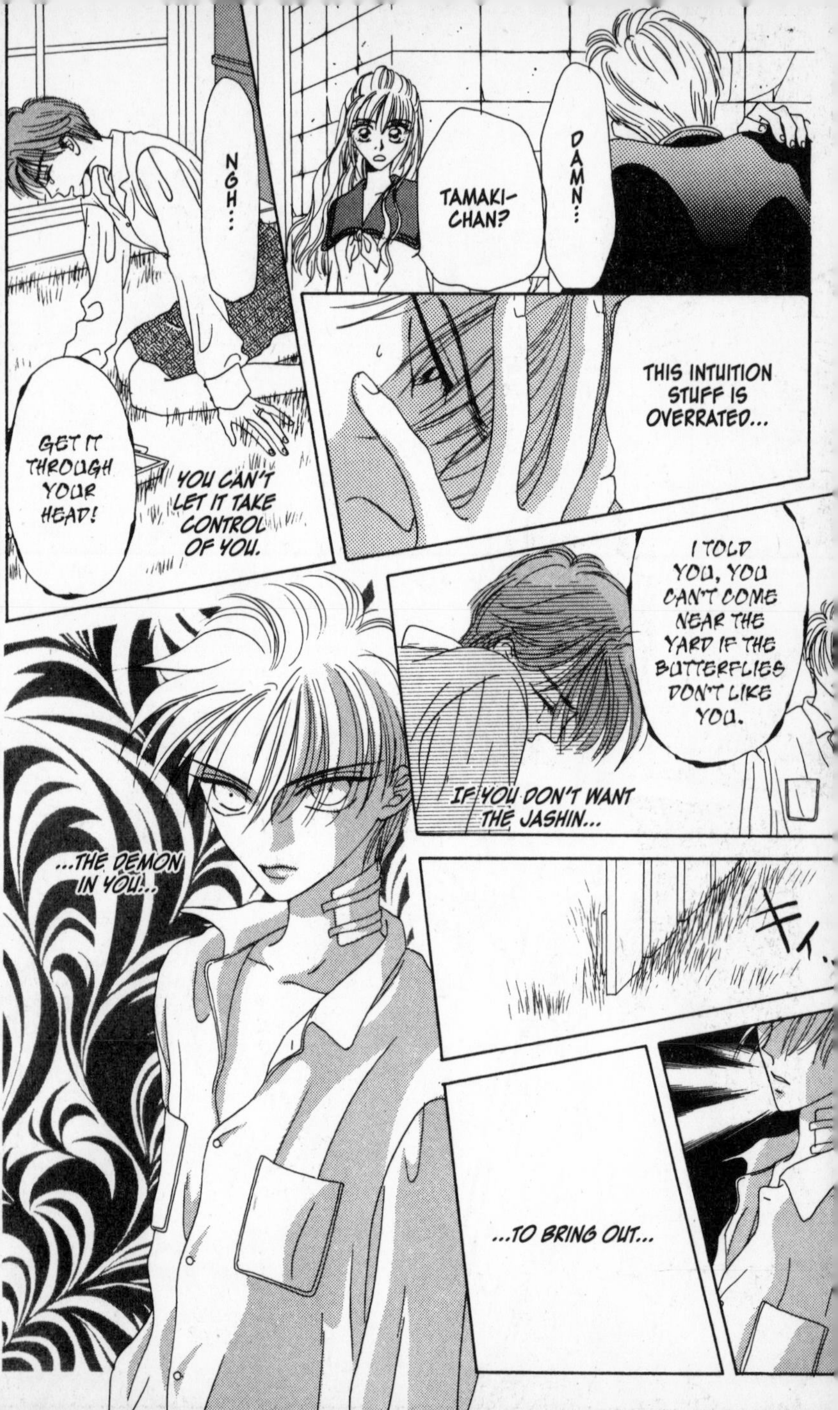
DAMN...
TAMAKI-CHAN?
NGH...
THIS INTUITION STUFF IS OVERRATED...
YOU CAN'T LET IT TAKE CONTROL OF YOU.
GET IT THROUGH YOUR HEAD!
I TOLD YOU, YOU CAN'T COME NEAR THE YARD IF THE BUTTERFLIES DON'T LIKE YOU.
IF YOU DON'T WANT THE JASHIN...
...TO BRING OUT...
...THE DEMON IN YOU...

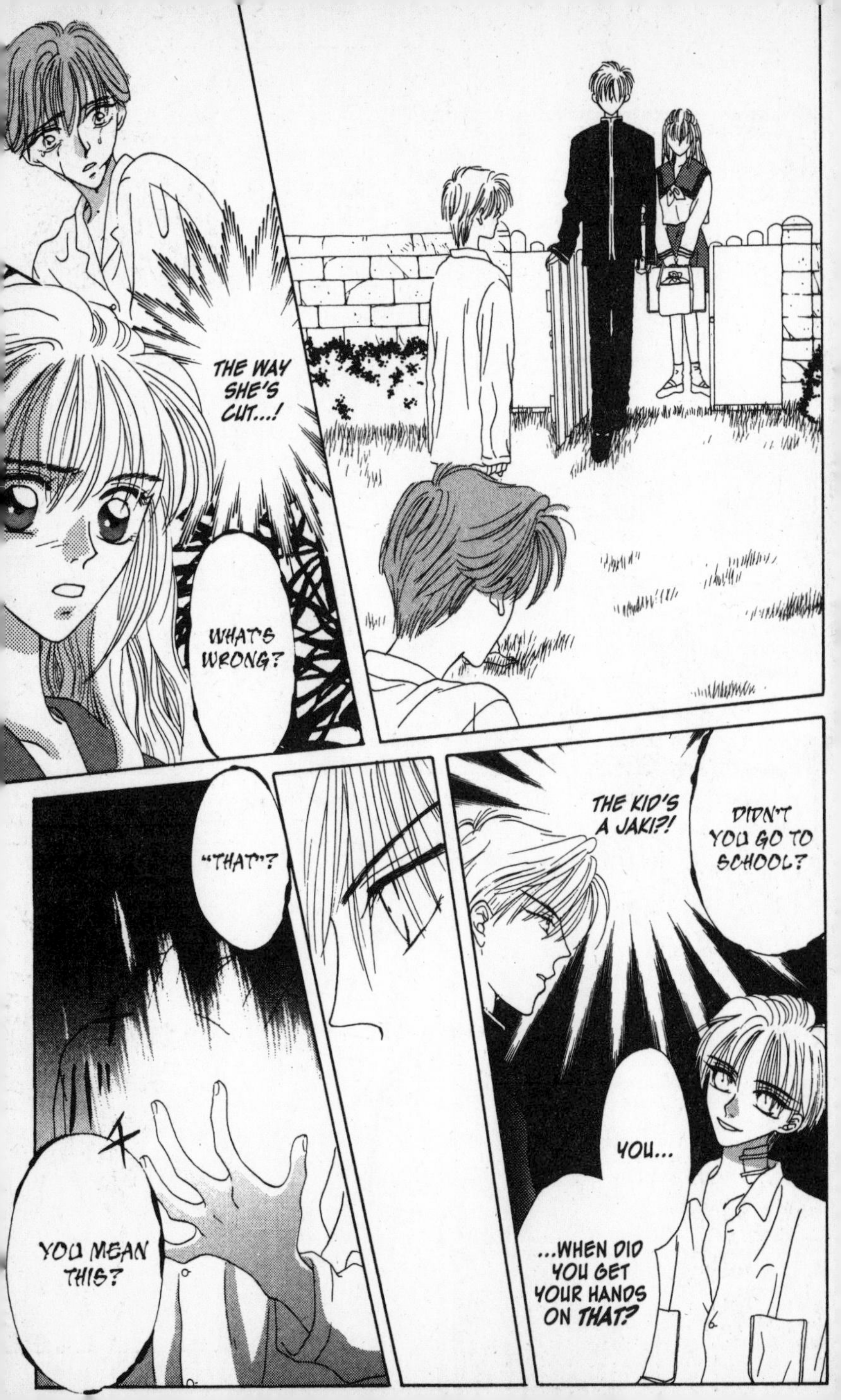
THE WAY SHE'S CUT...!
WHAT'S WRONG?
DIDN'T YOU GO TO SCHOOL?
THE KID'S A JAKI?!
YOU...
...WHEN DID YOU GET YOUR HANDS ON THAT?
"THAT"?
YOU MEAN THIS?

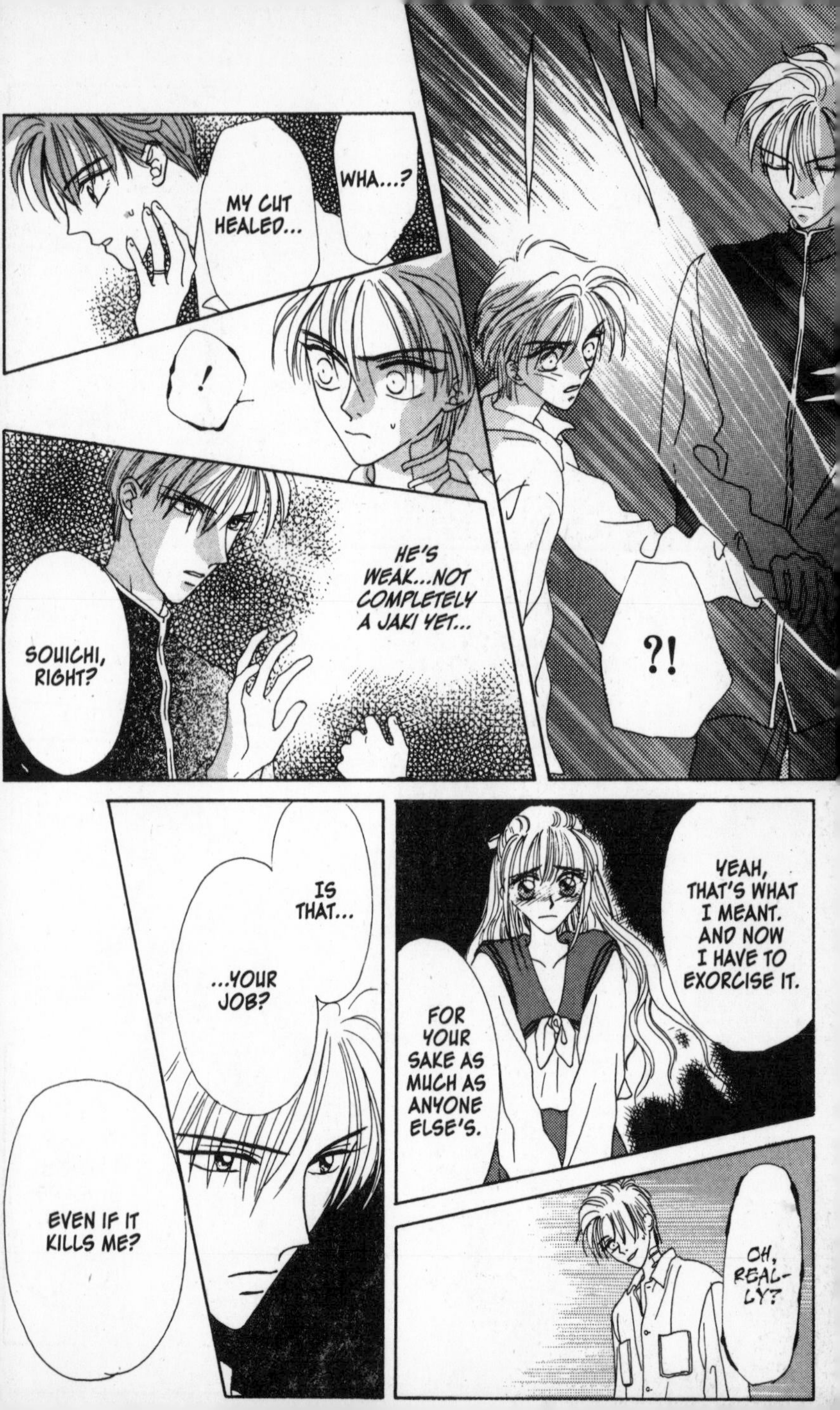
?!
WHA...?
MY CUT HEALED...
!
HE'S WEAK...NOT COMPLETELY A JAKI YET...
SOUICHI, RIGHT?
YEAH, THAT'S WHAT I MEANT. AND NOW I HAVE TO EXORCISE IT.
FOR YOUR SAKE AS MUCH AS ANYONE ELSE'S.
OH, REAL-LY?
IS THAT...
...YOUR JOB?
EVEN IF IT KILLS ME?

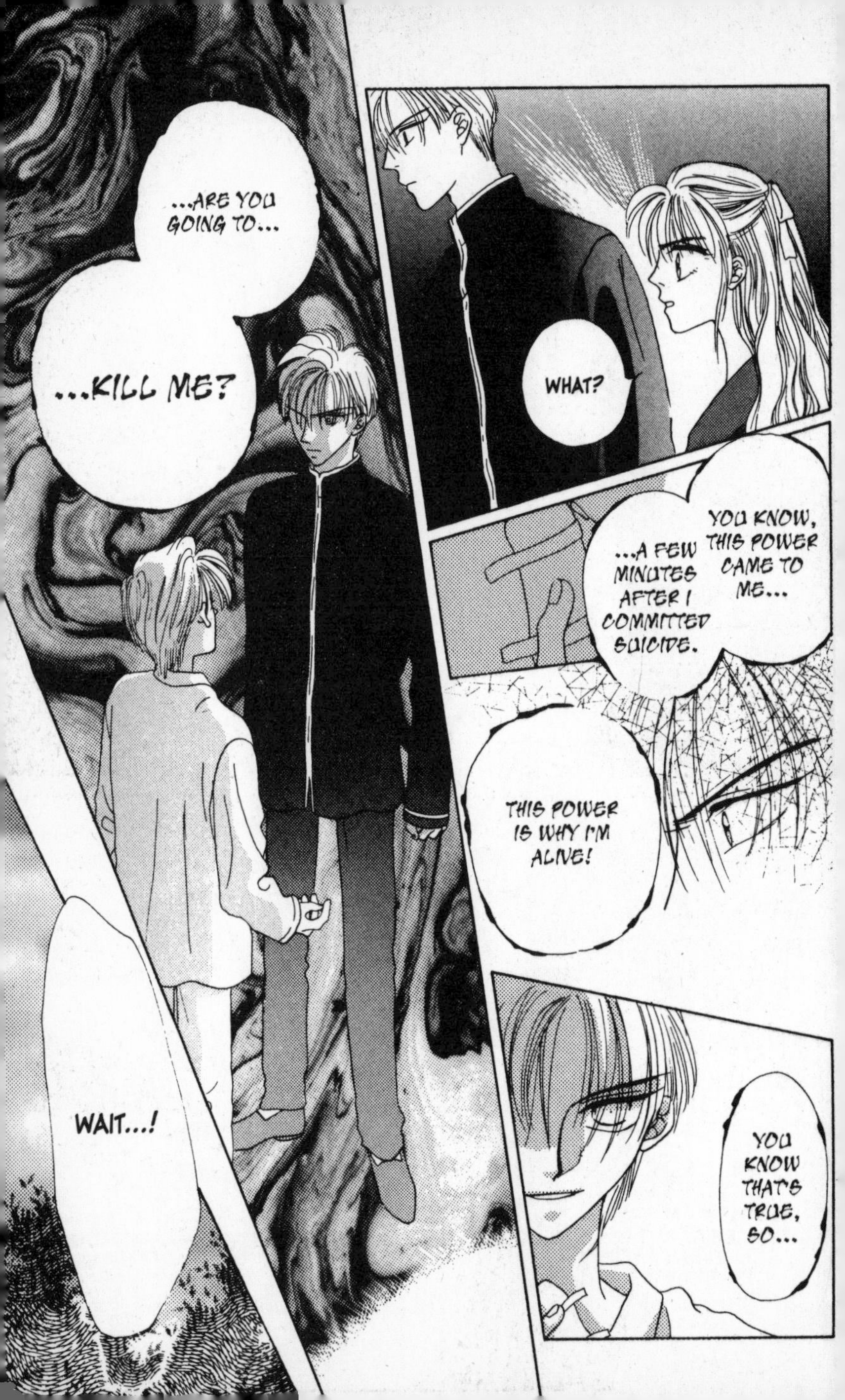
WHAT?
YOU KNOW, THIS POWER CAME TO ME...
...A FEW MINUTES AFTER I COMMITTED SUICIDE.
THIS POWER IS WHY I'M ALIVE!
YOU KNOW THAT'S TRUE, SO...
...ARE YOU GOING TO...
...KILL ME?
WAIT...!

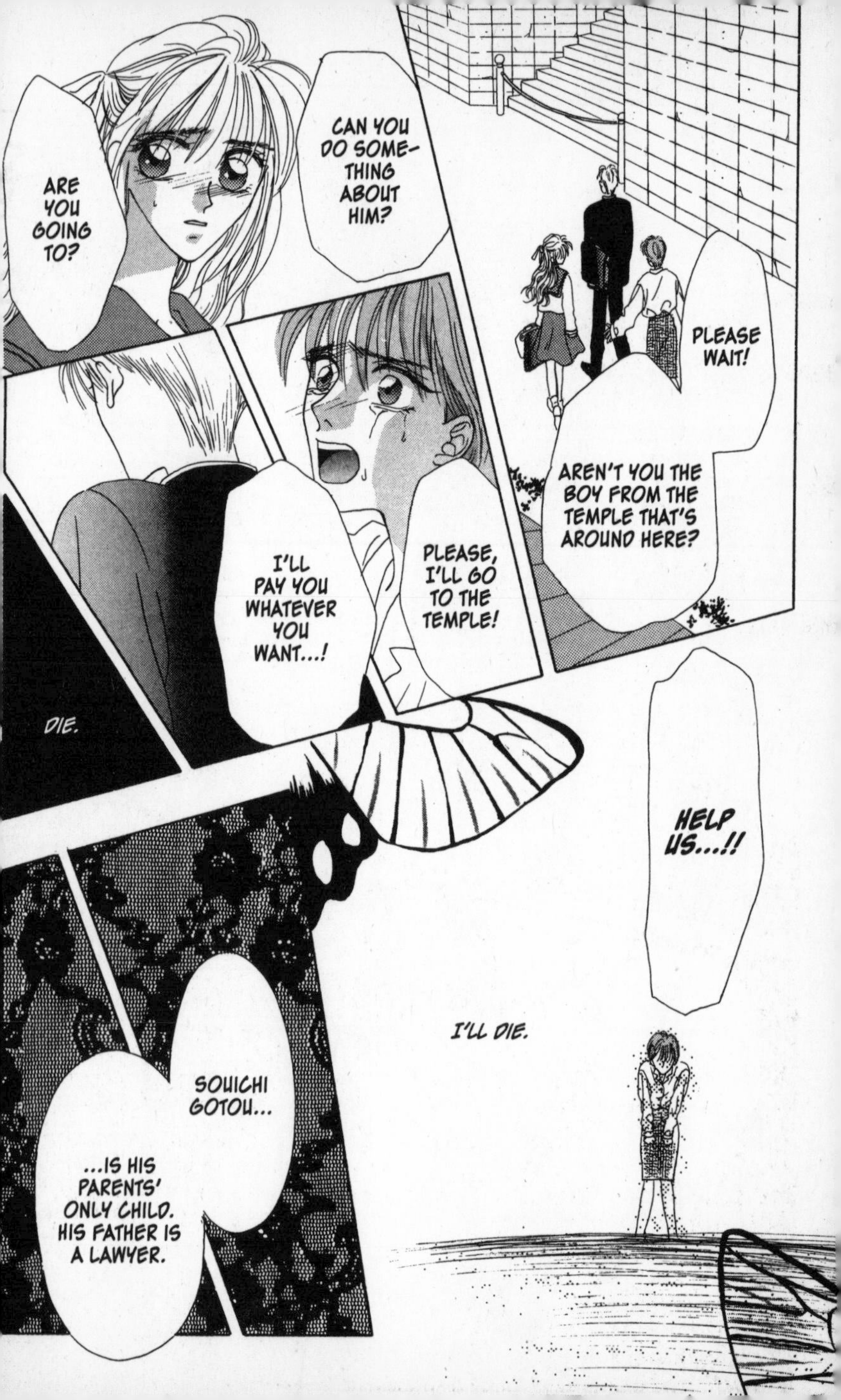
PLEASE WAIT!
AREN'T YOU THE BOY FROM THE TEMPLE THAT'S AROUND HERE?
CAN YOU DO SOME-THING ABOUT HIM?
ARE YOU GOING TO?
PLEASE, I'LL GO TO THE TEMPLE!
I'LL PAY YOU WHATEVER YOU WANT...!
DIE.
HELP US...!!
I'LL DIE.
SOUICHI GOTOU...
...IS HIS PARENTS' ONLY CHILD. HIS FATHER IS A LAWYER.

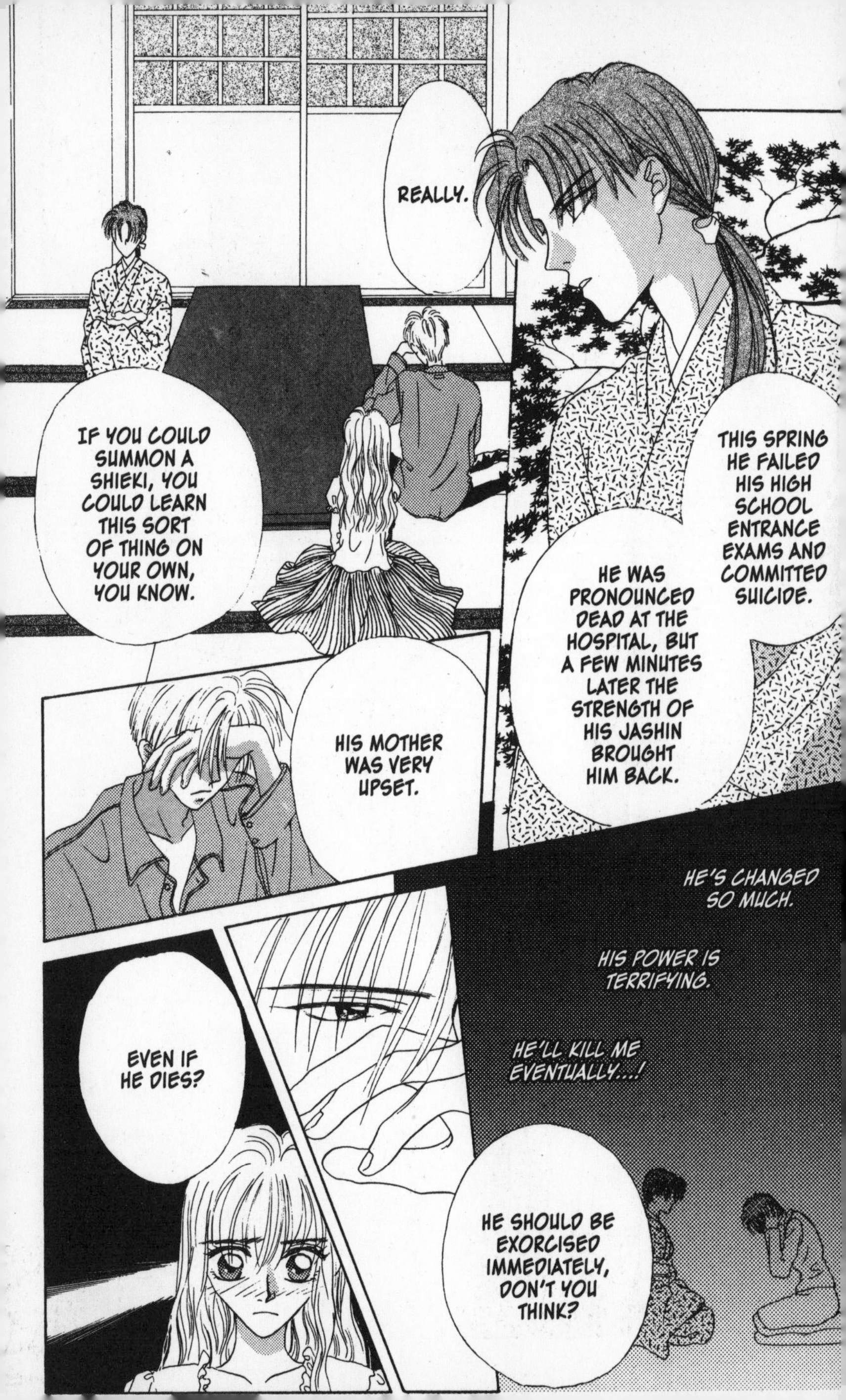
THIS SPRING HE FAILED HIS HIGH SCHOOL ENTRANCE EXAMS AND COMMITTED SUICIDE.
HE WAS PRONOUNCED DEAD AT THE HOSPITAL, BUT A FEW MINUTES LATER THE STRENGTH OF HIS JASHIN BROUGHT HIM BACK.
REALLY.
IF YOU COULD SUMMON A SHIEKI, YOU COULD LEARN THIS SORT OF THING ON YOUR OWN, YOU KNOW.
HIS MOTHER WAS VERY UPSET.
HE'S CHANGED SO MUCH.
HIS POWER IS TERRIFYING.
HE'LL KILL ME EVENTUALLY...!
HE SHOULD BE EXORCISED IMMEDIATELY, DON'T YOU THINK?
EVEN IF HE DIES?

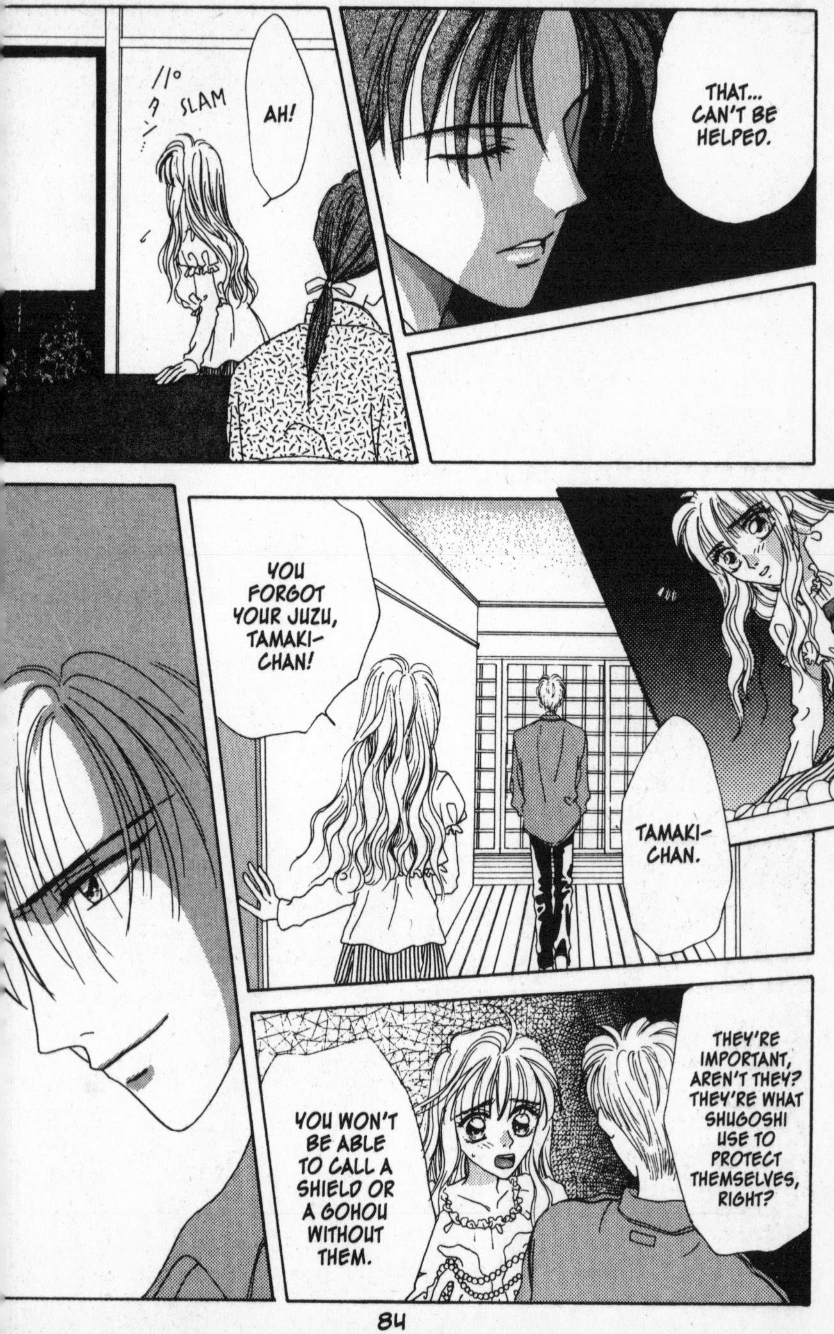

THAT... CAN'T BE HELPED.
SLAM
AH!
TAMAKI-CHAN.
YOU FORGOT YOUR JUZU, TAMAKI-CHAN!
THEY'RE IMPORTANT, AREN'T THEY? THEY'RE WHAT SHUGOSHI USE TO PROTECT THEMSELVES, RIGHT?
YOU WON'T BE ABLE TO CALL A SHIELD OR A GOHOU WITHOUT THEM.

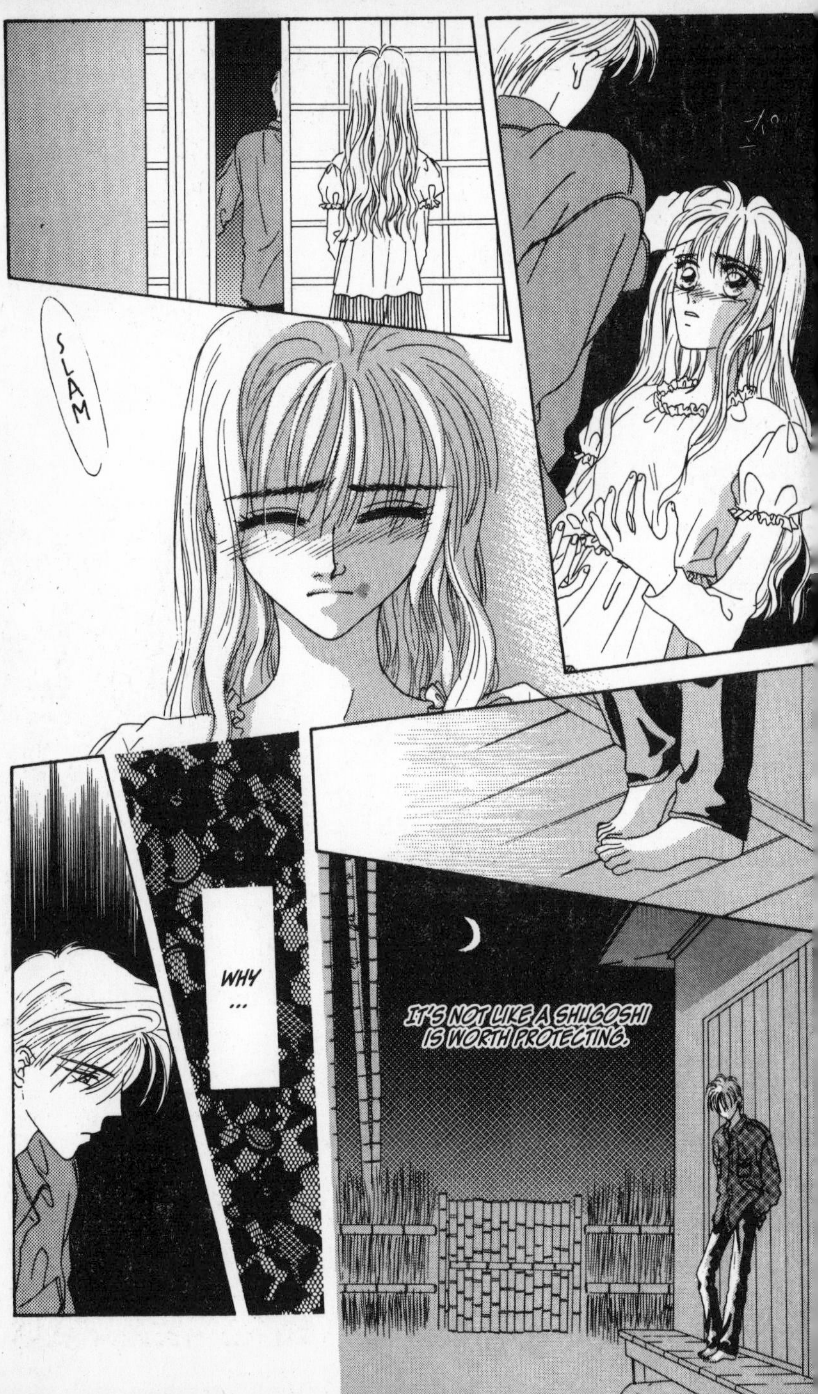
SLAM
IT'S NOT LIKE A SHUGOSHI IS WORTH PROTECTING.
WHY ...

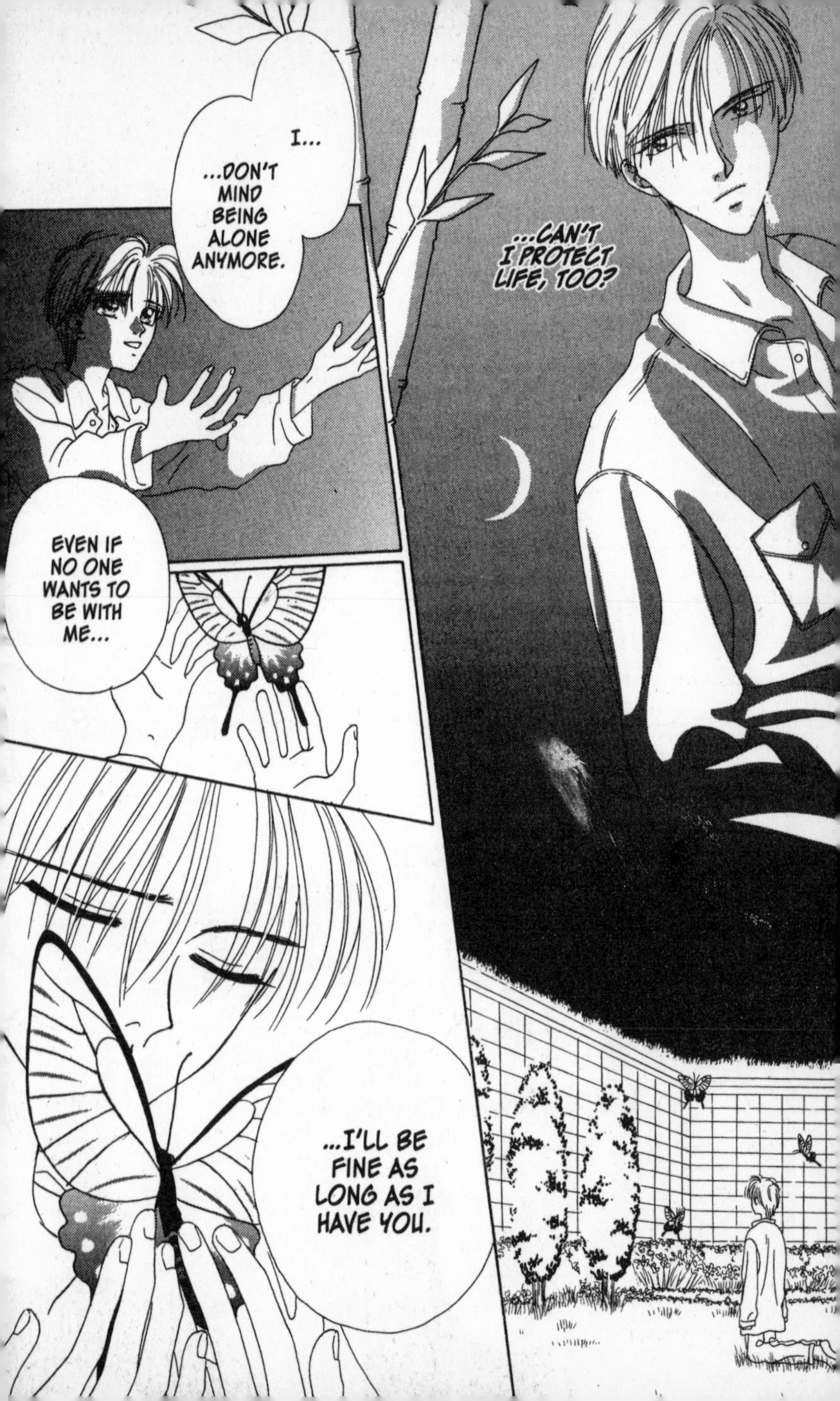
...CAN'T I PROTECT LIFE, TOO?
I...
...DON'T MIND BEING ALONE ANYMORE.
EVEN IF NO ONE WANTS TO BE WITH ME...
...I'LL BE FINE AS LONG AS I HAVE YOU.

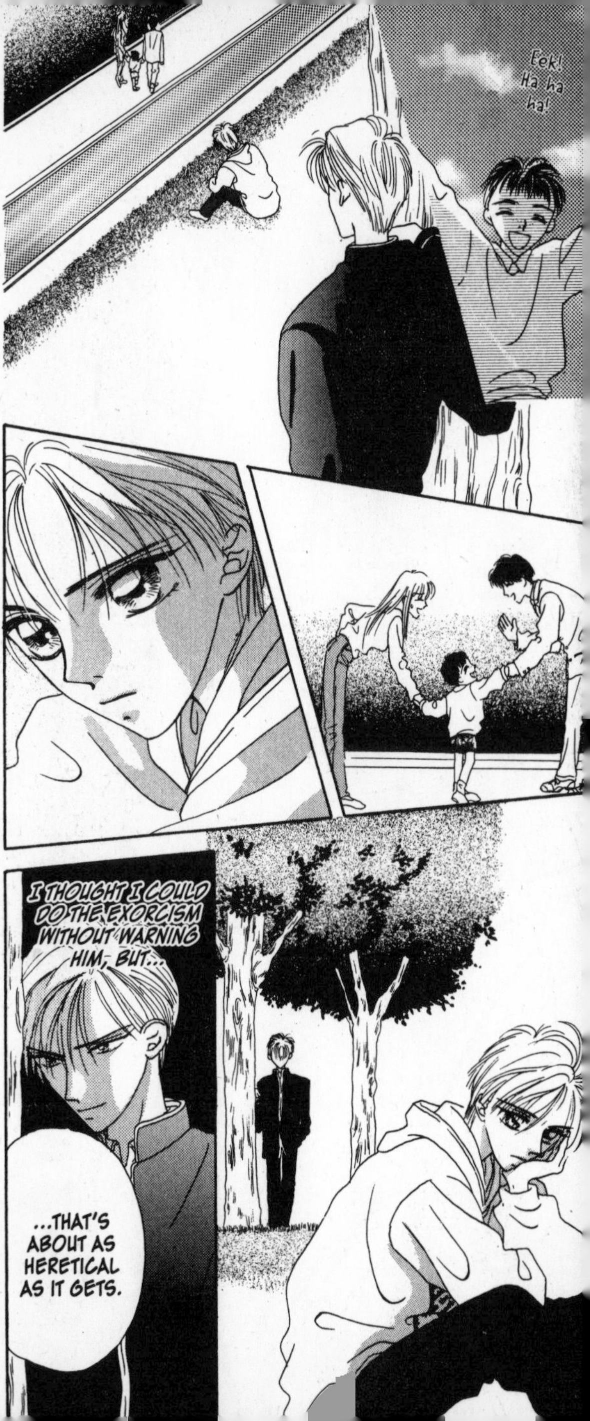
Eek! Ha ha ha!
I THOUGHT I COULD DO THE EXORCISM WITHOUT WARNING HIM, BUT...
...THAT'S ABOUT AS HERETICAL AS IT GETS.

Two

I tried my best and wrote it as well as I could. Looks like I can't stop talking about it. This story still gives me problems, like--

Who cares about your problems? Hurry up and get the story moving.

Oh, right.

I did some research and looked at other manga artists' first manga (not a good idea), but... I don't know. Should authors introduce themselves? What to do... Hmm... Maybe I'll just write one. ♥

What are you doing?

Oh, right.

This creature called Natsuki Takaya was born on July 7th, and has the mentality of a Cancer whose blood type is A. I live in the Edogawa district of Tokyo but I'm a staunch Tokyoite...probably. I like lots of things, and I'll probably come to like a lot more. I hate things like yuzu, kabosu* and bell peppers. Really, I'm such a baby. I faint when I put them in my mouth!

Incidentally, I'm left handed.

* Yuzu and kabosu are citrus fruits.

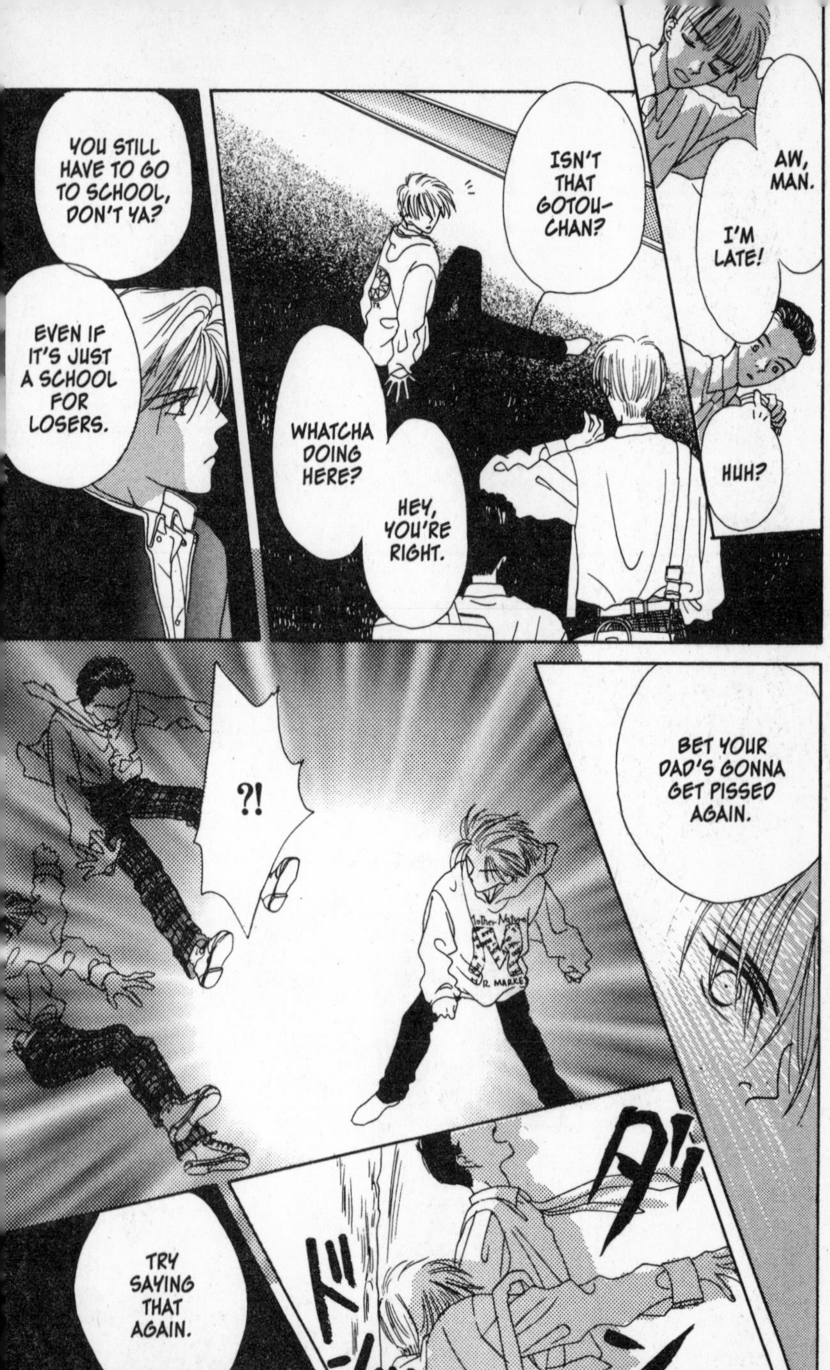

AW, MAN.
I'M LATE!
HUH?
ISN'T THAT GOTOU-CHAN?
HEY, YOU'RE RIGHT.
WHATCHA DOING HERE?
YOU STILL HAVE TO GO TO SCHOOL, DON'T YA?
EVEN IF IT'S JUST A SCHOOL FOR LOSERS.
BET YOUR DAD'S GONNA GET PISSED AGAIN.
?!
TRY SAYING THAT AGAIN.

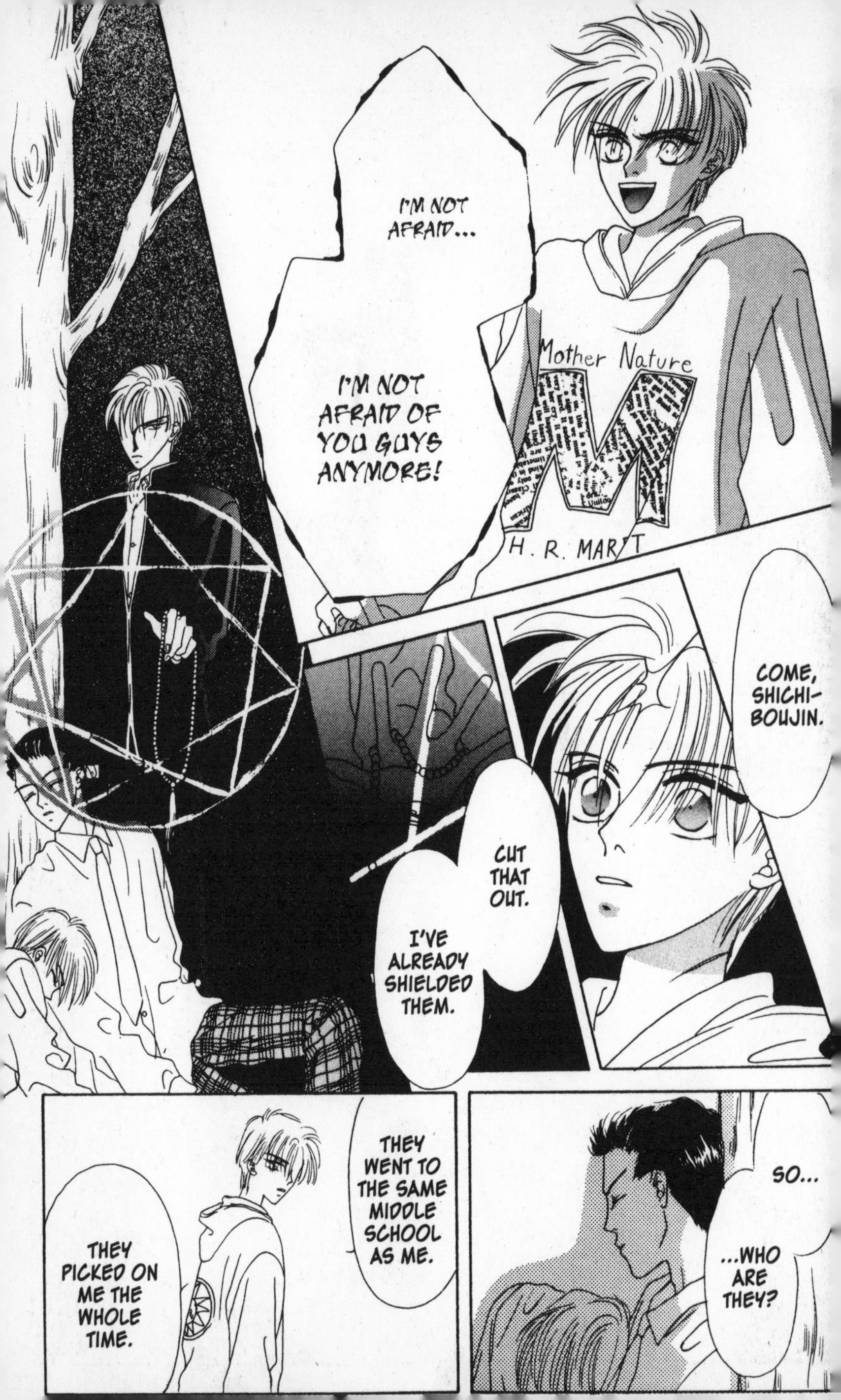
I'M NOT AFRAID...
I'M NOT AFRAID OF YOU GUYS ANYMORE!
Mother Nature
COME, SHICHI-BOUJIN.
CUT THAT OUT.
I'VE ALREADY SHIELDED THEM.
SO...
...WHO ARE THEY?
THEY WENT TO THE SAME MIDDLE SCHOOL AS ME.
THEY PICKED ON ME THE WHOLE TIME.

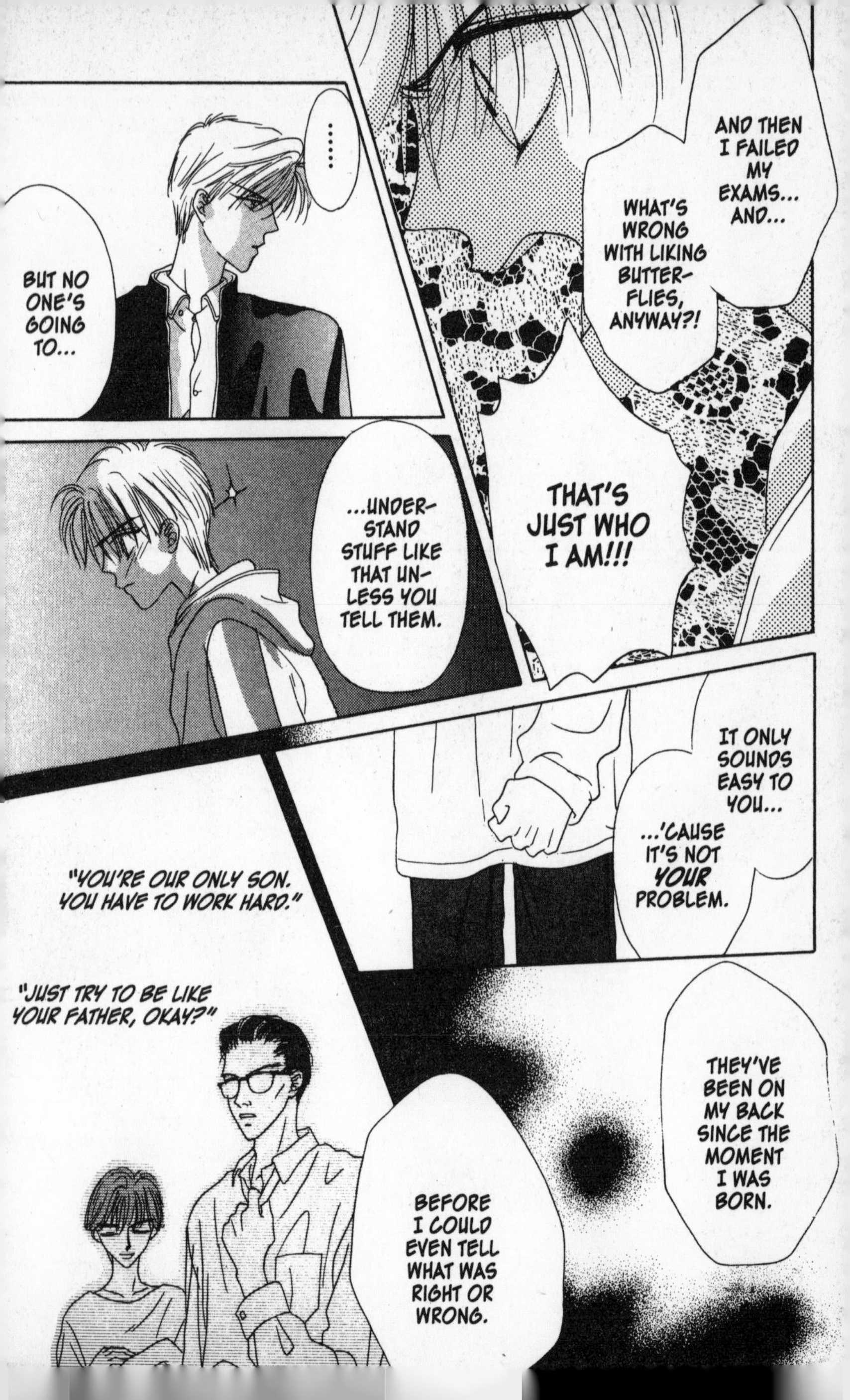
AND THEN I FAILED MY EXAMS... AND...
WHAT'S WRONG WITH LIKING BUTTER-FLIES, ANYWAY?!
THAT'S JUST WHO I AM!!!
......
BUT NO ONE'S GOING TO...
...UNDER-STAND STUFF LIKE THAT UN-LESS YOU TELL THEM.
IT ONLY SOUNDS EASY TO YOU...
...'CAUSE IT'S NOT YOUR PROBLEM.
"YOU'RE OUR ONLY SON. YOU HAVE TO WORK HARD."
THEY'VE BEEN ON MY BACK SINCE THE MOMENT I WAS BORN.
BEFORE I COULD EVEN TELL WHAT WAS RIGHT OR WRONG.
"JUST TRY TO BE LIKE YOUR FATHER, OKAY?"

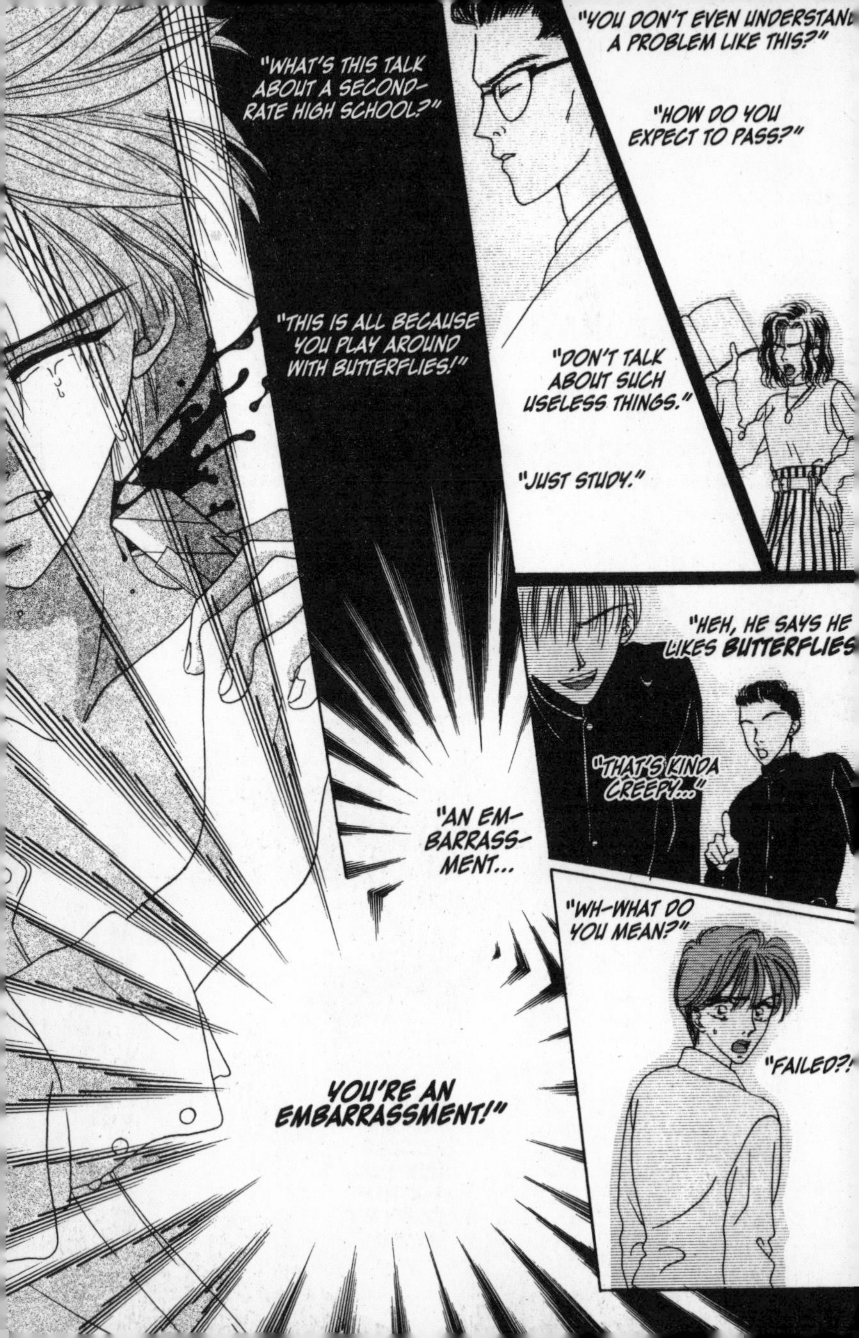
"YOU DON'T EVEN UNDERSTAN
A PROBLEM LIKE THIS?"
"HOW DO YOU EXPECT TO PASS?"
"DON'T TALK ABOUT SUCH USELESS THINGS."
"JUST STUDY."
"HEH, HE SAYS HE LIKES BUTTERFLIES
"THAT'S KINDA CREEPY..."
"WH-WHAT DO YOU MEAN?"
"FAILED?!
"WHAT'S THIS TALK ABOUT A SECOND-RATE HIGH SCHOOL?"
"THIS IS ALL BECAUSE YOU PLAY AROUND WITH BUTTERFLIES!"
"AN EM-BARRASS-MENT...
YOU'RE AN EMBARRASSMENT!"

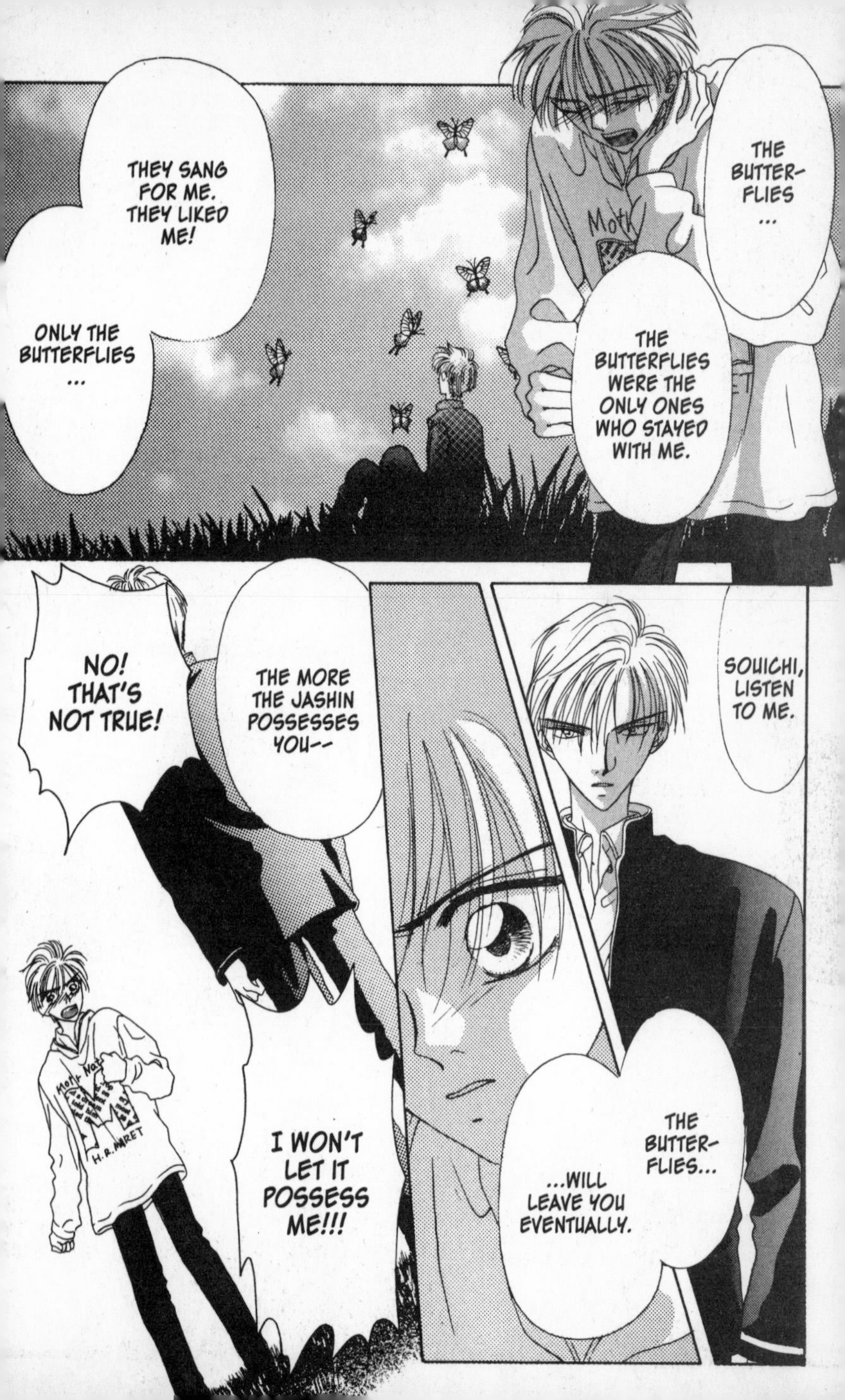
THE BUTTERFLIES...
THE BUTTERFLIES WERE THE ONLY ONES WHO STAYED WITH ME.
THEY SANG FOR ME. THEY LIKED ME!
ONLY THE BUTTERFLIES...
SOUICHI, LISTEN TO ME.
THE BUTTERFLIES...
...WILL LEAVE YOU EVENTUALLY.
THE MORE THE JASHIN POSSESSES YOU--
NO! THAT'S NOT TRUE!
I WON'T LET IT POSSESS ME!!!

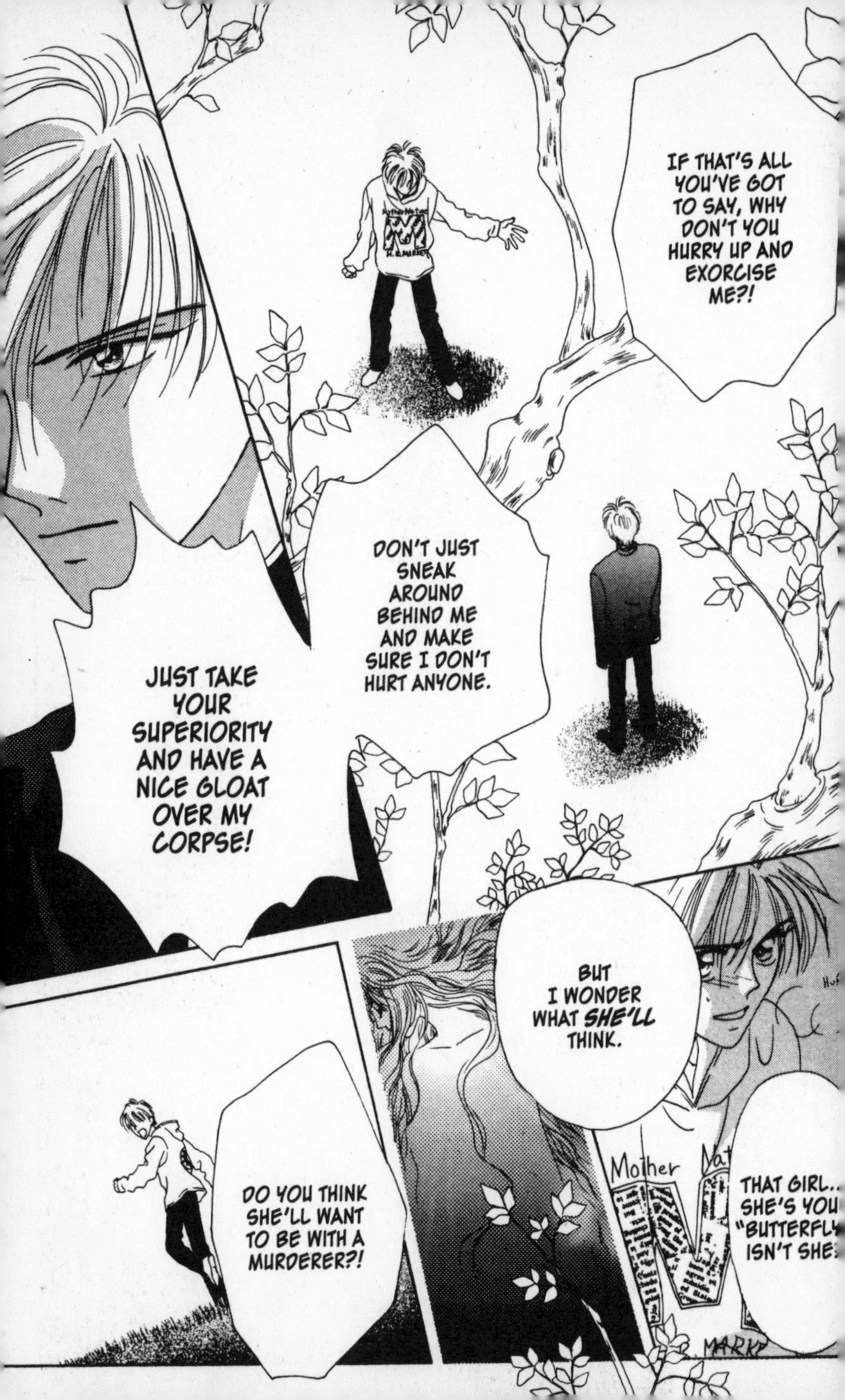
IF THAT'S ALL YOU'VE GOT TO SAY, WHY DON'T YOU HURRY UP AND EXORCISE ME?!
DON'T JUST SNEAK AROUND BEHIND ME AND MAKE SURE I DON'T HURT ANYONE.
JUST TAKE YOUR SUPERIORITY AND HAVE A NICE GLOAT OVER MY CORPSE!
THAT GIRL.. SHE'S YOU "BUTTERFL ISN'T SHE
BUT I WONDER WHAT *SHE'LL* THINK.
DO YOU THINK SHE'LL WANT TO BE WITH A MURDERER?!

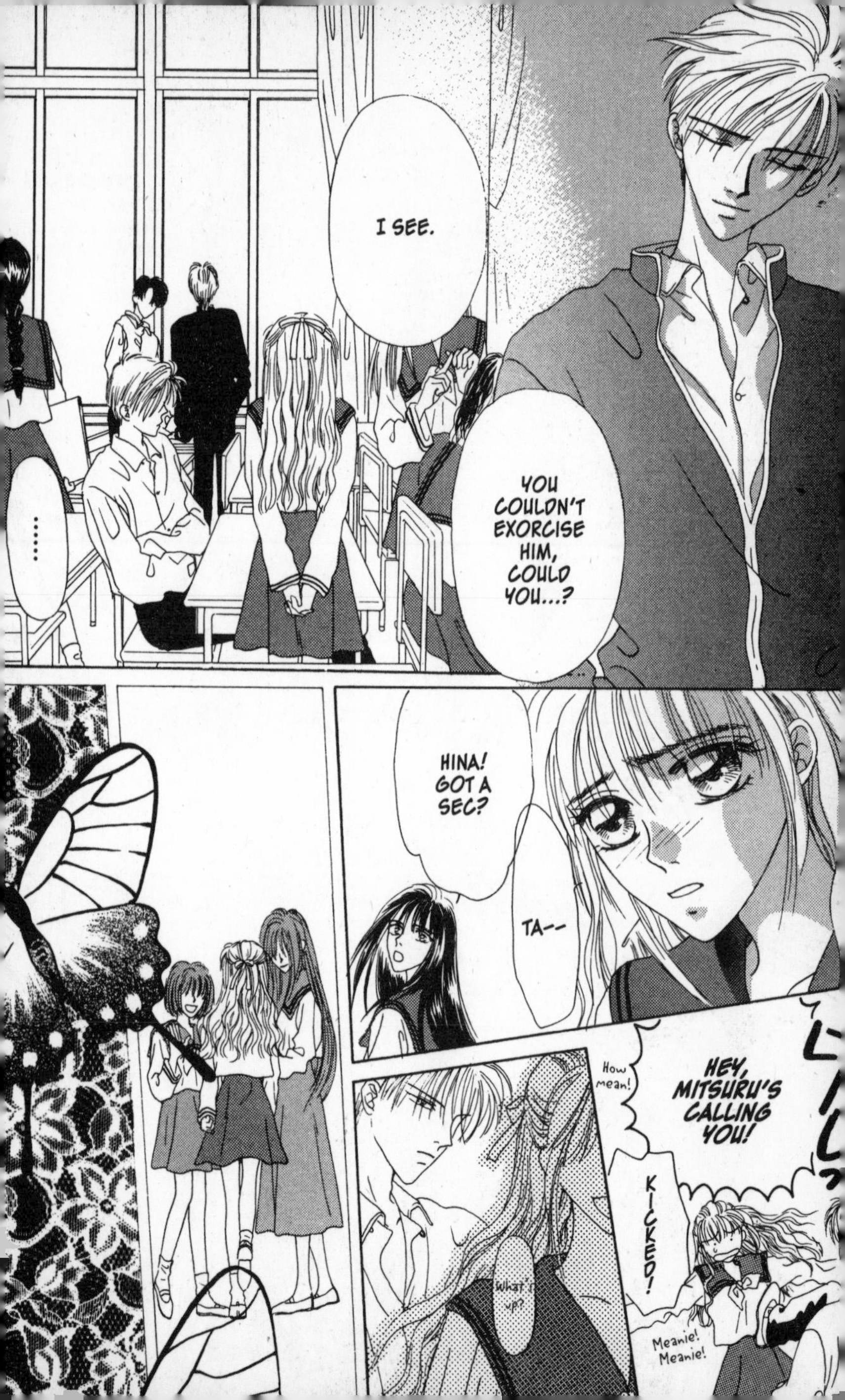
I SEE.
YOU COULDN'T EXORCISE HIM, COULD YOU...?
......
TA--
HINA! GOT A SEC?
HEY, MITSURU'S CALLING YOU!
How mean!
KICKED!
Meanie! Meanie!
What up?

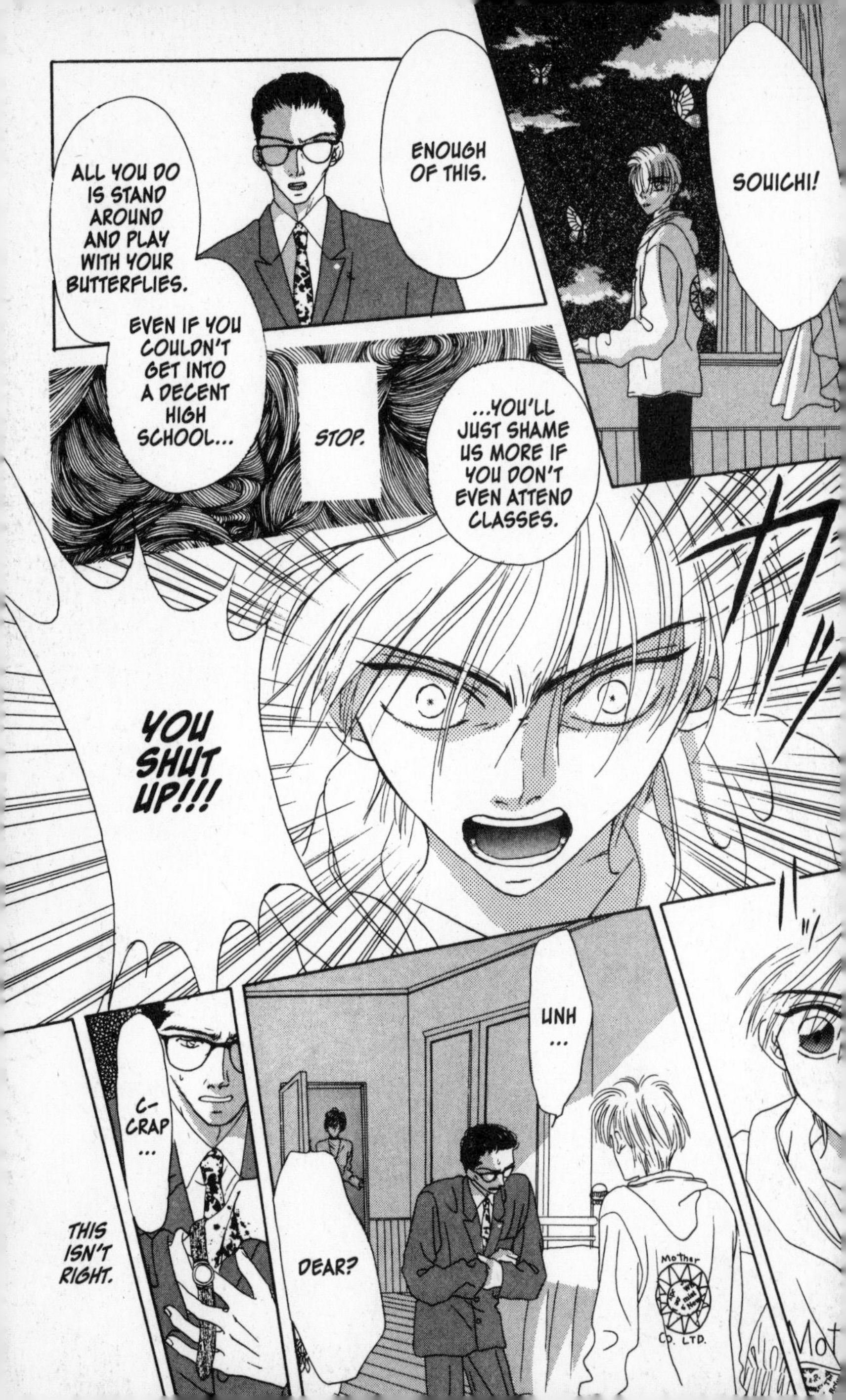

SOUICHI!
ENOUGH OF THIS.
ALL YOU DO IS STAND AROUND AND PLAY WITH YOUR BUTTERFLIES.
EVEN IF YOU COULDN'T GET INTO A DECENT HIGH SCHOOL...
STOP.
...YOU'LL JUST SHAME US MORE IF YOU DON'T EVEN ATTEND CLASSES.
YOU SHUT UP!!!
UNH ...
DEAR?
C-CRAP ...
THIS ISN'T RIGHT.

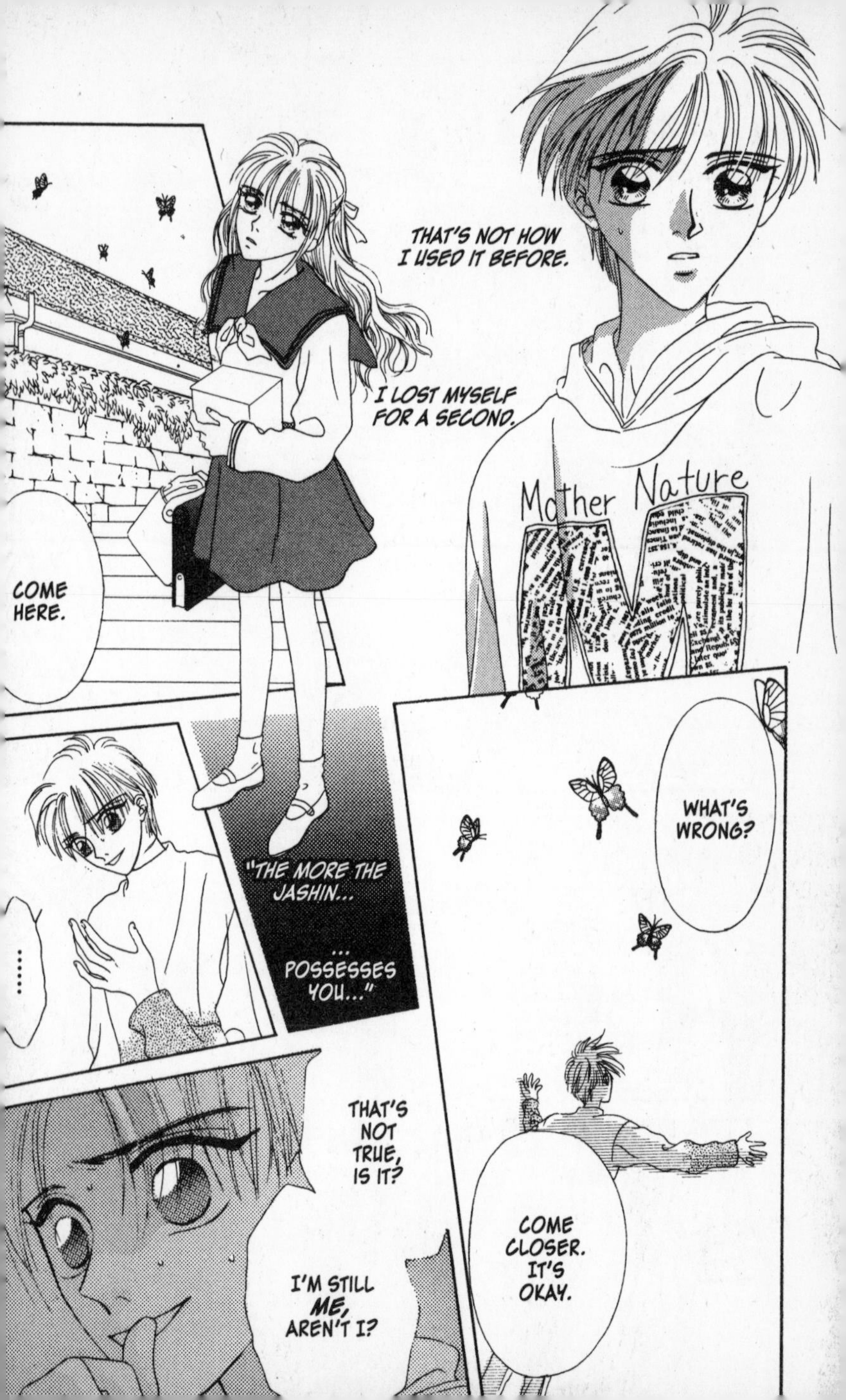
THAT'S NOT HOW I USED IT BEFORE.
I LOST MYSELF FOR A SECOND.
Mother Nature
COME HERE.
WHAT'S WRONG?
COME CLOSER. IT'S OKAY.
"THE MORE THE JASHIN...
... POSSESSES YOU..."
......
THAT'S NOT TRUE, IS IT?
I'M STILL *ME*, AREN'T I?

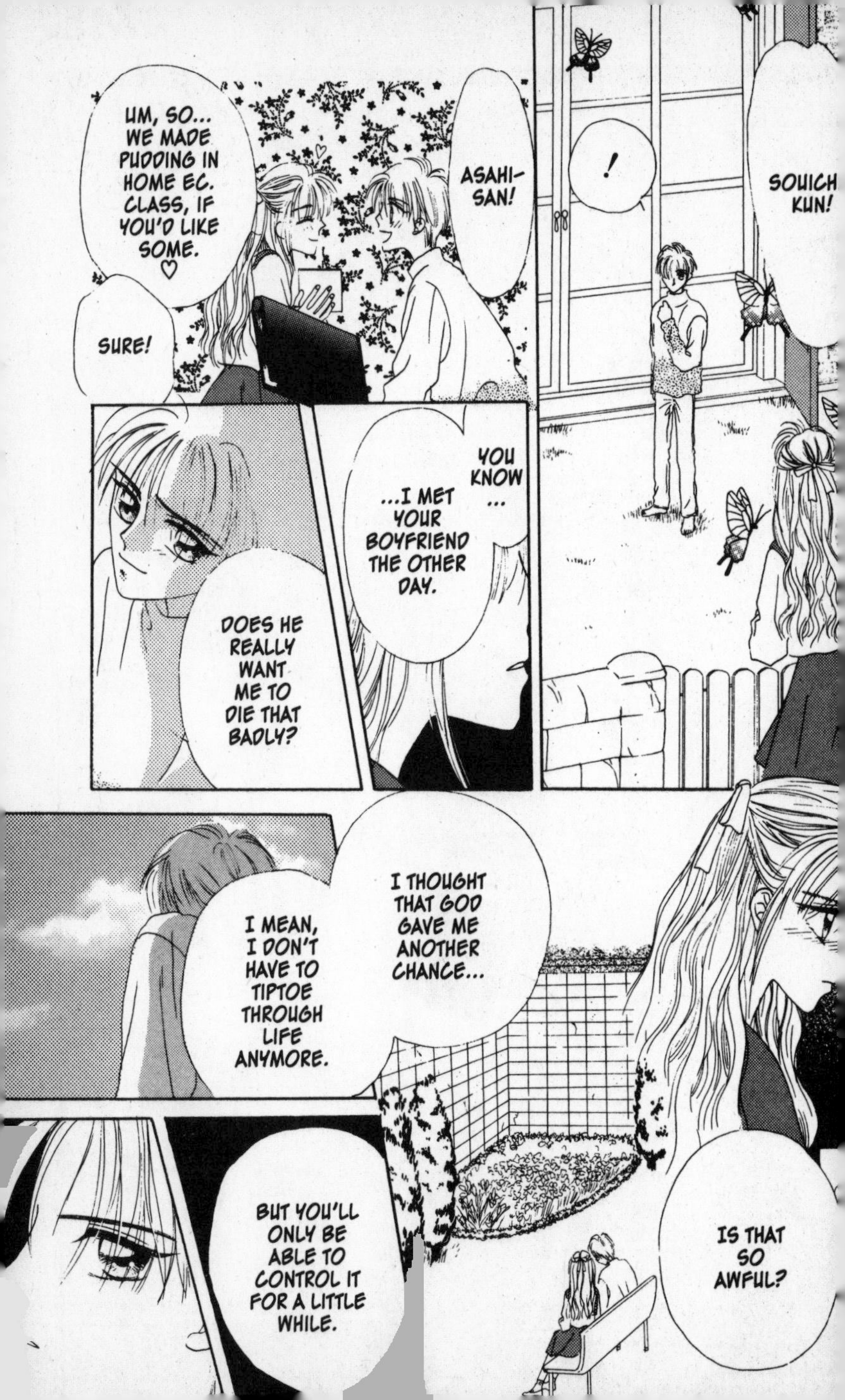
SOUICH KUN!
!
ASAHI-SAN!
UM, SO... WE MADE PUDDING IN HOME EC. CLASS, IF YOU'D LIKE SOME. ♡
SURE!
YOU KNOW...
...I MET YOUR BOYFRIEND THE OTHER DAY.
DOES HE REALLY WANT ME TO DIE THAT BADLY?
I THOUGHT THAT GOD GAVE ME ANOTHER CHANCE...
I MEAN, I DON'T HAVE TO TIPTOE THROUGH LIFE ANYMORE.
IS THAT SO AWFUL?
BUT YOU'LL ONLY BE ABLE TO CONTROL IT FOR A LITTLE WHILE.

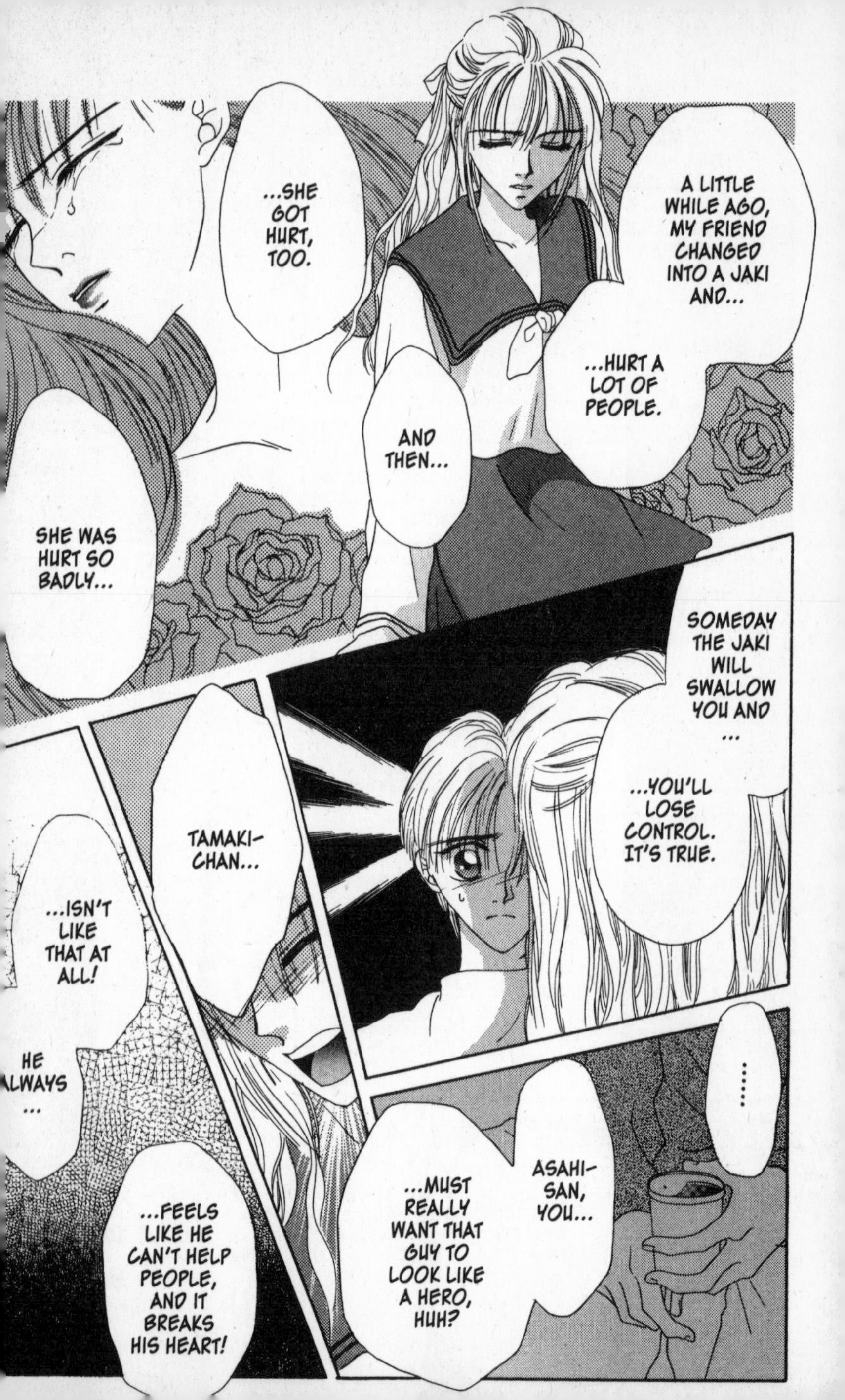
A LITTLE WHILE AGO, MY FRIEND CHANGED INTO A JAKI AND...
...HURT A LOT OF PEOPLE.
AND THEN...
...SHE GOT HURT, TOO.
SHE WAS HURT SO BADLY...
SOMEDAY THE JAKI WILL SWALLOW YOU AND ...
...YOU'LL LOSE CONTROL. IT'S TRUE.
TAMAKI-CHAN...
...ISN'T LIKE THAT AT ALL!
HE ALWAYS ...
...FEELS LIKE HE CAN'T HELP PEOPLE, AND IT BREAKS HIS HEART!
......
ASAHI-SAN, YOU...
...MUST REALLY WANT THAT GUY TO LOOK LIKE A HERO, HUH?

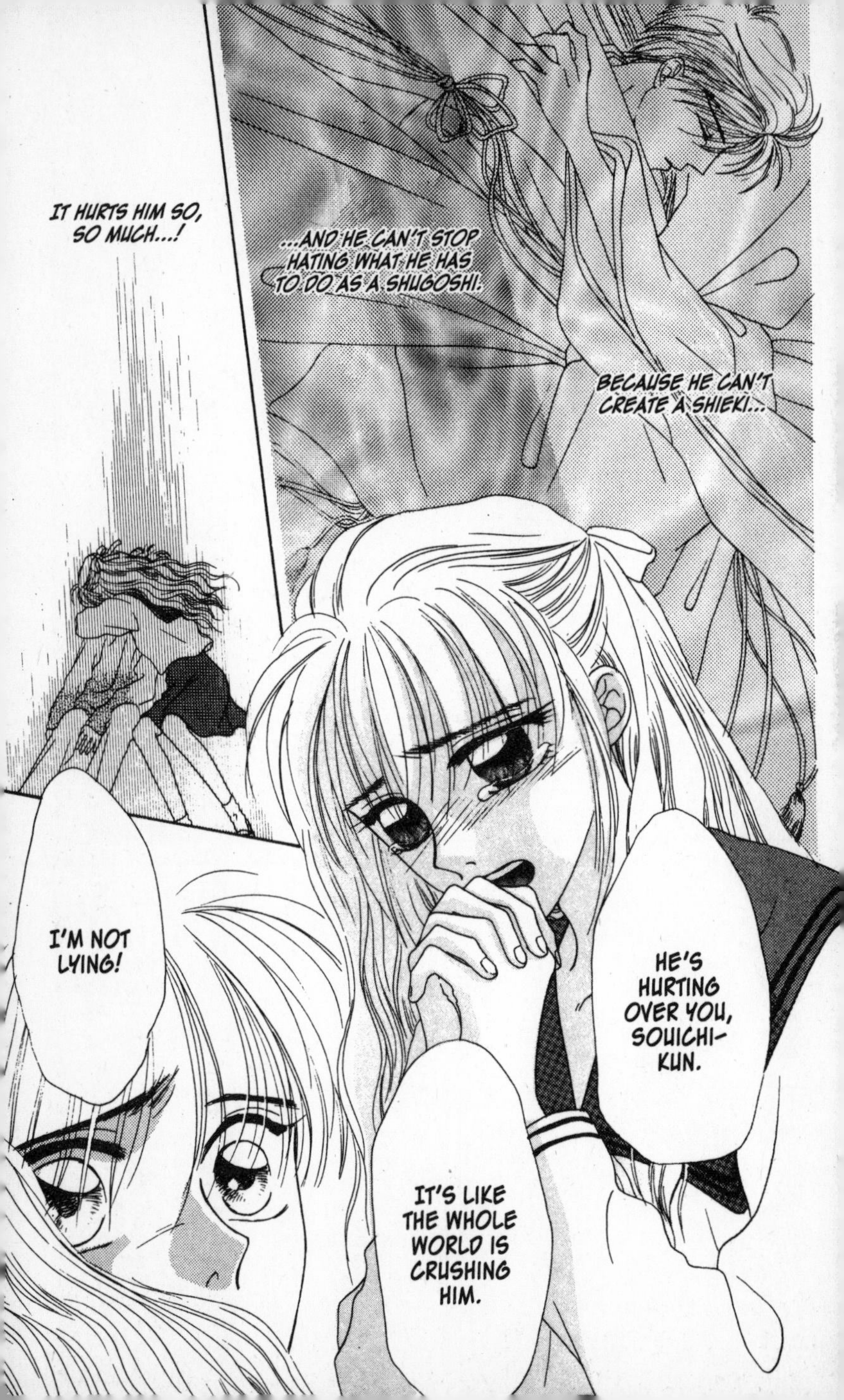
BECAUSE HE CAN'T CREATE A SHIEKI...
...AND HE CAN'T STOP HATING WHAT HE HAS TO DO AS A SHUGOSHI.
IT HURTS HIM SO, SO MUCH...!
HE'S HURTING OVER YOU, SOUICHI-KUN.
IT'S LIKE THE WHOLE WORLD IS CRUSHING HIM.
I'M NOT LYING!

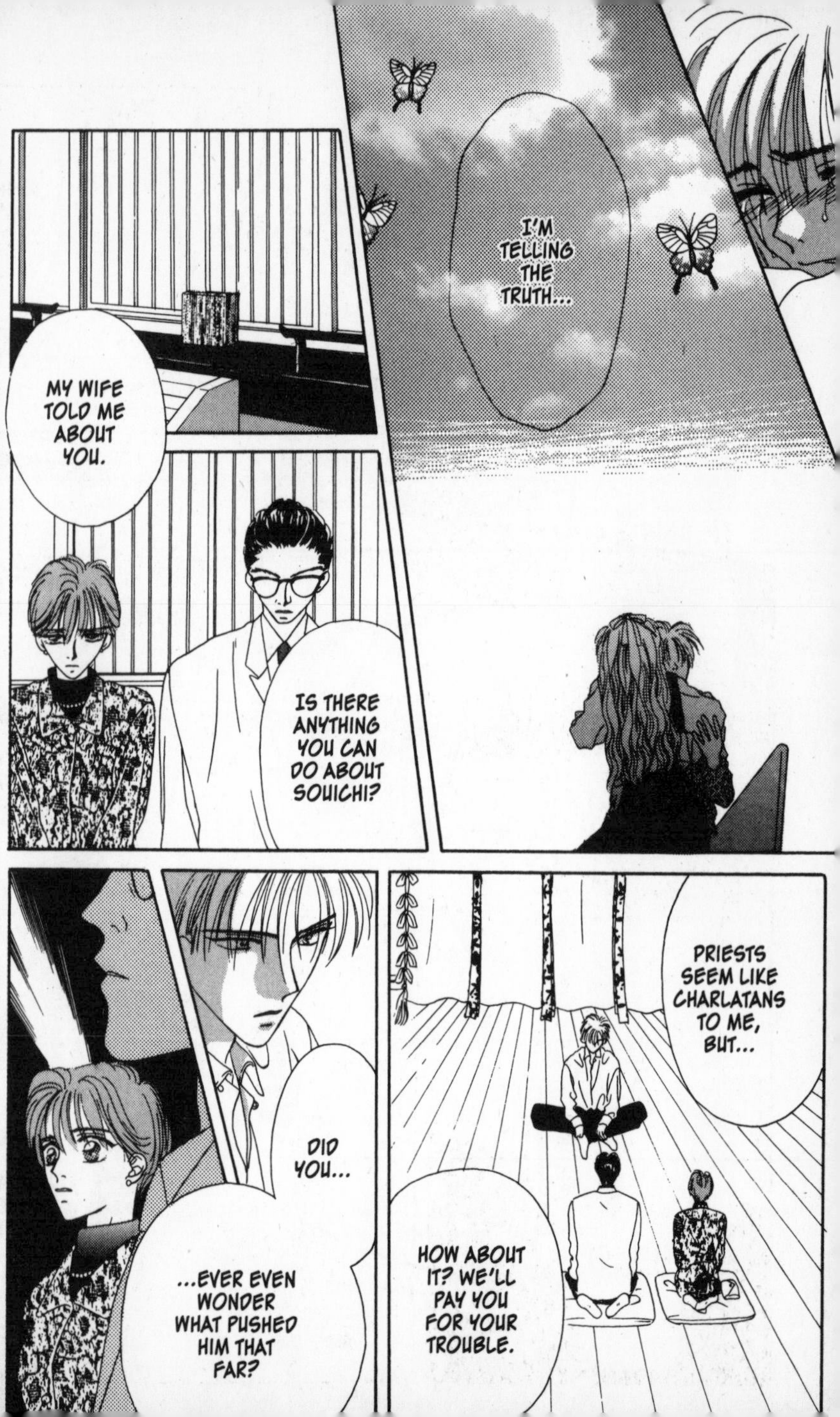
I'M TELLING THE TRUTH...
MY WIFE TOLD ME ABOUT YOU.
IS THERE ANYTHING YOU CAN DO ABOUT SOUICHI?
PRIESTS SEEM LIKE CHARLATANS TO ME, BUT...
HOW ABOUT IT? WE'LL PAY YOU FOR YOUR TROUBLE.
DID YOU...
...EVER EVEN WONDER WHAT PUSHED HIM THAT FAR?

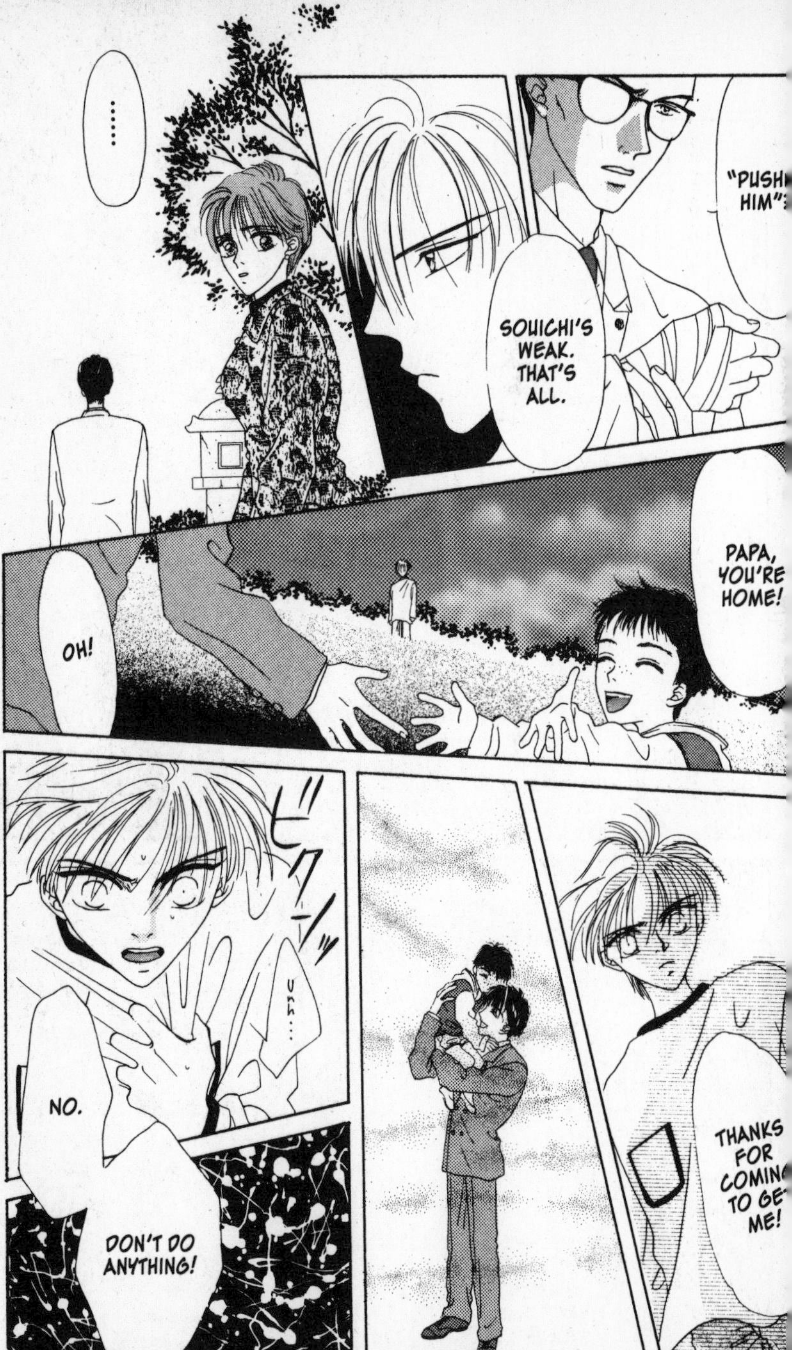
"PUSH HIM"
SOUICHI'S WEAK. THAT'S ALL.
......
PAPA, YOU'RE HOME!
OH!
THANKS FOR COMING TO GET ME!
ビクーッ
Uh...
NO.
DON'T DO ANYTHING!

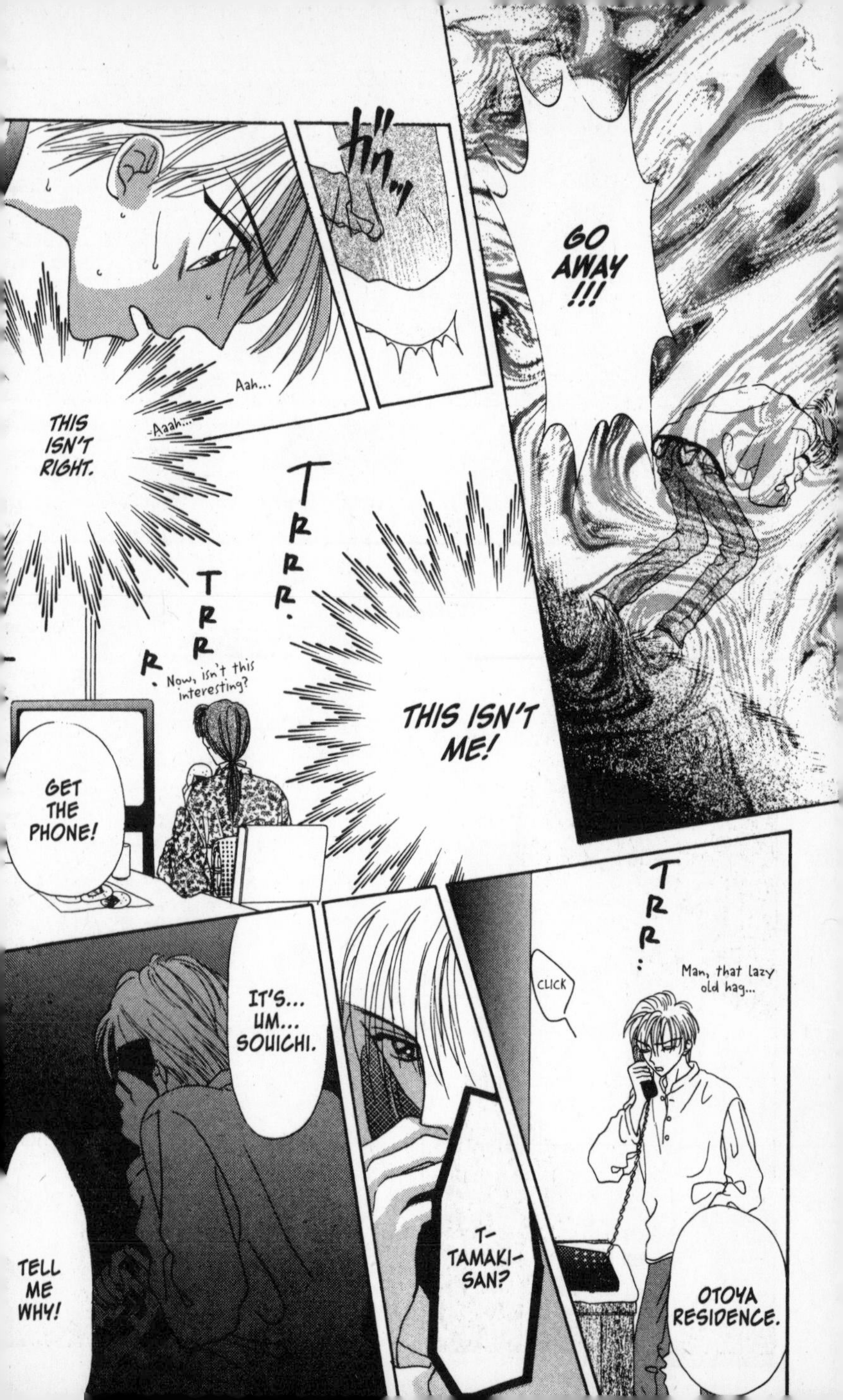
GO AWAY!!!
Aah...
-Aaah...
THIS ISN'T RIGHT.
TRRR.
THIS ISN'T ME!
TRRR.
Now, isn't this interesting?
GET THE PHONE!
TRR...
CLICK
Man, that lazy old hag...
OTOYA RESIDENCE.
IT'S... UM... SOUICHI.
T-TAMAKI-SAN?
TELL ME WHY!

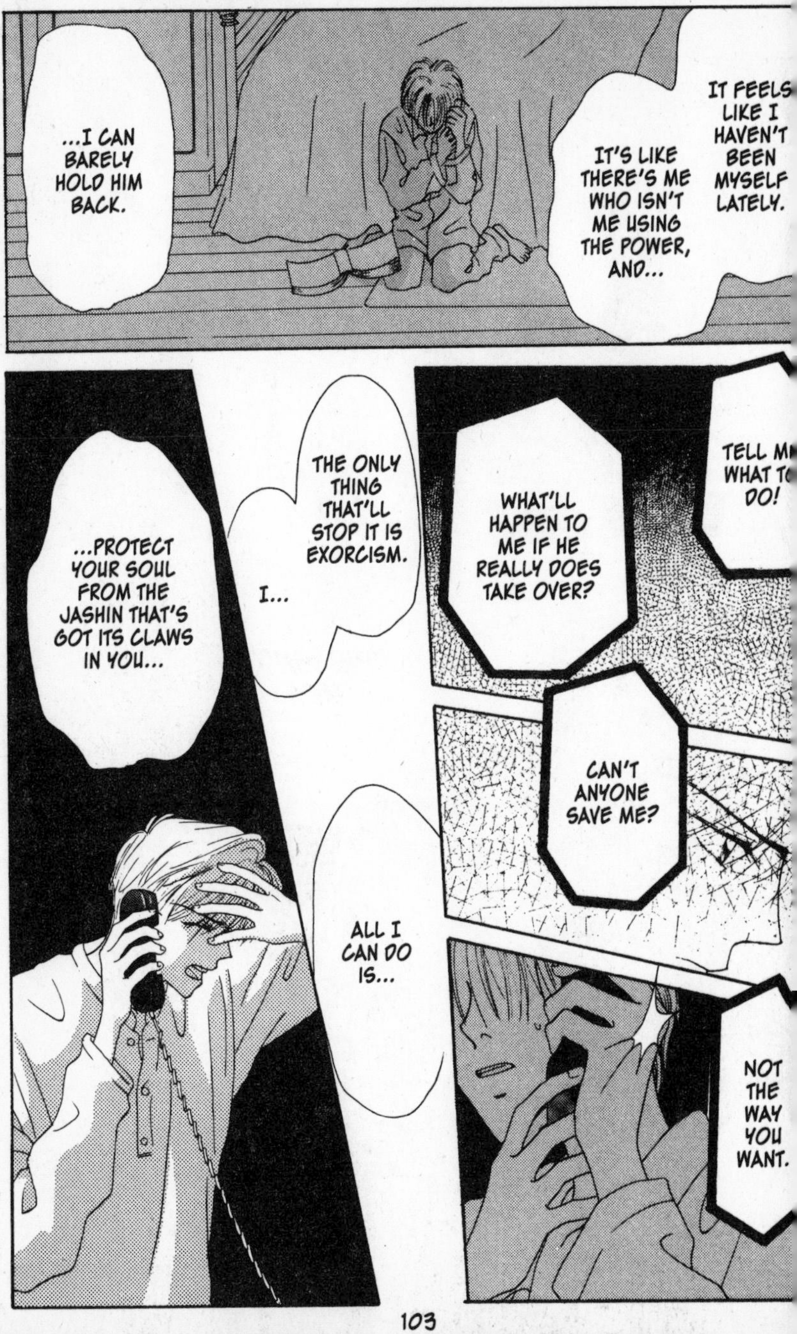
IT FEELS LIKE I HAVEN'T BEEN MYSELF LATELY.
IT'S LIKE THERE'S ME WHO ISN'T ME USING THE POWER, AND...
...I CAN BARELY HOLD HIM BACK.
TELL M WHAT T DO!
WHAT'LL HAPPEN TO ME IF HE REALLY DOES TAKE OVER?
CAN'T ANYONE SAVE ME?
NOT THE WAY YOU WANT.
THE ONLY THING THAT'LL STOP IT IS EXORCISM.
I...
ALL I CAN DO IS...
...PROTECT YOUR SOUL FROM THE JASHIN THAT'S GOT ITS CLAWS IN YOU...

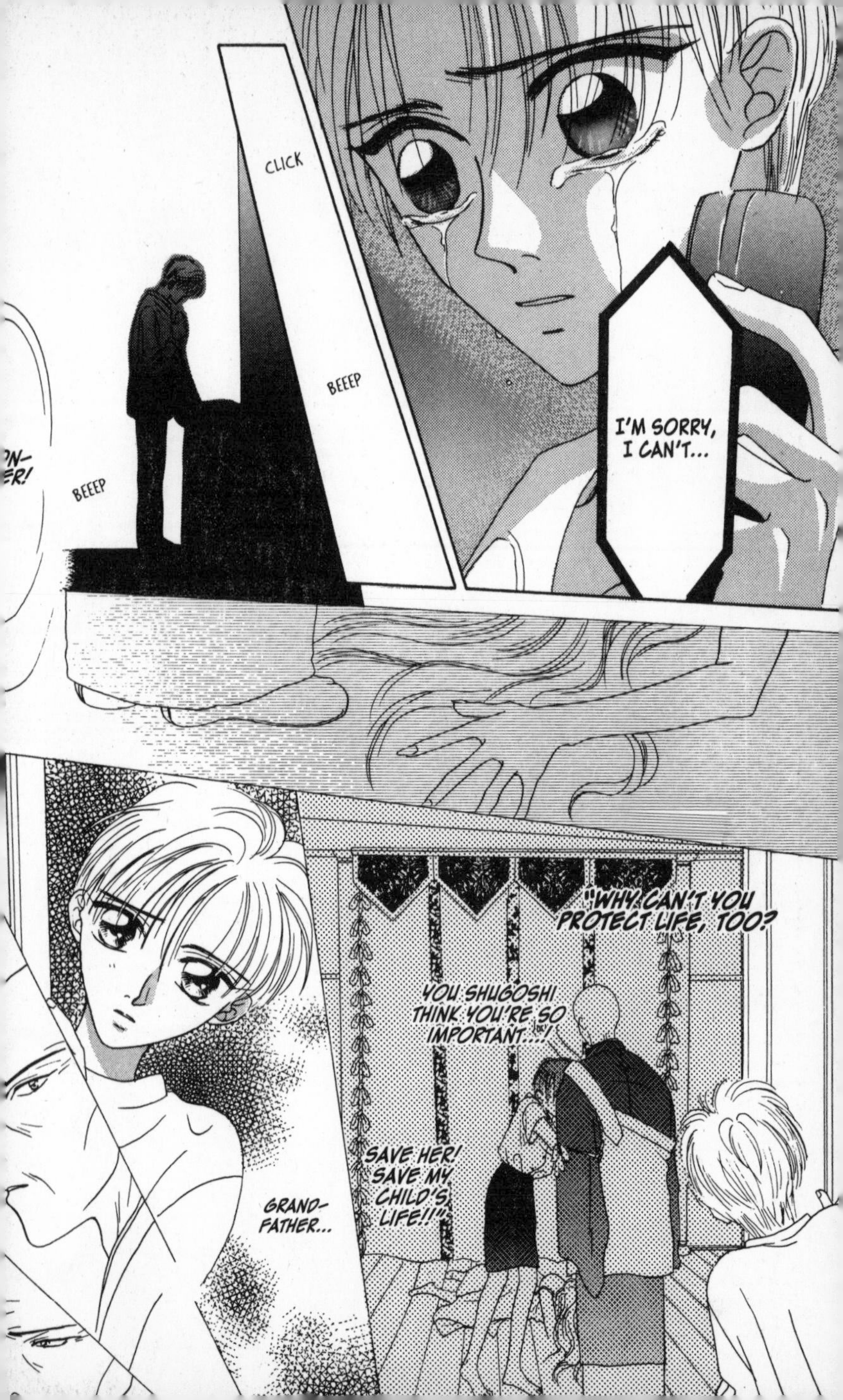
I'M SORRY, I CAN'T...
CLICK
BEEEP
BEEEP
"WHY CAN'T YOU PROTECT LIFE, TOO?
YOU SHUGOSHI THINK YOU'RE SO IMPORTANT...!
SAVE HER! SAVE MY CHILD'S LIFE!!"
GRAND-FATHER...

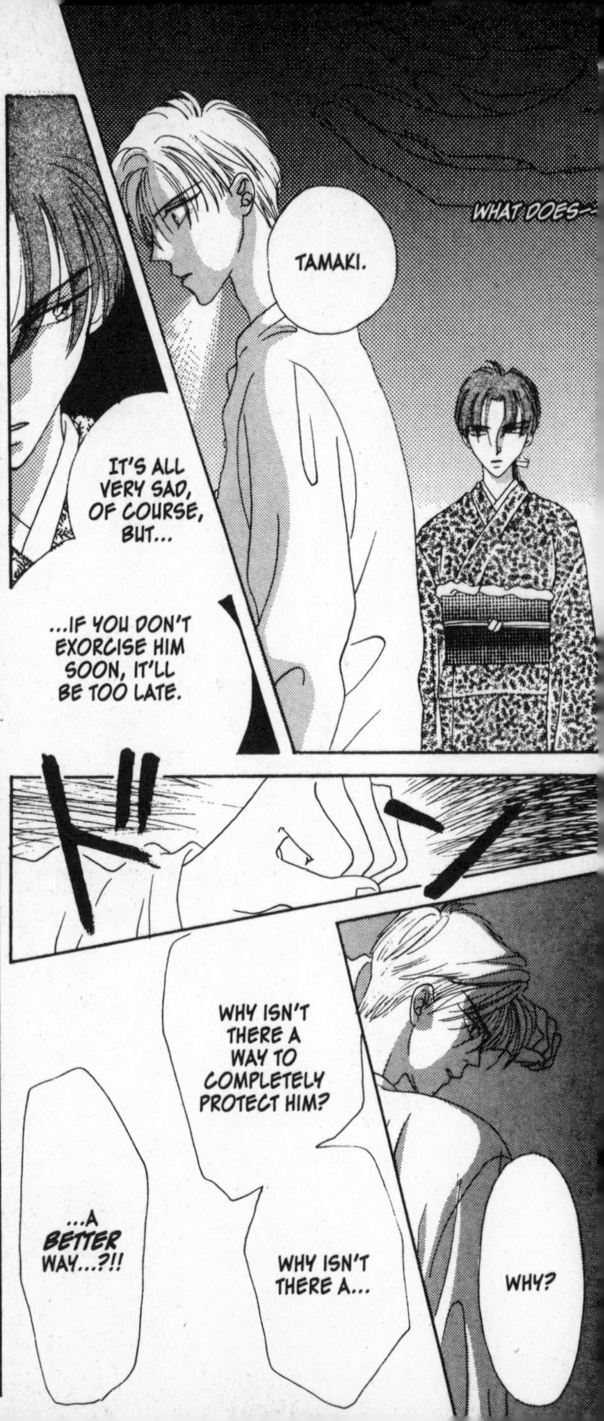
WHAT DOES—
TAMAKI.
IT'S ALL VERY SAD, OF COURSE, BUT...
...IF YOU DON'T EXORCISE HIM SOON, IT'LL BE TOO LATE.
WHY ISN'T THERE A WAY TO COMPLETELY PROTECT HIM?
WHY?
WHY ISN'T THERE A...
...A BETTER WAY...?!!

Three

Until now I've been throwing the name "Tamaki" around very casually, but the truth is...I borrowed my big sister's name. Okay?

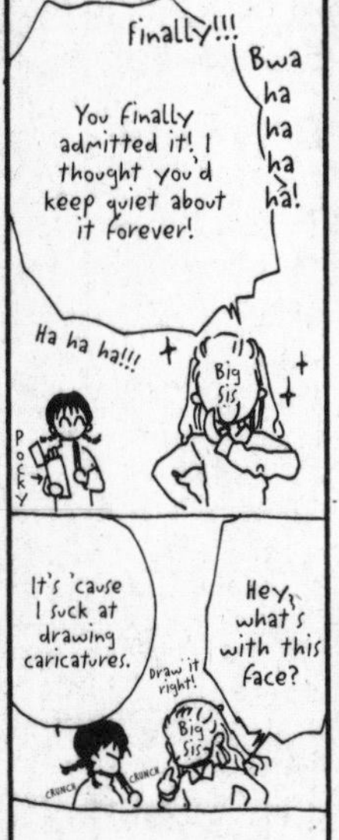
Finally!!!
Bwa ha ha ha ha!
You finally admitted it! I thought you'd keep quiet about it forever!
Ha ha ha!!!
Big Sis
POCKY
It's 'cause I suck at drawing caricatures.
Hey, what's with this face?
Draw it right!
Big Sis
CRUNCH
CRUNCH

Thanks, big sister! I hear you used to have a rough time because people thought you were a guy, but I guess it got easier after Haikara-san ga Tooru* had a girl named Tamaki. Maybe it's old, but it's a gender-neutral name, after all. And I think it's really nice! Not that it does any good to compliment your relatives. (Laughs.) Anyway, I've always been attracted to gender-neutral things.

* Manga by Waki Yamako.

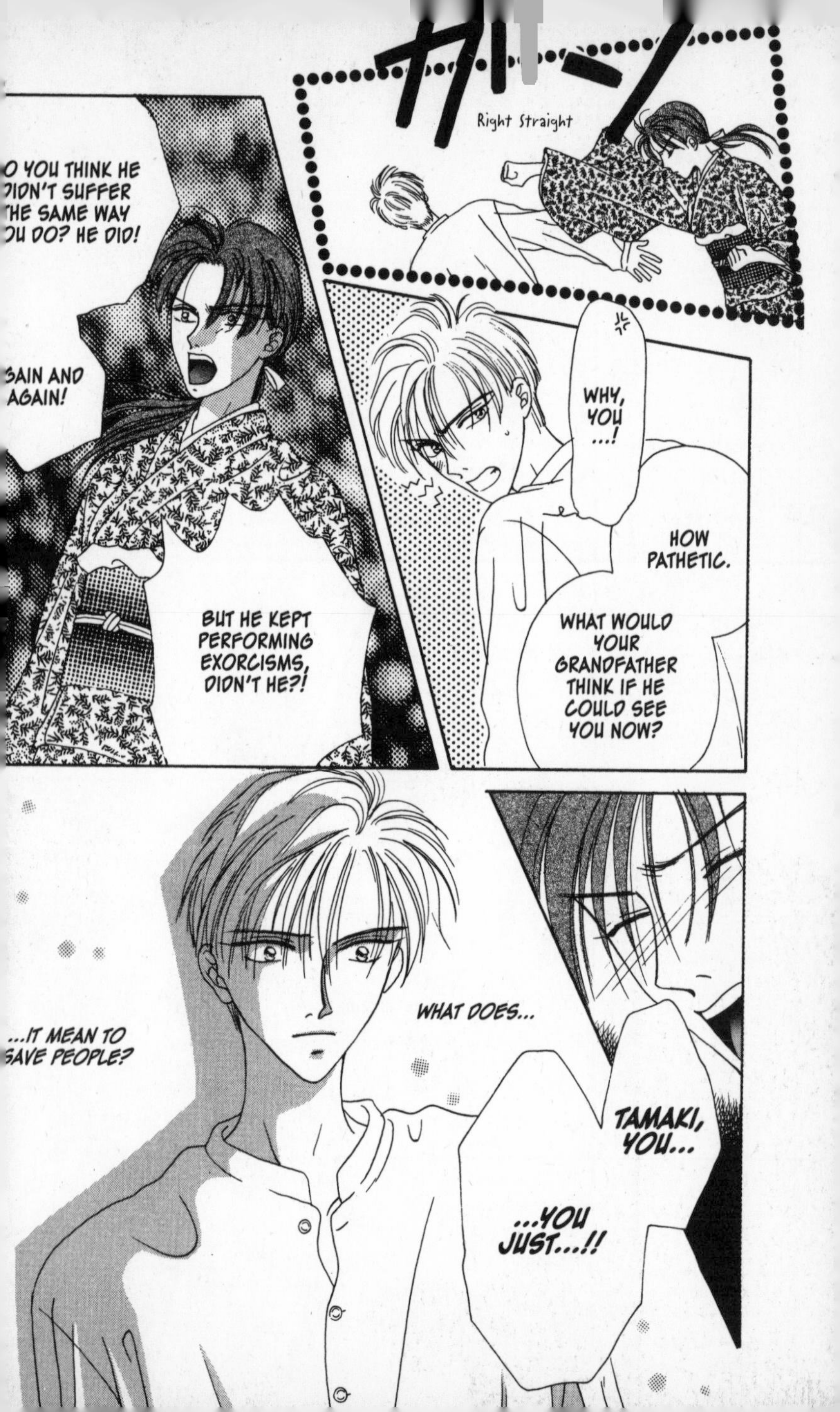

カーン
Right Straight
WHY, YOU ...!
HOW PATHETIC.
WHAT WOULD YOUR GRANDFATHER THINK IF HE COULD SEE YOU NOW?
O YOU THINK HE DIDN'T SUFFER THE SAME WAY OU DO? HE DID!
GAIN AND AGAIN!
BUT HE KEPT PERFORMING EXORCISMS, DIDN'T HE?!
TAMAKI, YOU...
...YOU JUST...!!
WHAT DOES...
...IT MEAN TO SAVE PEOPLE?

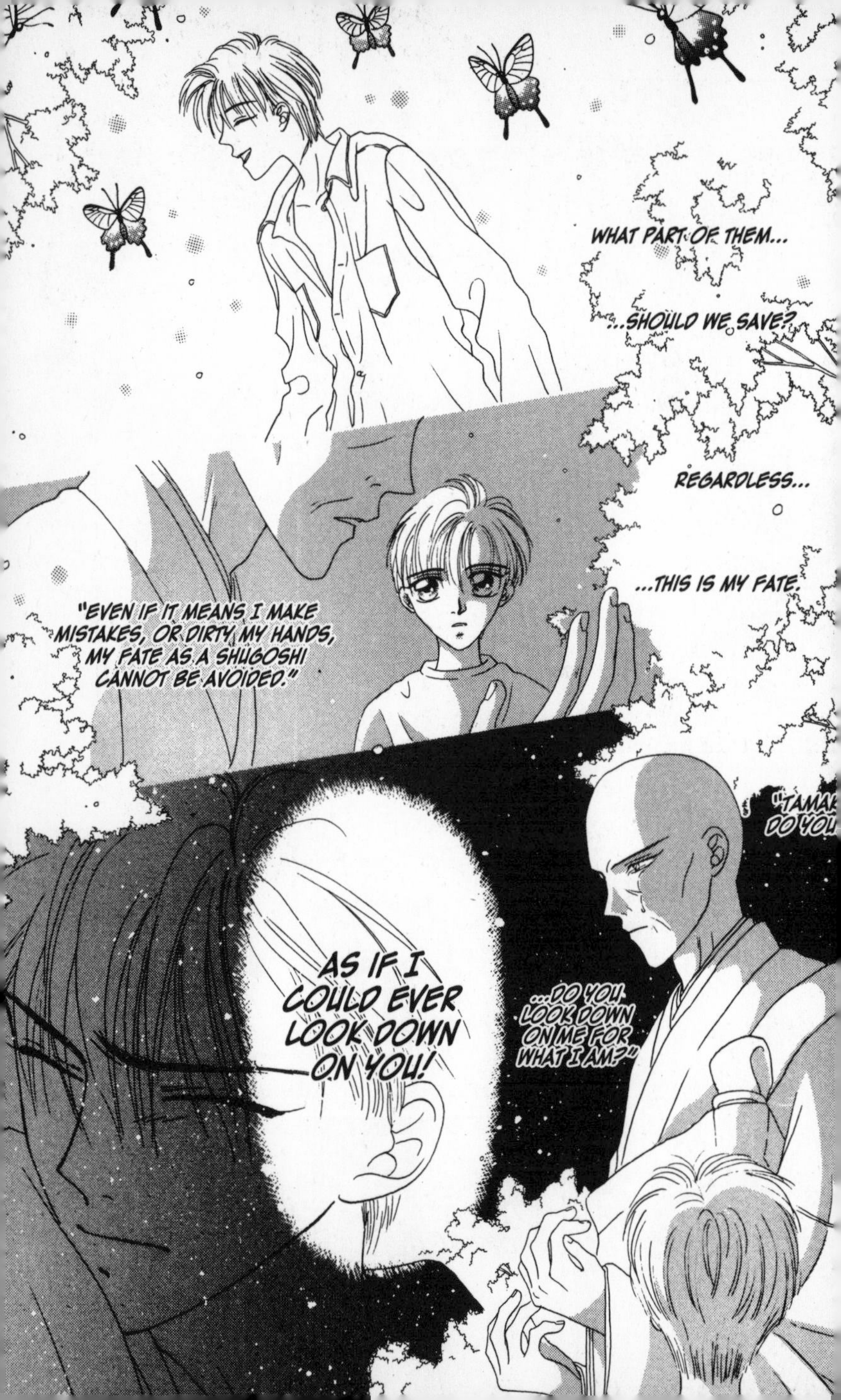
WHAT PART OF THEM...
...SHOULD WE SAVE?
REGARDLESS...
...THIS IS MY FATE.
"EVEN IF IT MEANS I MAKE MISTAKES, OR DIRTY MY HANDS, MY FATE AS A SHUGOSHI CANNOT BE AVOIDED."
"TAMAK
DO YOU
...DO YOU LOOK DOWN ON ME FOR WHAT I AM?"
AS IF I COULD EVER LOOK DOWN ON YOU!

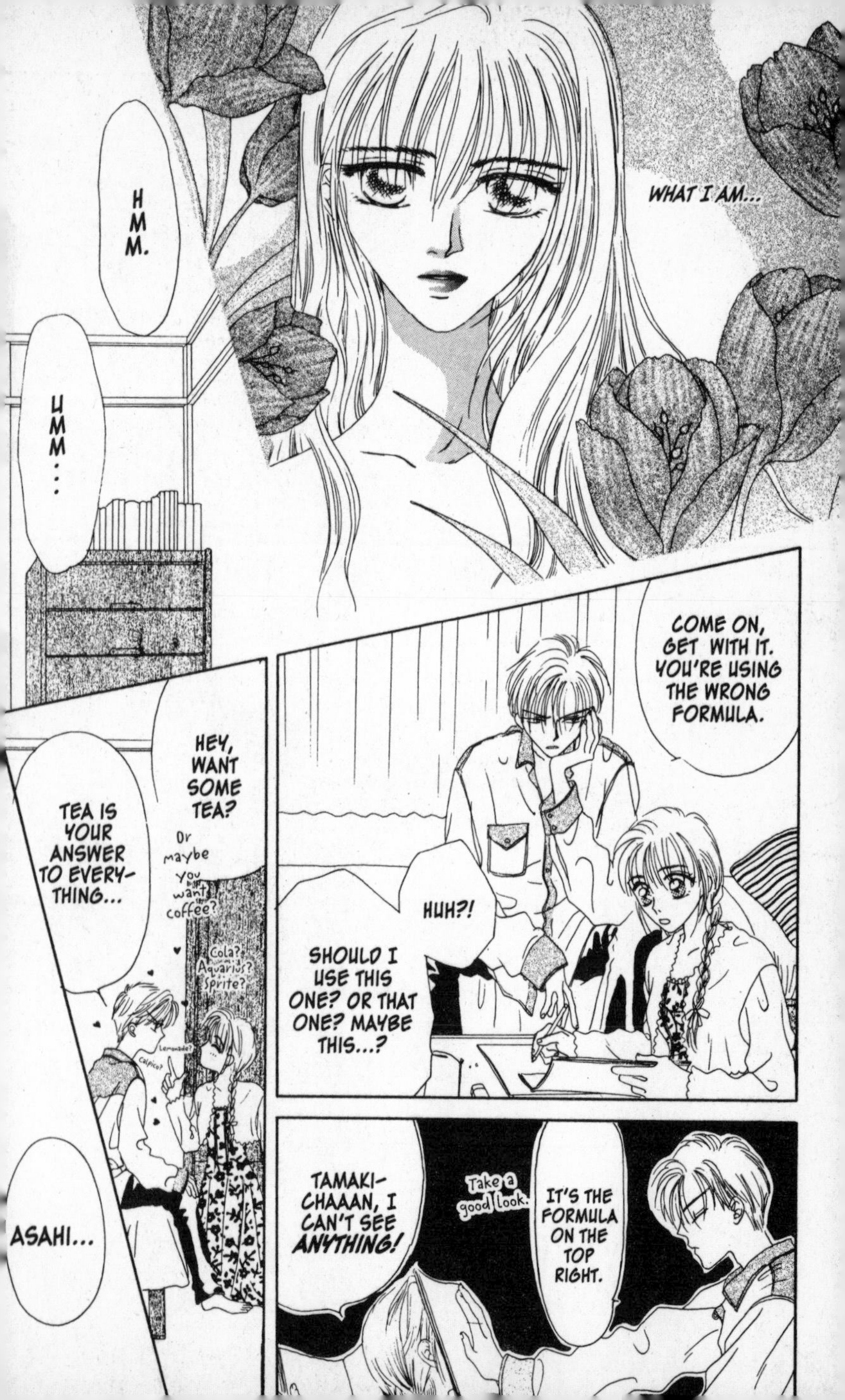
WHAT I AM...
HMM.
UMM...
COME ON, GET WITH IT. YOU'RE USING THE WRONG FORMULA.
HUH?!
SHOULD I USE THIS ONE? OR THAT ONE? MAYBE THIS...?
IT'S THE FORMULA ON THE TOP RIGHT.
Take a good look.
TAMAKI-CHAAAN, I CAN'T SEE *ANYTHING!*
HEY, WANT SOME TEA?
Or maybe you want coffee?
Cola? Aquarius? Sprite?
Lemonade?
Calpico?
TEA IS YOUR ANSWER TO EVERY-THING...
ASAHI...

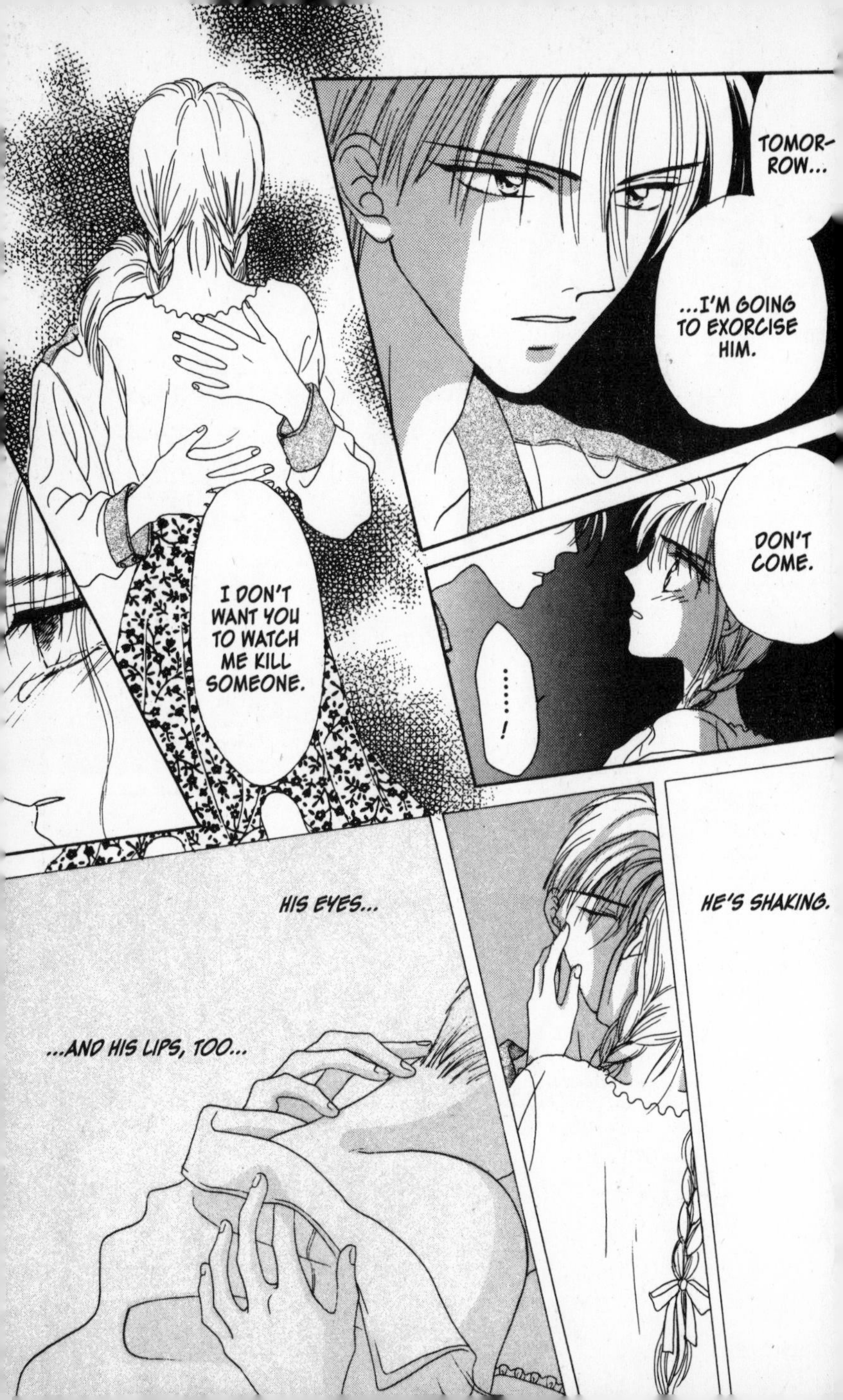
TOMOR-ROW...
...I'M GOING TO EXORCISE HIM.
DON'T COME.
......!
I DON'T WANT YOU TO WATCH ME KILL SOMEONE.
HE'S SHAKING.
HIS EYES...
...AND HIS LIPS, TOO...

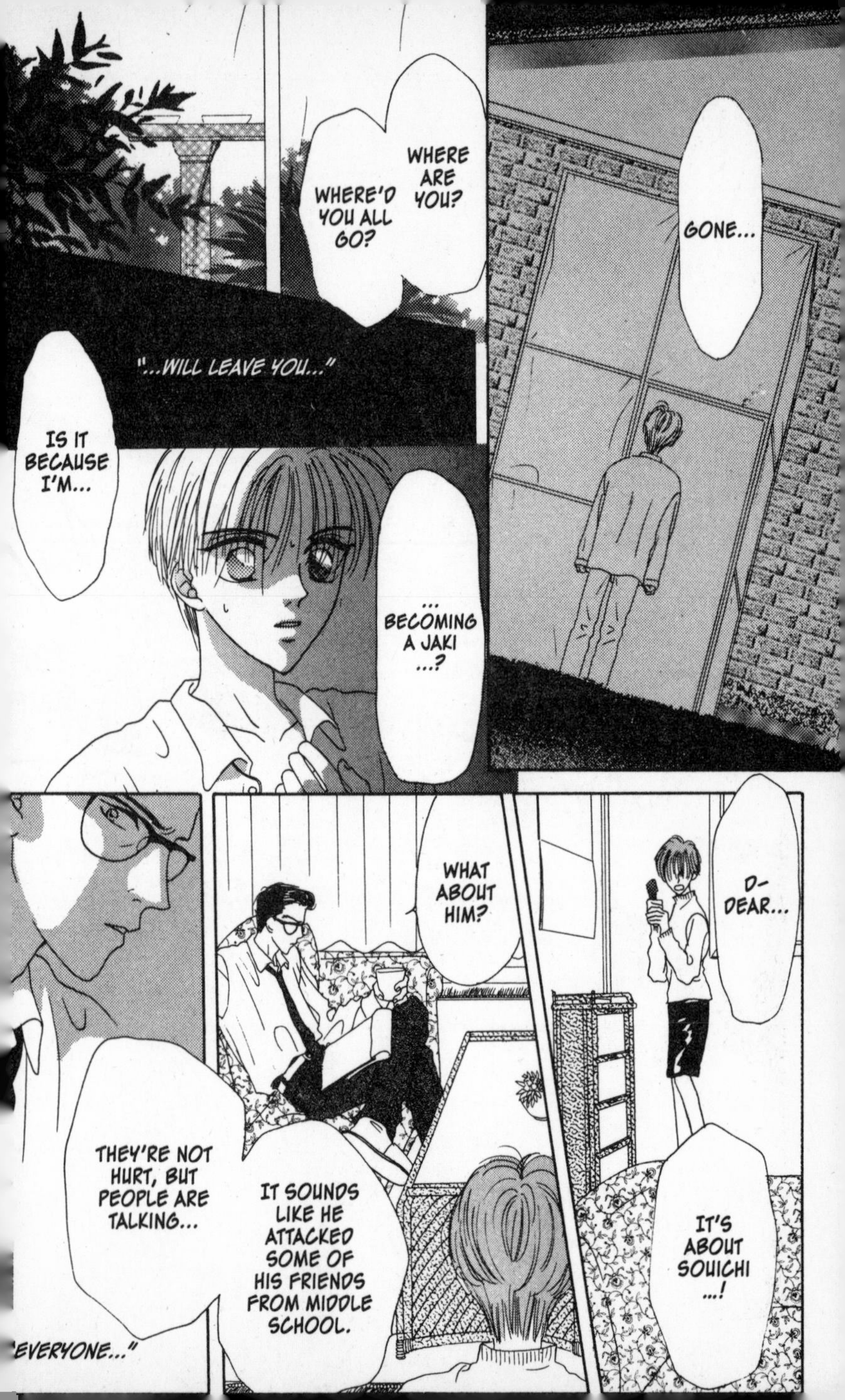
GONE...
WHERE ARE YOU?
WHERE'D YOU ALL GO?
"...WILL LEAVE YOU..."
IS IT BECAUSE I'M...
... BECOMING A JAKI ...?
D- DEAR...
IT'S ABOUT SOUICHI ...!
WHAT ABOUT HIM?
IT SOUNDS LIKE HE ATTACKED SOME OF HIS FRIENDS FROM MIDDLE SCHOOL.
THEY'RE NOT HURT, BUT PEOPLE ARE TALKING...
EVERYONE..."

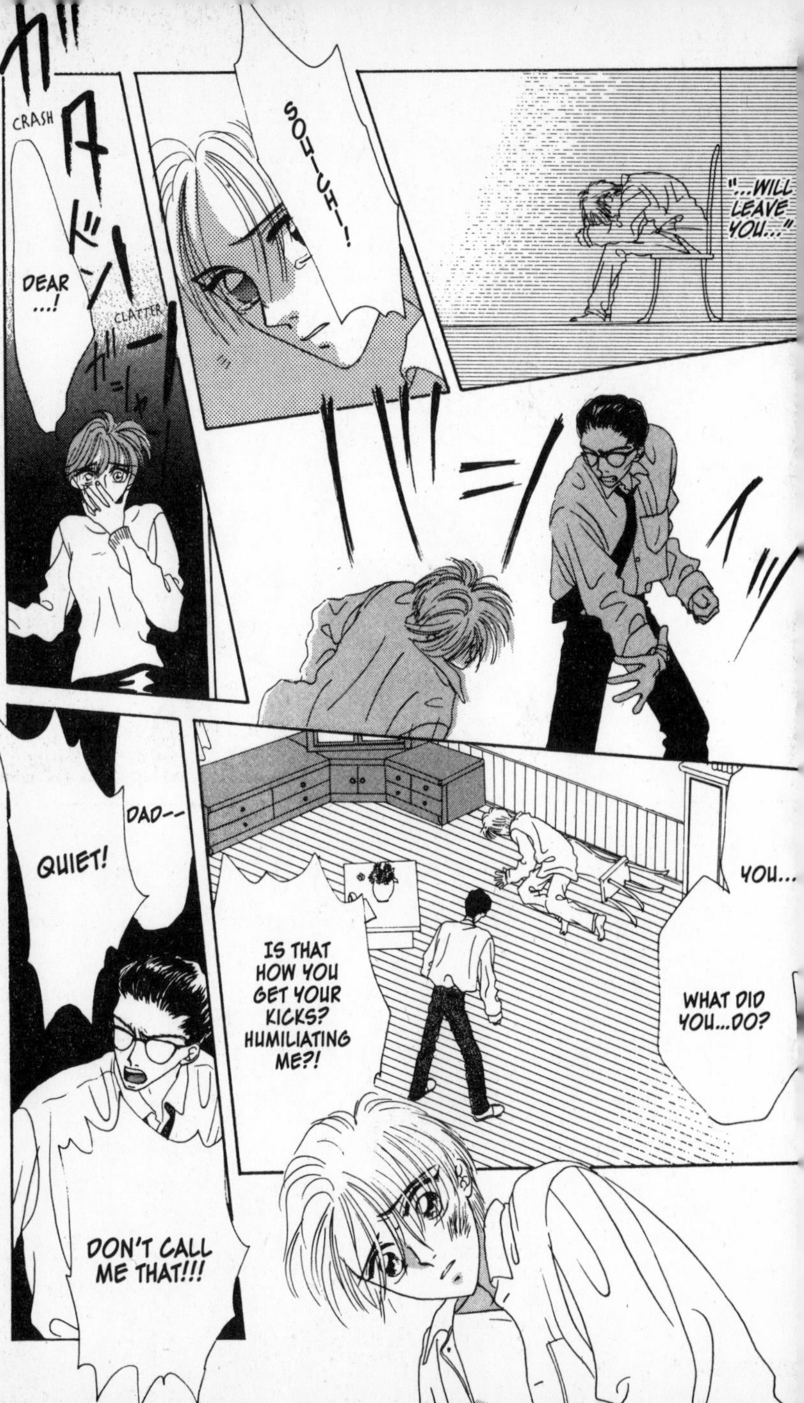
"...WILL LEAVE YOU..."
SOUICHI!
CRASH
DEAR ...!
CLATTER
YOU...
WHAT DID YOU...DO?
IS THAT HOW YOU GET YOUR KICKS? HUMILIATING ME?!
DAD--
QUIET!
DON'T CALL ME THAT!!!

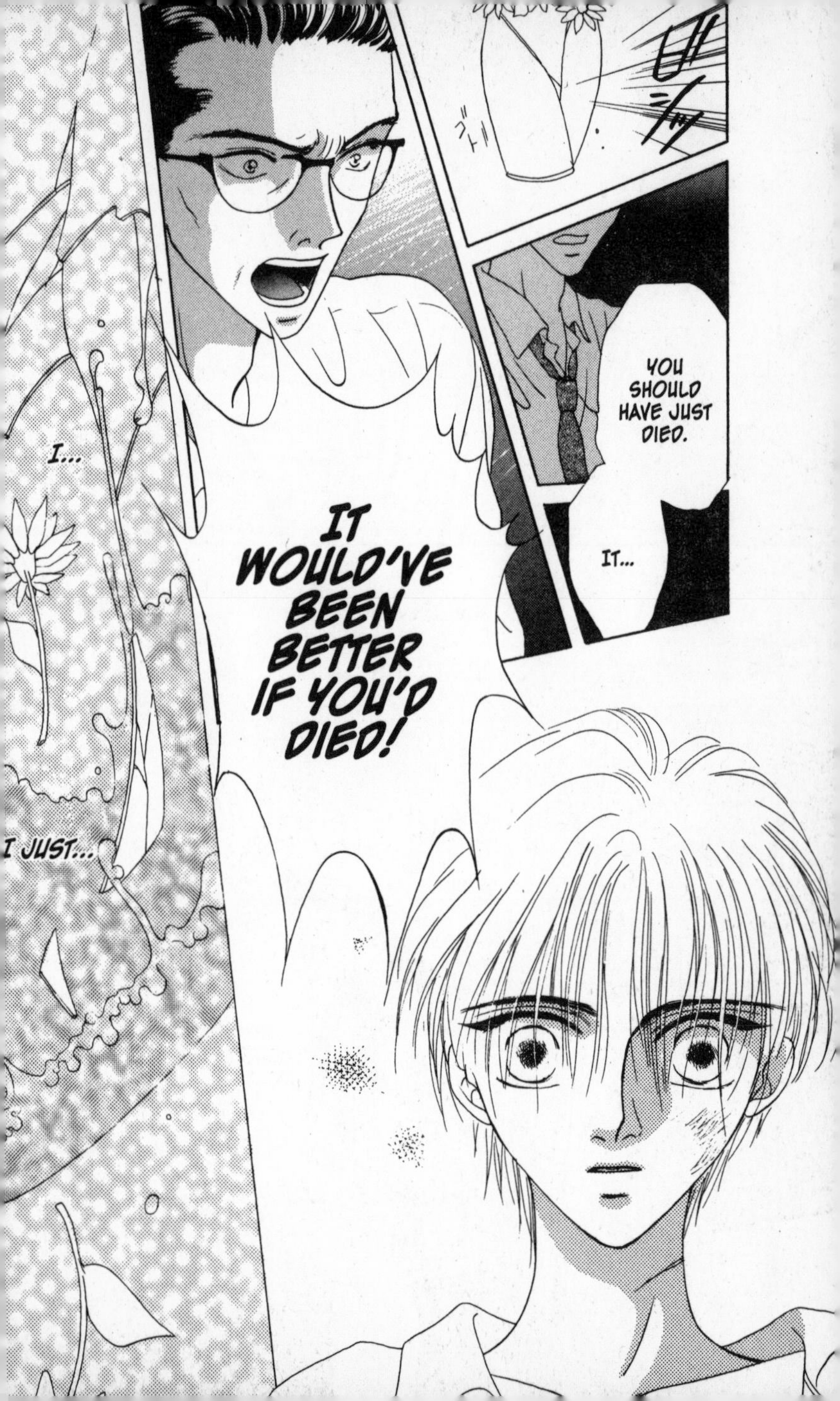

YOU SHOULD HAVE JUST DIED.
IT...
IT WOULD'VE BEEN BETTER IF YOU'D DIED!
I...
I JUST...

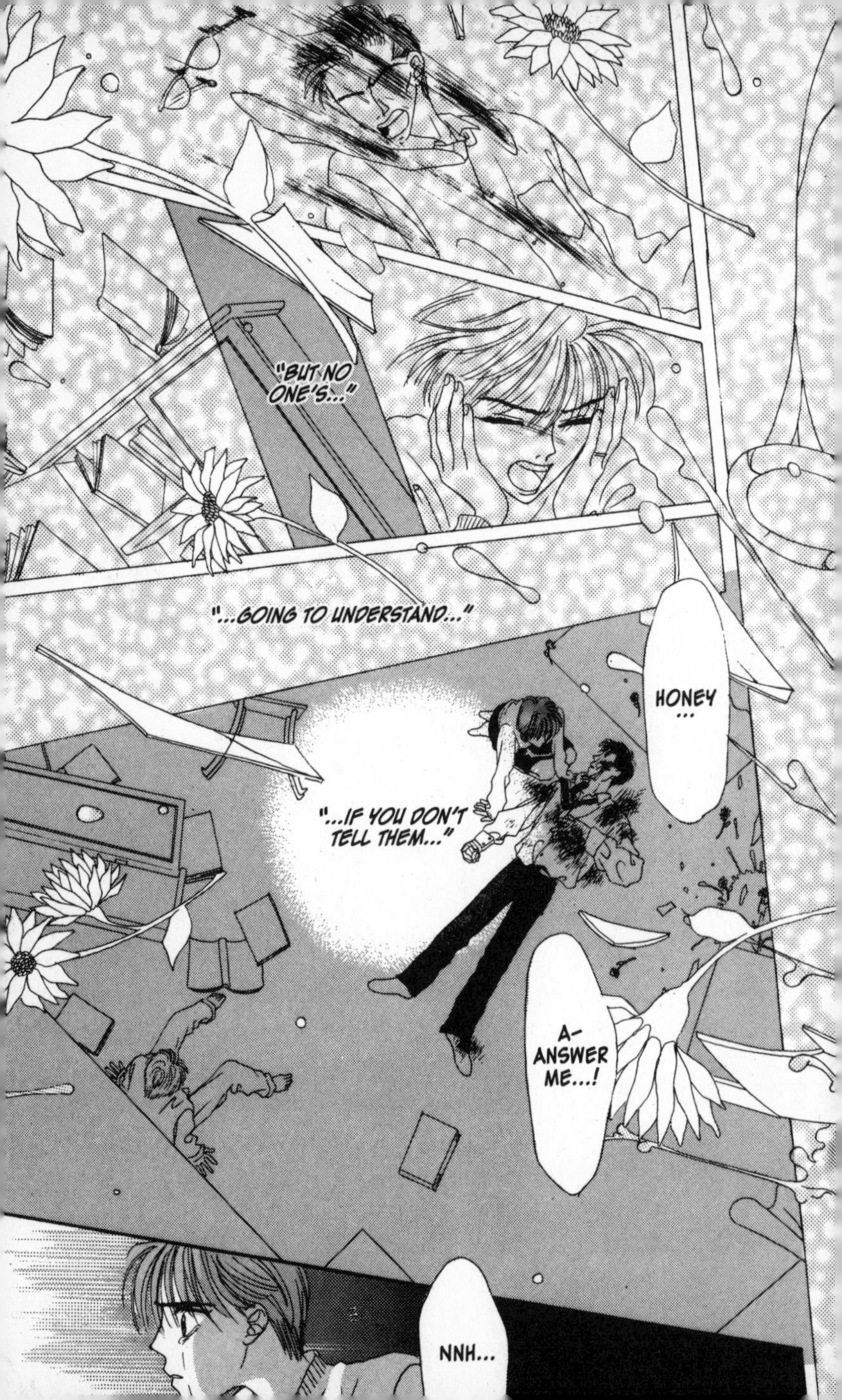
"BUT NO ONE'S..."
"...GOING TO UNDERSTAND..."
HONEY...
"...IF YOU DON'T TELL THEM..."
A- ANSWER ME...!
NNH...

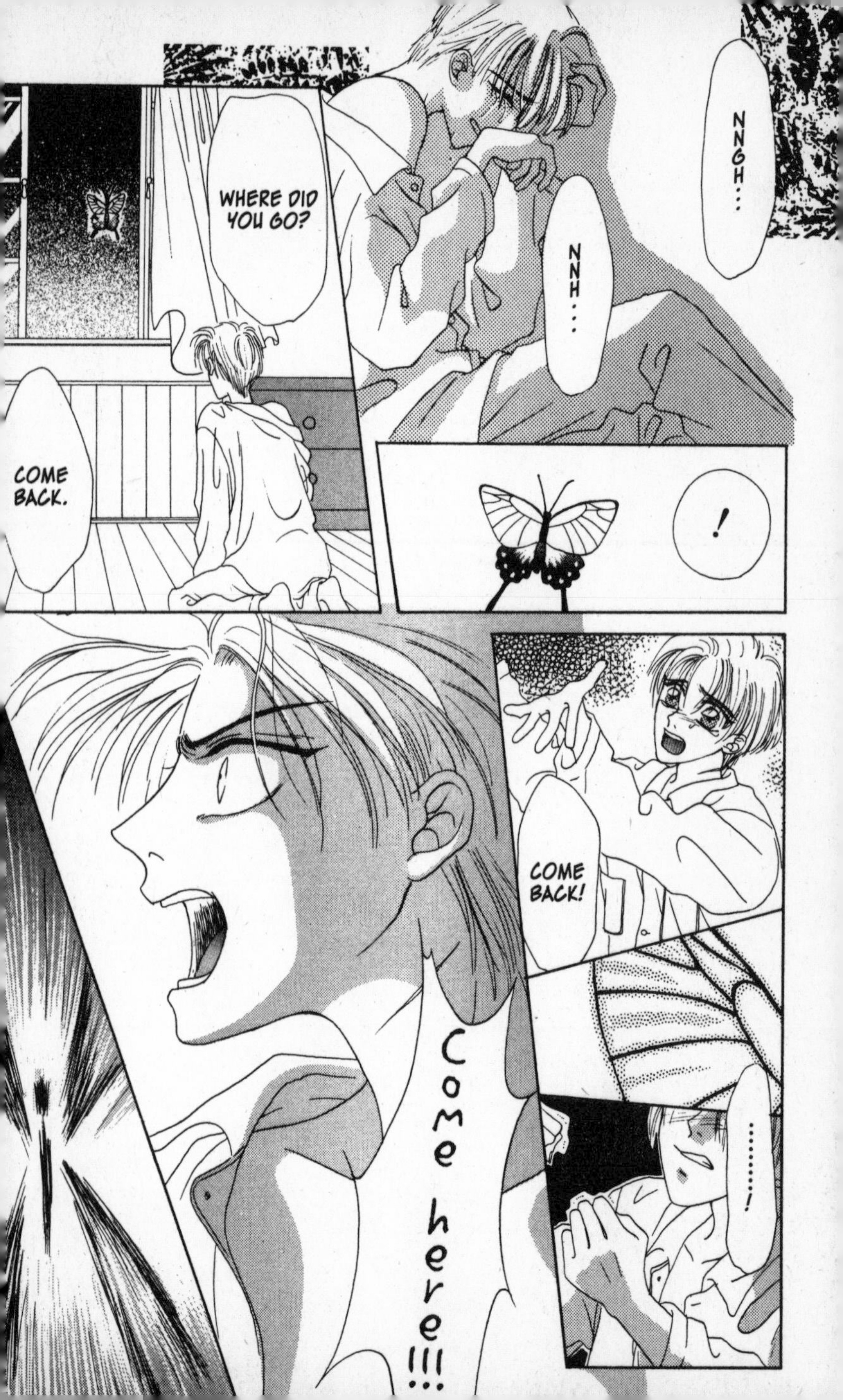
NNGH...
NNH...
!
WHERE DID YOU GO?
COME BACK.
COME BACK!
......!
Come here!!!

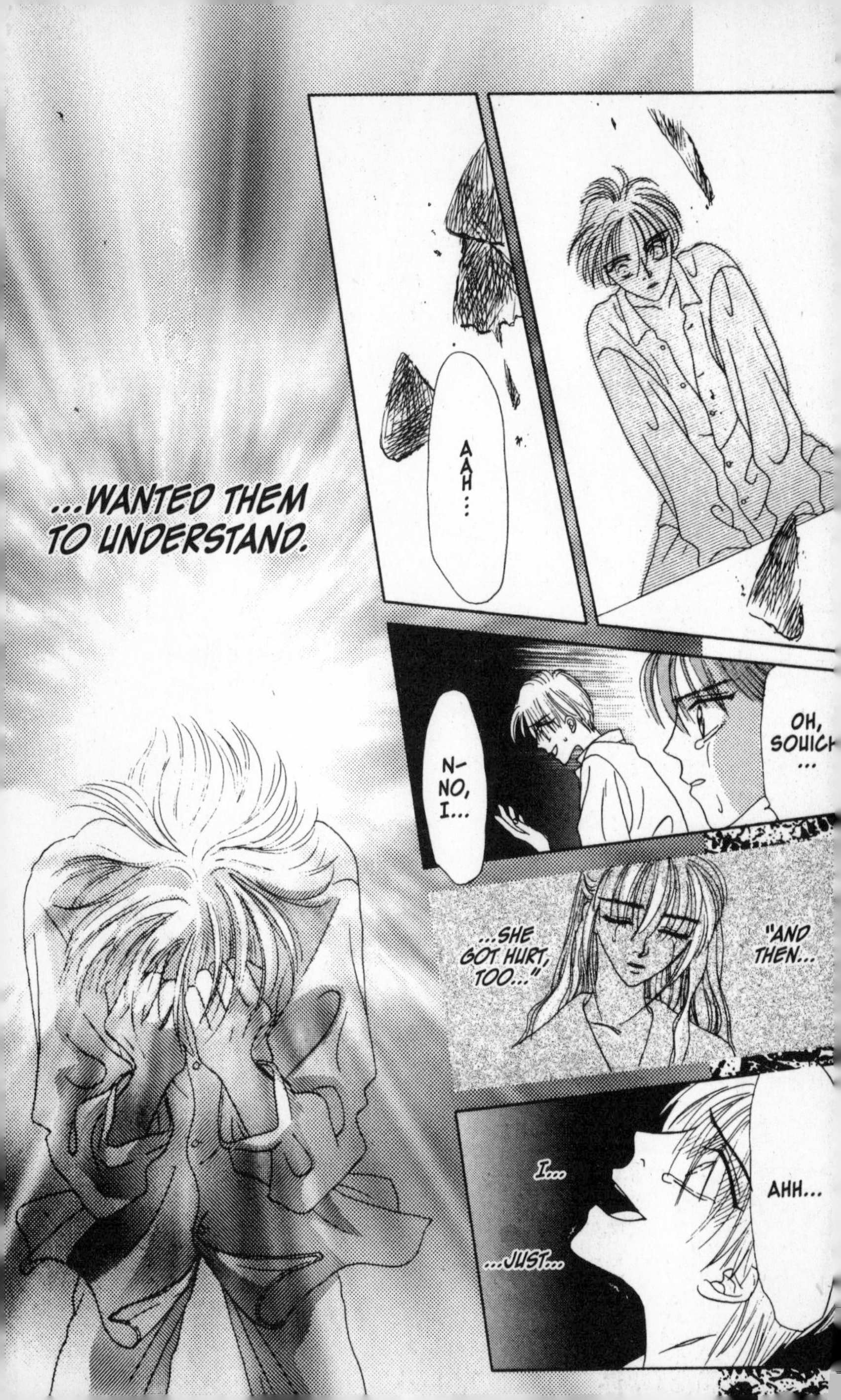
AAH...
OH, SOUICH...
N-NO, I...
"AND THEN...
...SHE GOT HURT, TOO..."
AHH...
I...
...JUST...
...WANTED THEM TO UNDERSTAND.

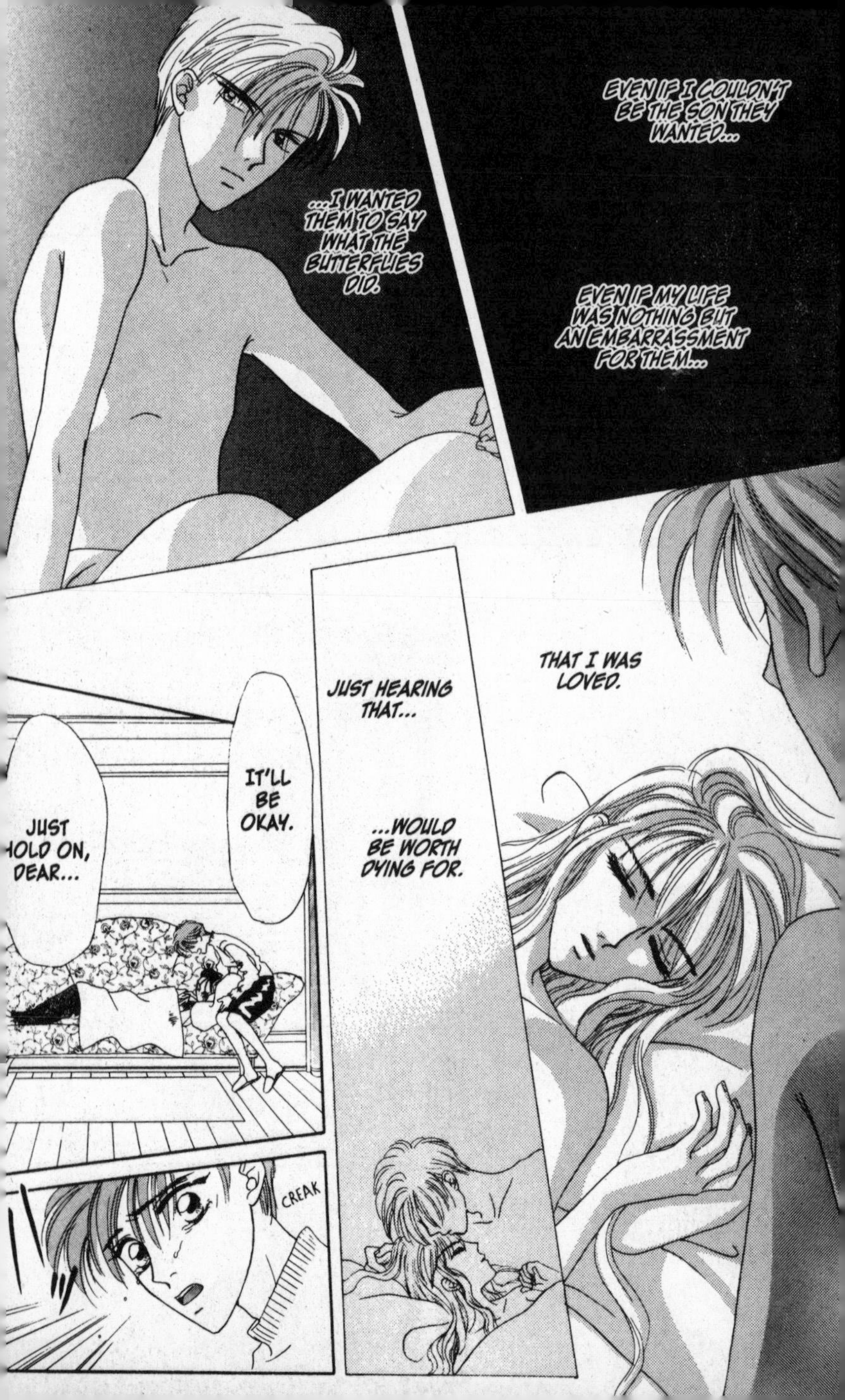
EVEN IF I COULDN'T BE THE SON THEY WANTED...
EVEN IF MY LIFE WAS NOTHING BUT AN EMBARRASSMENT FOR THEM...
...I WANTED THEM TO SAY WHAT THE BUTTERFLIES DID.
THAT I WAS LOVED.
JUST HEARING THAT...
...WOULD BE WORTH DYING FOR.
IT'LL BE OKAY.
JUST HOLD ON, DEAR...
CREAK

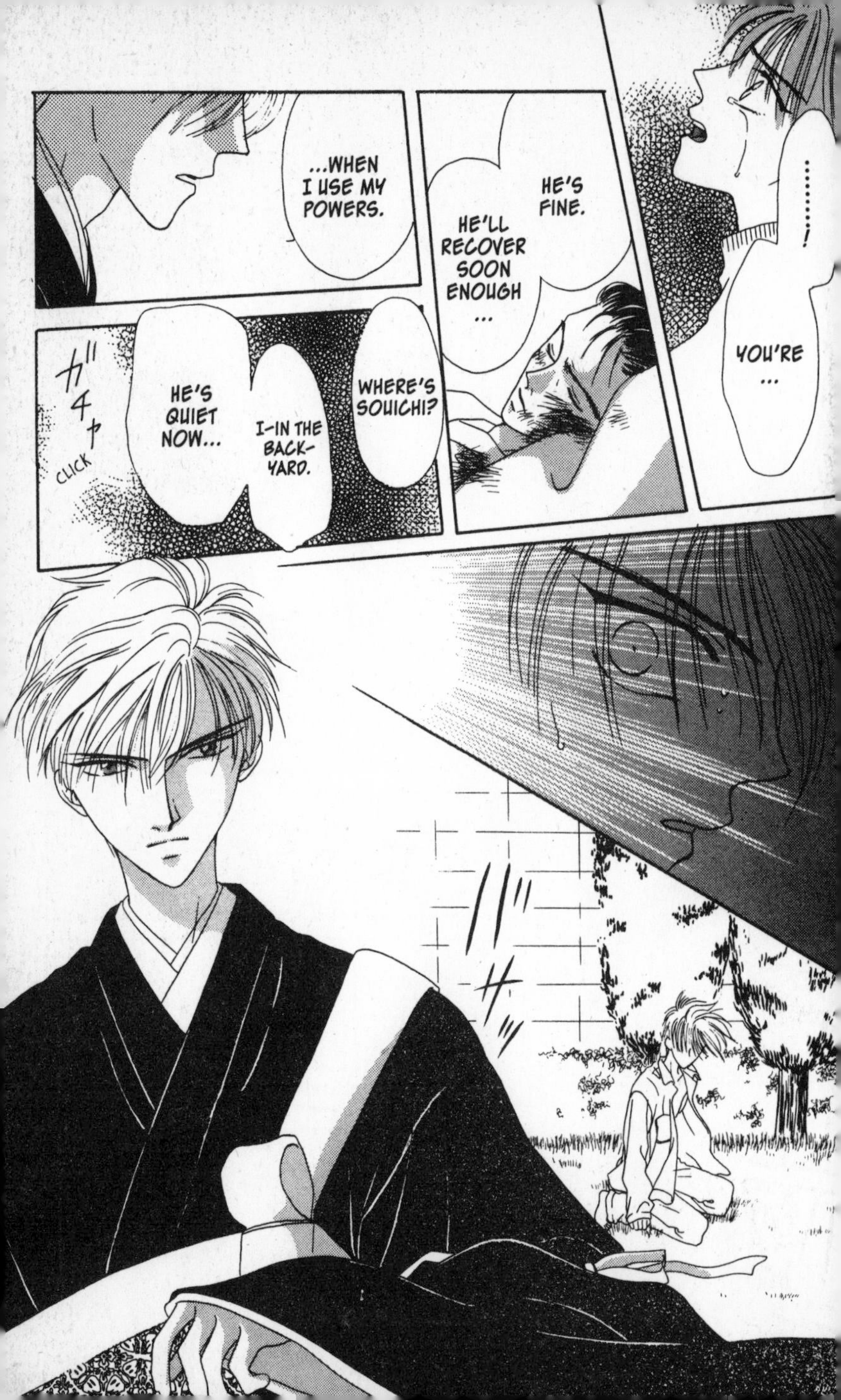

......!
YOU'RE ...
HE'S FINE.
HE'LL RECOVER SOON ENOUGH ...
...WHEN I USE MY POWERS.
WHERE'S SOUICHI?
I-IN THE BACK-YARD.
HE'S QUIET NOW...
ガチャ
CLICK

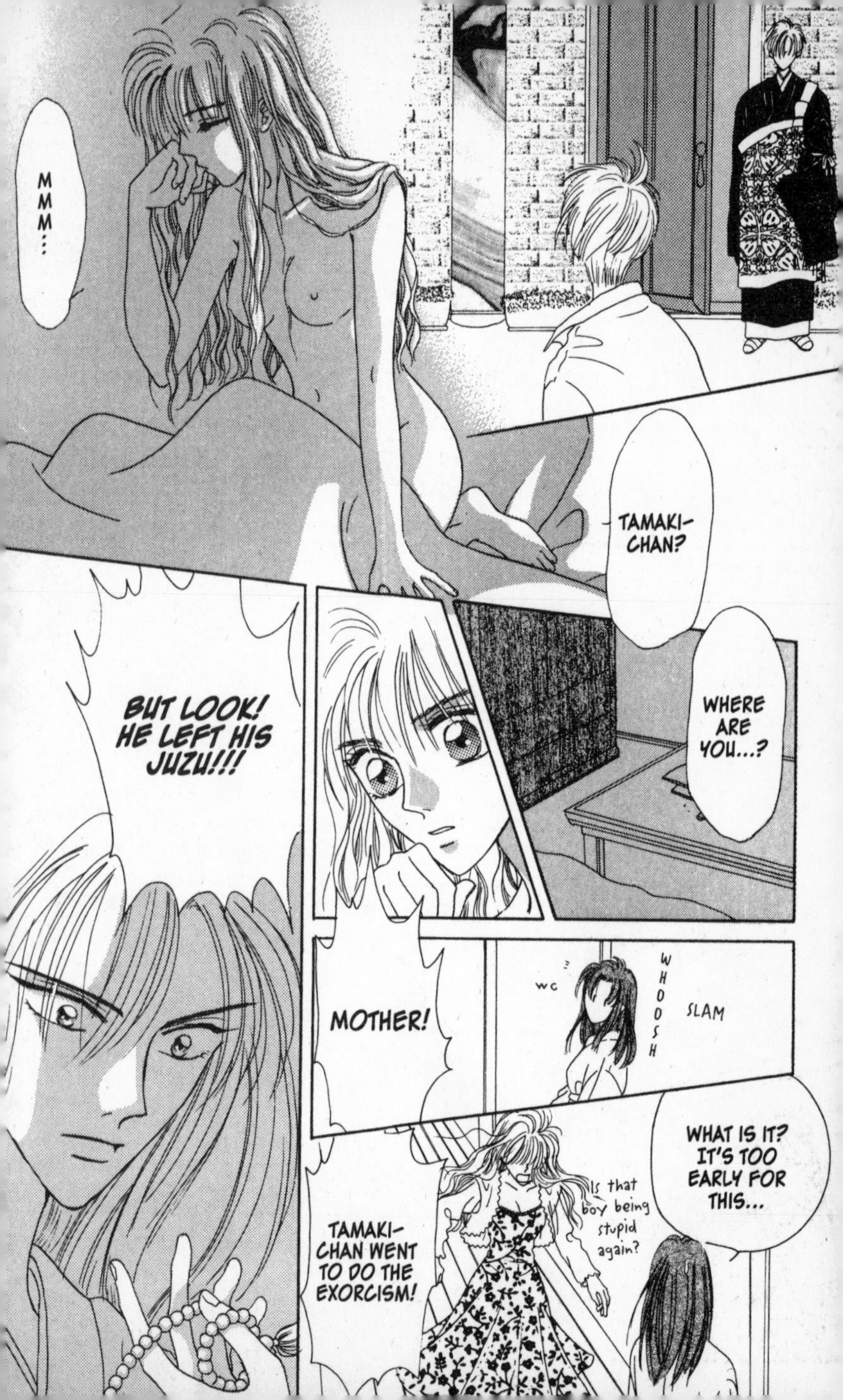
MMM...
TAMAKI-CHAN?
WHERE ARE YOU...?
BUT LOOK! HE LEFT HIS JUZU!!!
WHOOSH
SLAM
MOTHER!
WHAT IS IT? IT'S TOO EARLY FOR THIS...
Is that boy being stupid again?
TAMAKI-CHAN WENT TO DO THE EXORCISM!

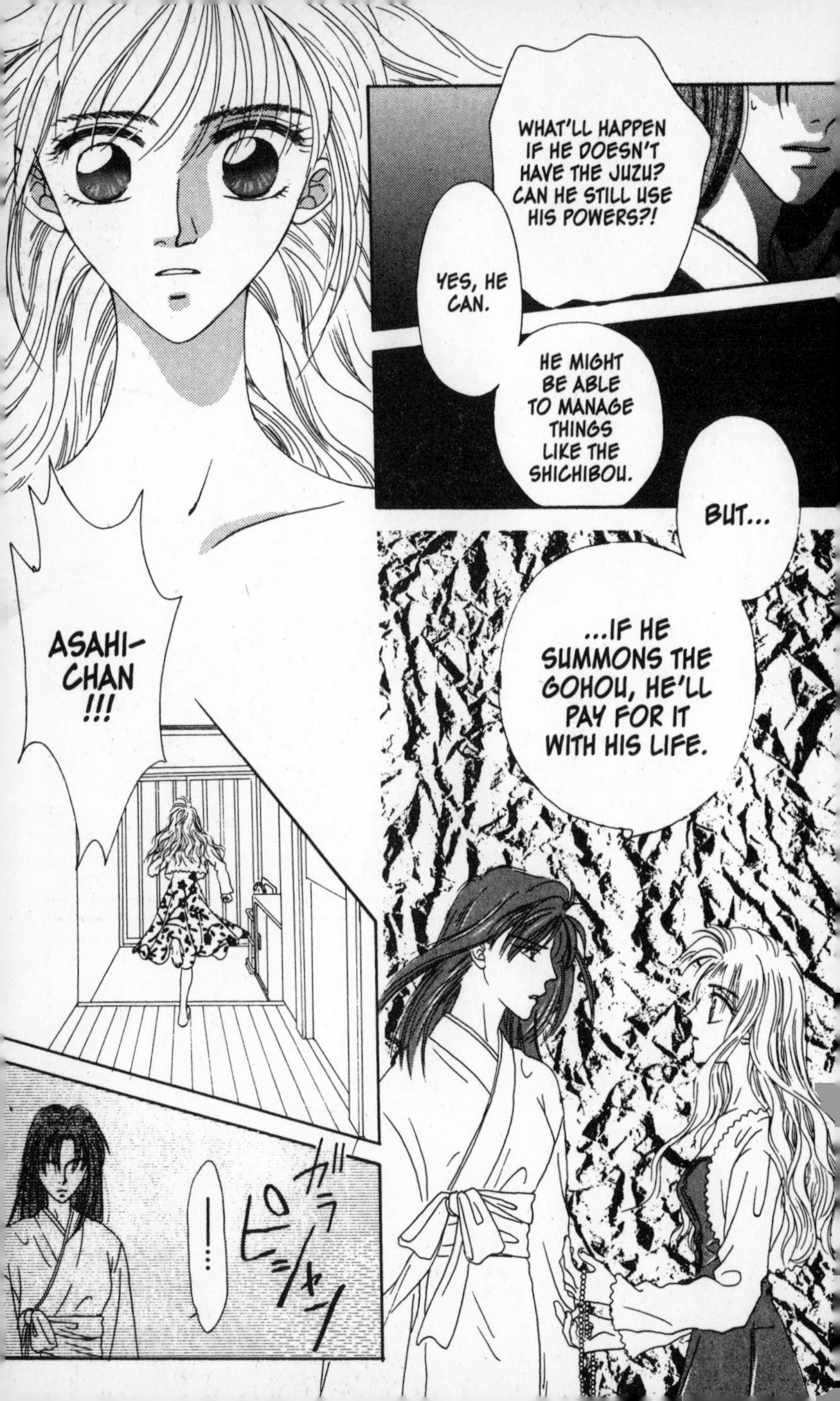

WHAT'LL HAPPEN IF HE DOESN'T HAVE THE JUZU? CAN HE STILL USE HIS POWERS?!
YES, HE CAN.
HE MIGHT BE ABLE TO MANAGE THINGS LIKE THE SHICHIBOU.
BUT...
...IF HE SUMMONS THE GOHOU, HE'LL PAY FOR IT WITH HIS LIFE.
ASAHI-CHAN!!!
ガラピシャン
!...

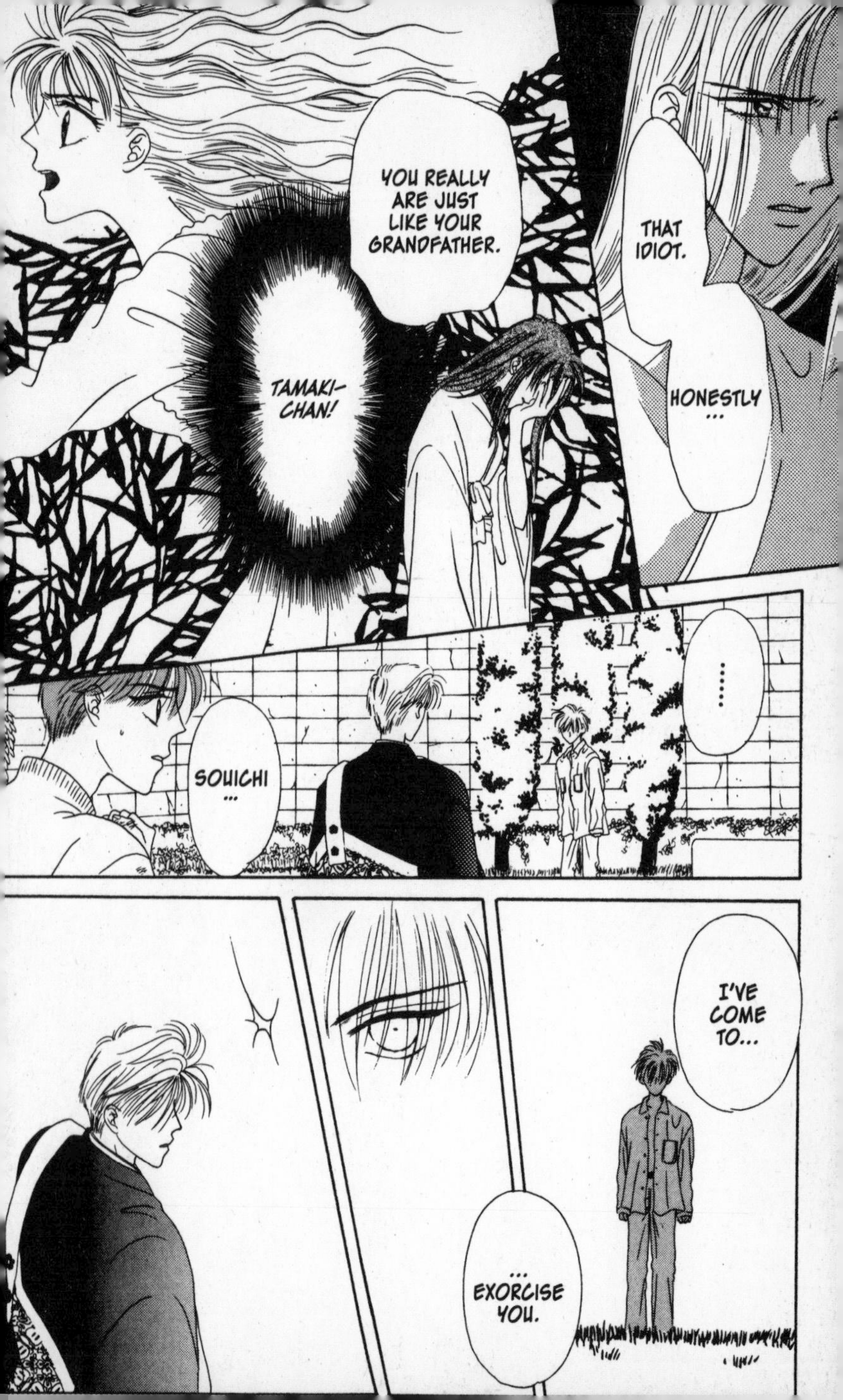
THAT IDIOT.
HONESTLY ...
YOU REALLY ARE JUST LIKE YOUR GRANDFATHER.
TAMAKI-CHAN!
......
SOUICHI ...
I'VE COME TO...
... EXORCISE YOU.

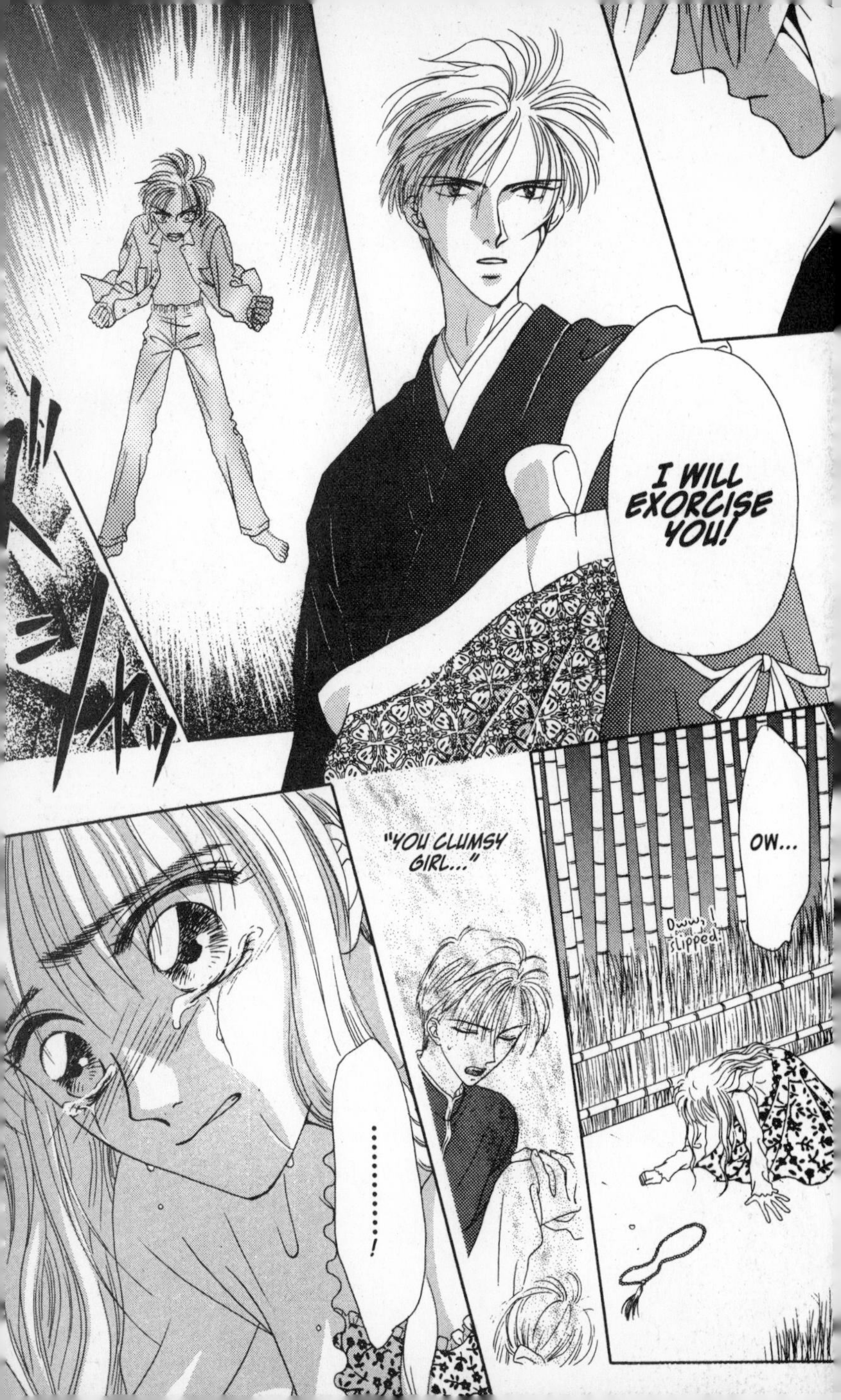
I WILL EXORCISE YOU!
OW...
Owww, I slipped!
"YOU CLUMSY GIRL..."
.......!

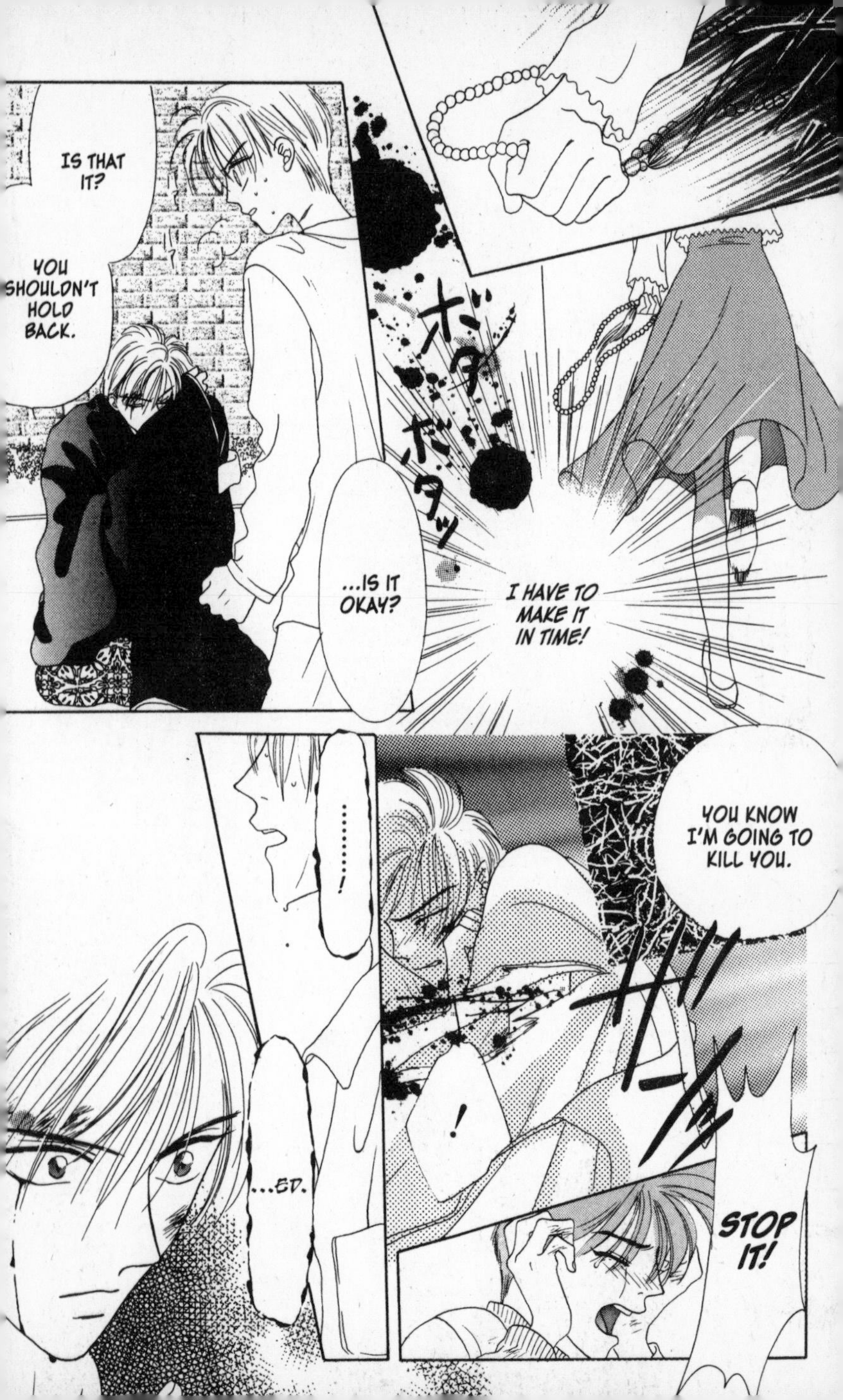
ボダ
ボタッ
I HAVE TO MAKE IT IN TIME!
IS THAT IT?
YOU SHOULDN'T HOLD BACK.
...IS IT OKAY?
YOU KNOW I'M GOING TO KILL YOU.
!
STOP IT!
......!
...ED.

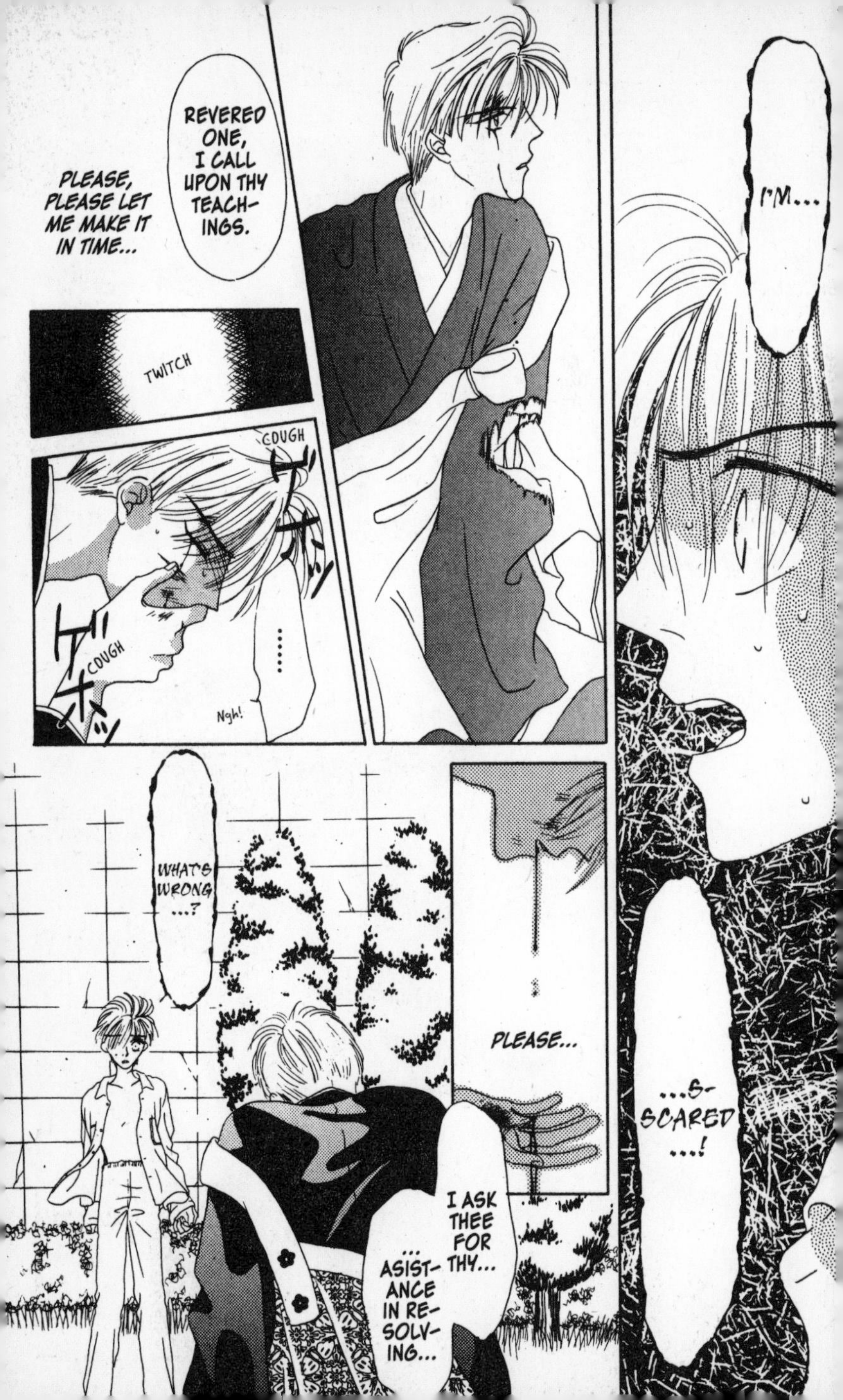
I'M...
...S-SCARED...!
REVERED ONE, I CALL UPON THY TEACHINGS.
PLEASE, PLEASE LET ME MAKE IT IN TIME...
TWITCH
COUGH
......
COUGH
Ngh!
PLEASE...
I ASK THEE FOR THY...
...ASIST-ANCE IN RE-SOLV-ING...
WHAT'S WRONG...?

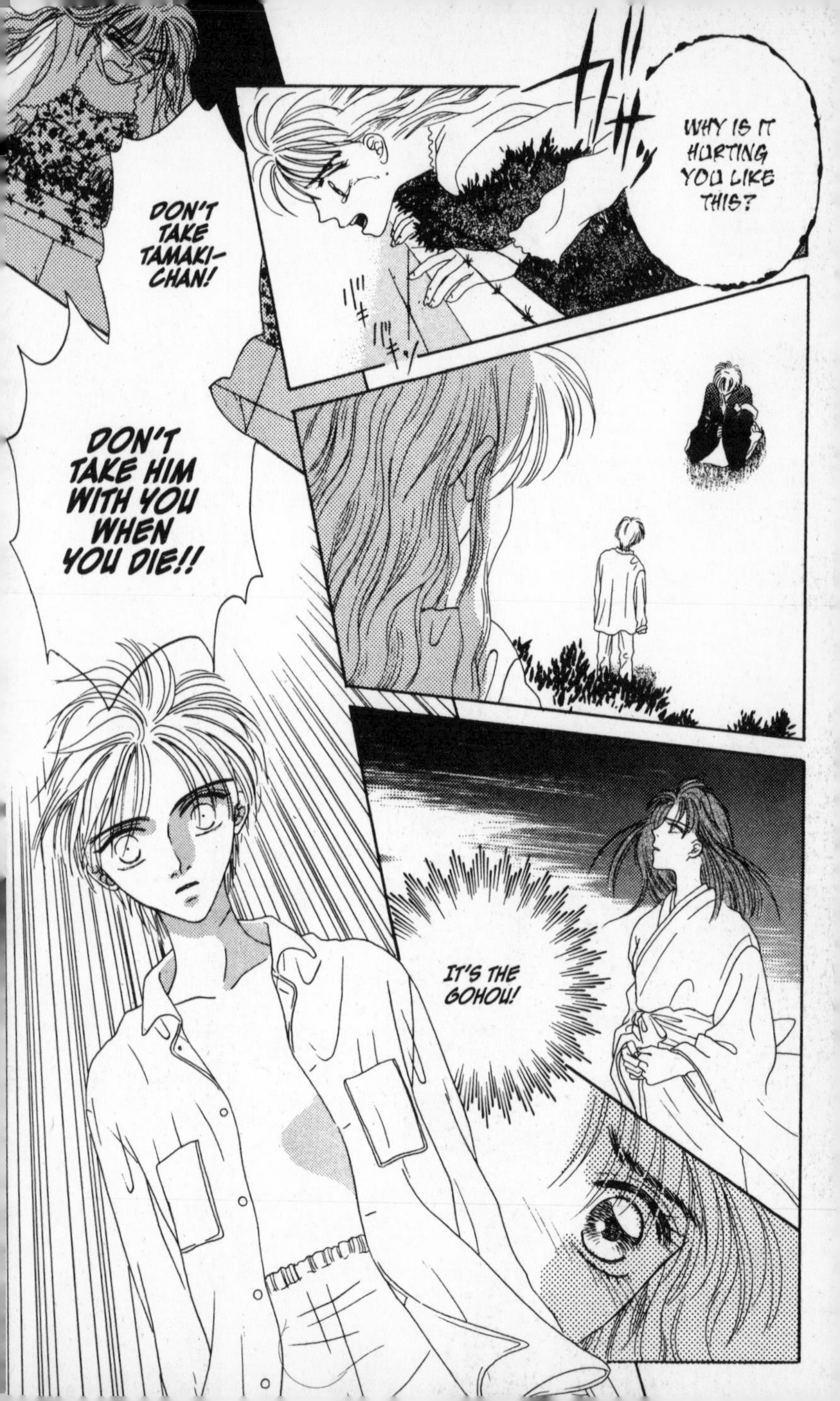

WHY IS IT HURTING YOU LIKE THIS?
DON'T TAKE TAMAKI-CHAN!
DON'T TAKE HIM WITH YOU WHEN YOU DIE!!
IT'S THE GOHOU!

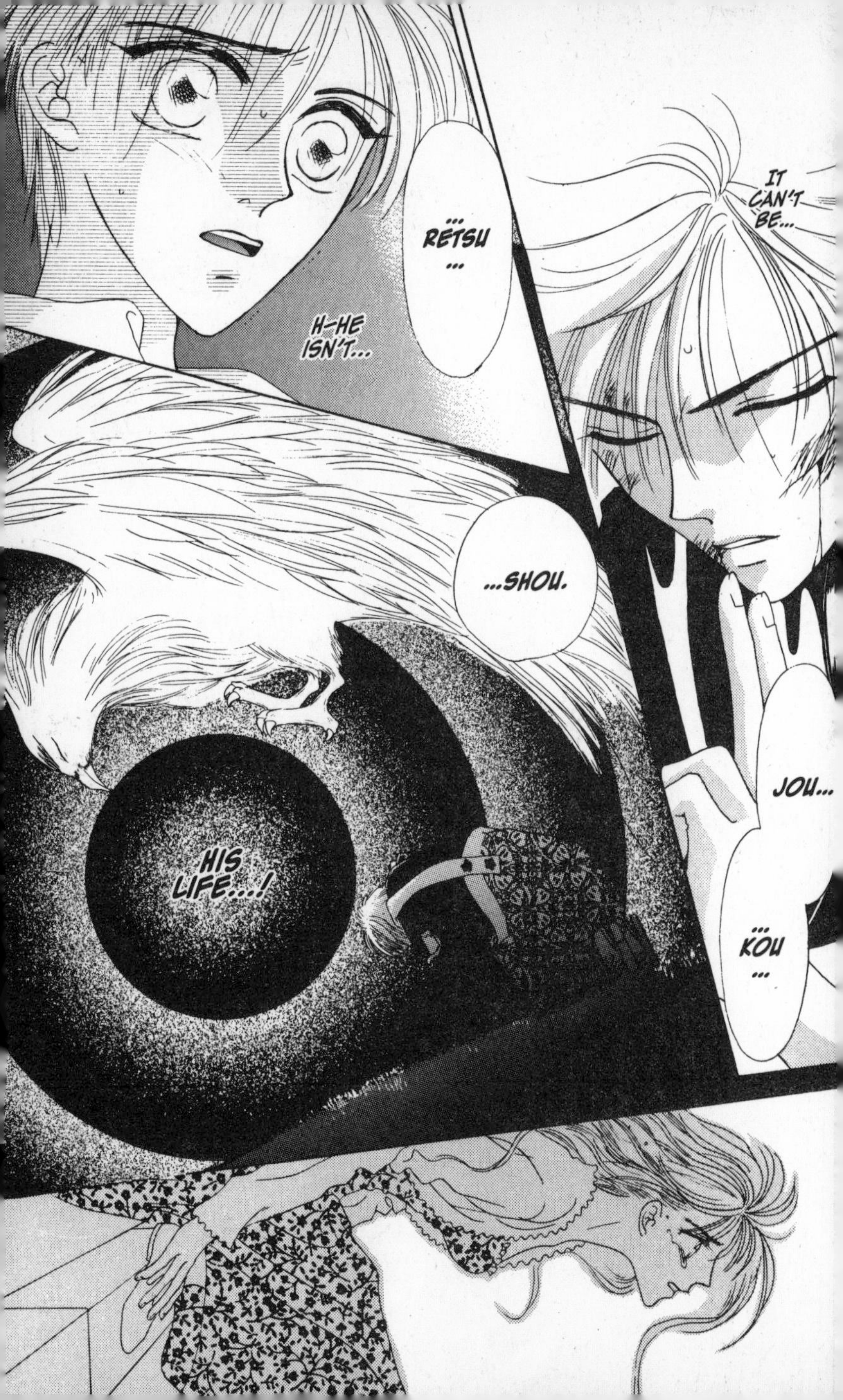
IT CAN'T BE...
...RETSU...
H-HE ISN'T...
...SHOU.
JOU...
...KOU...
HIS LIFE...!

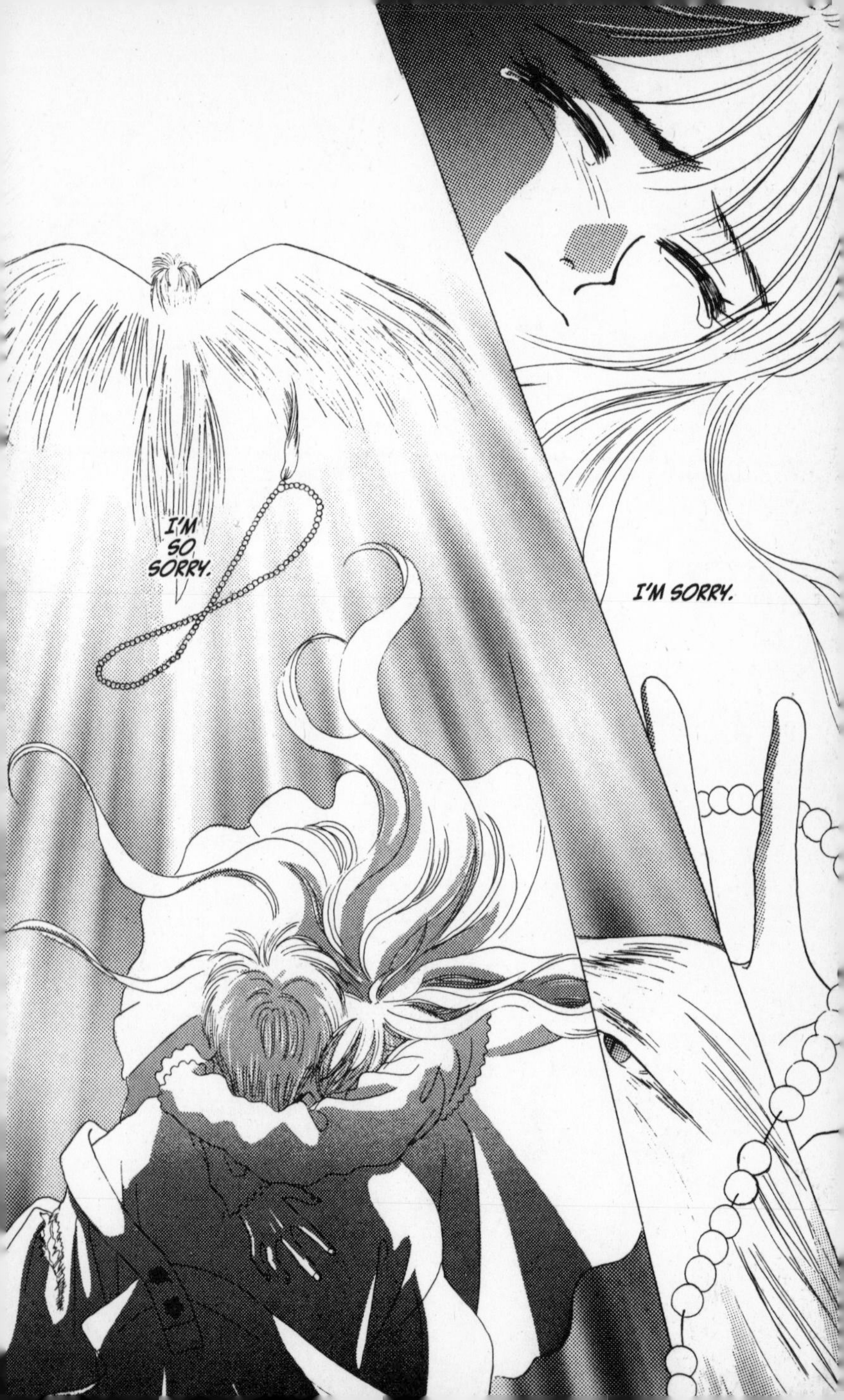
I'M SORRY.
I'M SO SORRY.

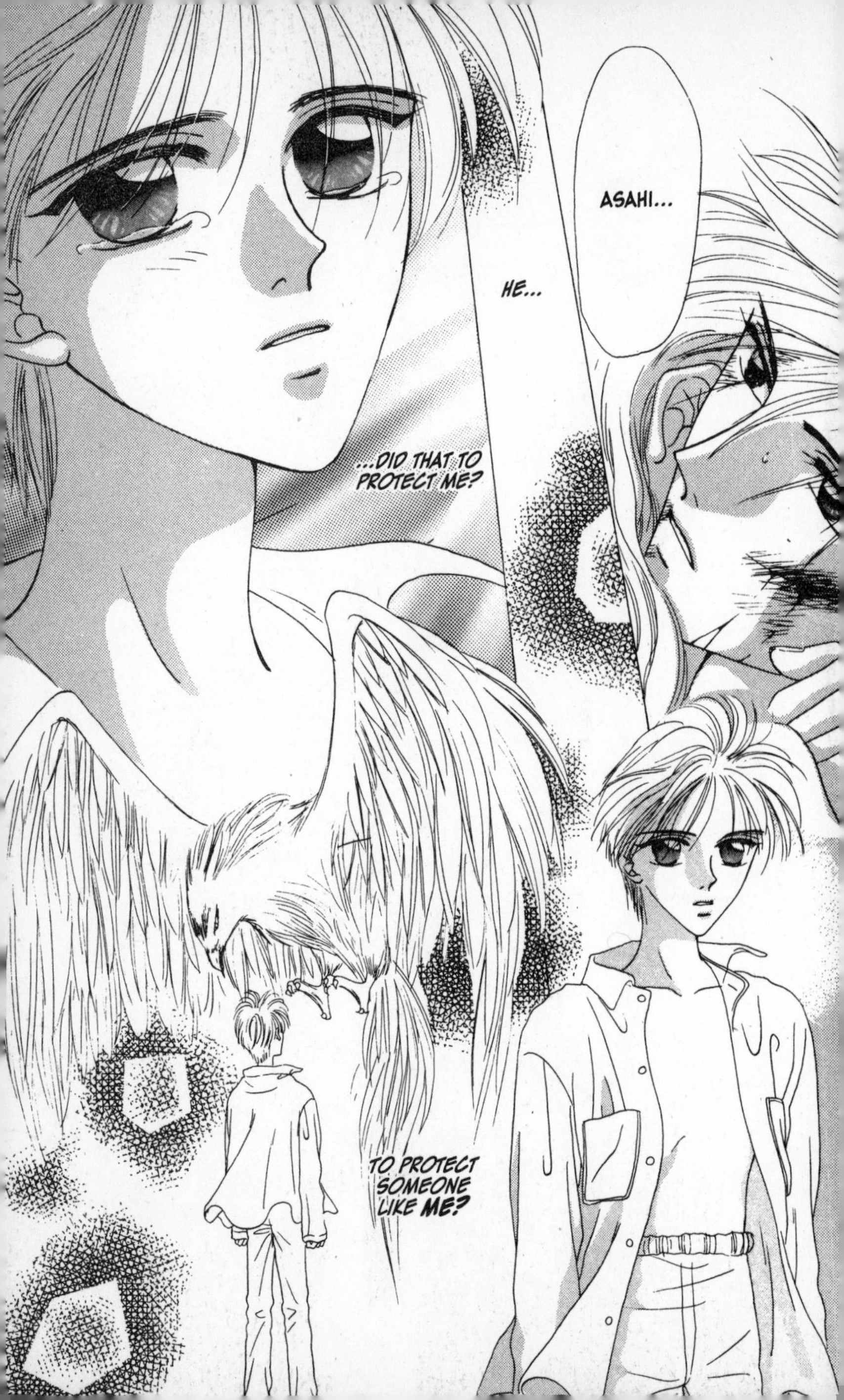
ASAHI...
HE...
...DID THAT TO PROTECT ME?
TO PROTECT SOMEONE LIKE ME?

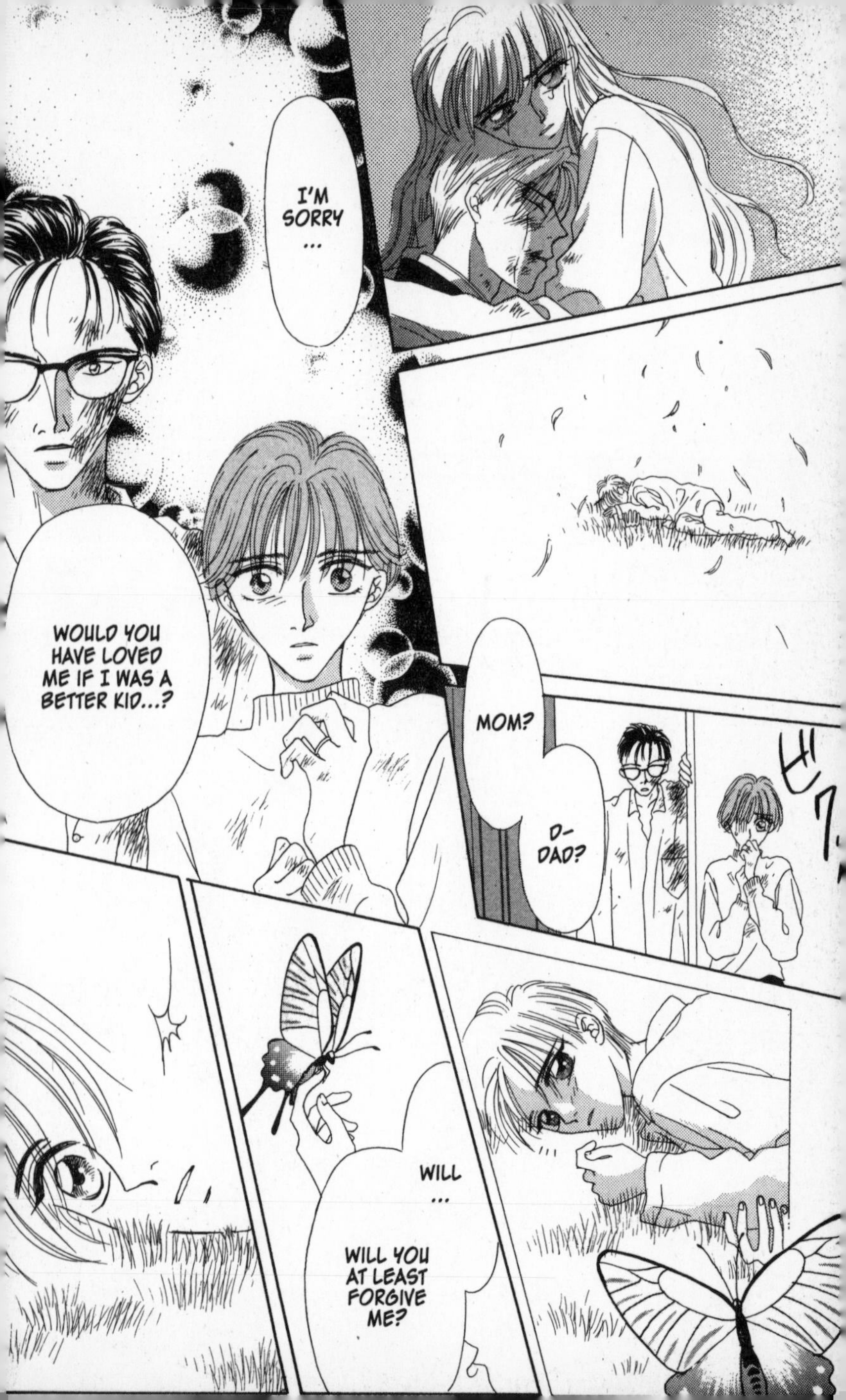
MOM?
D- DAD?
ビク
I'M SORRY ...
WOULD YOU HAVE LOVED ME IF I WAS A BETTER KID...?
WILL ...
WILL YOU AT LEAST FORGIVE ME?

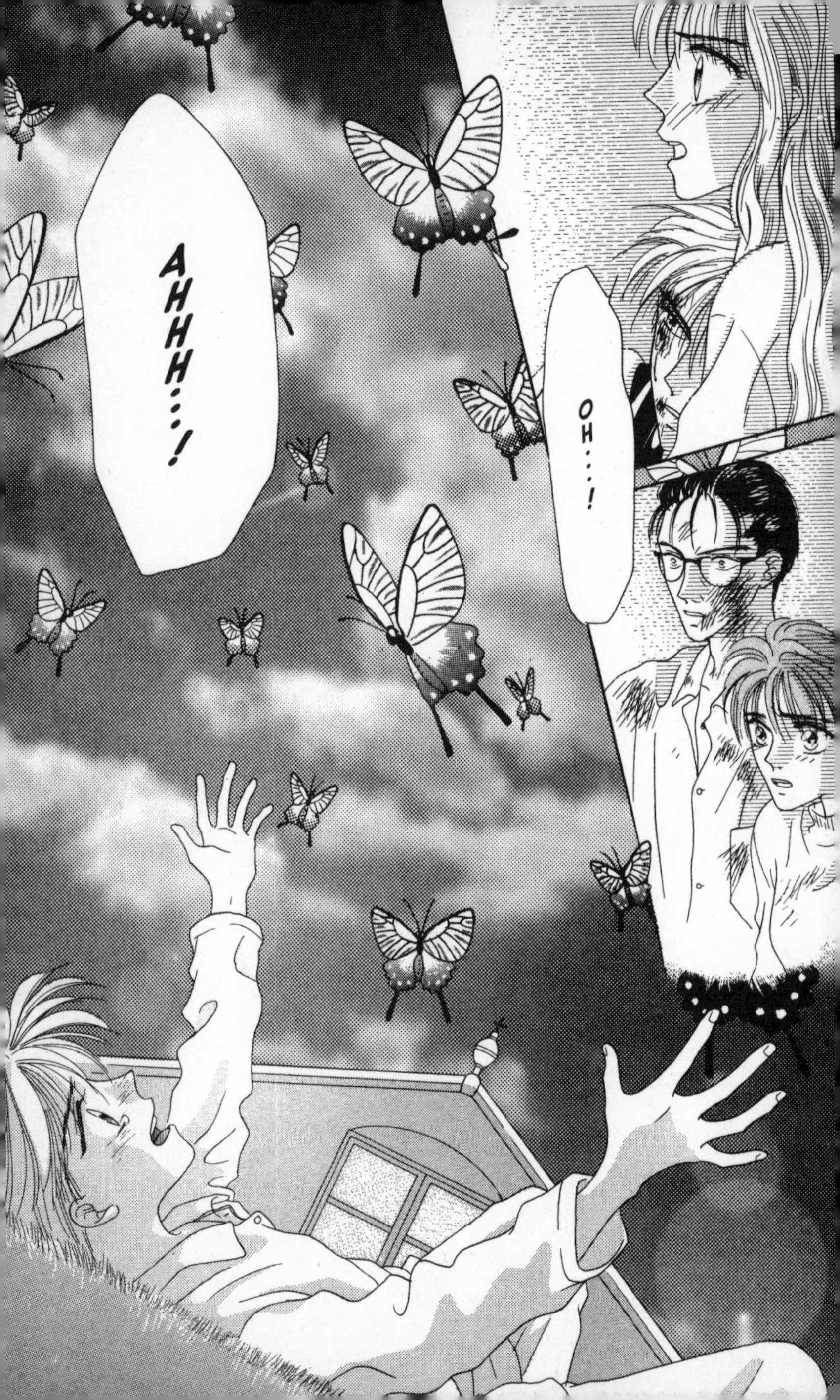
OH...!
AHHHH...!

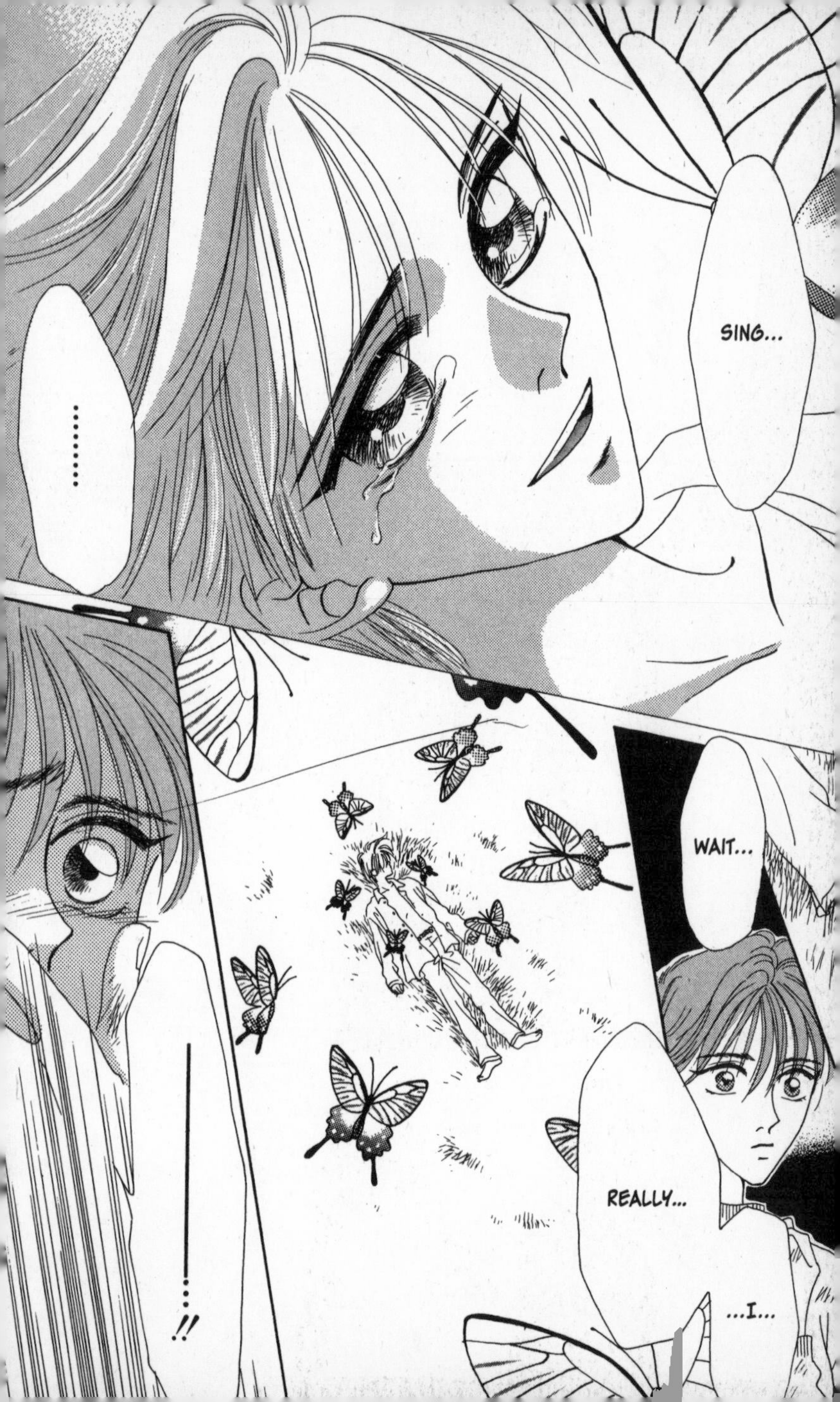
SING...
......
WAIT...
REALLY...
...I...
......!!

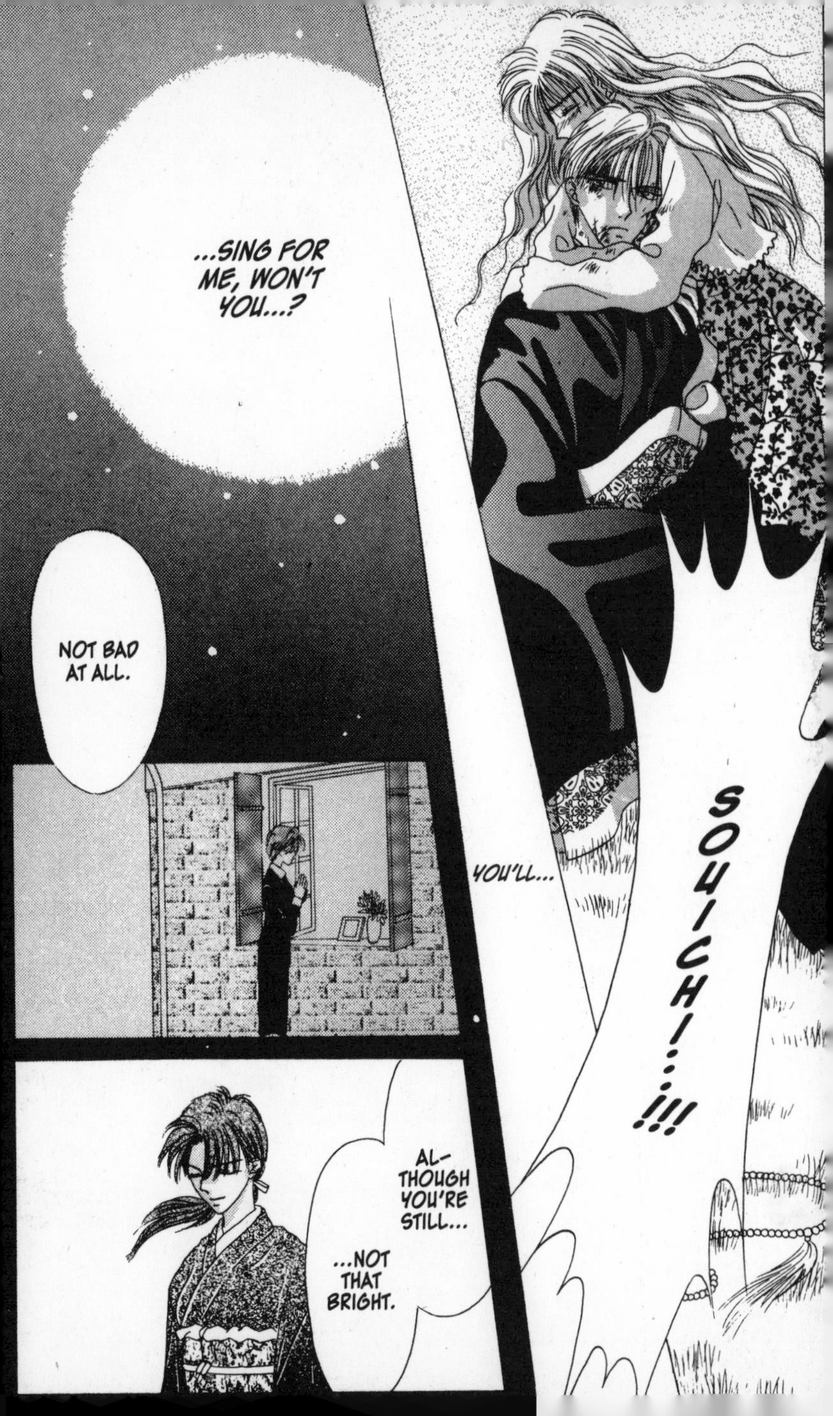
SOUICHI...!!!
YOU'LL...
...SING FOR ME, WON'T YOU...?
NOT BAD AT ALL.
AL-THOUGH YOU'RE STILL...
...NOT THAT BRIGHT.

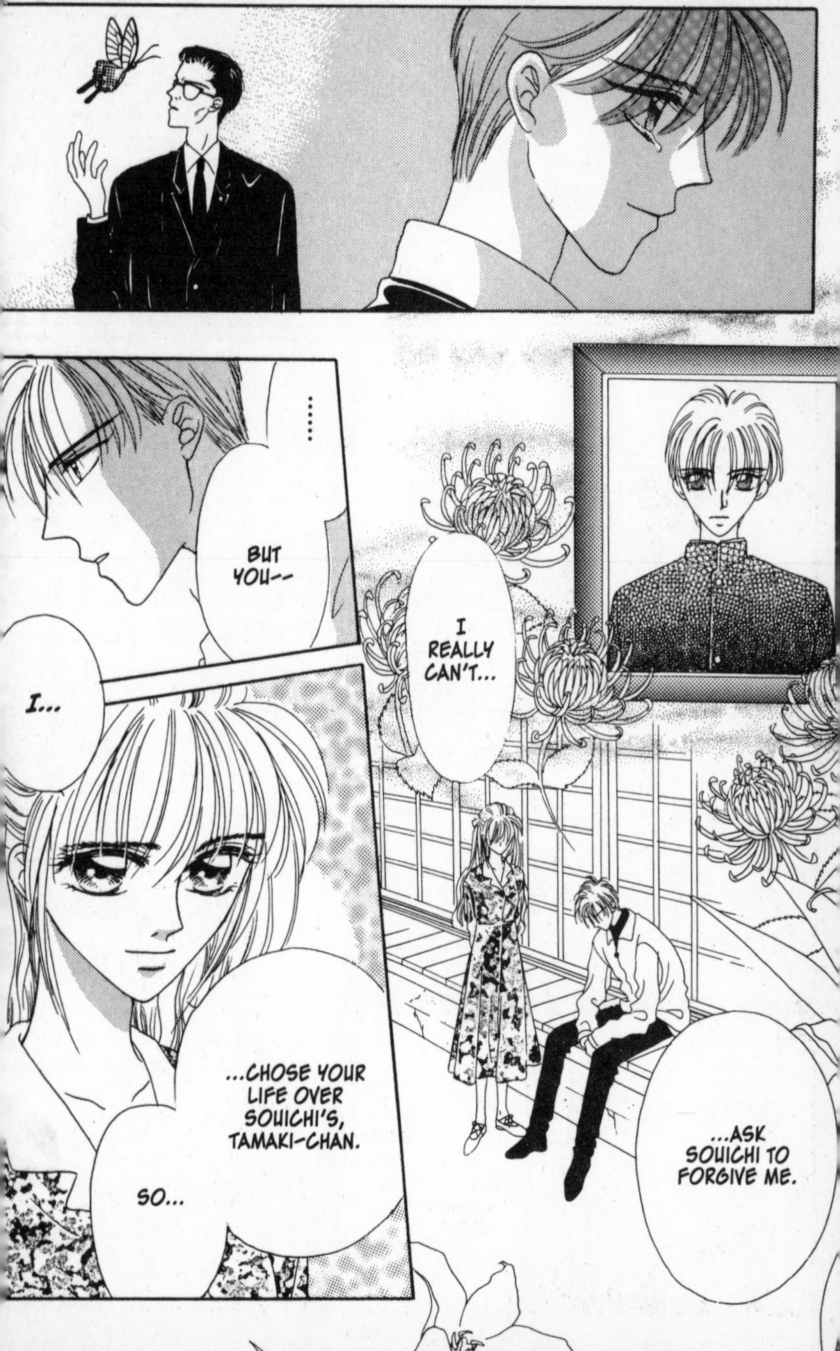
I REALLY CAN'T...
...ASK SOUICHI TO FORGIVE ME.
......
BUT YOU--
I...
...CHOSE YOUR LIFE OVER SOUICHI'S, TAMAKI-CHAN.
SO...

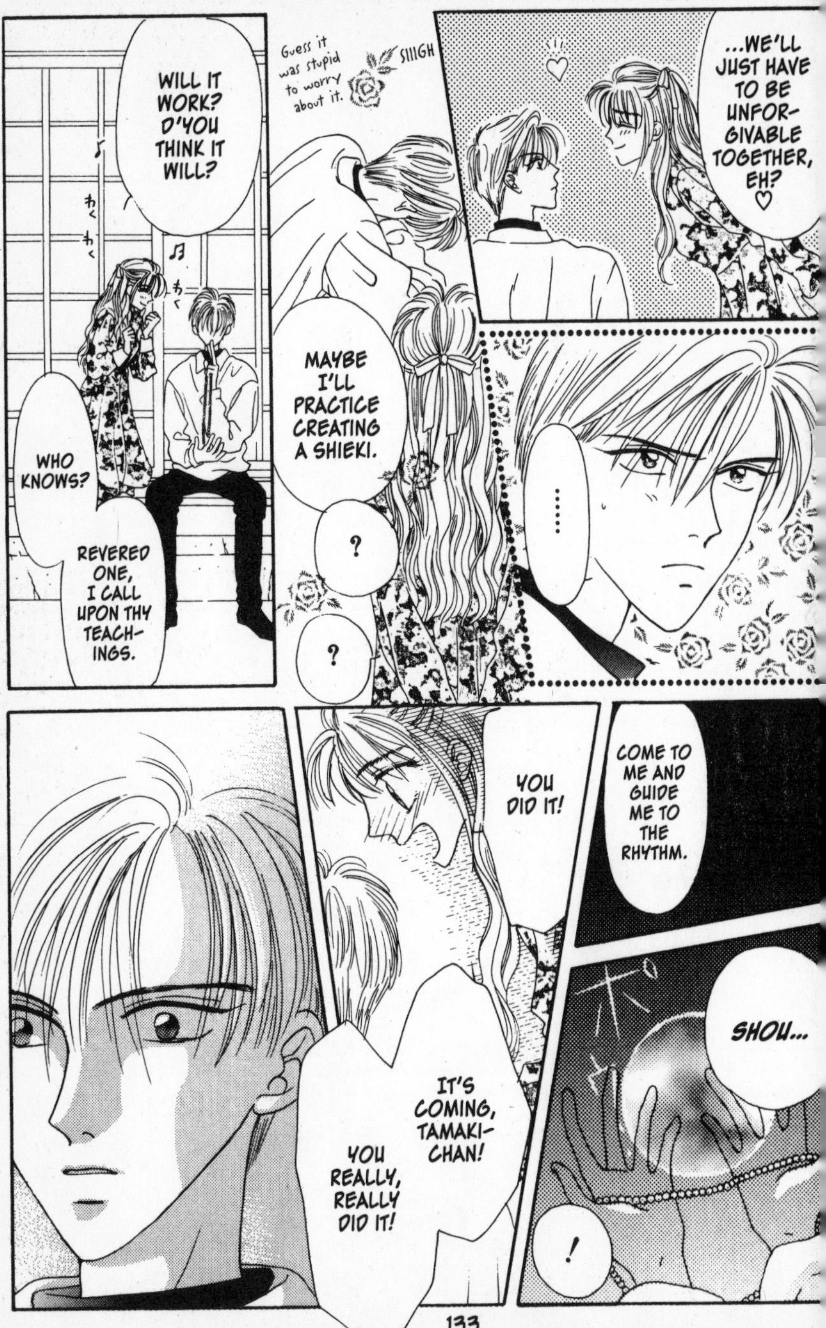
...WE'LL JUST HAVE TO BE UNFORGIVABLE TOGETHER, EH? ♡
......
Guess it was stupid to worry about it.
SIIIGH
MAYBE I'LL PRACTICE CREATING A SHIEKI.
?
?
WILL IT WORK? D'YOU THINK IT WILL?
わく わく
わく
WHO KNOWS?
REVERED ONE, I CALL UPON THY TEACHINGS.
COME TO ME AND GUIDE ME TO THE RHYTHM.
SHOU...
!
YOU DID IT!
IT'S COMING, TAMAKI-CHAN!
YOU REALLY, REALLY DID IT!

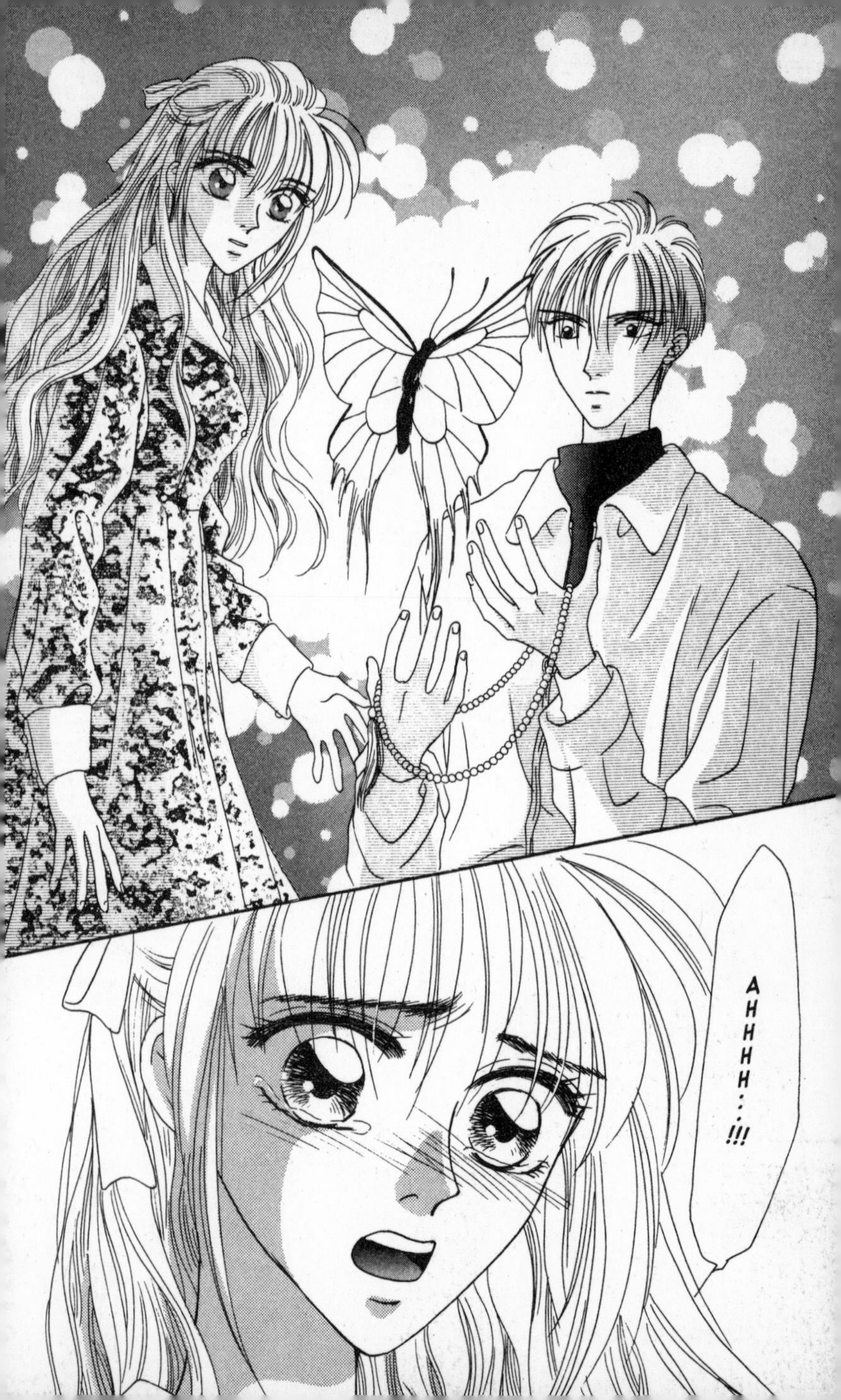
AHHHH...!!!

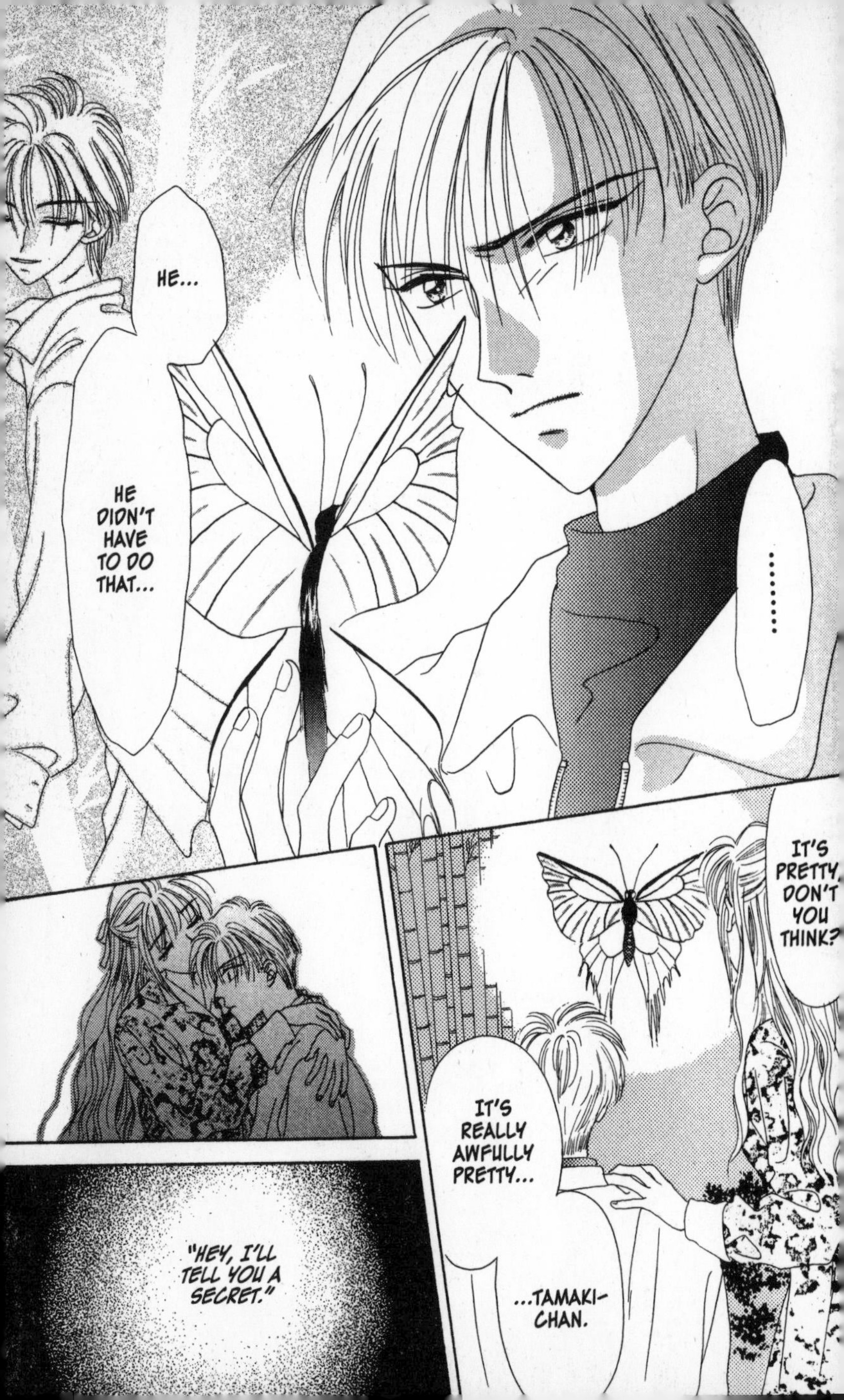
HE...
HE DIDN'T HAVE TO DO THAT...
......
IT'S PRETTY, DON'T YOU THINK?
IT'S REALLY AWFULLY PRETTY...
...TAMAKI-CHAN.
"HEY, I'LL TELL YOU A SECRET."

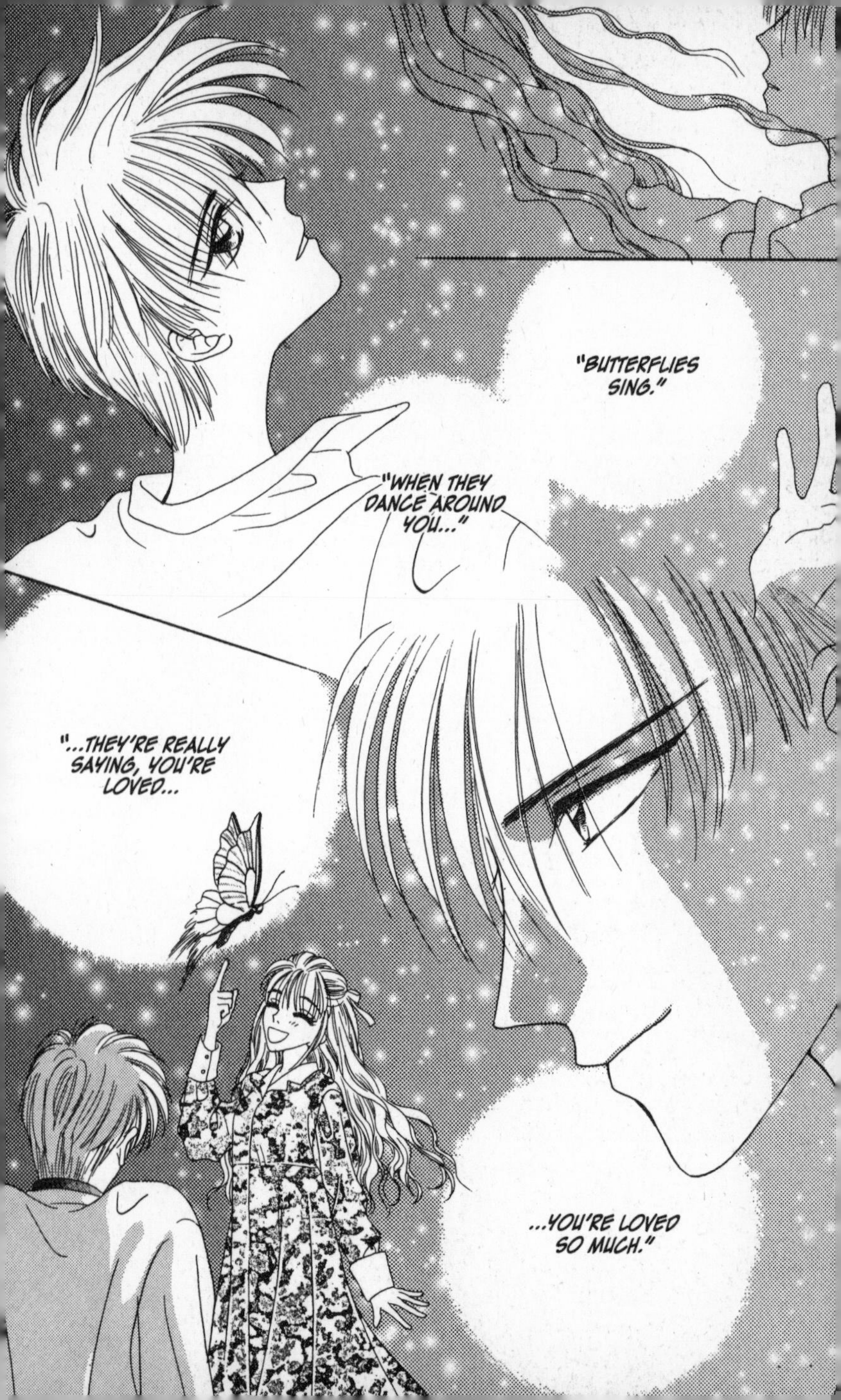
"BUTTERFLIES SING."
"WHEN THEY DANCE AROUND YOU..."
"...THEY'RE REALLY SAYING, YOU'RE LOVED...
...YOU'RE LOVED SO MUCH."

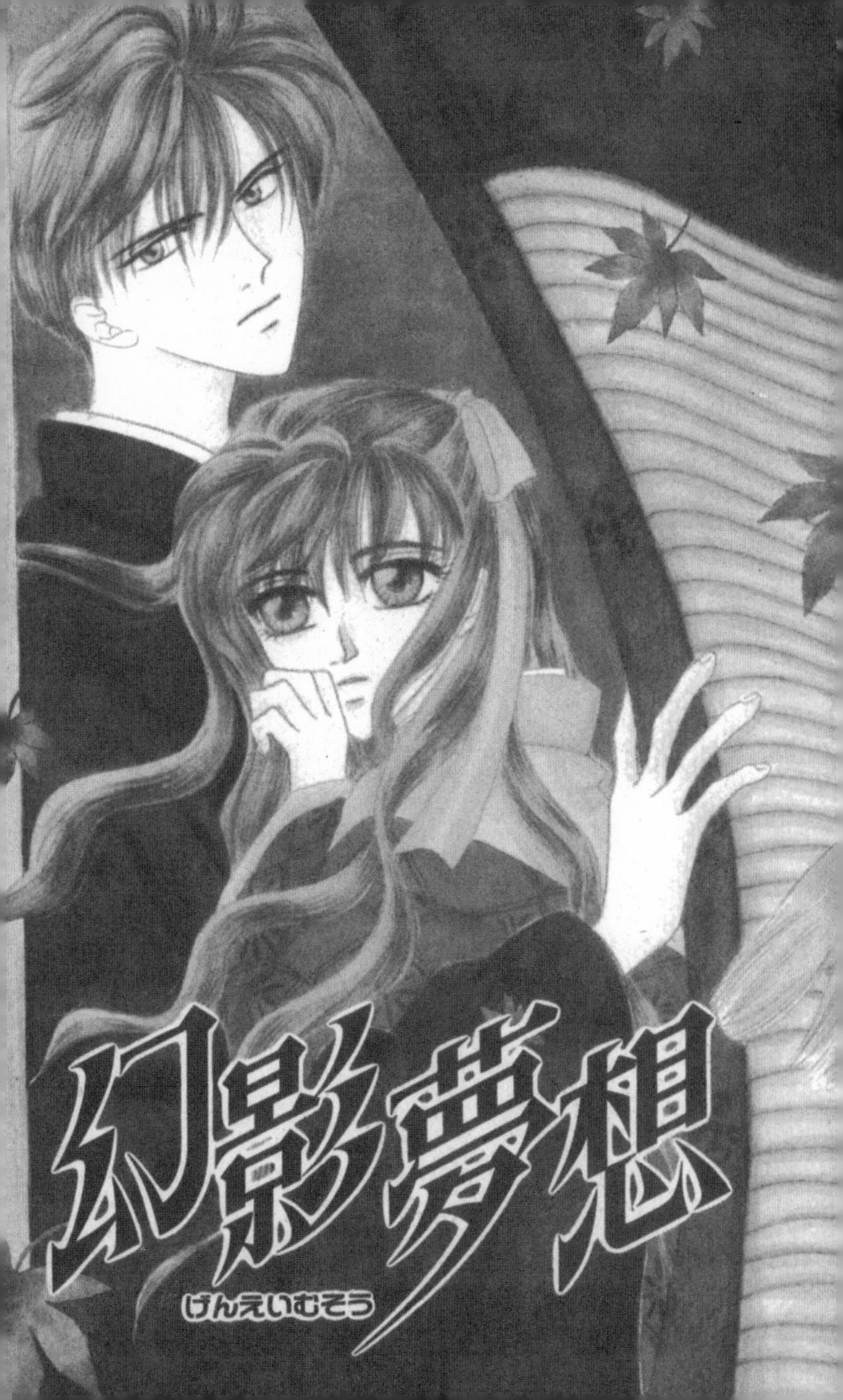
幻影夢想
げんえいむそう

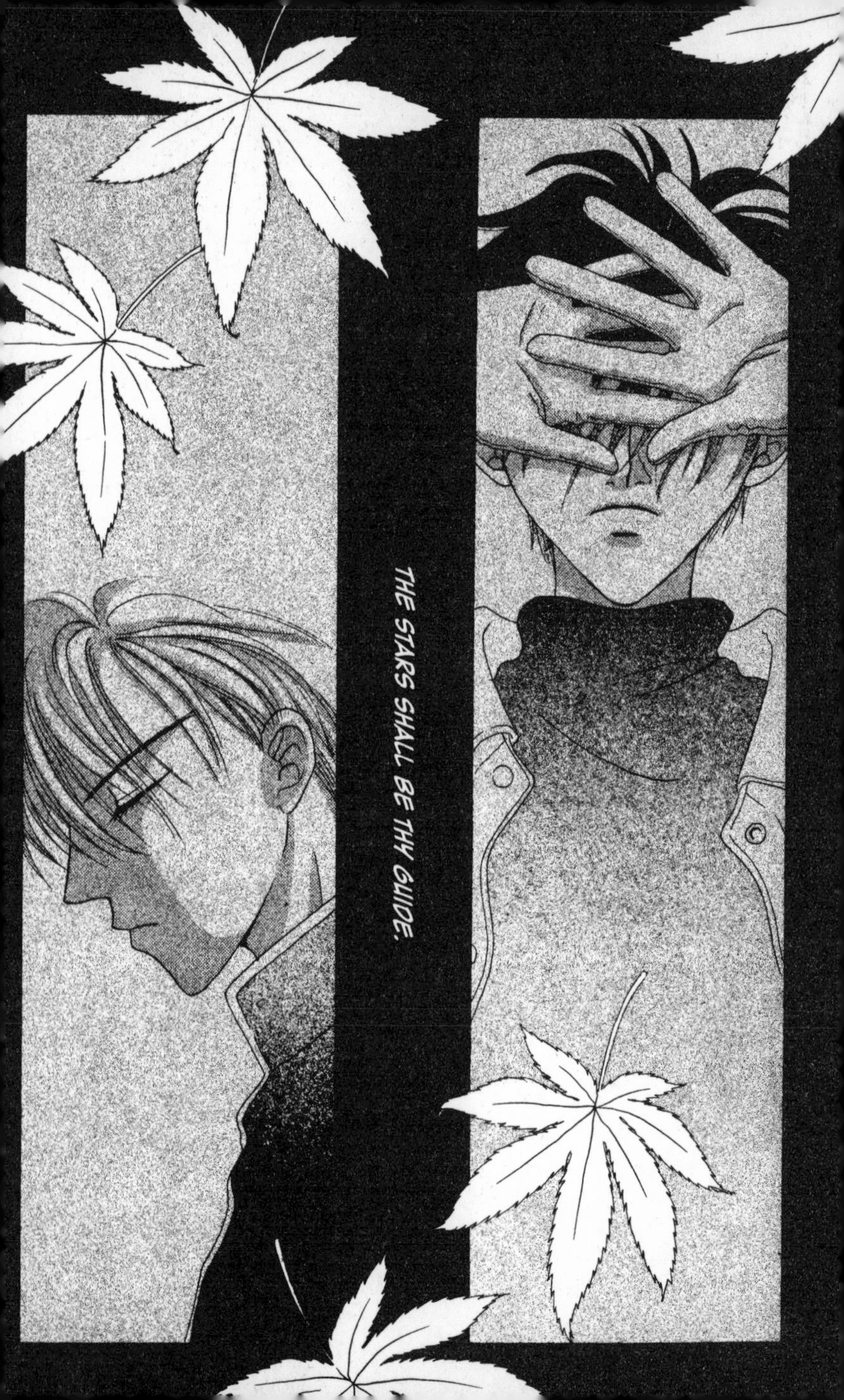
THE STARS SHALL BE THY GUIDE.

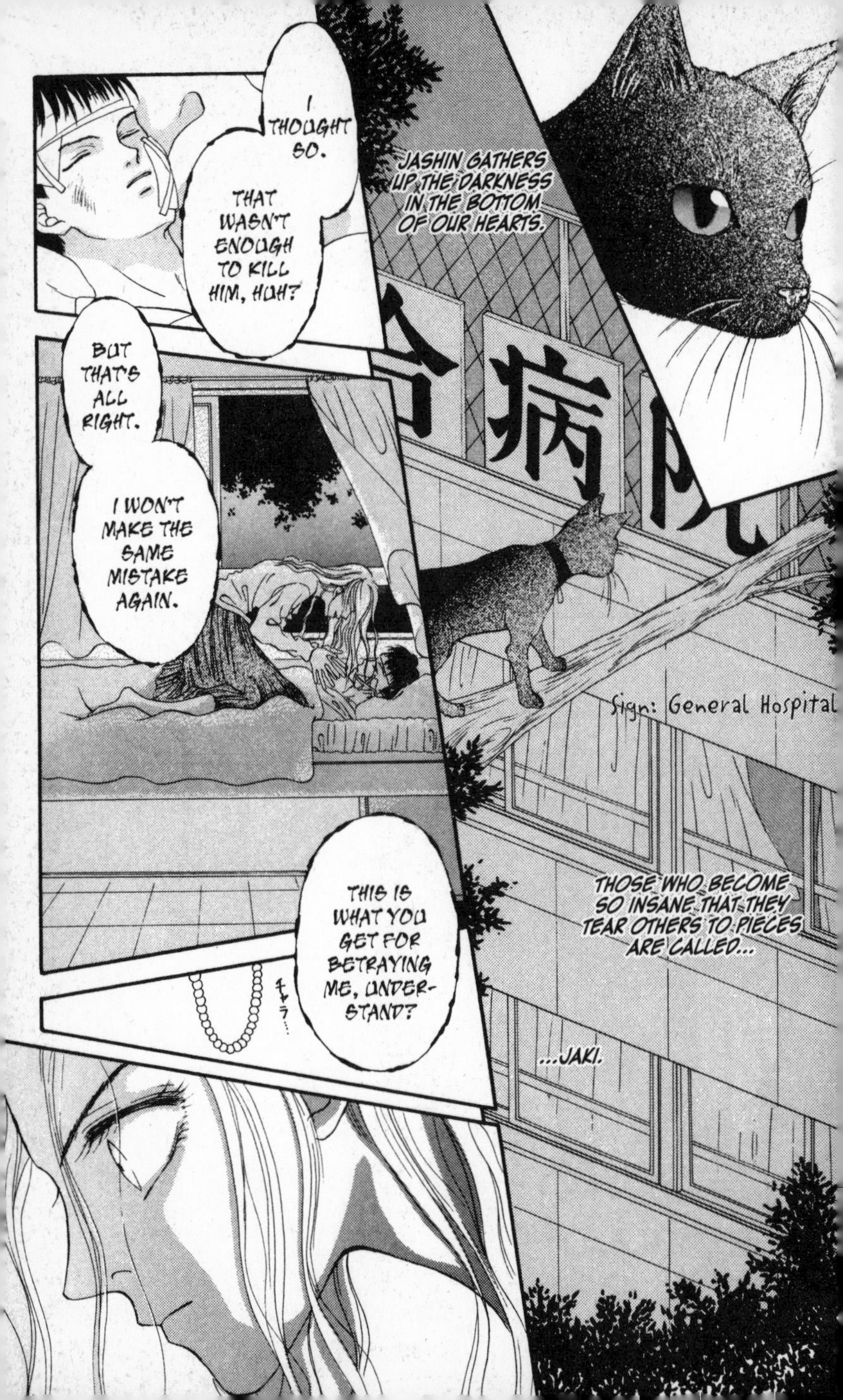

JASHIN GATHERS UP THE DARKNESS IN THE BOTTOM OF OUR HEARTS.
Sign: General Hospital
THOSE WHO BECOME SO INSANE THAT THEY TEAR OTHERS TO PIECES ARE CALLED...
...JAKI.
I THOUGHT SO.
THAT WASN'T ENOUGH TO KILL HIM, HUH?
BUT THAT'S ALL RIGHT.
I WON'T MAKE THE SAME MISTAKE AGAIN.
THIS IS WHAT YOU GET FOR BETRAYING ME, UNDER-STAND?
チャラ…

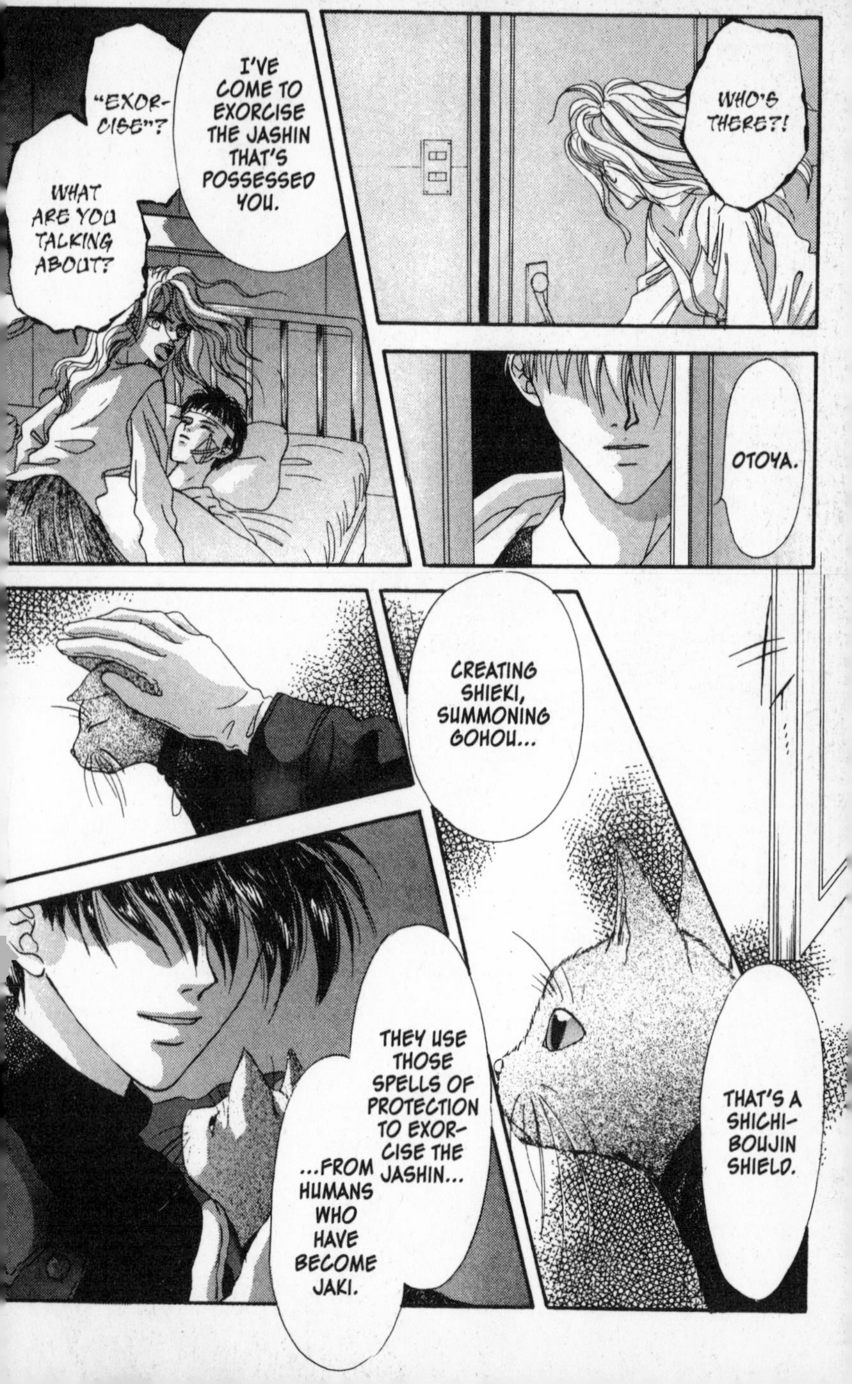
WHO'S THERE?!
OTOYA.
I'VE COME TO EXORCISE THE JASHIN THAT'S POSSESSED YOU.
"EXOR-CISE"?
WHAT ARE YOU TALKING ABOUT?
CREATING SHIEKI, SUMMONING GOHOU...
THAT'S A SHICHI-BOUJIN SHIELD.
THEY USE THOSE SPELLS OF PROTECTION TO EXOR-CISE THE JASHIN...
...FROM HUMANS WHO HAVE BECOME JAKI.

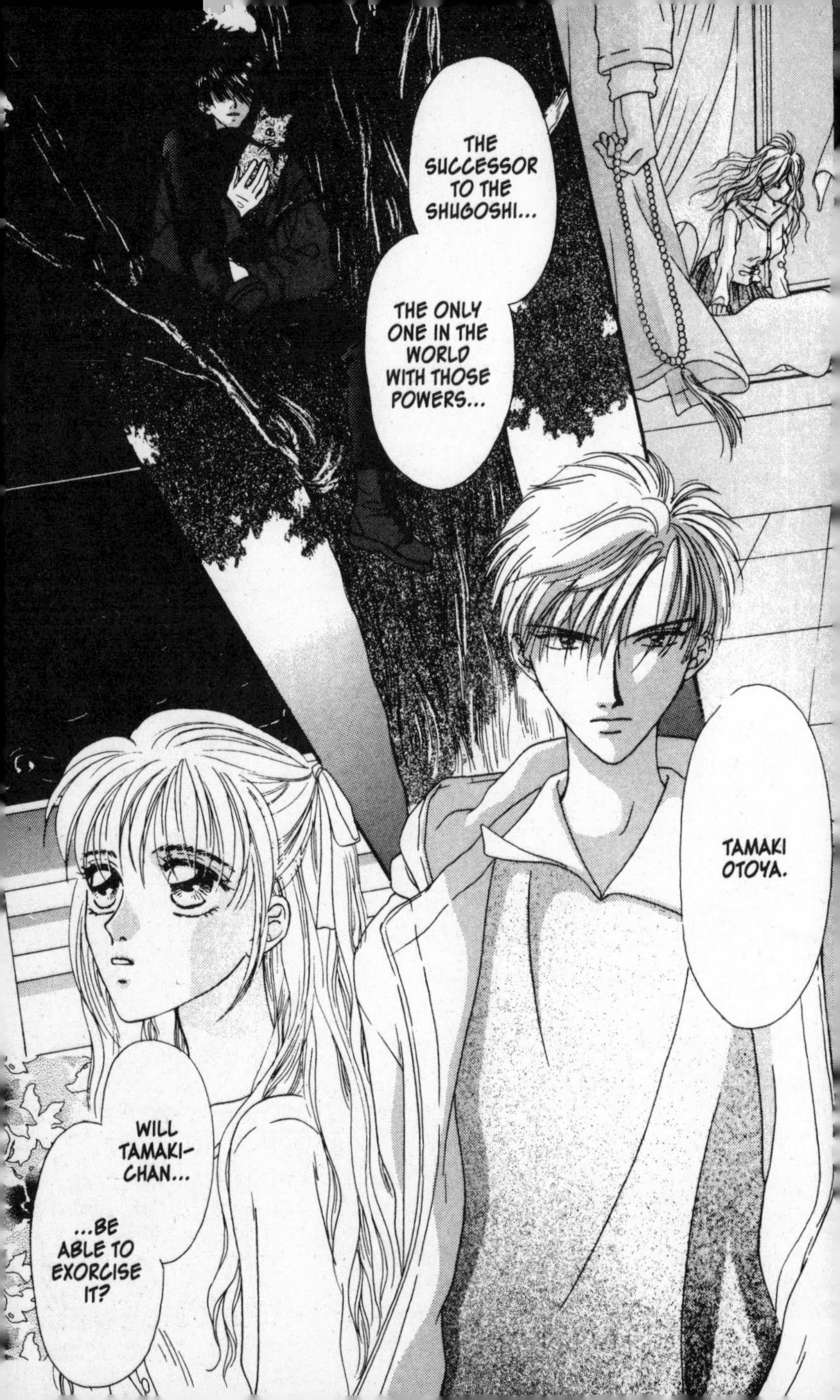
THE SUCCESSOR TO THE SHUGOSHI...
THE ONLY ONE IN THE WORLD WITH THOSE POWERS...
TAMAKI OTOYA.
WILL TAMAKI-CHAN...
...BE ABLE TO EXORCISE IT?

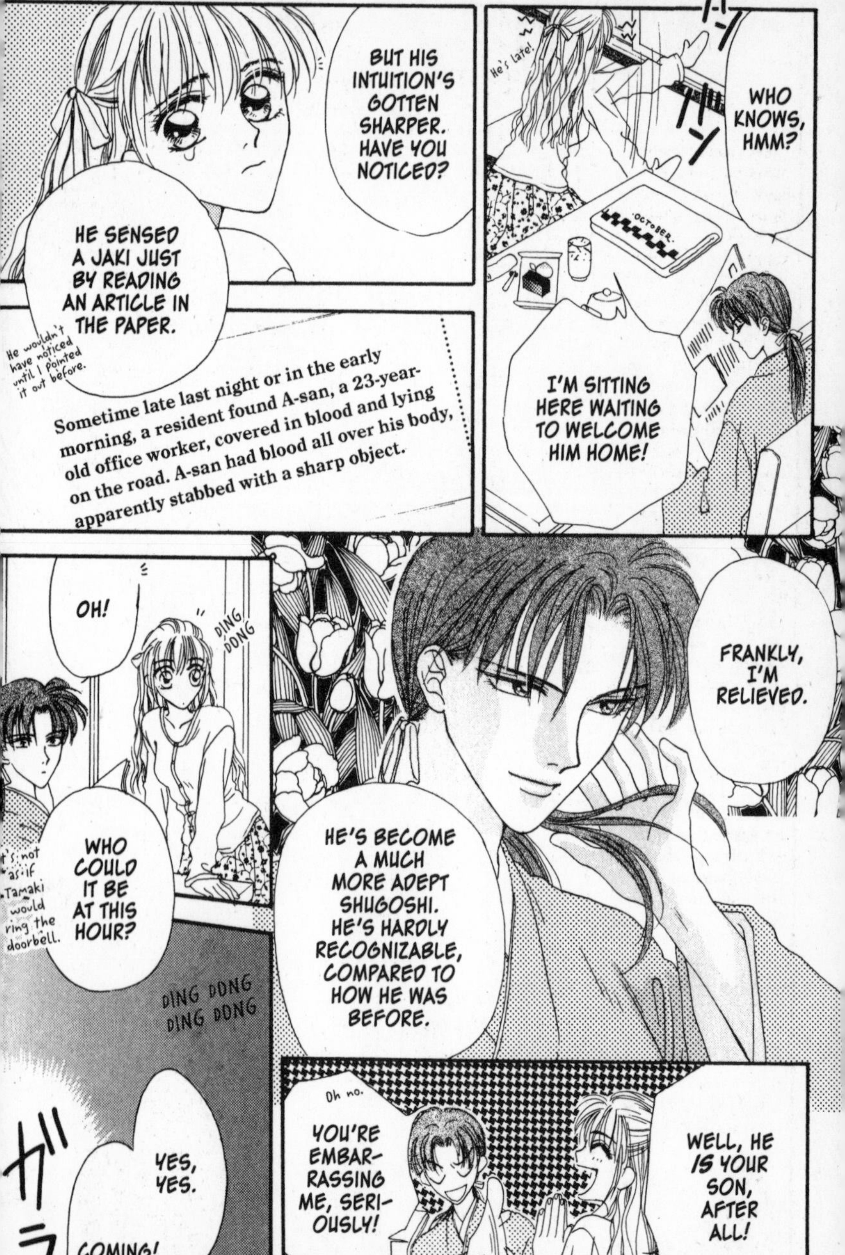
He's late!
WHO KNOWS, HMM?
I'M SITTING HERE WAITING TO WELCOME HIM HOME!
OCTOBER
BUT HIS INTUITION'S GOTTEN SHARPER. HAVE YOU NOTICED?
HE SENSED A JAKI JUST BY READING AN ARTICLE IN THE PAPER.
He wouldn't have noticed until I pointed it out before.
Sometime late last night or in the early morning, a resident found A-san, a 23-year-old office worker, covered in blood and lying on the road. A-san had blood all over his body, apparently stabbed with a sharp object.
FRANKLY, I'M RELIEVED.
HE'S BECOME A MUCH MORE ADEPT SHUGOSHI. HE'S HARDLY RECOGNIZABLE, COMPARED TO HOW HE WAS BEFORE.
OH!
DING DONG
WHO COULD IT BE AT THIS HOUR?
It's not as if Tamaki would ring the doorbell.
Oh no.
WELL, HE IS YOUR SON, AFTER ALL!
YOU'RE EMBARRASSING ME, SERIOUSLY!
DING DONG DING DONG
YES, YES.
COMING!

Four

I love video games although I don't have as much time to immerse myself in them as I used to. Maybe I can blame it on simulation games? I wonder if I'll finish *Fujimaru Jigokuhen* by the time this book is released (I bet I won't be done). It's got 30 chapters, and I've only made it through seven so far. Oh! And there's new hardware coming out this spring. First I'll play *Silver Fox*, and then I want to get *Final Fantasy 7* when it comes out. But before that, I'll finish *Fujimaru*, *Tactics Ogre* and *Bahamut Lagoon*, and then I'll overdose on *Vampire Hunter* and play the PS version of *Robot Taisen!* But maybe it's impossible to do all of that. (laughs) If you think I must be pretty good to get through all those games, well...sorry for the misunderstanding! (laughs)

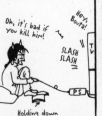

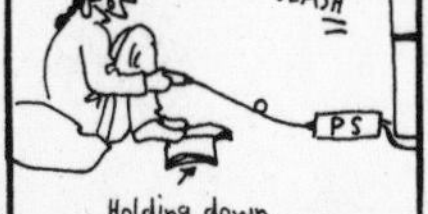
Hey, Bouta!
Oh, it's bad if you kill him!
SLASH SLASH
TV
PS
Holding down

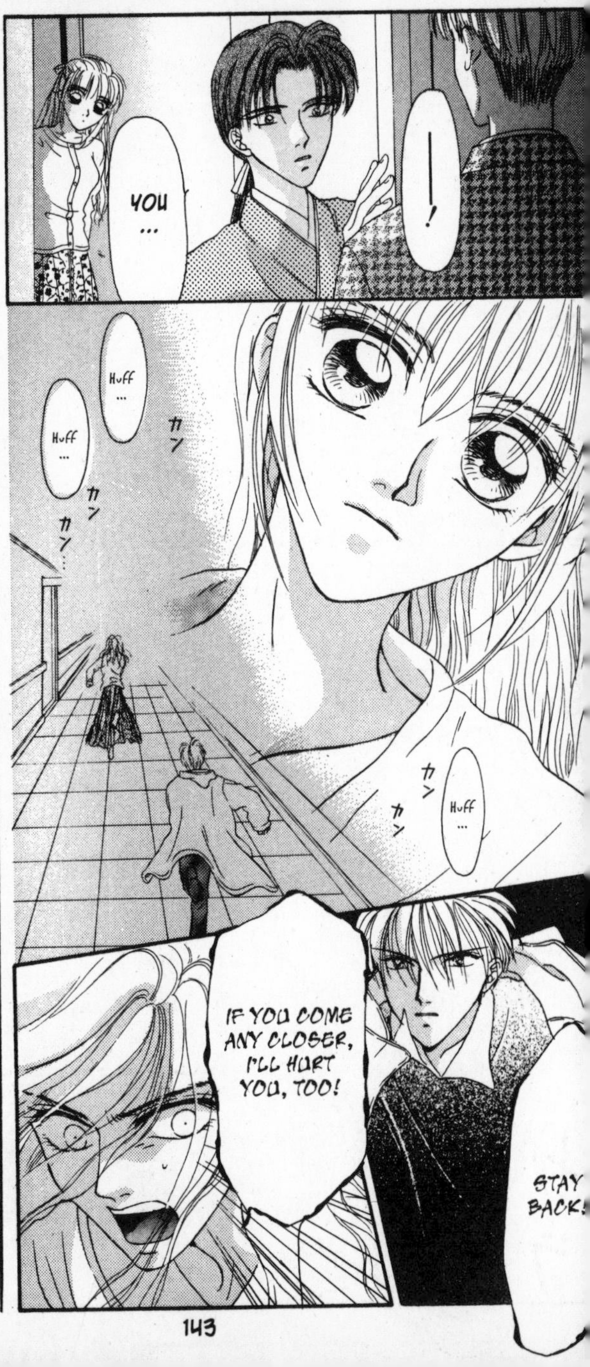
—!
YOU ...
Huff ...
Huff ...
カン
カン
カン...
カン
カン
Huff ...
STAY BACK!
IF YOU COME ANY CLOSER, I'LL HURT YOU, TOO!

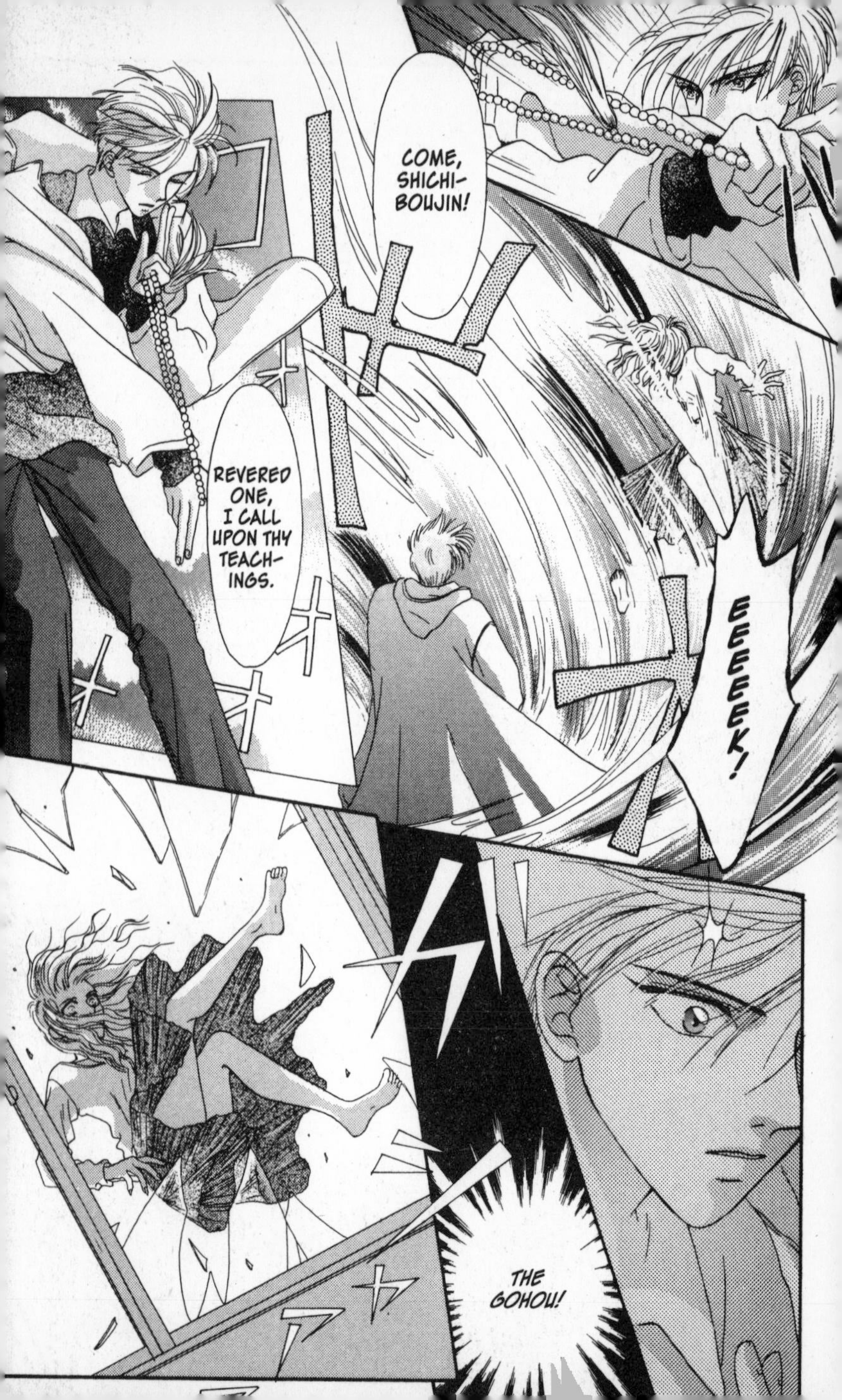
COME, SHICHI-BOUJIN!
REVERED ONE, I CALL UPON THY TEACHINGS.
EEEEEEK!
THE GOHOU!

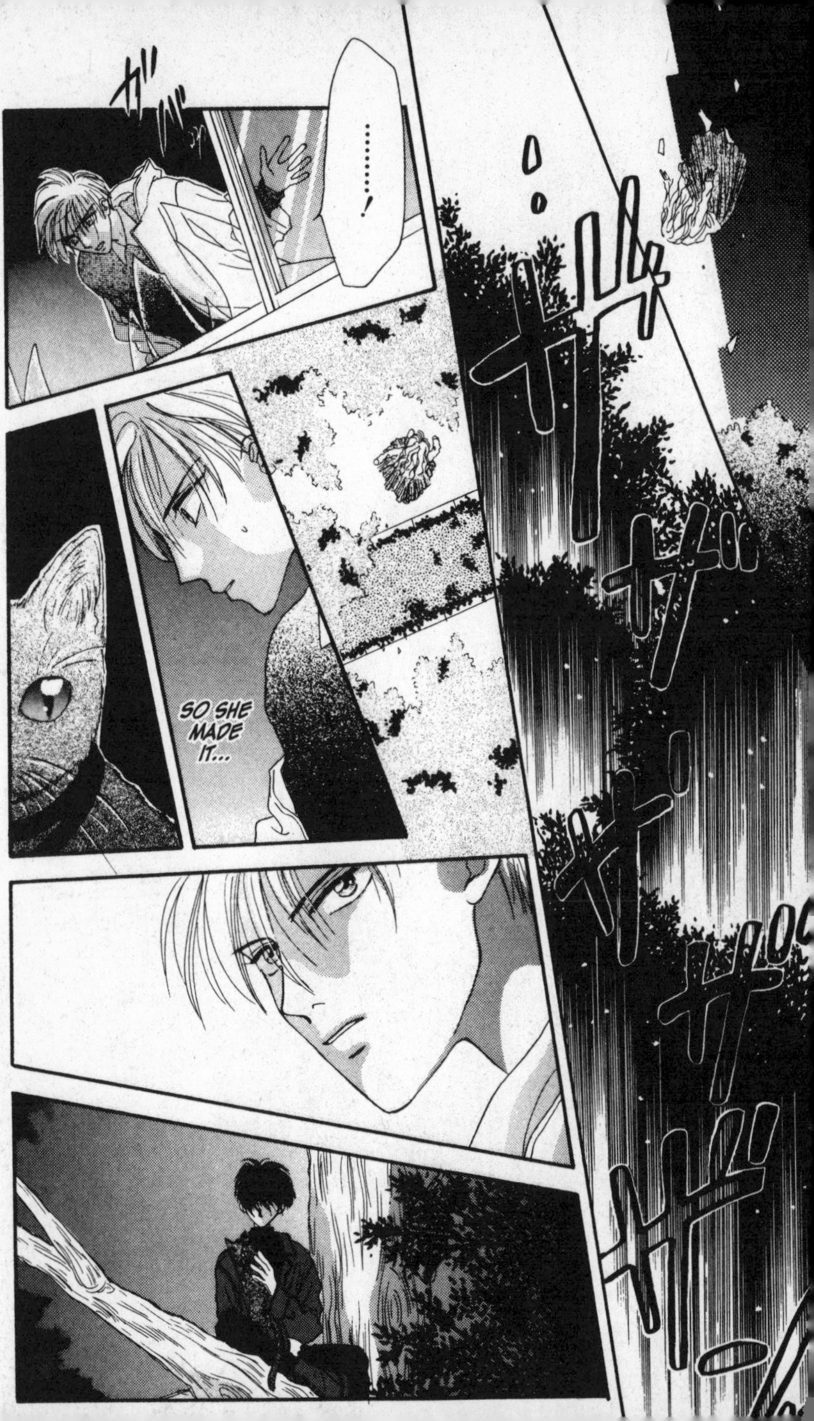

ガバッ
......!
SO SHE MADE IT...

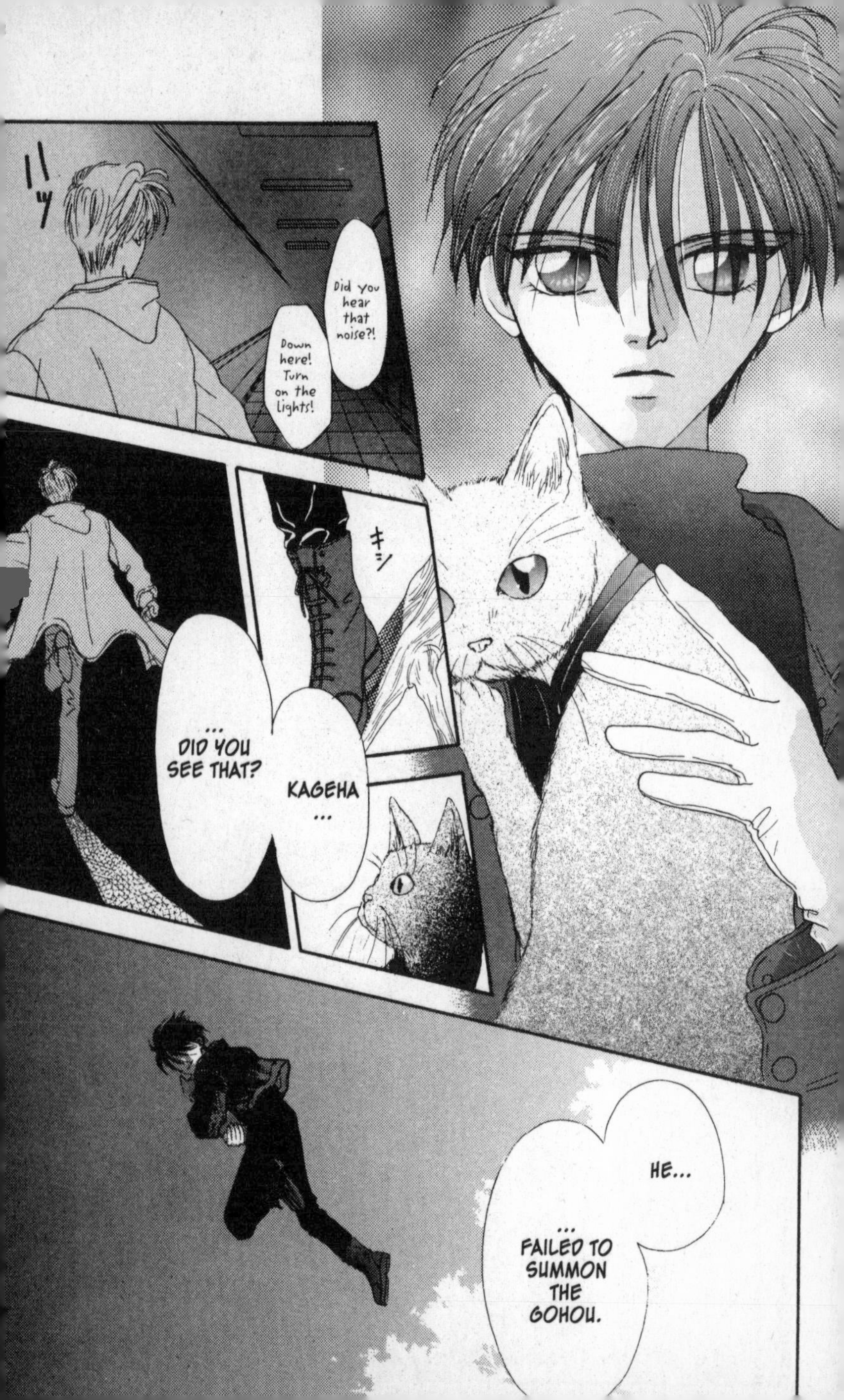
Did you hear that noise?!
Down here! Turn on the lights!
ハッ
キシ
KAGEHA ...
... DID YOU SEE THAT?
HE...
... FAILED TO SUMMON THE GOHOU.

Five

So, about music... Which musicians do I like? I get that kind of question a lot, so let me just say that I like a lot of them! I can't pick a favorite--I like them all! I'm not too into indie artists, though. It's mostly major, mainstream people. As for what type of music, I'd have to say it's across the board. I could start naming musicians I like here, but I don't think the list would fit in this space, so I won't. (laughs) Besides, I don't have any more room for them--CDs, I mean. And I've been getting more and more manga and books, so now it looks like a tornado's passed through my room. If I could use magic, the first thing I'd do is clean this room! I take my habit of relying on others to do stuff for me to an extreme. But... you know how it is. And you're babbling again, Takaya-san! (laughs)

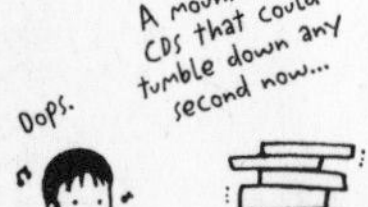
A mountain of CDs that could tumble down any second now...
Oops.

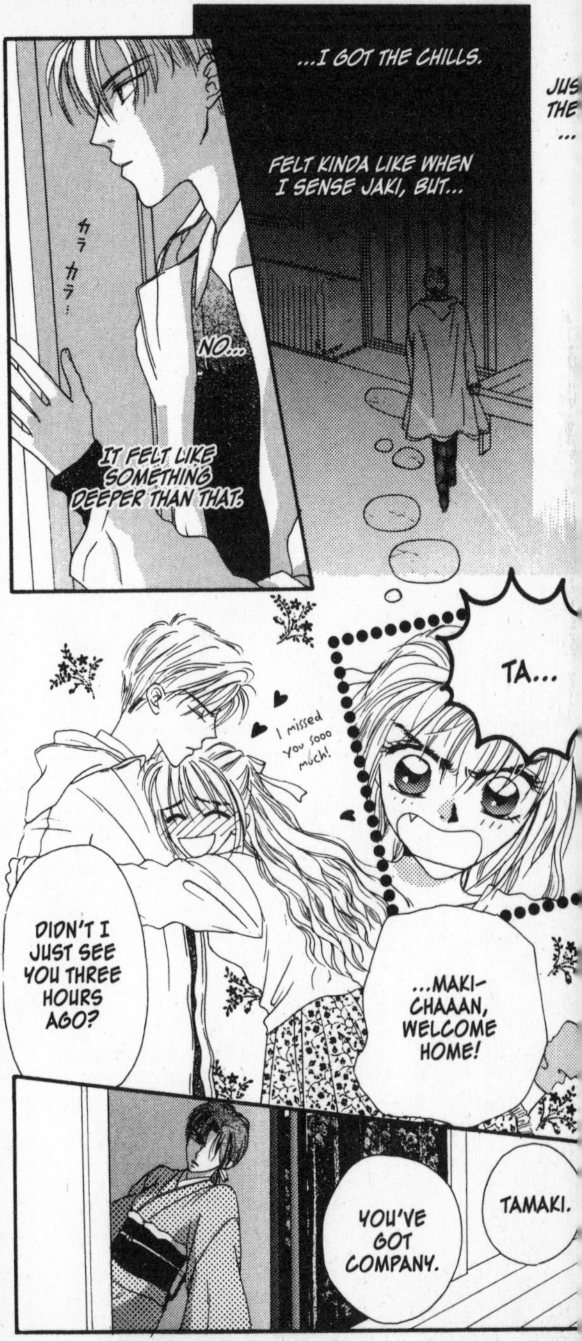
...I GOT THE CHILLS.
FELT KINDA LIKE WHEN I SENSE JAKI, BUT...
カラ カラ...
NO...
IT FELT LIKE SOMETHING DEEPER THAN THAT.
TA...
...MAKI-CHAAAN, WELCOME HOME!
I missed you sooo much!
DIDN'T I JUST SEE YOU THREE HOURS AGO?
TAMAKI.
YOU'VE GOT COMPANY.

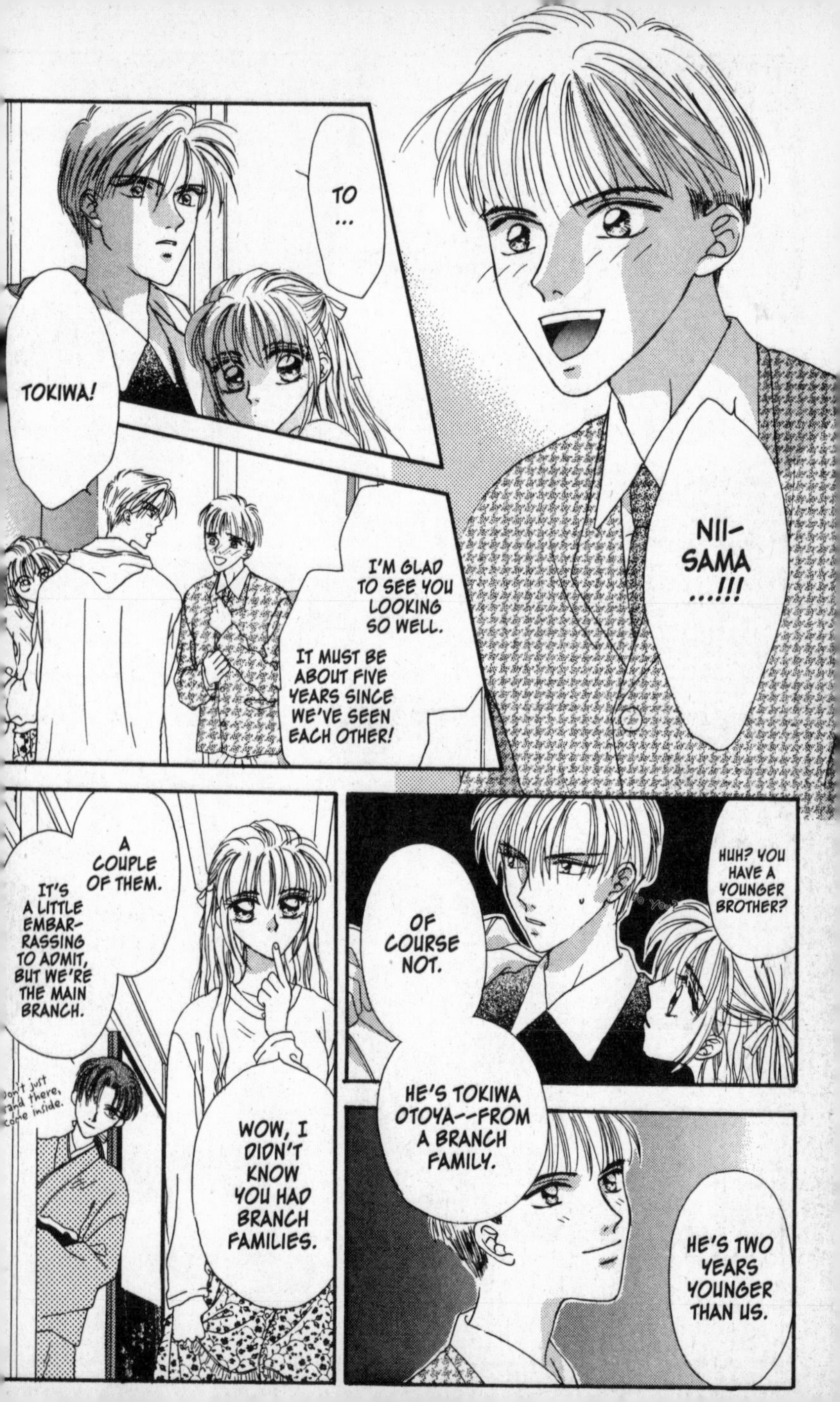
NII-SAMA ...!!!
TO ...
TOKIWA!
I'M GLAD TO SEE YOU LOOKING SO WELL.
IT MUST BE ABOUT FIVE YEARS SINCE WE'VE SEEN EACH OTHER!
HUH? YOU HAVE A YOUNGER BROTHER?
OF COURSE NOT.
HE'S TOKIWA OTOYA--FROM A BRANCH FAMILY.
HE'S TWO YEARS YOUNGER THAN US.
WOW, I DIDN'T KNOW YOU HAD BRANCH FAMILIES.
A COUPLE OF THEM.
IT'S A LITTLE EMBAR-RASSING TO ADMIT, BUT WE'RE THE MAIN BRANCH.
on't just and there, come inside.

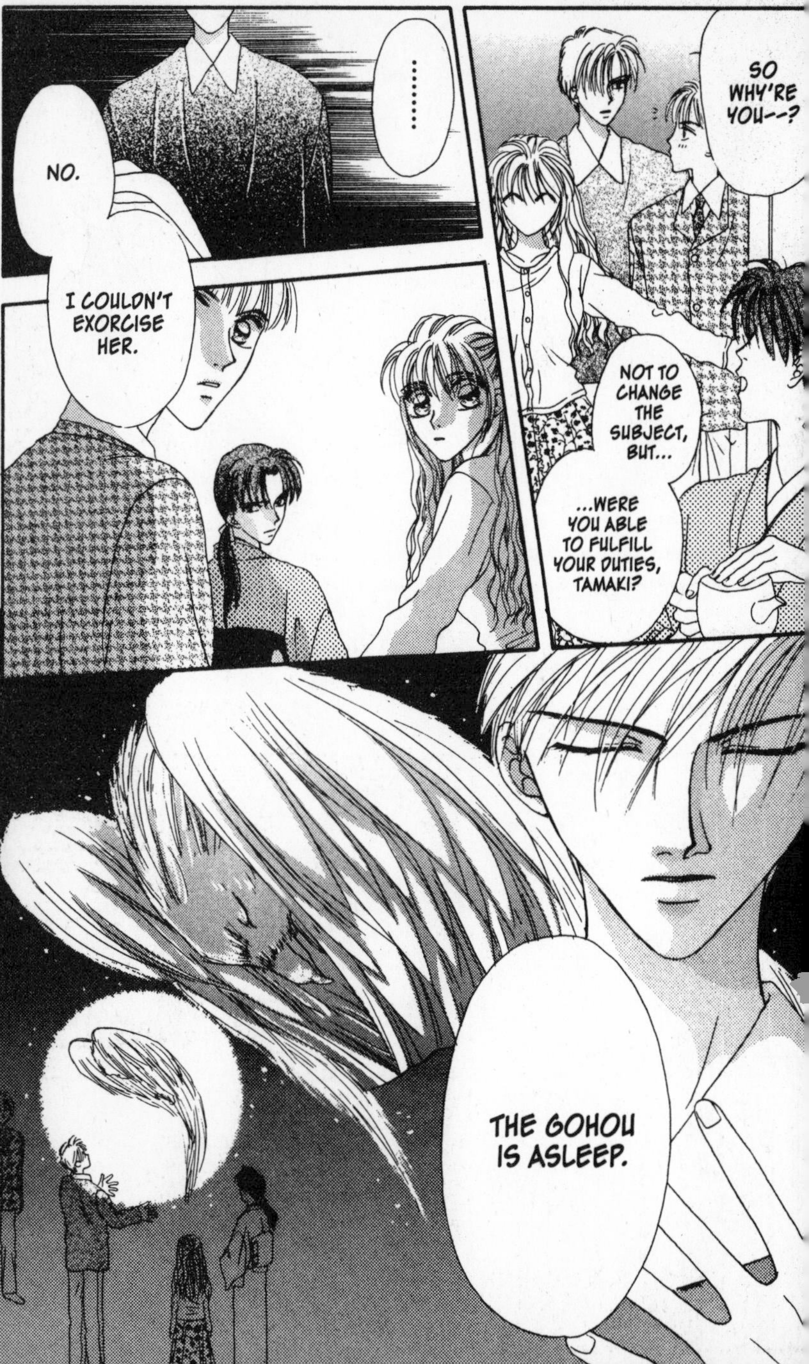
SO WHY'RE YOU--?
NOT TO CHANGE THE SUBJECT, BUT...
...WERE YOU ABLE TO FULFILL YOUR DUTIES, TAMAKI?
......
NO.
I COULDN'T EXORCISE HER.
THE GOHOU IS ASLEEP.

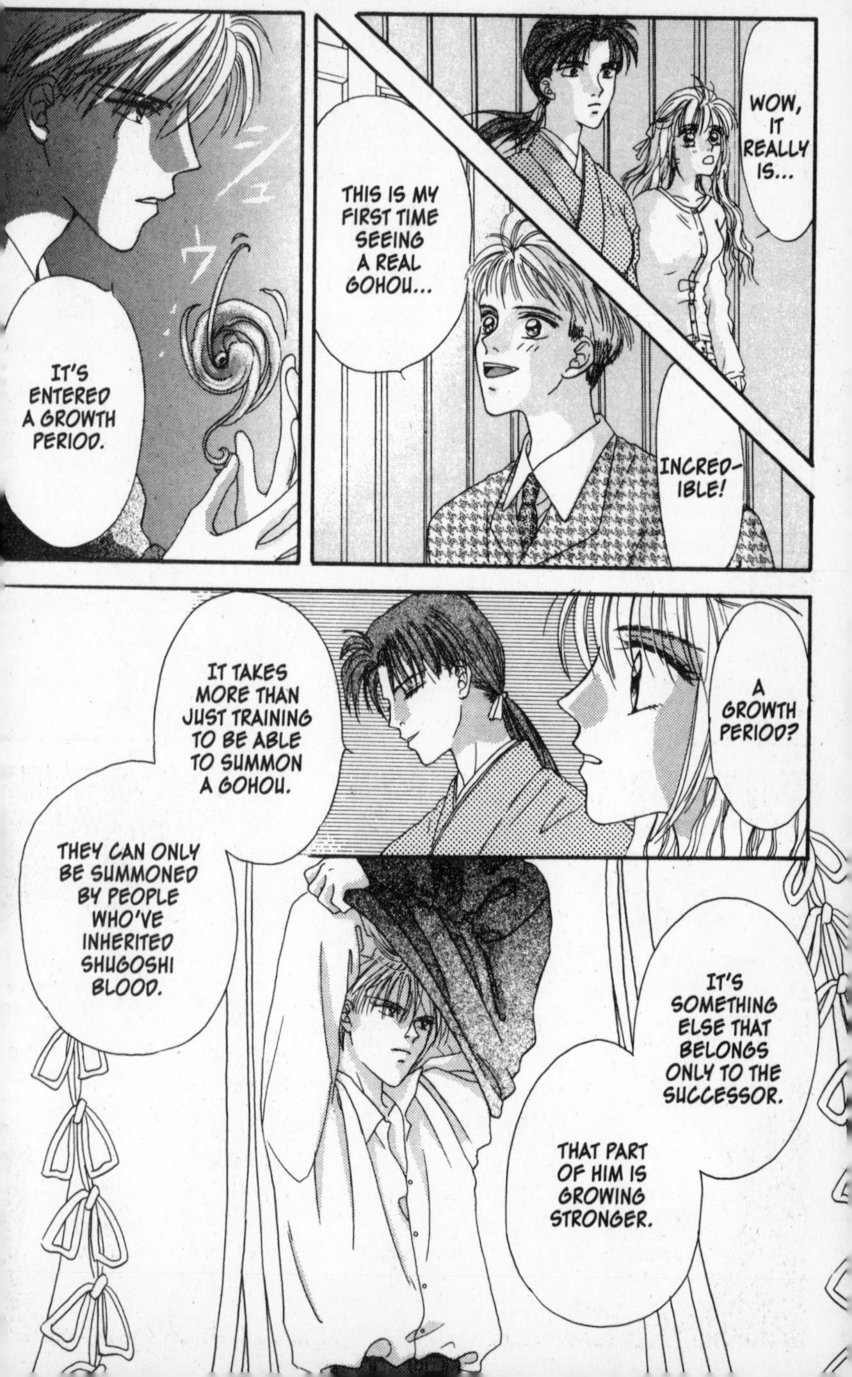
WOW, IT REALLY IS...
INCREDIBLE!
THIS IS MY FIRST TIME SEEING A REAL GOHOU...
IT'S ENTERED A GROWTH PERIOD.
A GROWTH PERIOD?
IT TAKES MORE THAN JUST TRAINING TO BE ABLE TO SUMMON A GOHOU.
THEY CAN ONLY BE SUMMONED BY PEOPLE WHO'VE INHERITED SHUGOSHI BLOOD.
IT'S SOMETHING ELSE THAT BELONGS ONLY TO THE SUCCESSOR.
THAT PART OF HIM IS GROWING STRONGER.

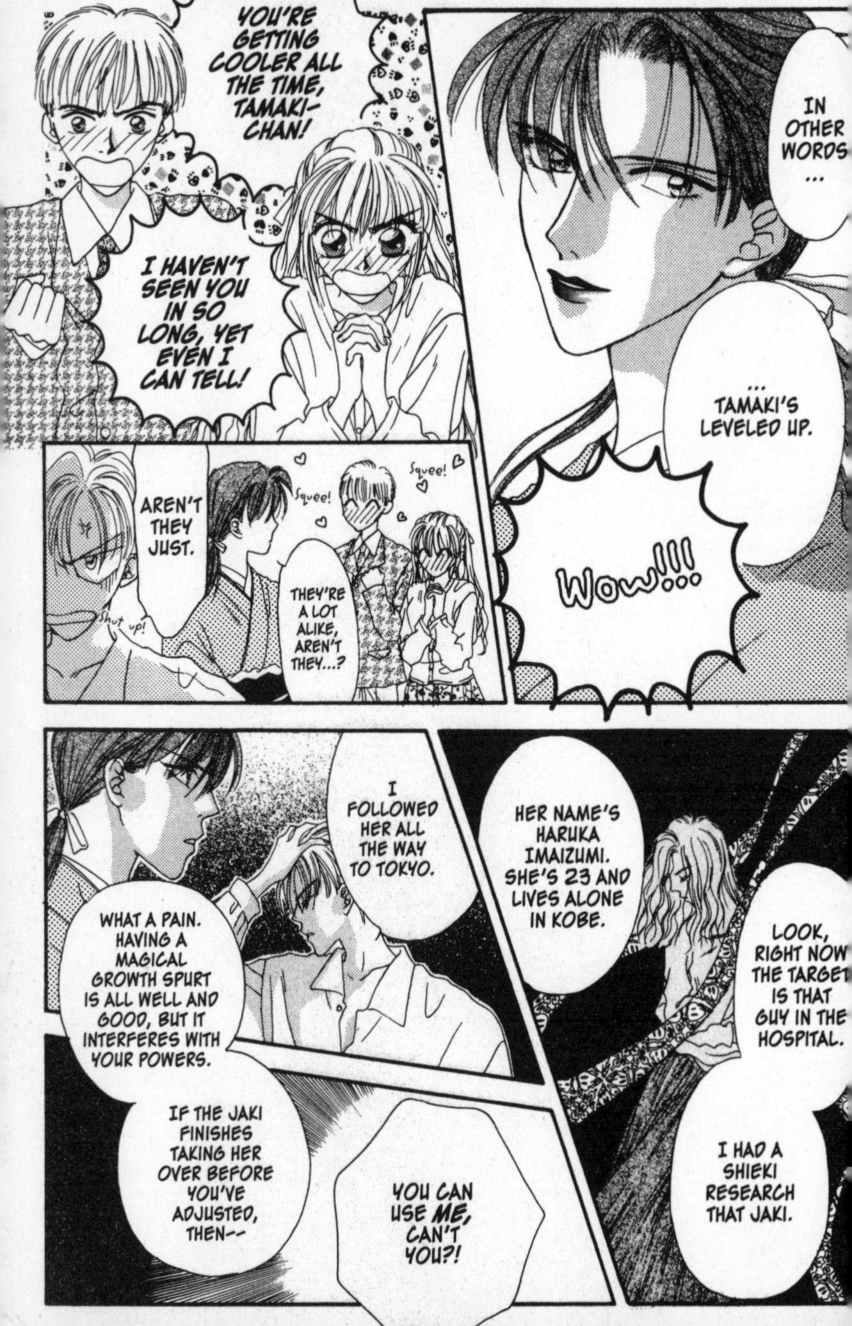
IN OTHER WORDS...
...TAMAKI'S LEVELED UP.
Wow!!!
YOU'RE GETTING COOLER ALL THE TIME, TAMAKI-CHAN!
I HAVEN'T SEEN YOU IN SO LONG, YET EVEN I CAN TELL!
Squee!
Squee!
THEY'RE A LOT ALIKE, AREN'T THEY...?
AREN'T THEY JUST.
Shut up!
LOOK, RIGHT NOW THE TARGET IS THAT GUY IN THE HOSPITAL.
HER NAME'S HARUKA IMAIZUMI. SHE'S 23 AND LIVES ALONE IN KOBE.
I HAD A SHIEKI RESEARCH THAT JAKI.
I FOLLOWED HER ALL THE WAY TO TOKYO.
WHAT A PAIN. HAVING A MAGICAL GROWTH SPURT IS ALL WELL AND GOOD, BUT IT INTERFERES WITH YOUR POWERS.
YOU CAN USE ME, CAN'T YOU?!
IF THE JAKI FINISHES TAKING HER OVER BEFORE YOU'VE ADJUSTED, THEN--

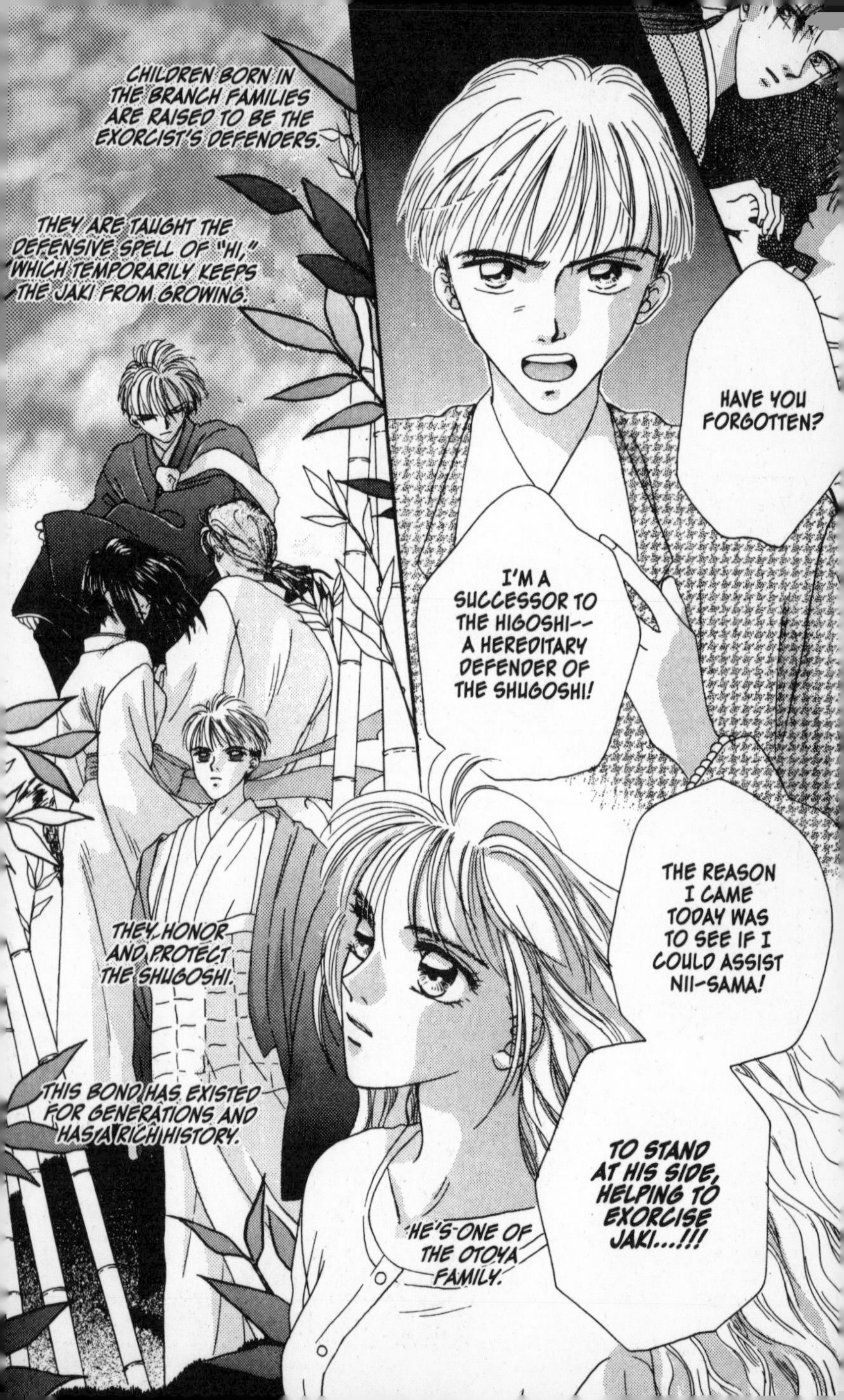
HAVE YOU FORGOTTEN?
I'M A SUCCESSOR TO THE HIGOSHI-- A HEREDITARY DEFENDER OF THE SHUGOSHI!
THE REASON I CAME TODAY WAS TO SEE IF I COULD ASSIST NII-SAMA!
TO STAND AT HIS SIDE, HELPING TO EXORCISE JAKI...!!!
HE'S ONE OF THE OTOYA FAMILY.
CHILDREN BORN IN THE BRANCH FAMILIES ARE RAISED TO BE THE EXORCIST'S DEFENDERS.
THEY ARE TAUGHT THE DEFENSIVE SPELL OF "HI," WHICH TEMPORARILY KEEPS THE JAKI FROM GROWING.
THEY HONOR AND PROTECT THE SHUGOSHI.
THIS BOND HAS EXISTED FOR GENERATIONS AND HAS A RICH HISTORY.

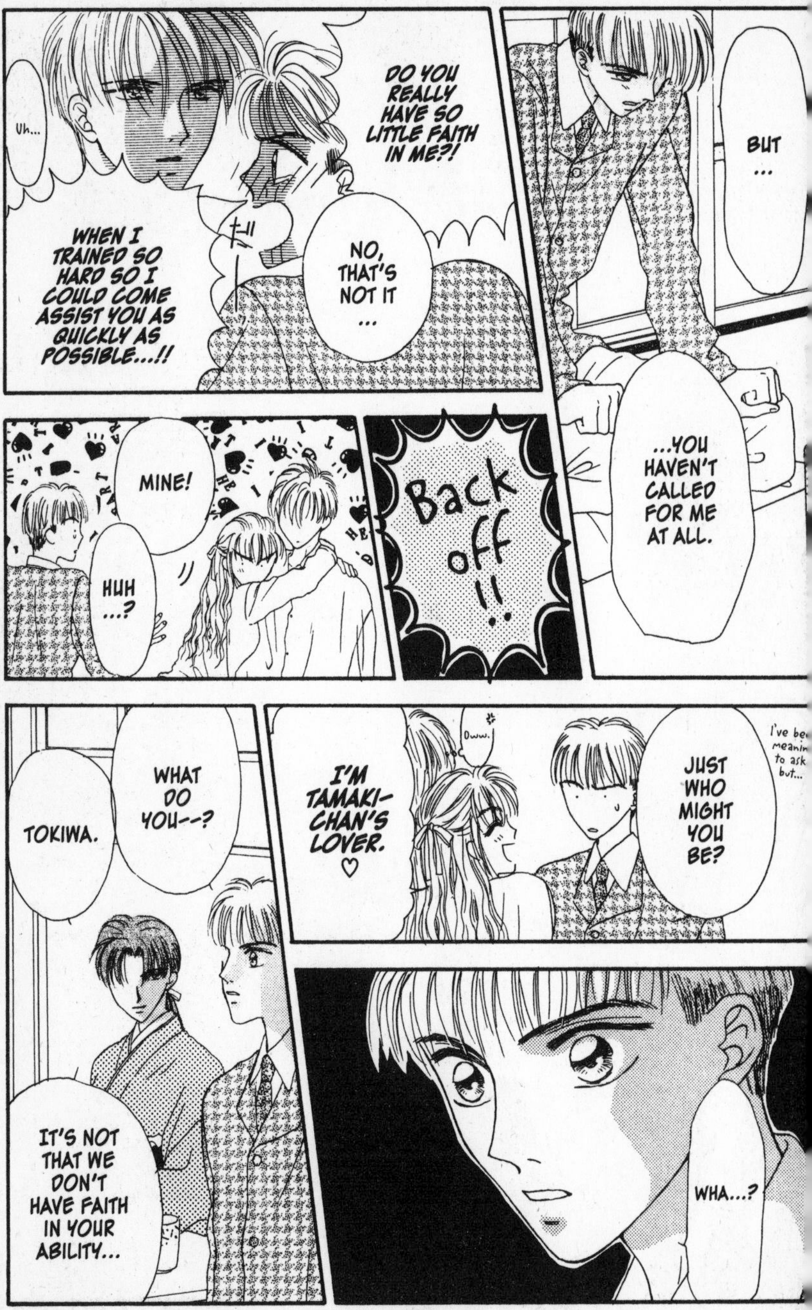
BUT ...
...YOU HAVEN'T CALLED FOR ME AT ALL.
DO YOU REALLY HAVE SO LITTLE FAITH IN ME?!
Uh...
NO, THAT'S NOT IT ...
WHEN I TRAINED SO HARD SO I COULD COME ASSIST YOU AS QUICKLY AS POSSIBLE...!!
Back off!!
MINE!
HUH ...?
I've be meanin to ask but...
JUST WHO MIGHT YOU BE?
Oww.
I'M TAMAKI-CHAN'S LOVER. ♡
WHA...?
WHAT DO YOU--?
TOKIWA.
IT'S NOT THAT WE DON'T HAVE FAITH IN YOUR ABILITY...

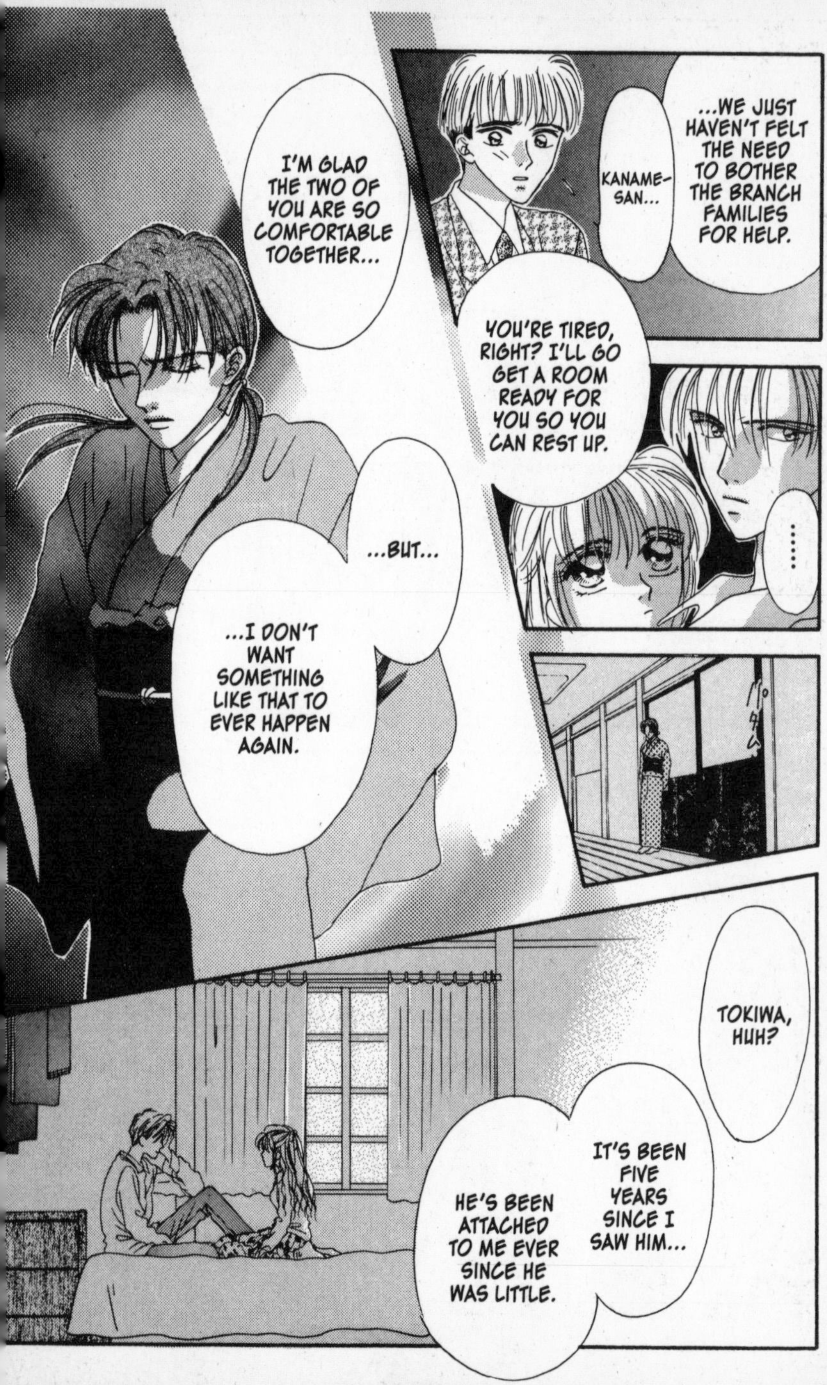
...WE JUST HAVEN'T FELT THE NEED TO BOTHER THE BRANCH FAMILIES FOR HELP.
KANAME-SAN...
YOU'RE TIRED, RIGHT? I'LL GO GET A ROOM READY FOR YOU SO YOU CAN REST UP.
......
I'M GLAD THE TWO OF YOU ARE SO COMFORTABLE TOGETHER...
...BUT...
...I DON'T WANT SOMETHING LIKE THAT TO EVER HAPPEN AGAIN.
TOKIWA, HUH?
IT'S BEEN FIVE YEARS SINCE I SAW HIM...
HE'S BEEN ATTACHED TO ME EVER SINCE HE WAS LITTLE.

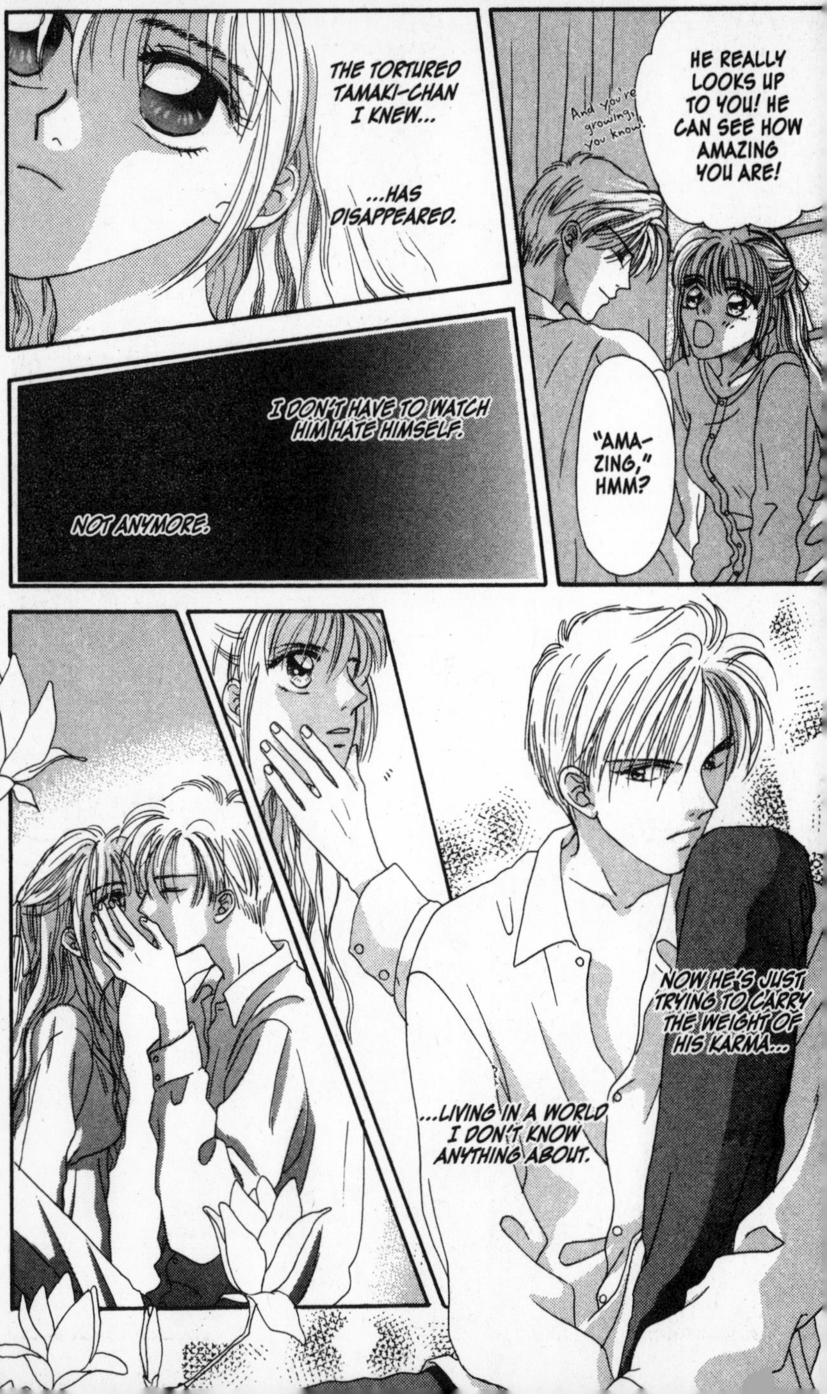
HE REALLY LOOKS UP TO YOU! HE CAN SEE HOW AMAZING YOU ARE!
And you're growing, you know!
"AMA-ZING," HMM?
THE TORTURED TAMAKI-CHAN I KNEW...
...HAS DISAPPEARED.
I DON'T HAVE TO WATCH HIM HATE HIMSELF.
NOT ANYMORE.
NOW HE'S JUST TRYING TO CARRY THE WEIGHT OF HIS KARMA...
...LIVING IN A WORLD I DON'T KNOW ANYTHING ABOUT.

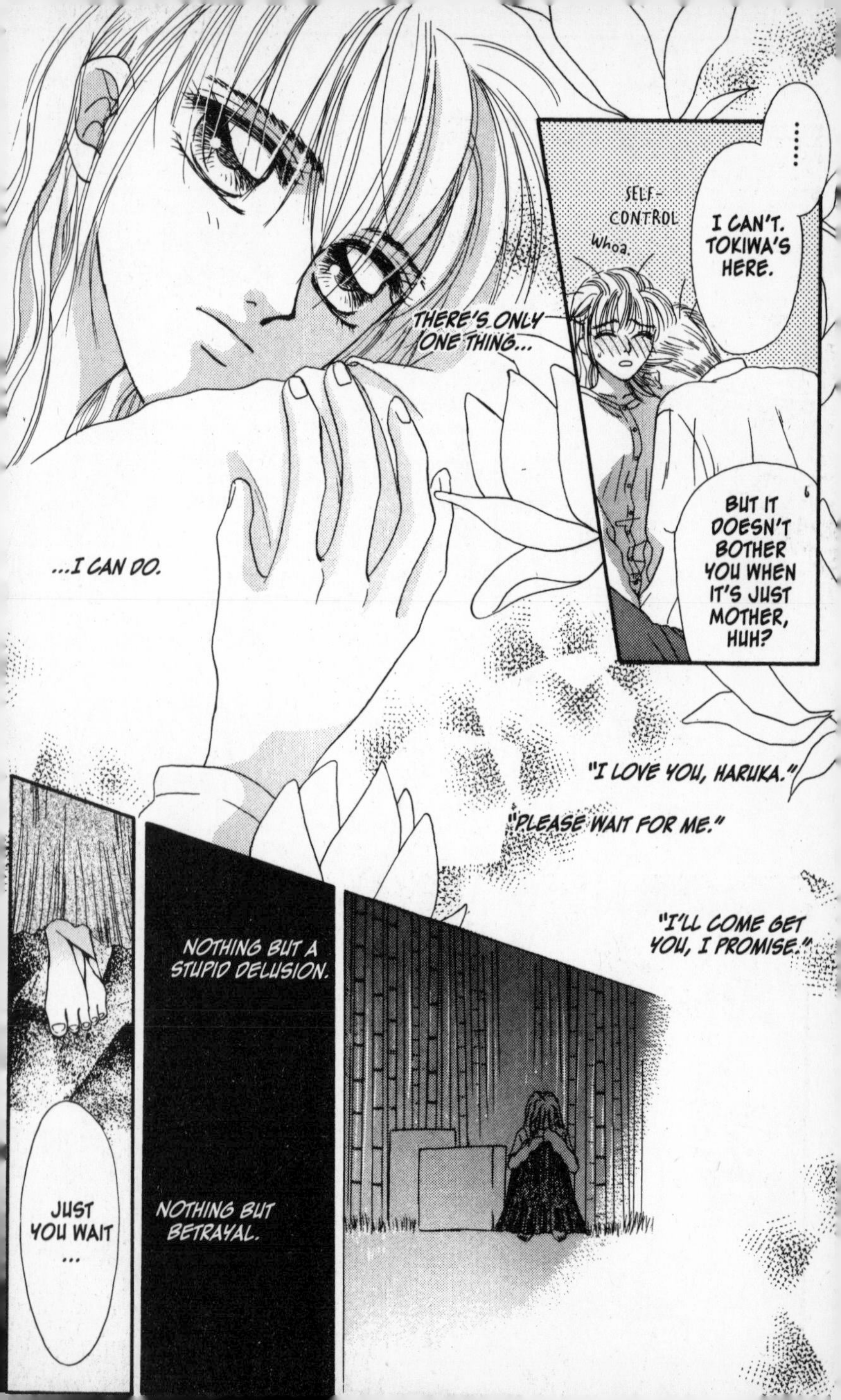
......
I CAN'T. TOKIWA'S HERE.
SELF-CONTROL
Whoa.
BUT IT DOESN'T BOTHER YOU WHEN IT'S JUST MOTHER, HUH?
THERE'S ONLY ONE THING...
...I CAN DO.
"I LOVE YOU, HARUKA."
"PLEASE WAIT FOR ME."
"I'LL COME GET YOU, I PROMISE."
NOTHING BUT A STUPID DELUSION.
NOTHING BUT BETRAYAL.
JUST YOU WAIT ...

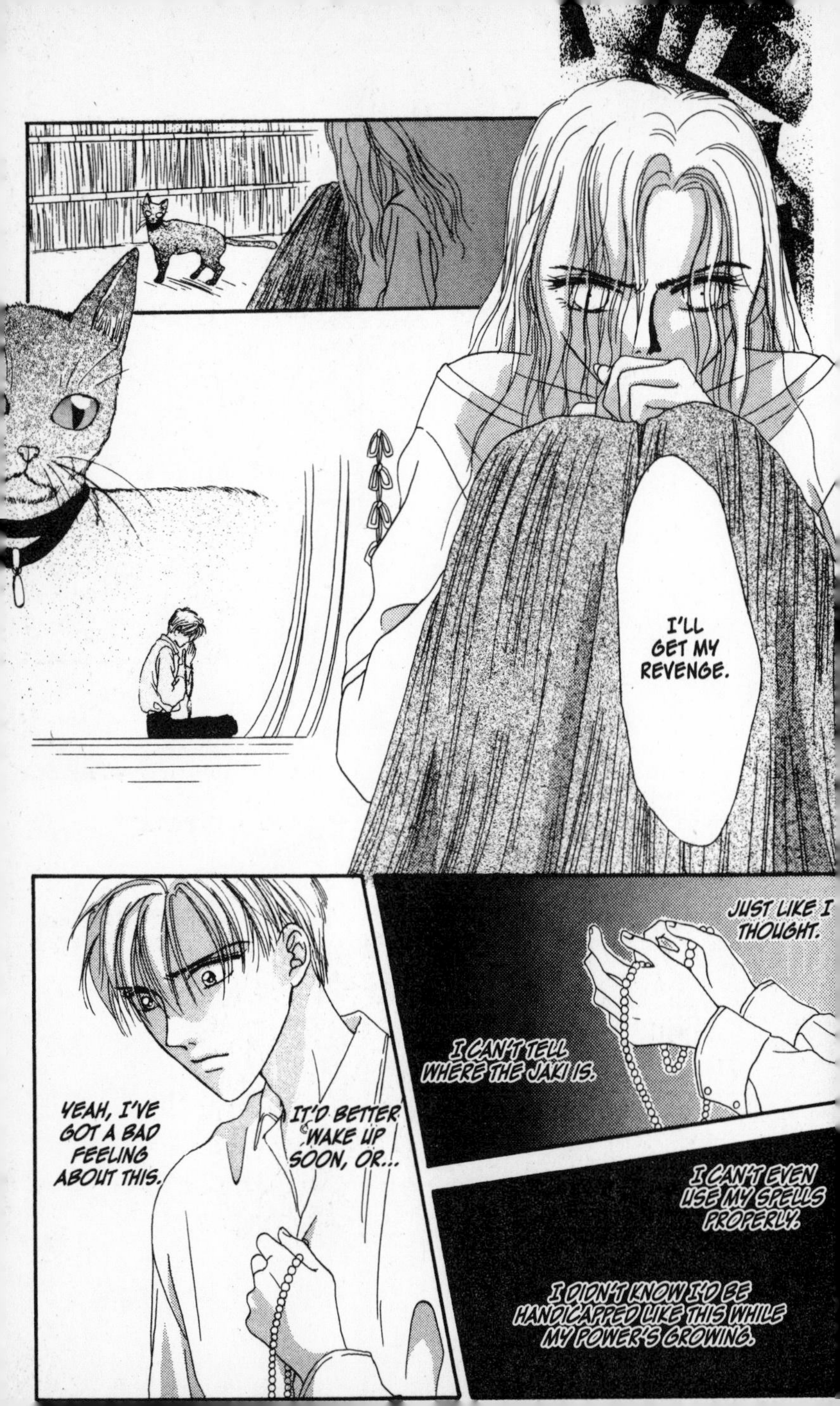
I'LL GET MY REVENGE.
JUST LIKE I THOUGHT.
I CAN'T TELL WHERE THE JAKI IS.
I CAN'T EVEN USE MY SPELLS PROPERLY.
I DIDN'T KNOW I'D BE HANDICAPPED LIKE THIS WHILE MY POWER'S GROWING.
IT'D BETTER WAKE UP SOON, OR...
YEAH, I'VE GOT A BAD FEELING ABOUT THIS.

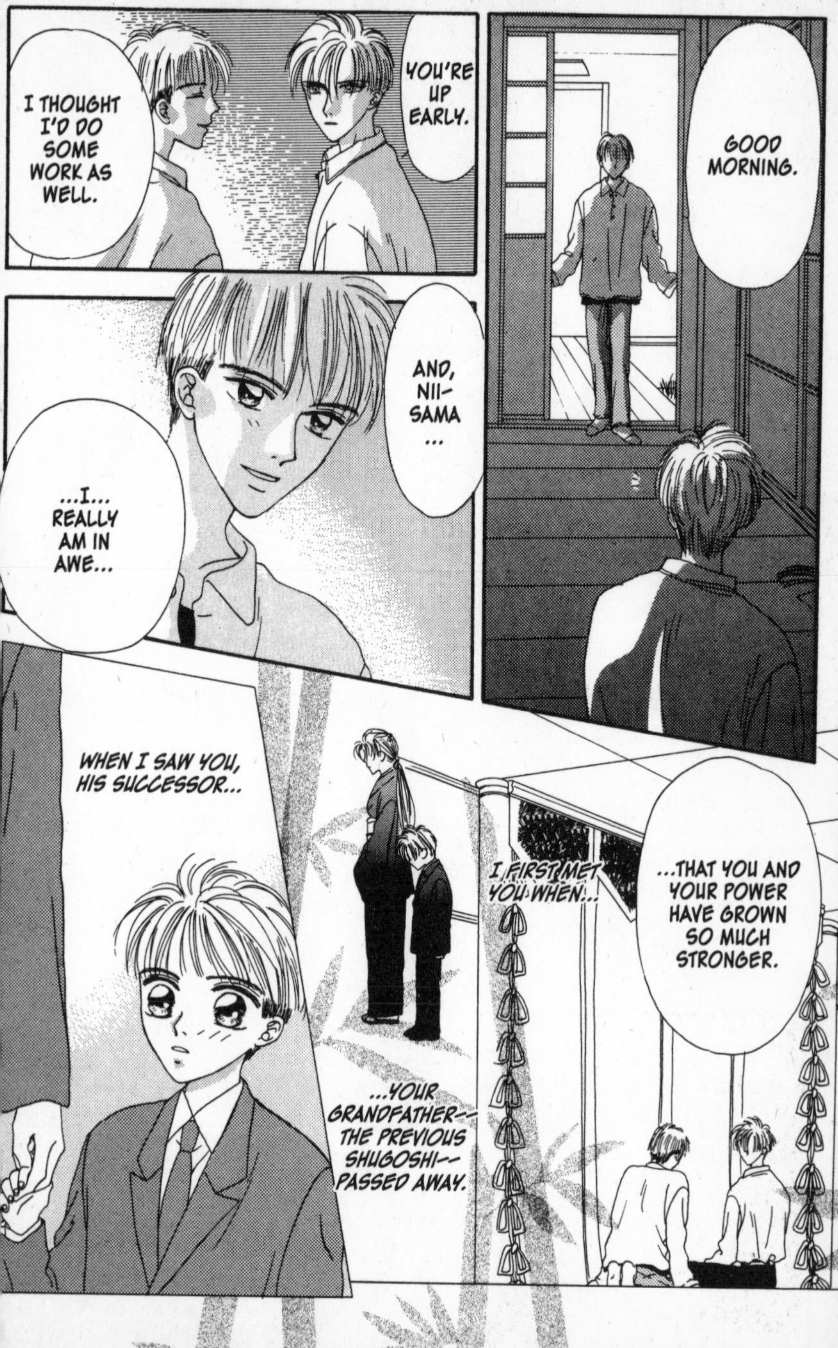
GOOD MORNING.
YOU'RE UP EARLY.
I THOUGHT I'D DO SOME WORK AS WELL.
AND, NII-SAMA ...
...I... REALLY AM IN AWE...
...THAT YOU AND YOUR POWER HAVE GROWN SO MUCH STRONGER.
I FIRST MET YOU WHEN...
...YOUR GRANDFATHER--THE PREVIOUS SHUGOSHI--PASSED AWAY.
WHEN I SAW YOU, HIS SUCCESSOR...

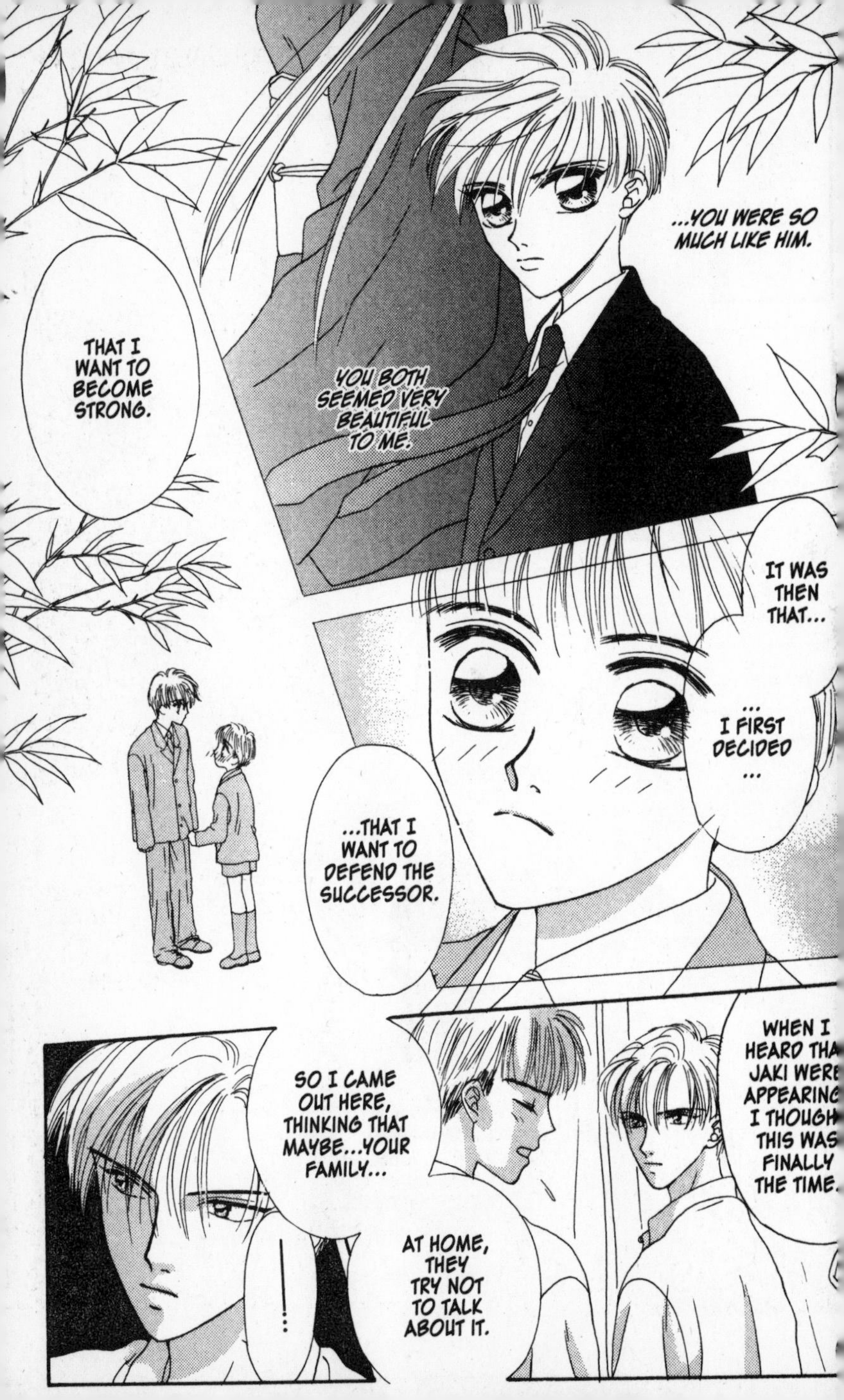
...YOU WERE SO MUCH LIKE HIM.
YOU BOTH SEEMED VERY BEAUTIFUL TO ME.
IT WAS THEN THAT...
... I FIRST DECIDED ...
...THAT I WANT TO DEFEND THE SUCCESSOR.
THAT I WANT TO BECOME STRONG.
WHEN I HEARD THA JAKI WERE APPEARING I THOUGH THIS WAS FINALLY THE TIME.
SO I CAME OUT HERE, THINKING THAT MAYBE...YOUR FAMILY...
AT HOME, THEY TRY NOT TO TALK ABOUT IT.
!...

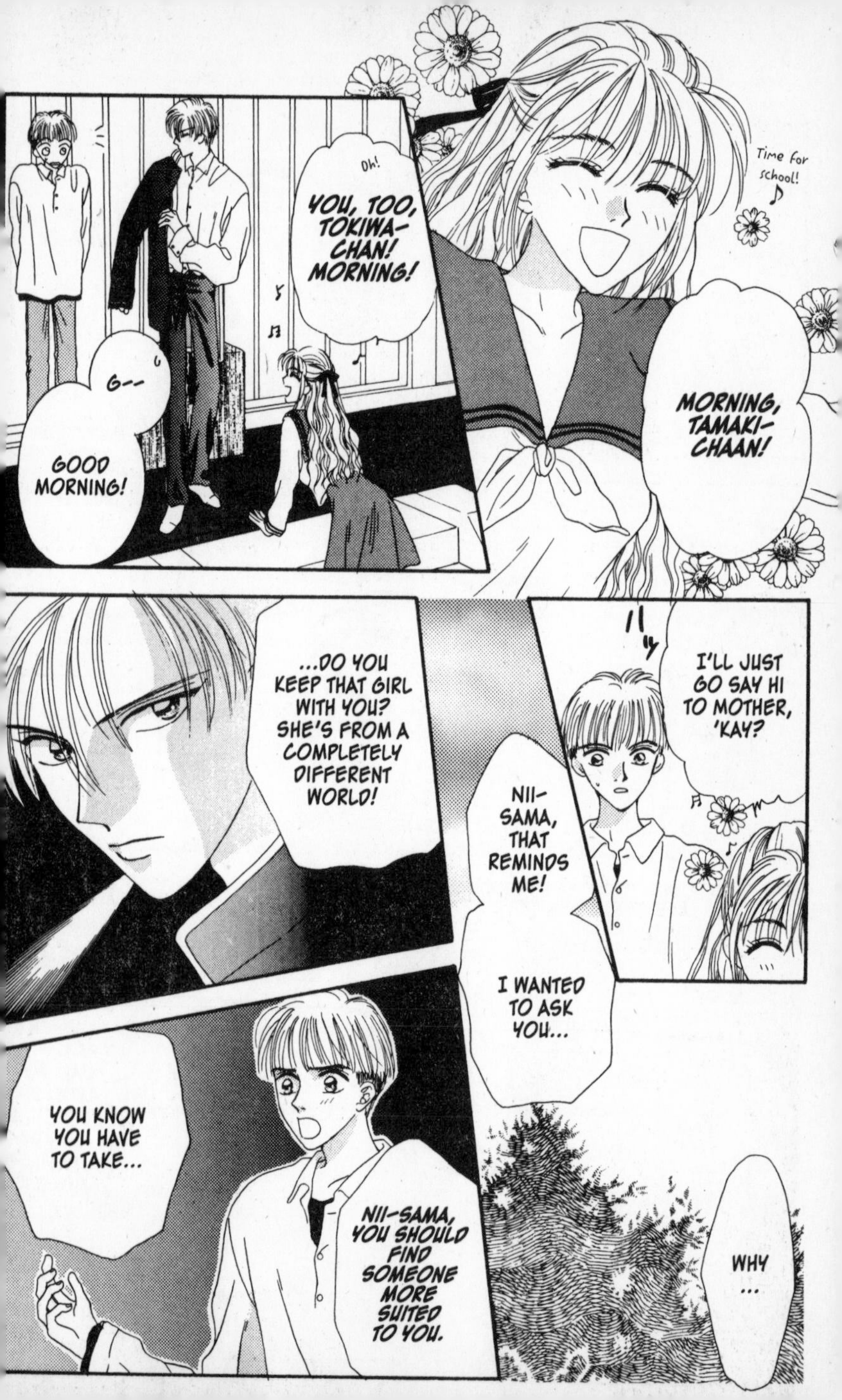
Time for school! ♪
MORNING, TAMAKI-CHAAN!
Oh!
YOU, TOO, TOKIWA-CHAN! MORNING!
G--
GOOD MORNING!
I'LL JUST GO SAY HI TO MOTHER, 'KAY?
NII-SAMA, THAT REMINDS ME!
I WANTED TO ASK YOU...
WHY ...
...DO YOU KEEP THAT GIRL WITH YOU? SHE'S FROM A COMPLETELY DIFFERENT WORLD!
NII-SAMA, YOU SHOULD FIND SOMEONE MORE SUITED TO YOU.
YOU KNOW YOU HAVE TO TAKE...

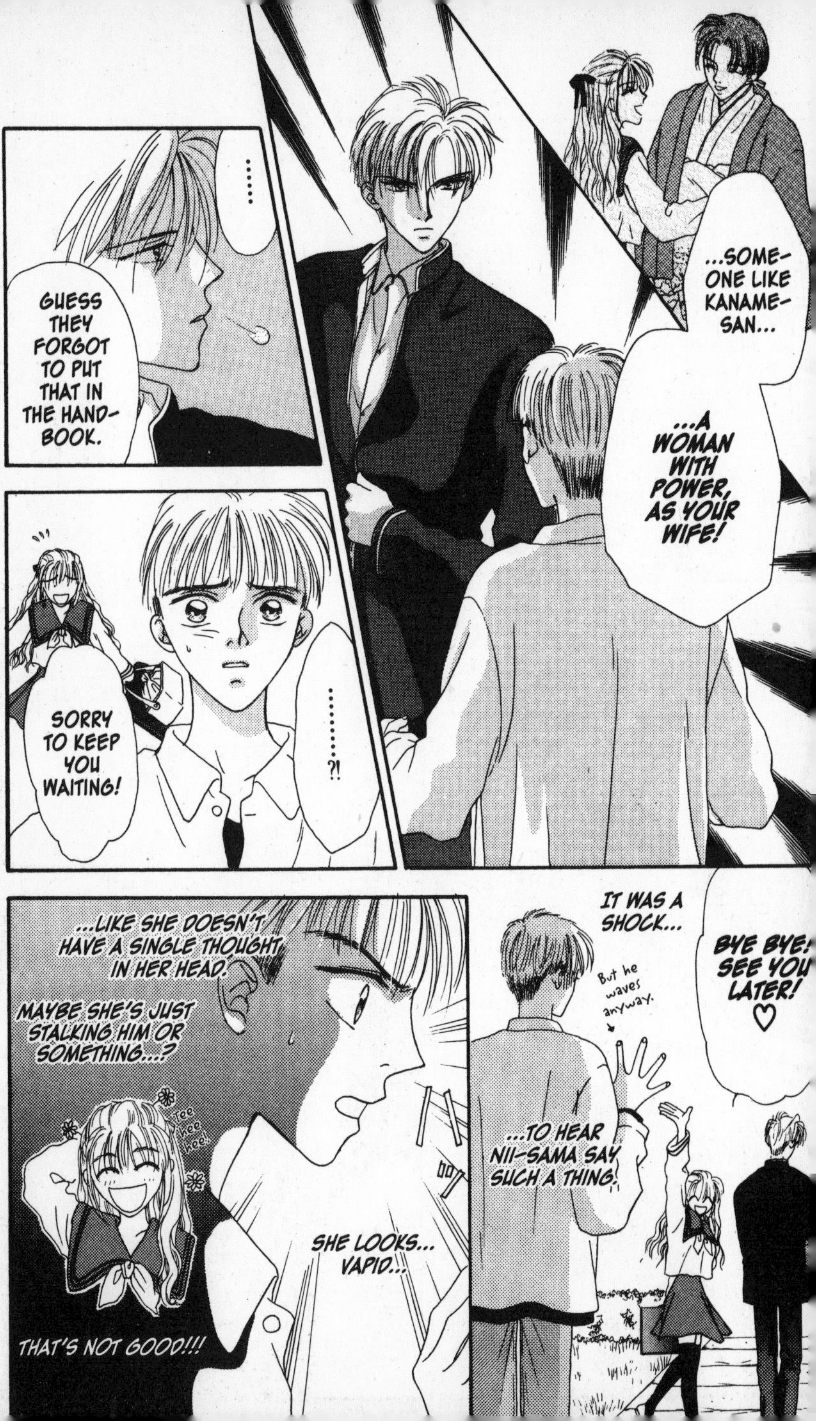
...SOME-ONE LIKE KANAME-SAN...
...A WOMAN WITH POWER, AS YOUR WIFE!
......
GUESS THEY FORGOT TO PUT THAT IN THE HAND-BOOK.
SORRY TO KEEP YOU WAITING!
........?!
BYE BYE! SEE YOU LATER! ♡
IT WAS A SHOCK...
But he waves anyway.
...TO HEAR NII-SAMA SAY SUCH A THING.
...LIKE SHE DOESN'T HAVE A SINGLE THOUGHT IN HER HEAD.
MAYBE SHE'S JUST STALKING HIM OR SOMETHING...?
Tee hee hee.
SHE LOOKS... VAPID...
THAT'S NOT GOOD!!!

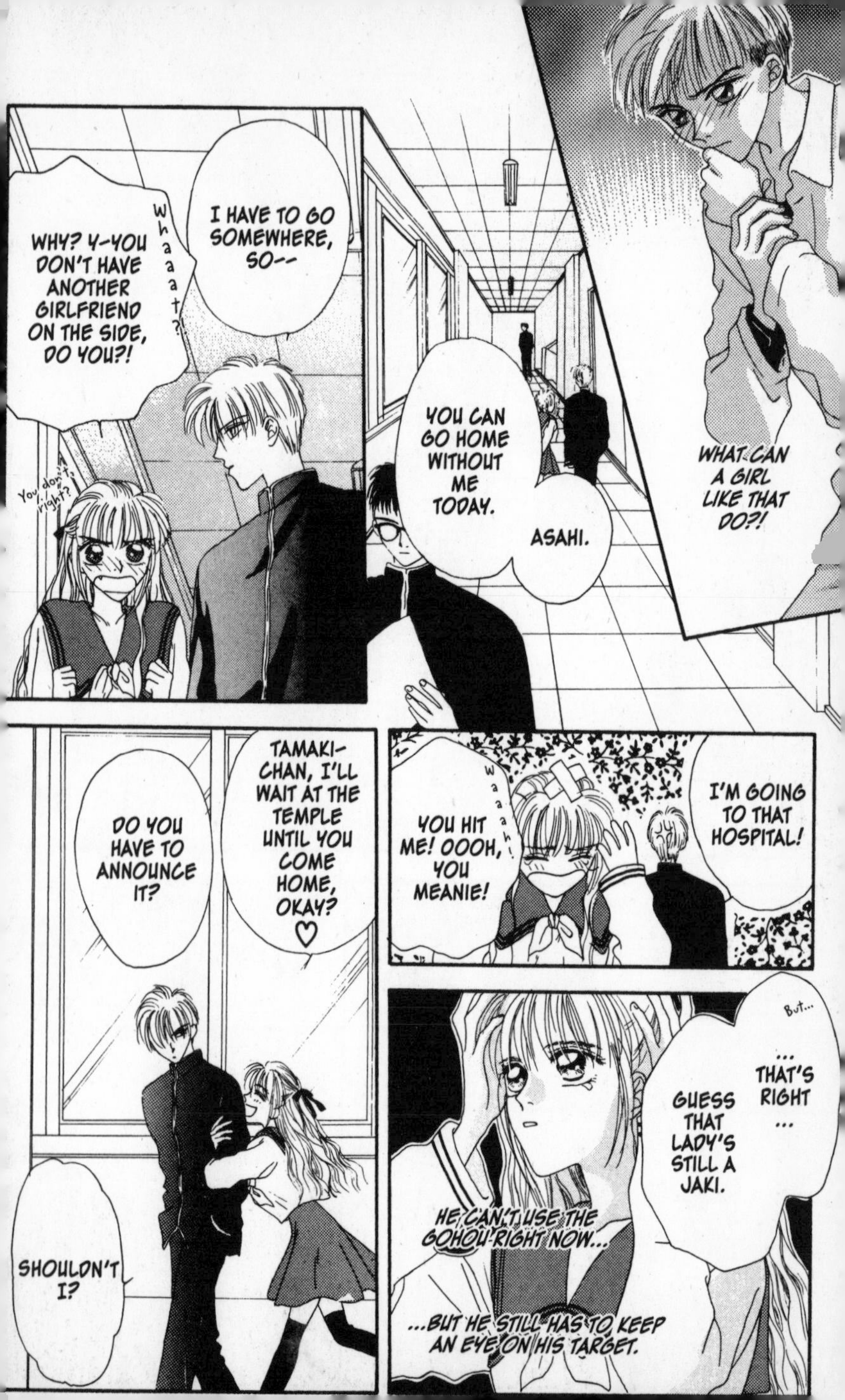
WHAT CAN A GIRL LIKE THAT DO?!
YOU CAN GO HOME WITHOUT ME TODAY.
ASAHI.
I HAVE TO GO SOMEWHERE, SO--
Whaaaat?!
WHY? Y-YOU DON'T HAVE ANOTHER GIRLFRIEND ON THE SIDE, DO YOU?!
You don't, right?
I'M GOING TO THAT HOSPITAL!
Waaaah!
YOU HIT ME! OOOH, YOU MEANIE!
But...
...THAT'S RIGHT...
GUESS THAT LADY'S STILL A JAKI.
HE CAN'T USE THE GOHOU RIGHT NOW...
...BUT HE STILL HAS TO KEEP AN EYE ON HIS TARGET.
TAMAKI-CHAN, I'LL WAIT AT THE TEMPLE UNTIL YOU COME HOME, OKAY? ♡
DO YOU HAVE TO ANNOUNCE IT?
SHOULDN'T I?

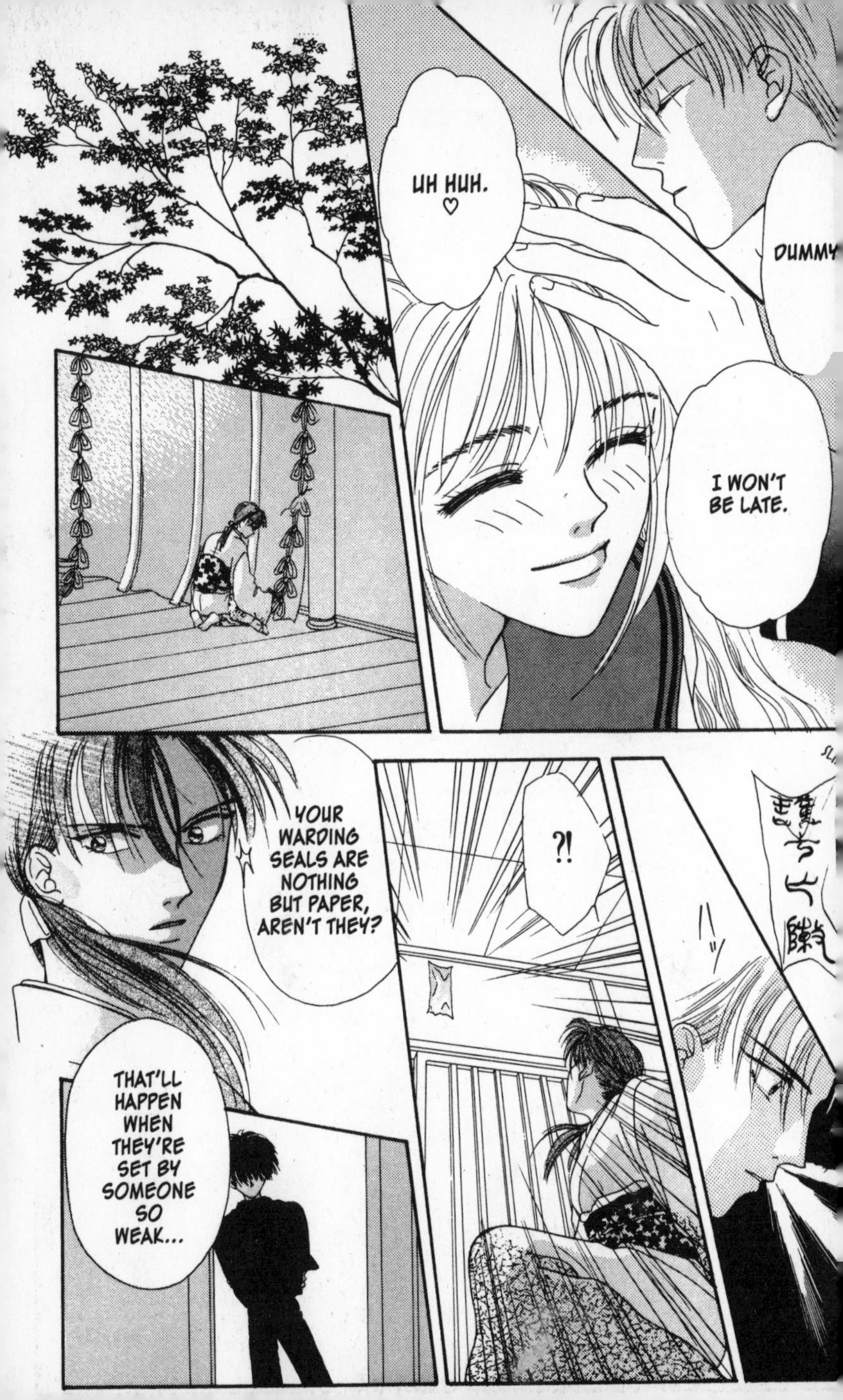
I WON'T BE LATE.
DUMMY
UH HUH. ♡
ハッ
?!
YOUR WARDING SEALS ARE NOTHING BUT PAPER, AREN'T THEY?
THAT'LL HAPPEN WHEN THEY'RE SET BY SOMEONE SO WEAK...

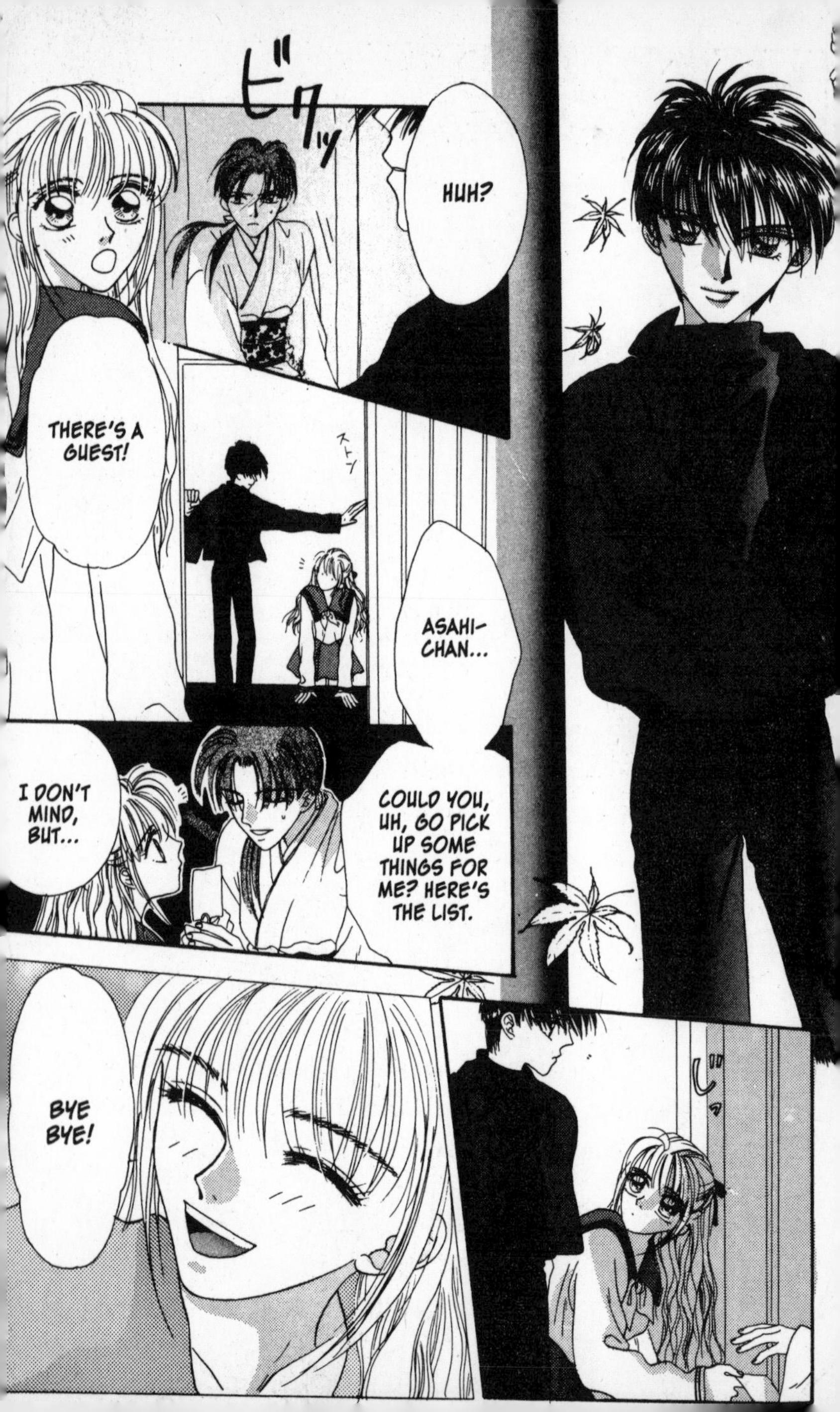

ビクッ
HUH?
THERE'S A GUEST!
ASAHI-CHAN...
COULD YOU, UH, GO PICK UP SOME THINGS FOR ME? HERE'S THE LIST.
I DON'T MIND, BUT...
BYE BYE!

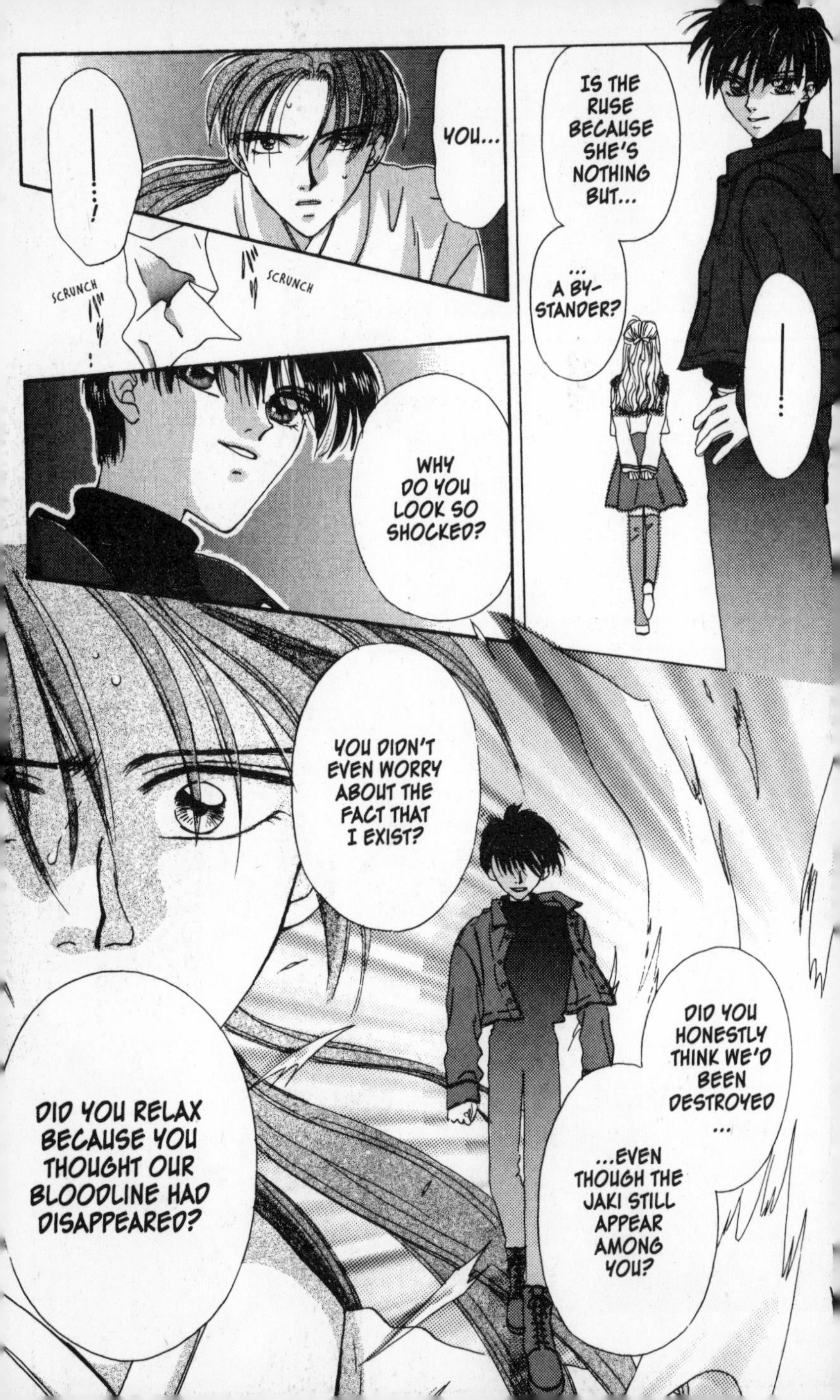
IS THE RUSE BECAUSE SHE'S NOTHING BUT...
...A BY-STANDER?
...!
YOU...
...!
SCRUNCH
SCRUNCH
WHY DO YOU LOOK SO SHOCKED?
YOU DIDN'T EVEN WORRY ABOUT THE FACT THAT I EXIST?
DID YOU HONESTLY THINK WE'D BEEN DESTROYED...
...EVEN THOUGH THE JAKI STILL APPEAR AMONG YOU?
DID YOU RELAX BECAUSE YOU THOUGHT OUR BLOODLINE HAD DISAPPEARED?

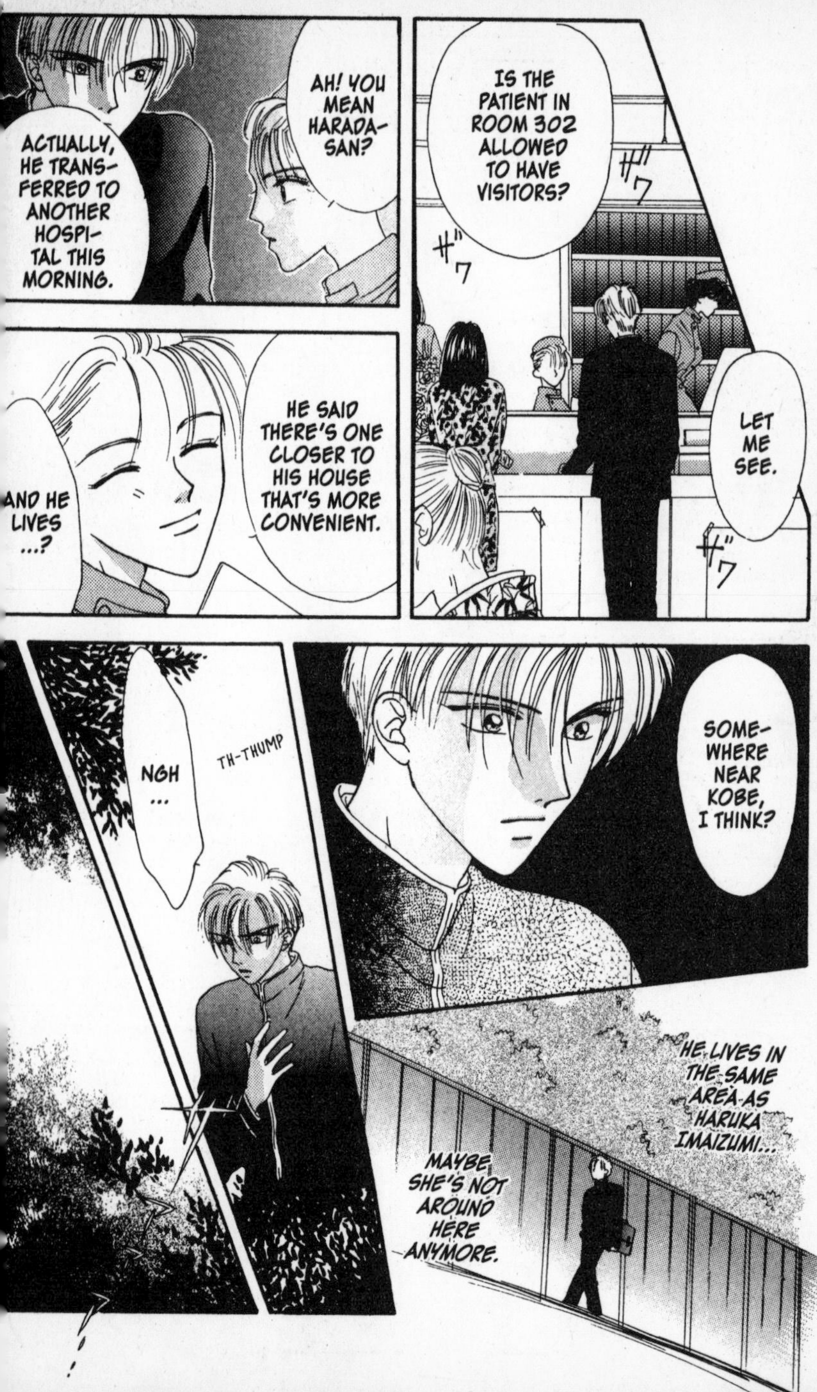

IS THE PATIENT IN ROOM 302 ALLOWED TO HAVE VISITORS?
ザワ
ザワ
LET ME SEE.
ザワ
AH! YOU MEAN HARADA-SAN?
ACTUALLY, HE TRANSFERRED TO ANOTHER HOSPITAL THIS MORNING.
HE SAID THERE'S ONE CLOSER TO HIS HOUSE THAT'S MORE CONVENIENT.
AND HE LIVES ...?
SOMEWHERE NEAR KOBE, I THINK?
HE LIVES IN THE SAME AREA AS HARUKA IMAIZUMI...
MAYBE SHE'S NOT AROUND HERE ANYMORE.
NGH ...
TH-THUMP

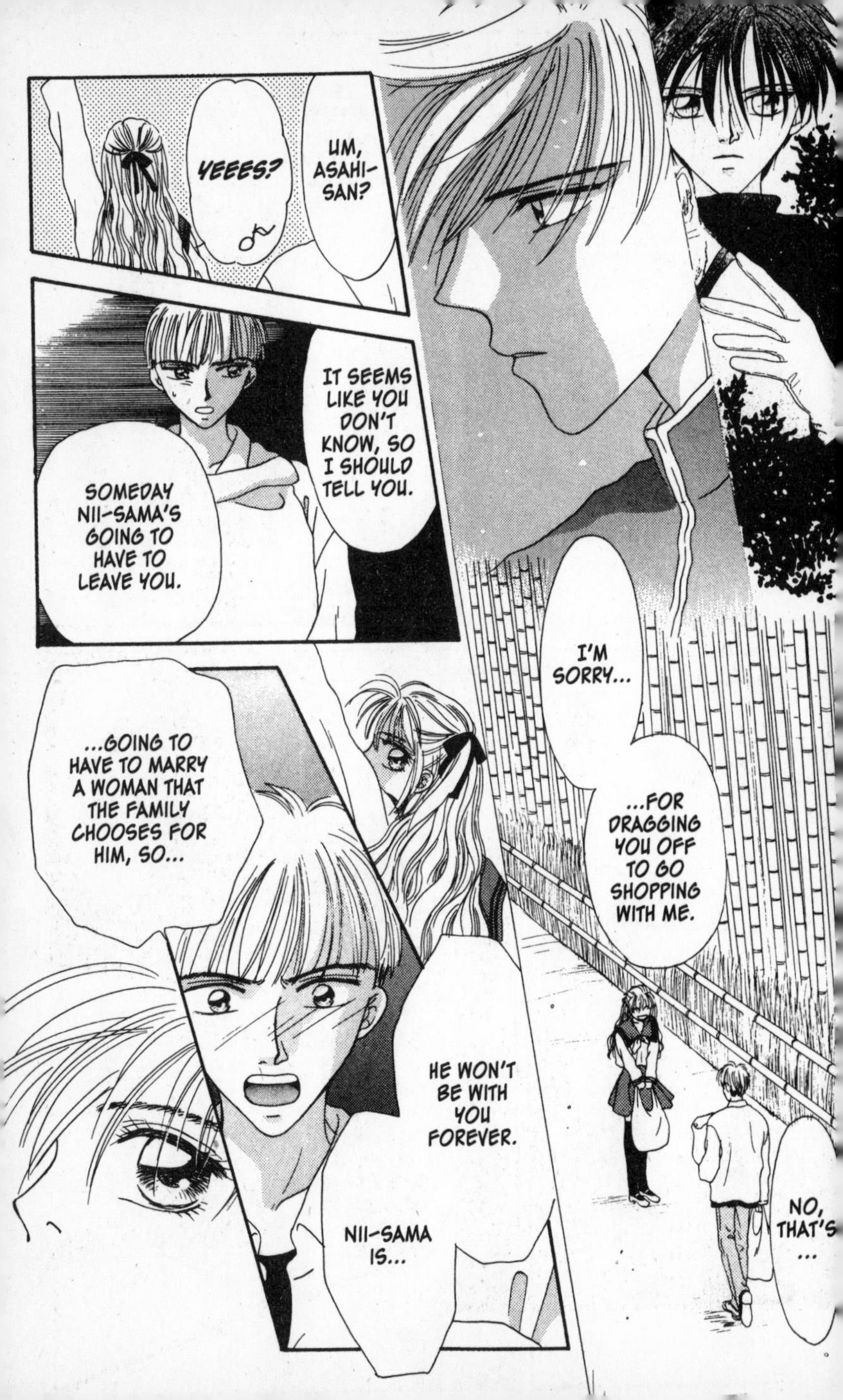
I'M SORRY...
...FOR DRAGGING YOU OFF TO GO SHOPPING WITH ME.
NO, THAT'S ...
UM, ASAHI-SAN?
YEEES?
IT SEEMS LIKE YOU DON'T KNOW, SO I SHOULD TELL YOU.
SOMEDAY NII-SAMA'S GOING TO HAVE TO LEAVE YOU.
NII-SAMA IS...
...GOING TO HAVE TO MARRY A WOMAN THAT THE FAMILY CHOOSES FOR HIM, SO...
HE WON'T BE WITH YOU FOREVER.

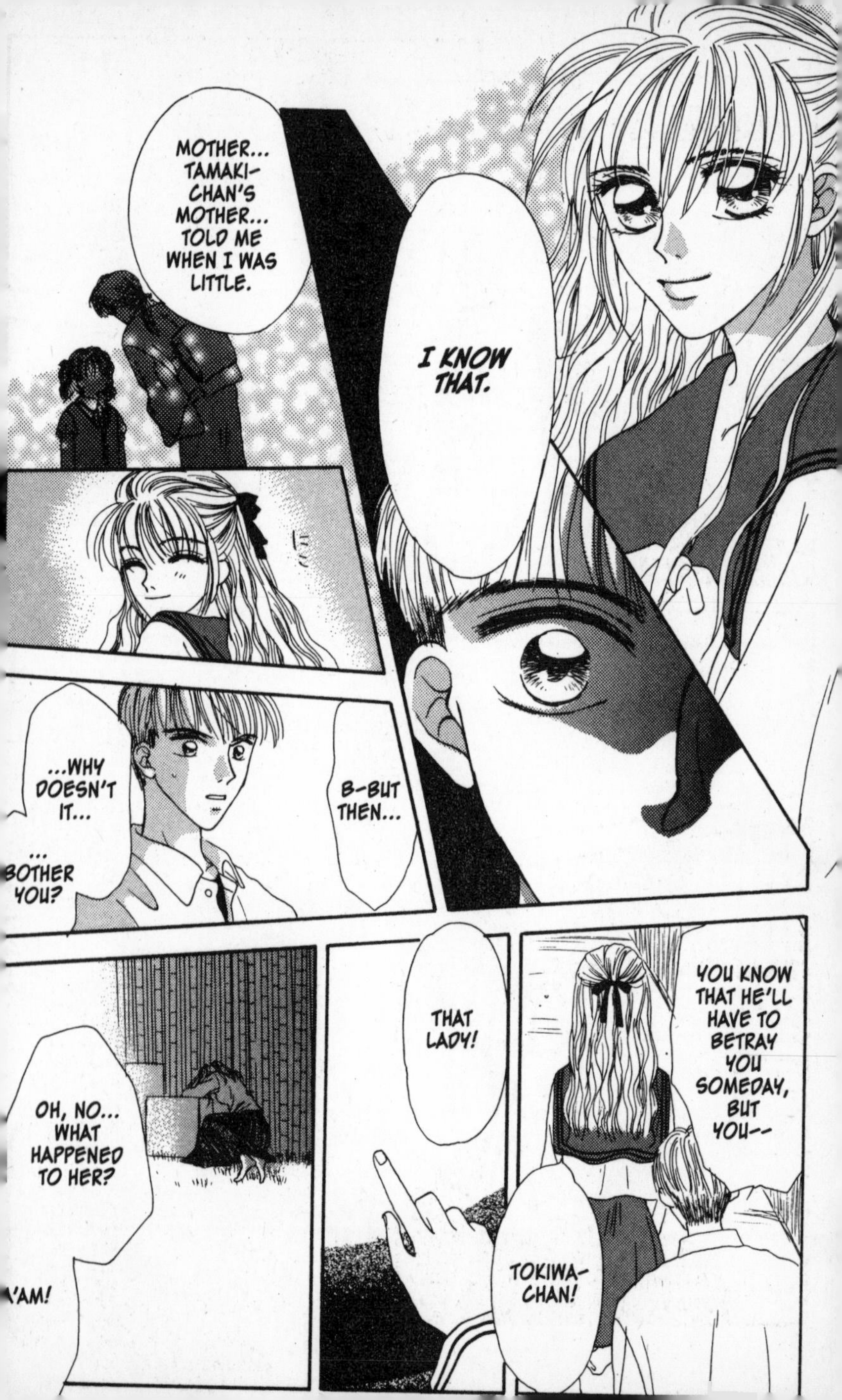

I KNOW THAT.
MOTHER... TAMAKI-CHAN'S MOTHER... TOLD ME WHEN I WAS LITTLE.
B-BUT THEN...
...WHY DOESN'T IT...
...BOTHER YOU?
YOU KNOW THAT HE'LL HAVE TO BETRAY YOU SOMEDAY, BUT YOU--
TOKIWA-CHAN!
THAT LADY!
OH, NO... WHAT HAPPENED TO HER?
'AM!

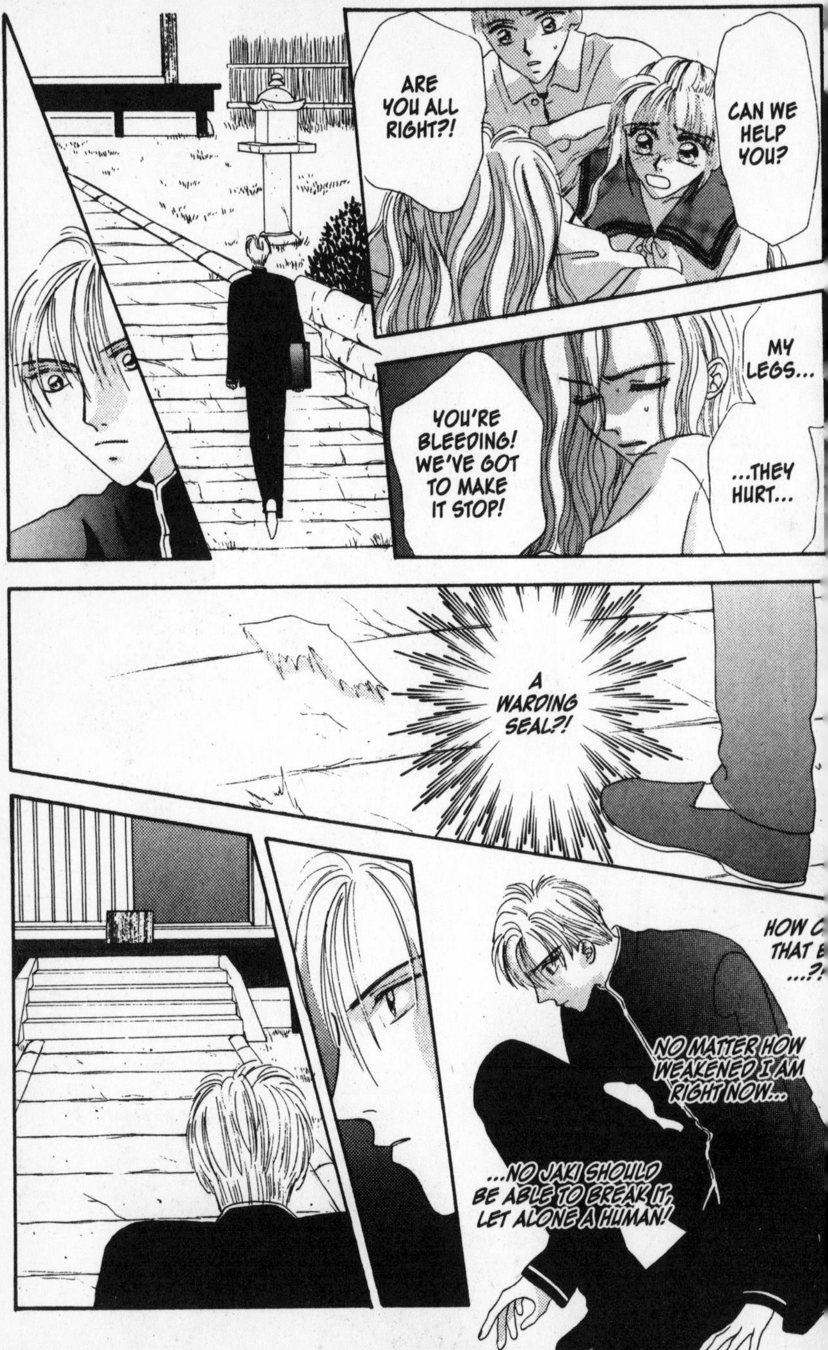
CAN WE HELP YOU?
ARE YOU ALL RIGHT?!
MY LEGS...
...THEY HURT...
YOU'RE BLEEDING! WE'VE GOT TO MAKE IT STOP!
A WARDING SEAL?!
HOW C THAT B ...?!
NO MATTER HOW WEAKENED I AM RIGHT NOW...
...NO JAKI SHOULD BE ABLE TO BREAK IT, LET ALONE A HUMAN!

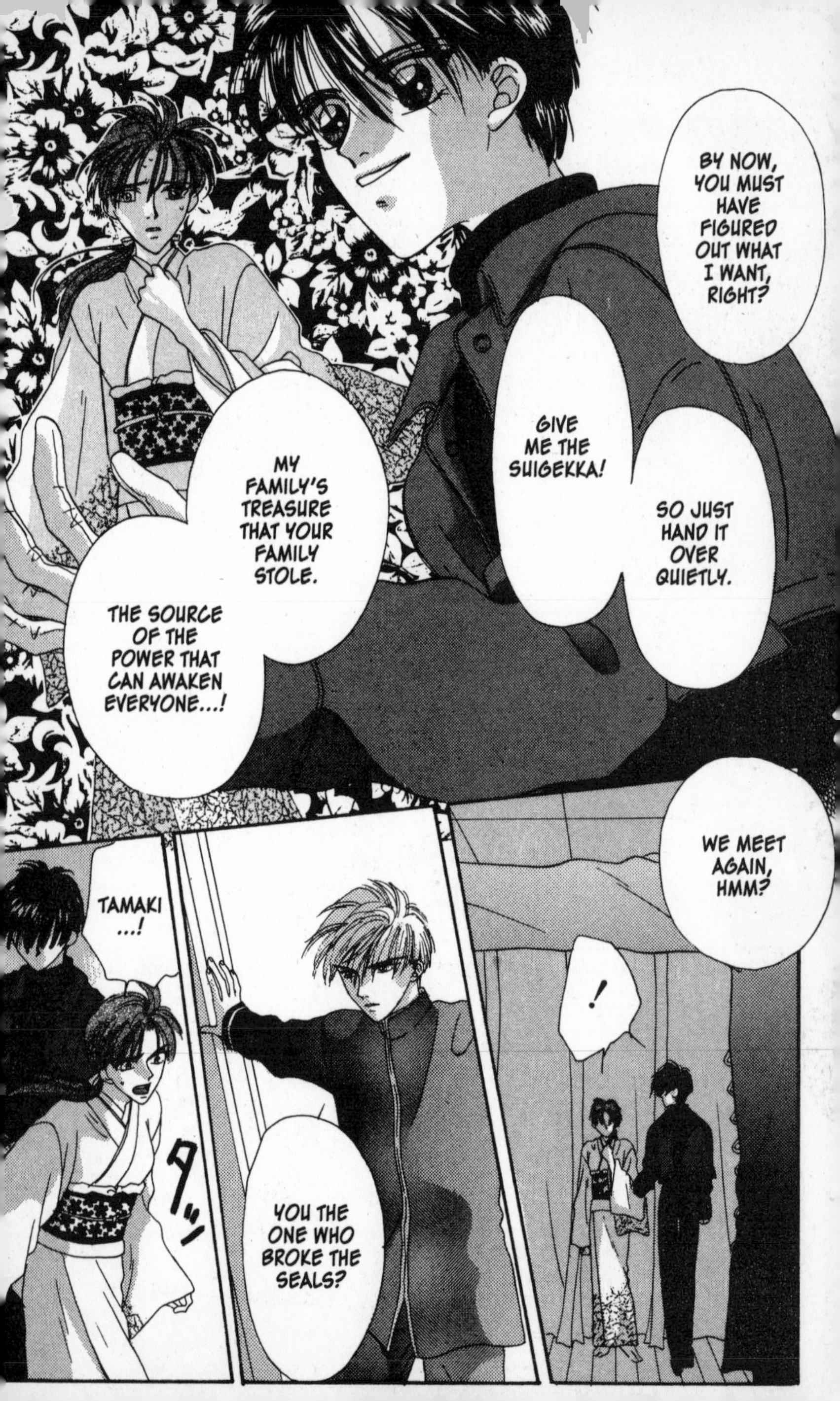
BY NOW, YOU MUST HAVE FIGURED OUT WHAT I WANT, RIGHT?
GIVE ME THE SUIGEKKA!
SO JUST HAND IT OVER QUIETLY.
MY FAMILY'S TREASURE THAT YOUR FAMILY STOLE.
THE SOURCE OF THE POWER THAT CAN AWAKEN EVERYONE...!
WE MEET AGAIN, HMM?
!
YOU THE ONE WHO BROKE THE SEALS?
TAMAKI ...!

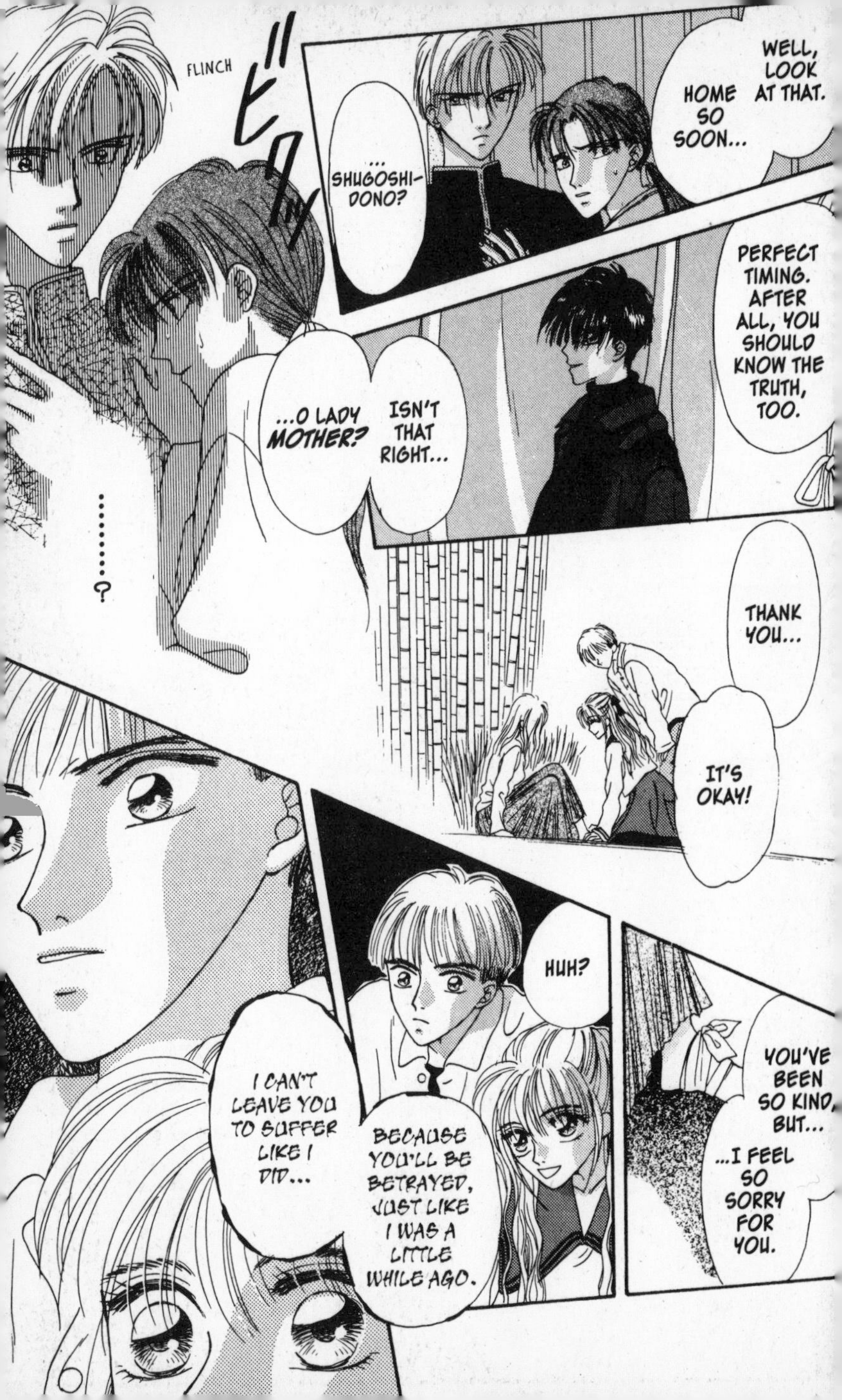

WELL, LOOK AT THAT.
HOME SO SOON...
...SHUGOSHI-DONO?
PERFECT TIMING. AFTER ALL, YOU SHOULD KNOW THE TRUTH, TOO.
ISN'T THAT RIGHT...
...O LADY *MOTHER?*
FLINCH
......?
THANK YOU...
IT'S OKAY!
YOU'VE BEEN SO KIND, BUT...
...I FEEL SO SORRY FOR YOU.
HUH?
BECAUSE YOU'LL BE BETRAYED, JUST LIKE I WAS A LITTLE WHILE AGO.
I CAN'T LEAVE YOU TO SUFFER LIKE I DID...

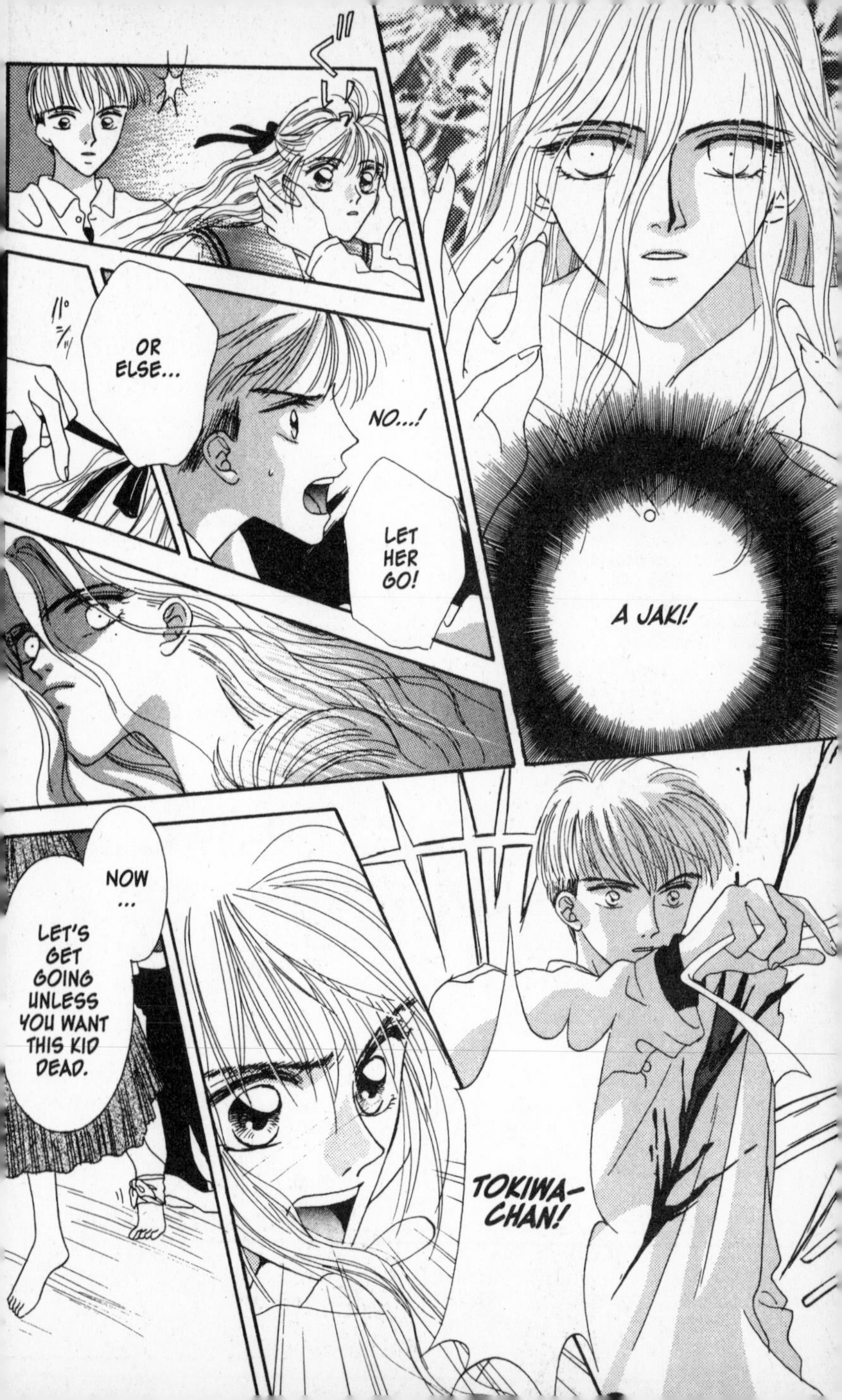

A JAKI!
OR ELSE...
NO...!
LET HER GO!
TOKIWA-CHAN!
NOW ...
LET'S GET GOING UNLESS YOU WANT THIS KID DEAD.

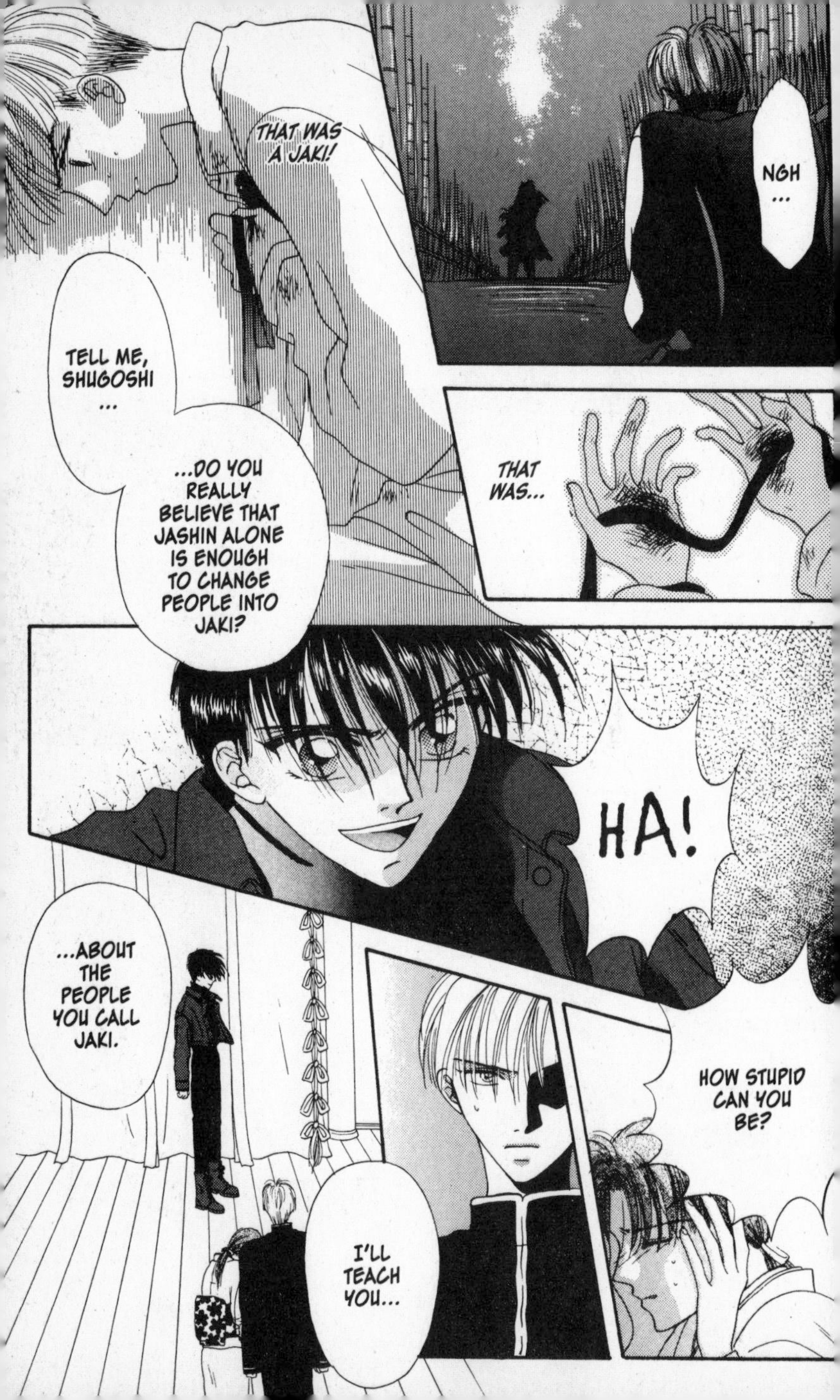
NGH ...
THAT WAS...
THAT WAS A JAKI!
TELL ME, SHUGOSHI ...
...DO YOU REALLY BELIEVE THAT JASHIN ALONE IS ENOUGH TO CHANGE PEOPLE INTO JAKI?
HA!
HOW STUPID CAN YOU BE?
I'LL TEACH YOU...
...ABOUT THE PEOPLE YOU CALL JAKI.

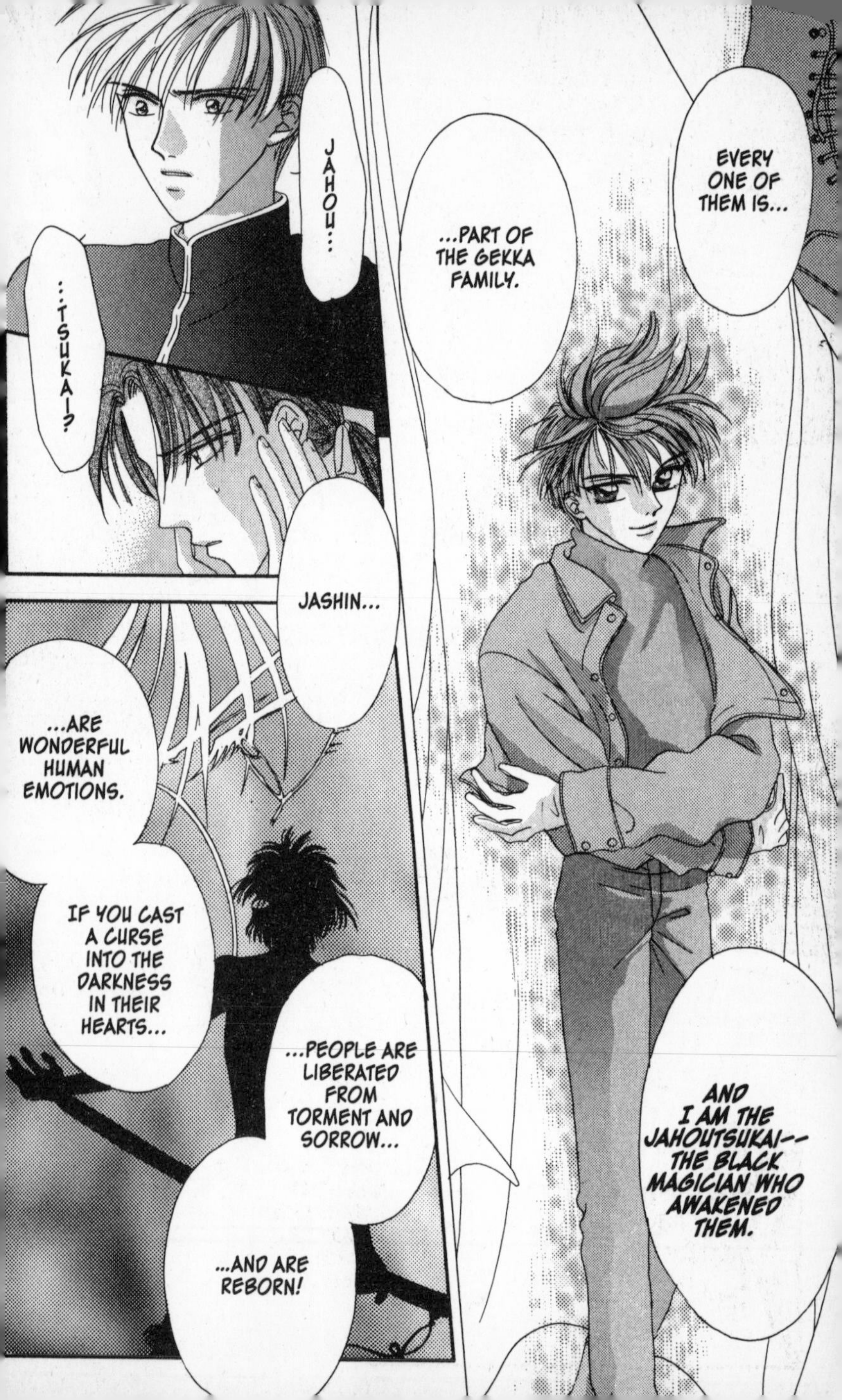
EVERY ONE OF THEM IS...
...PART OF THE GEKKA FAMILY.
AND I AM THE JAHOUTSUKAI-- THE BLACK MAGICIAN WHO AWAKENED THEM.
JAHOU...
...TSUKAI?
JASHIN...
...ARE WONDERFUL HUMAN EMOTIONS.
IF YOU CAST A CURSE INTO THE DARKNESS IN THEIR HEARTS...
...PEOPLE ARE LIBERATED FROM TORMENT AND SORROW...
...AND ARE REBORN!

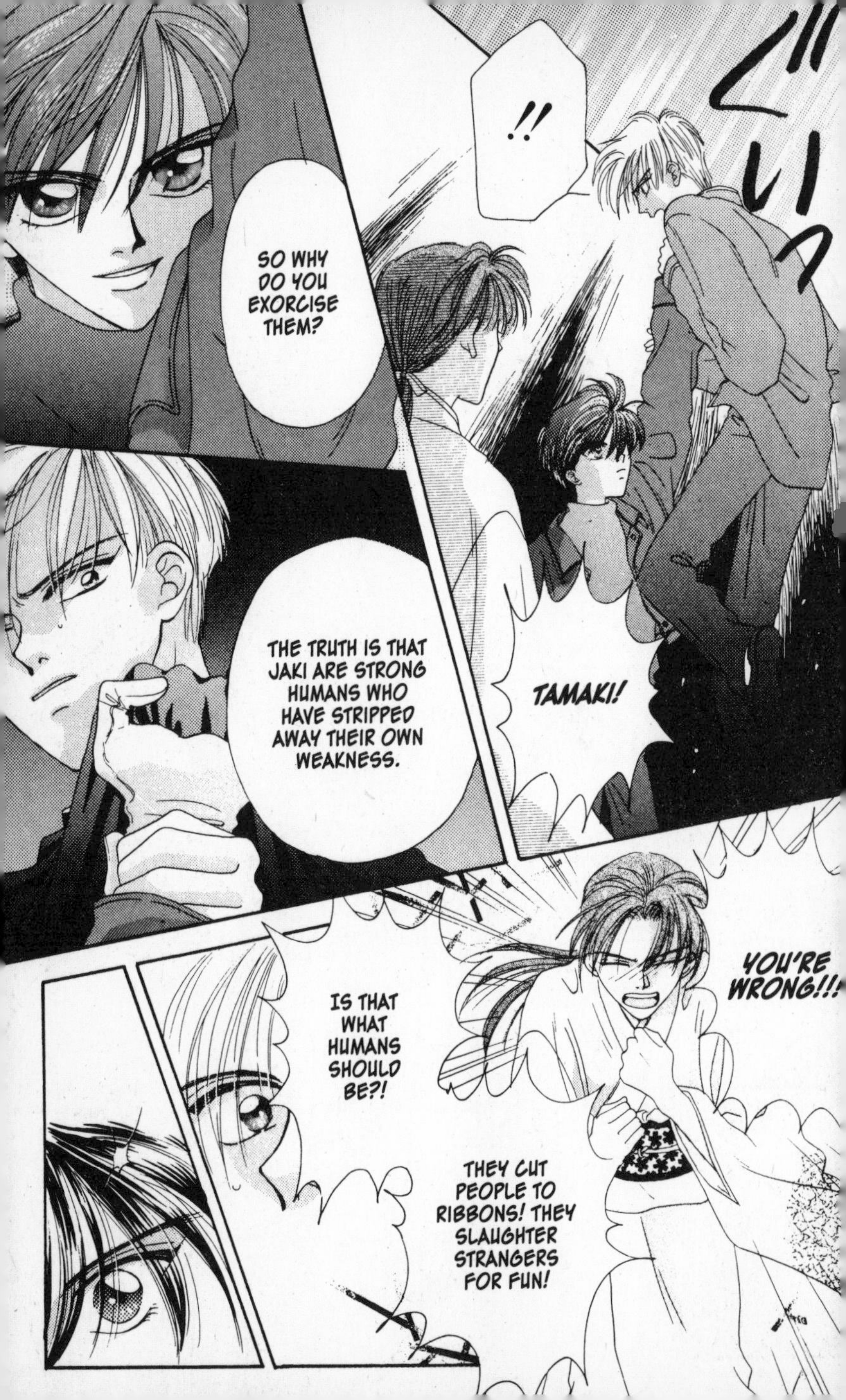
!!
TAMAKI!
SO WHY DO YOU EXORCISE THEM?
THE TRUTH IS THAT JAKI ARE STRONG HUMANS WHO HAVE STRIPPED AWAY THEIR OWN WEAKNESS.
YOU'RE WRONG!!!
IS THAT WHAT HUMANS SHOULD BE?!
THEY CUT PEOPLE TO RIBBONS! THEY SLAUGHTER STRANGERS FOR FUN!

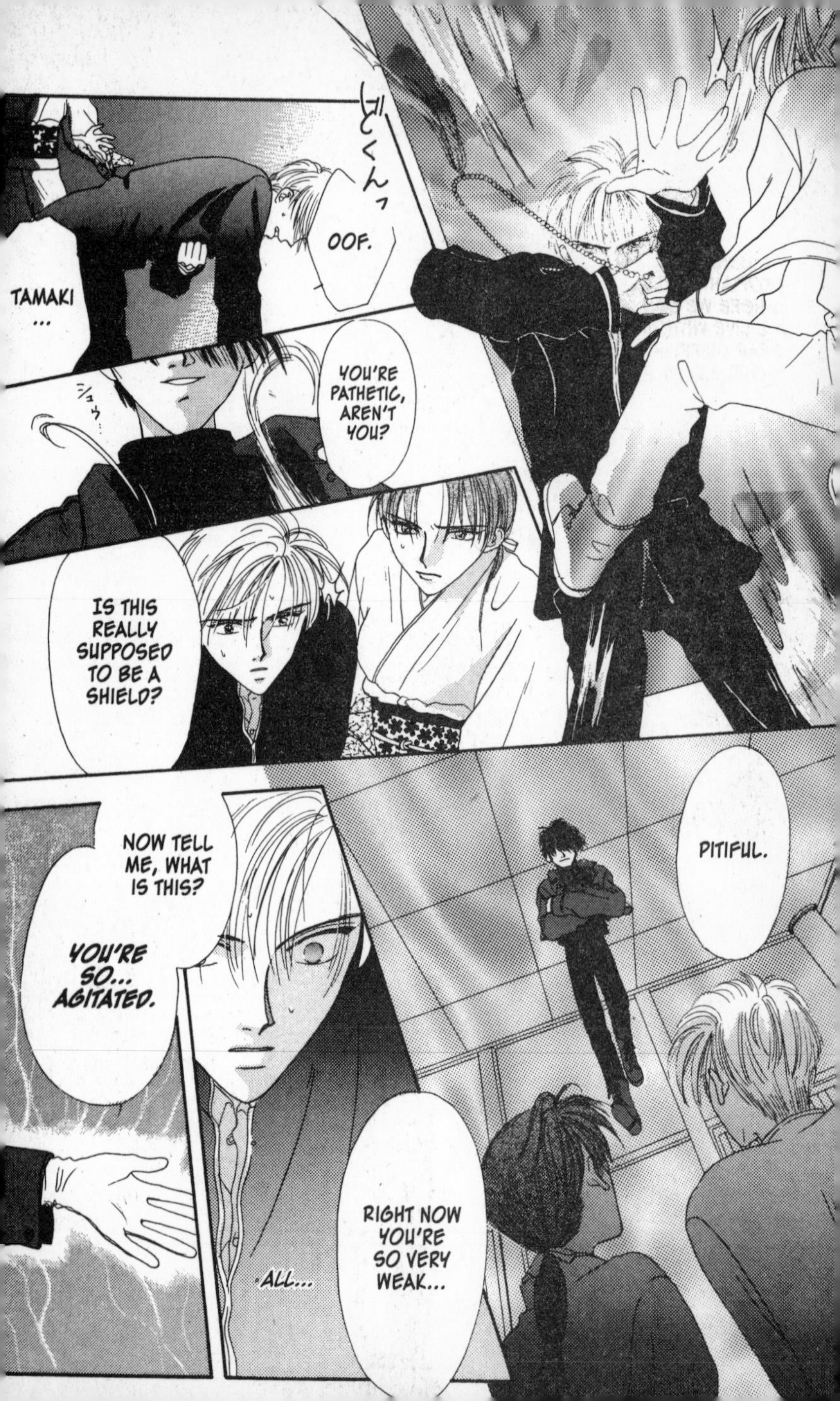
ごしん、
OOF.
TAMAKI ...
YOU'RE PATHETIC, AREN'T YOU?
シュウ…
IS THIS REALLY SUPPOSED TO BE A SHIELD?
PITIFUL.
RIGHT NOW YOU'RE SO VERY WEAK...
NOW TELL ME, WHAT IS THIS?
YOU'RE SO... AGITATED.
ALL...

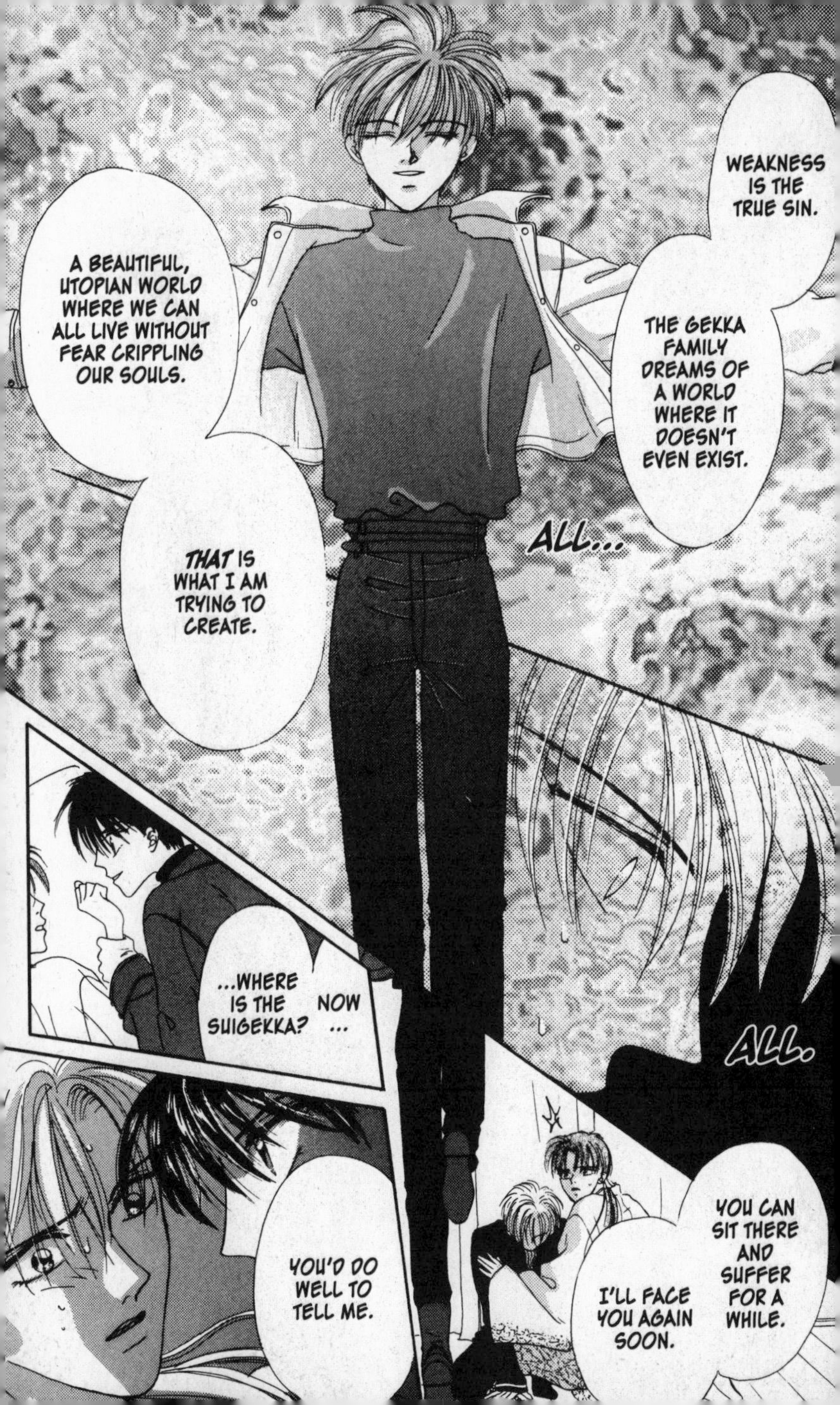
WEAKNESS IS THE TRUE SIN.
THE GEKKA FAMILY DREAMS OF A WORLD WHERE IT DOESN'T EVEN EXIST.
A BEAUTIFUL, UTOPIAN WORLD WHERE WE CAN ALL LIVE WITHOUT FEAR CRIPPLING OUR SOULS.
THAT IS WHAT I AM TRYING TO CREATE.
ALL...
ALL.
NOW ...
...WHERE IS THE SUIGEKKA?
YOU CAN SIT THERE AND SUFFER FOR A WHILE.
I'LL FACE YOU AGAIN SOON.
YOU'D DO WELL TO TELL ME.

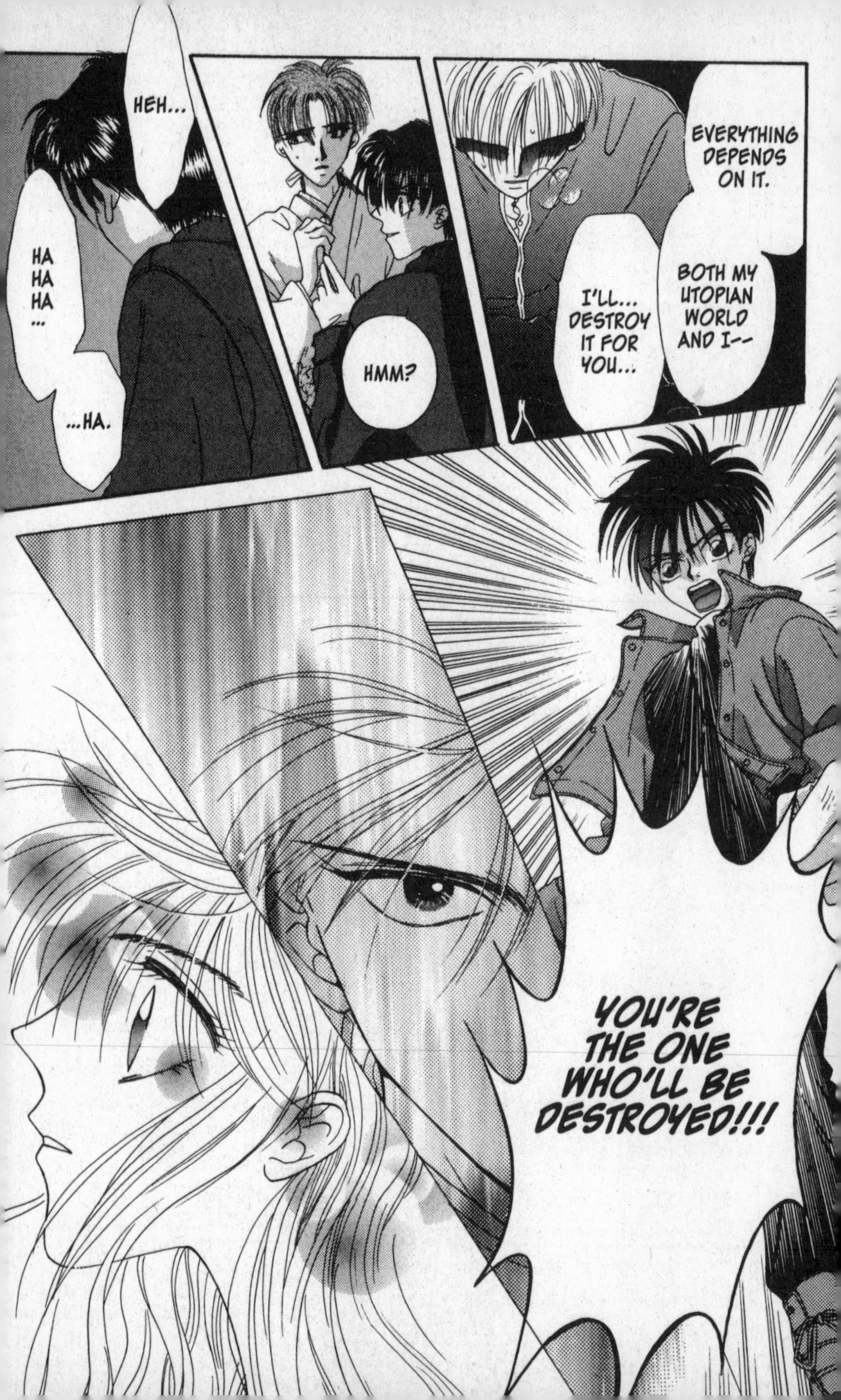
EVERYTHING DEPENDS ON IT.
BOTH MY UTOPIAN WORLD AND I--
I'LL... DESTROY IT FOR YOU...
HMM?
HEH...
HA HA HA ...
...HA.
YOU'RE THE ONE WHO'LL BE DESTROYED!!!

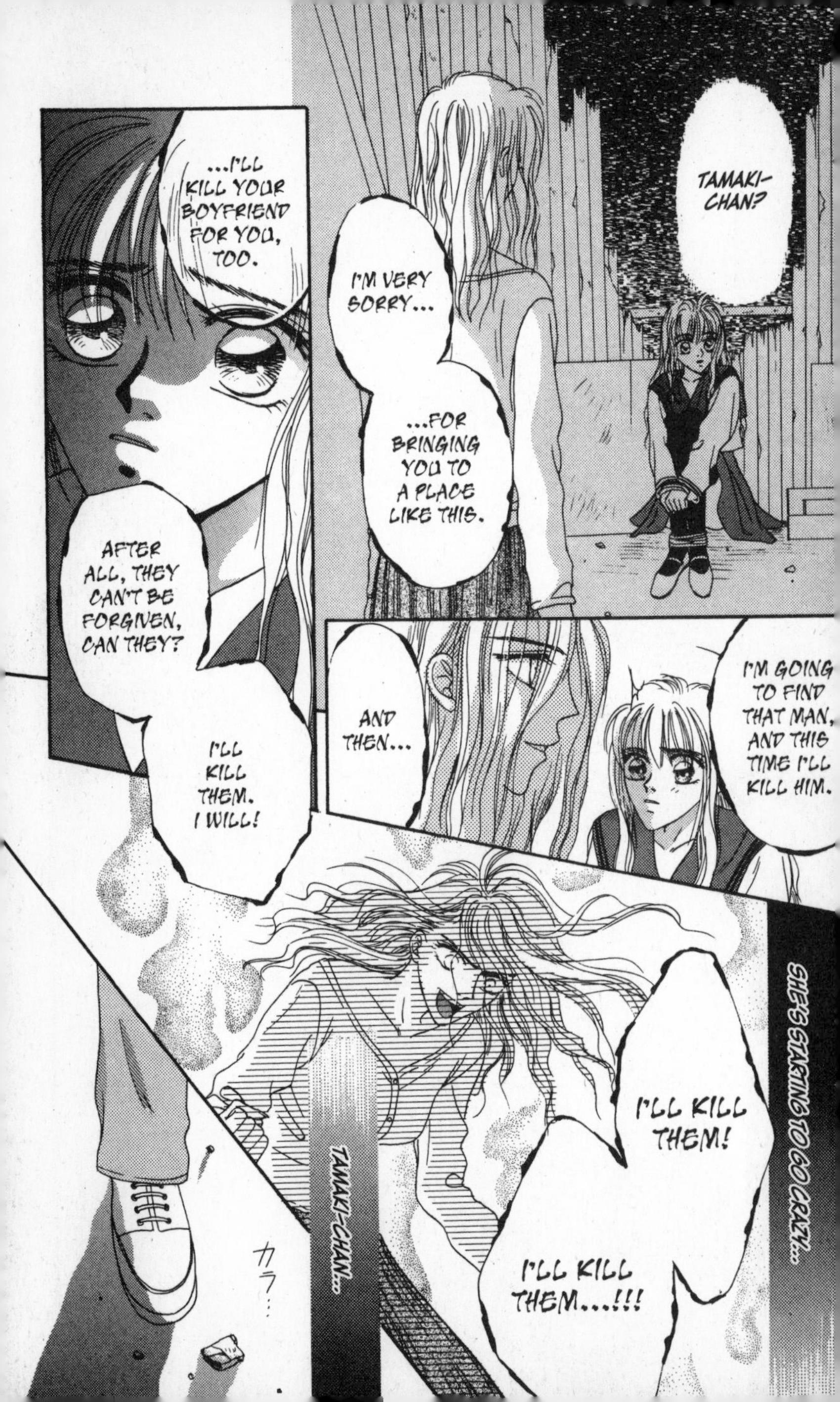
TAMAKI-CHAN?
I'M VERY SORRY...
...FOR BRINGING YOU TO A PLACE LIKE THIS.
I'M GOING TO FIND THAT MAN, AND THIS TIME I'LL KILL HIM.
AND THEN...
...I'LL KILL YOUR BOYFRIEND FOR YOU, TOO.
AFTER ALL, THEY CAN'T BE FORGIVEN, CAN THEY?
I'LL KILL THEM. I WILL!
SHE'S STARTING TO GO CRAZY...
I'LL KILL THEM!
I'LL KILL THEM...!!!
TAMAKI-CHAN...
カラ…

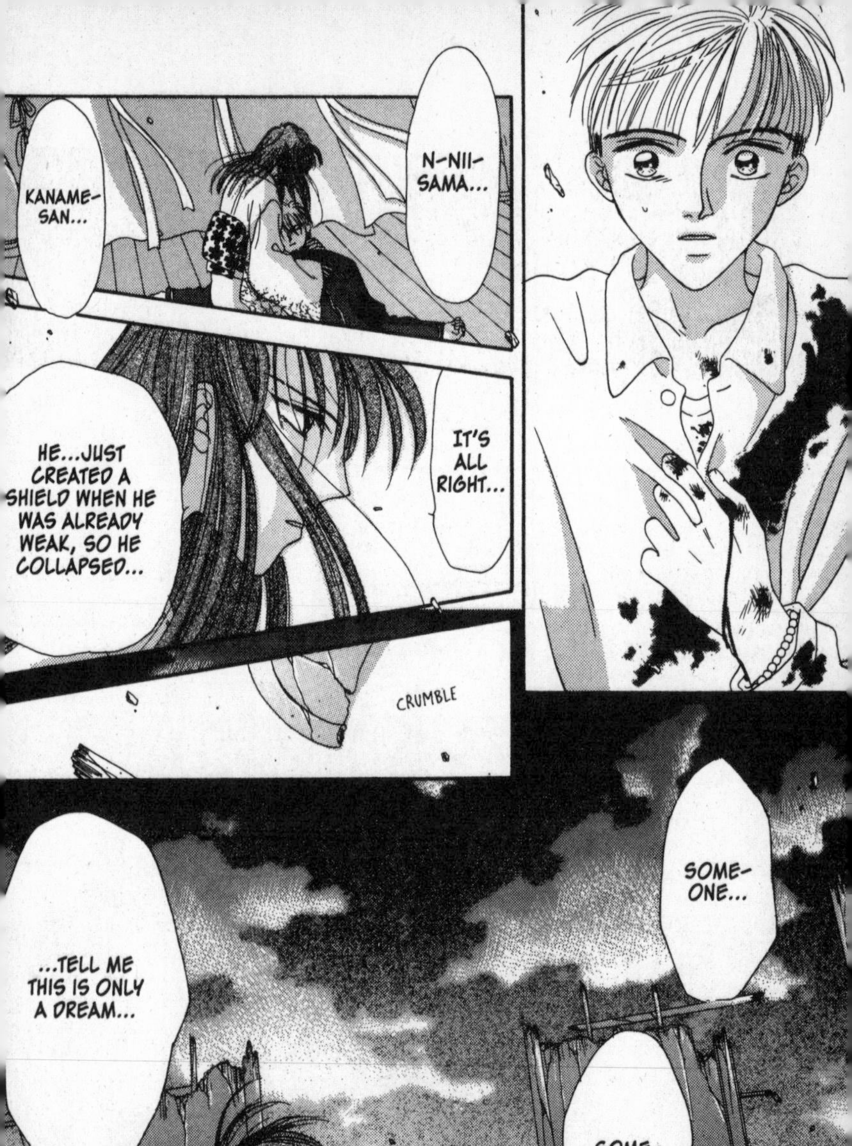
N-NII-SAMA...
KANAME-SAN...
IT'S ALL RIGHT...
HE...JUST CREATED A SHIELD WHEN HE WAS ALREADY WEAK, SO HE COLLAPSED...
CRUMBLE
SOME-ONE...
SOME-ONE...
...TELL ME THIS IS ONLY A DREAM...

PHANTOM DREAM 1 / THE END

REQUEST

ON THE WAY HOME FROM SCHOOL...

...I WAS OVERWHELMED BY DESPAIR.

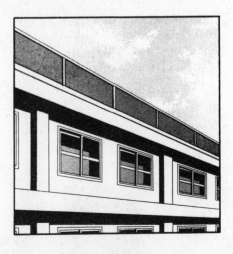

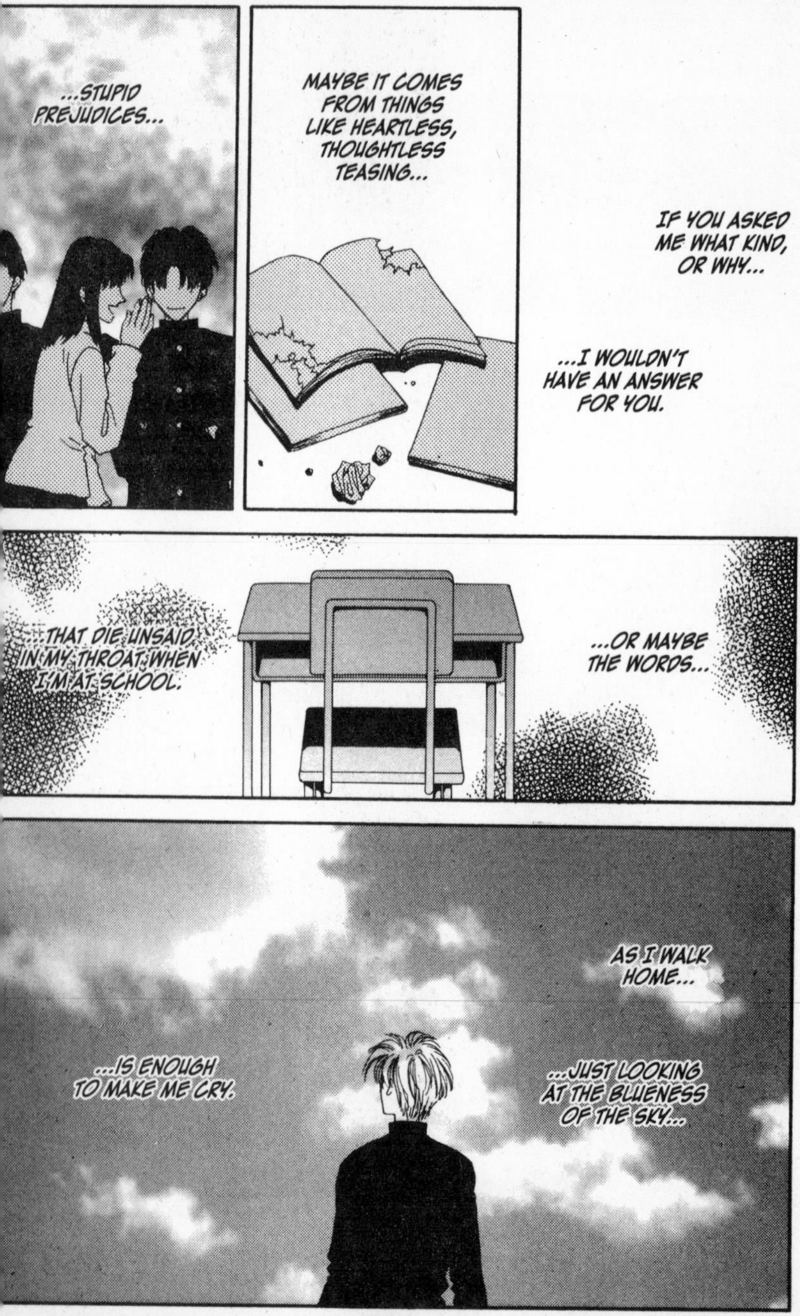
IF YOU ASKED ME WHAT KIND, OR WHY...
...I WOULDN'T HAVE AN ANSWER FOR YOU.
MAYBE IT COMES FROM THINGS LIKE HEARTLESS, THOUGHTLESS TEASING...
...STUPID PREJUDICES...
...OR MAYBE THE WORDS...
...THAT DIE UNSAID IN MY THROAT WHEN I'M AT SCHOOL.
AS I WALK HOME...
...JUST LOOKING AT THE BLUENESS OF THE SKY...
...IS ENOUGH TO MAKE ME CRY.

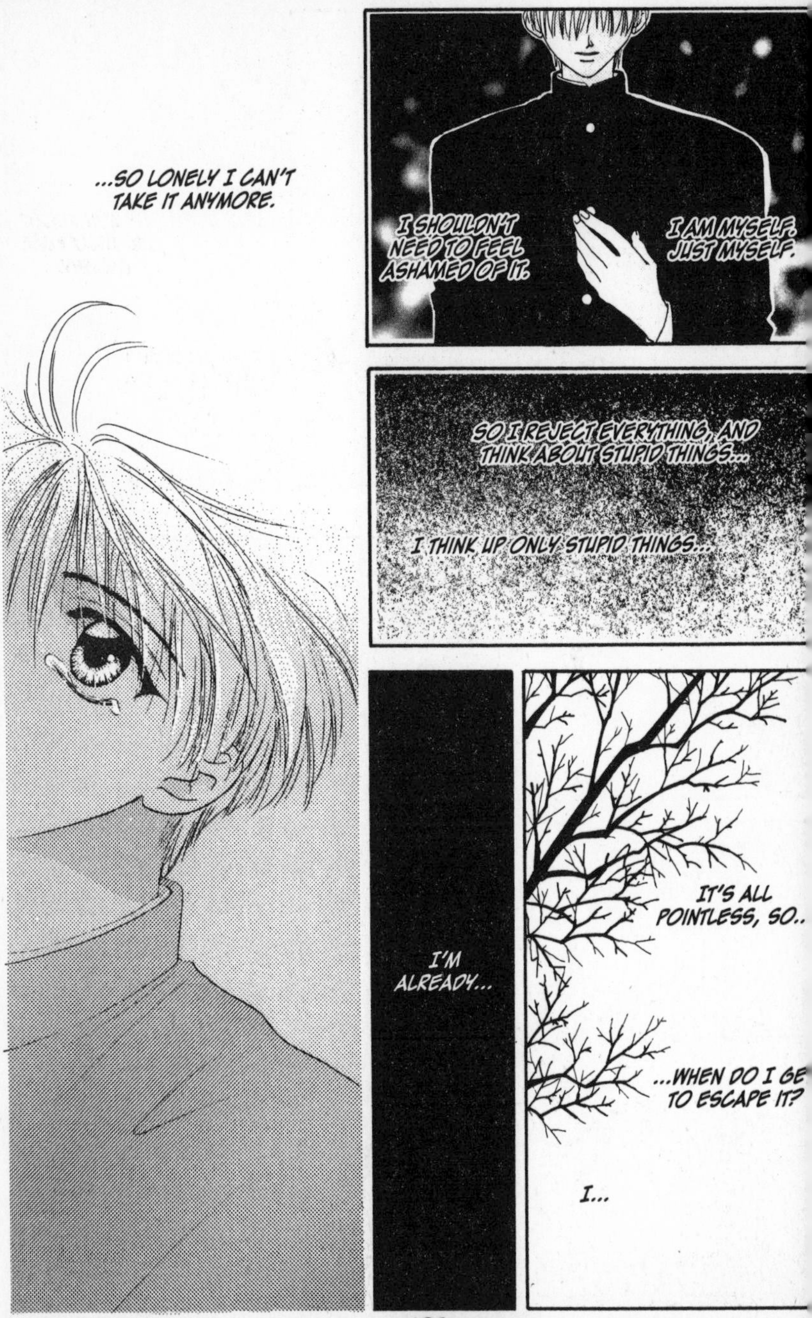

I AM MYSELF. JUST MYSELF.
I SHOULDN'T NEED TO FEEL ASHAMED OF IT.
SO I REJECT EVERYTHING, AND THINK ABOUT STUPID THINGS...
I THINK UP ONLY STUPID THINGS...
IT'S ALL POINTLESS, SO..
...WHEN DO I GE TO ESCAPE IT?
I...
I'M ALREADY...
...SO LONELY I CAN'T TAKE IT ANYMORE.

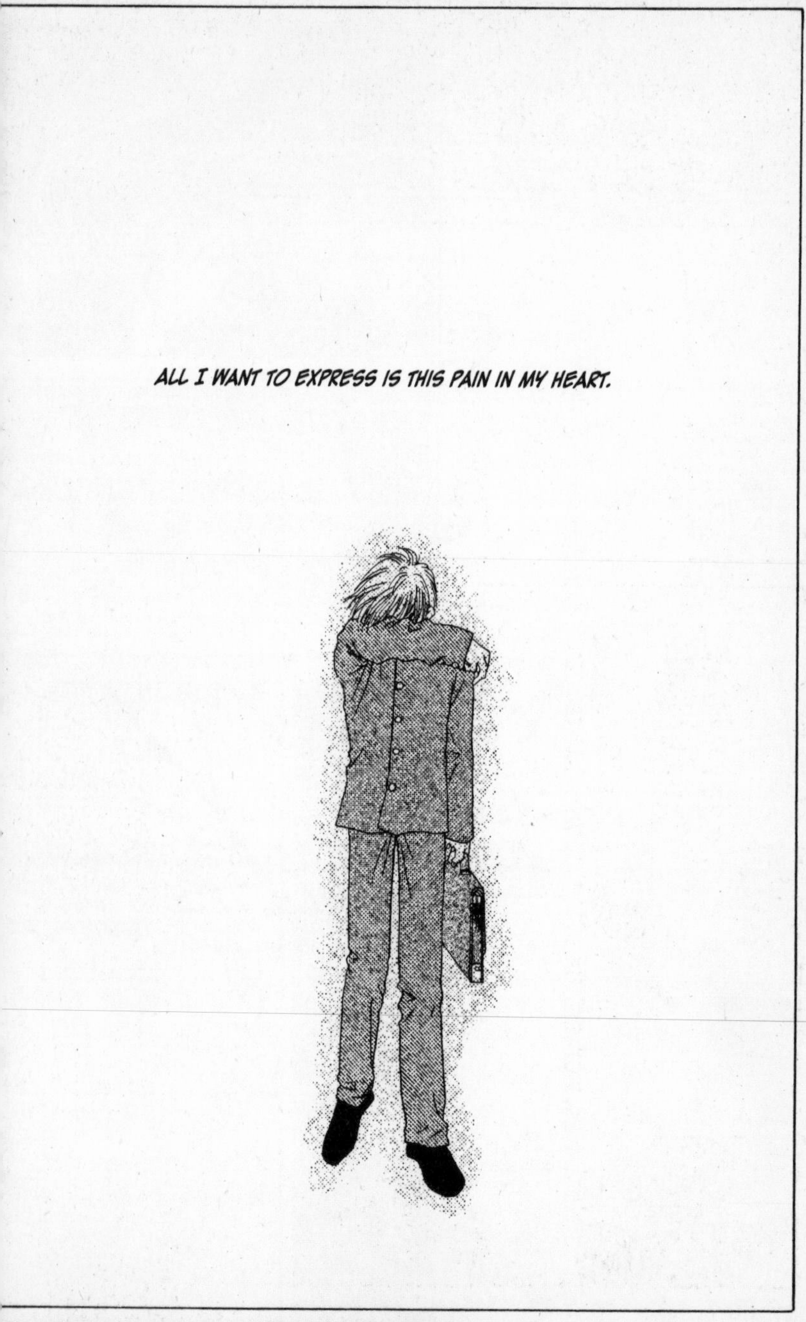
ALL I WANT TO EXPRESS IS THIS PAIN IN MY HEART.

"REQUEST" / THE END

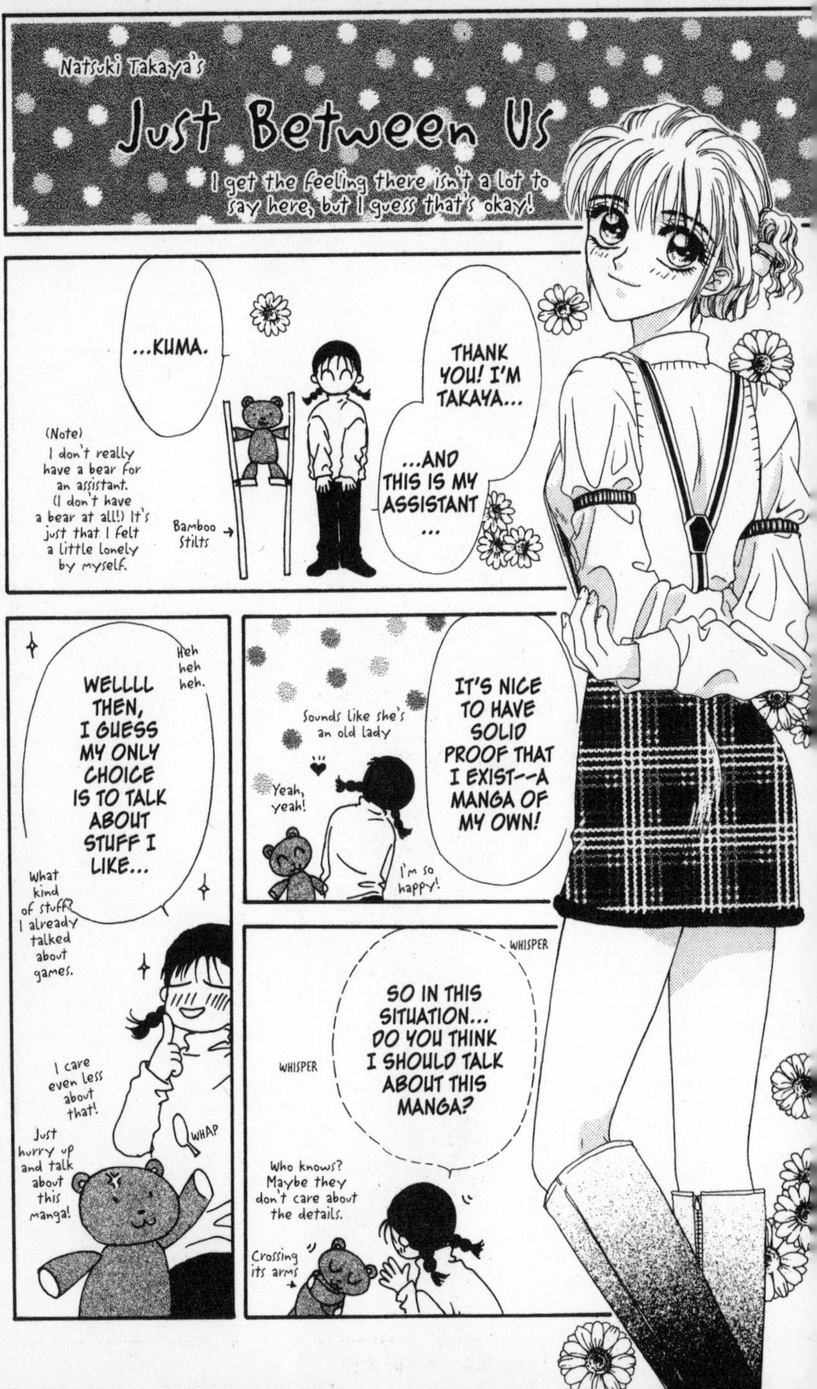
Natsuki Takaya's
Just Between Us
I get the feeling there isn't a lot to say here, but I guess that's okay!
THANK YOU! I'M TAKAYA...
...AND THIS IS MY ASSISTANT ...
...KUMA.
Bamboo stilts
(Note) I don't really have a bear for an assistant. (I don't have a bear at all!) It's just that I felt a little lonely by myself.
IT'S NICE TO HAVE SOLID PROOF THAT I EXIST--A MANGA OF MY OWN!
Sounds like she's an old lady
Yeah, yeah!
I'm so happy!
WHISPER
SO IN THIS SITUATION... DO YOU THINK I SHOULD TALK ABOUT THIS MANGA?
WHISPER
Who knows? Maybe they don't care about the details.
Crossing its arms
Heh heh heh.
WELLLL THEN, I GUESS MY ONLY CHOICE IS TO TALK ABOUT STUFF I LIKE...
What kind of stuff? I already talked about games.
I care even less about that!
WHAP
Just hurry up and talk about this manga!

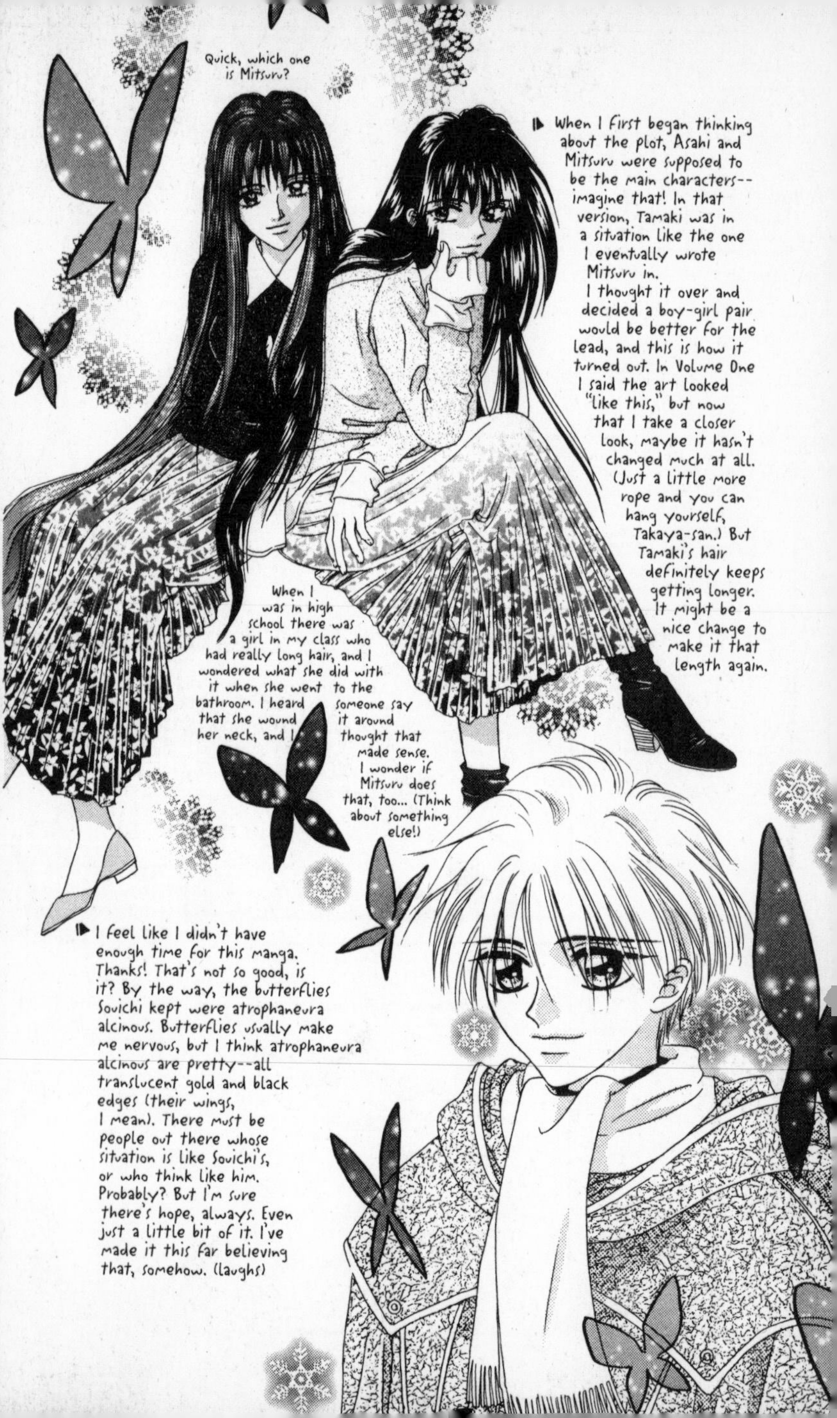

Quick, which one is Mitsuru?

When I first began thinking about the plot, Asahi and Mitsuru were supposed to be the main characters--imagine that! In that version, Tamaki was in a situation like the one I eventually wrote Mitsuru in. I thought it over and decided a boy-girl pair would be better for the lead, and this is how it turned out. In Volume One I said the art looked "like this," but now that I take a closer look, maybe it hasn't changed much at all. (Just a little more rope and you can hang yourself, Takaya-san.) But Tamaki's hair definitely keeps getting longer. It might be a nice change to make it that length again.

When I was in high school there was a girl in my class who had really long hair, and I wondered what she did with it when she went to the bathroom. I heard someone say that she wound it around her neck, and I thought that made sense. I wonder if Mitsuru does that, too... (Think about something else!)

I feel like I didn't have enough time for this manga. Thanks! That's not so good, is it? By the way, the butterflies Souichi kept were atrophaneura alcinous. Butterflies usually make me nervous, but I think atrophaneura alcinous are pretty--all translucent gold and black edges (their wings, I mean). There must be people out there whose situation is like Souichi's, or who think like him. Probably? But I'm sure there's hope, always. Even just a little bit of it. I've made it this far believing that, somehow. (laughs)

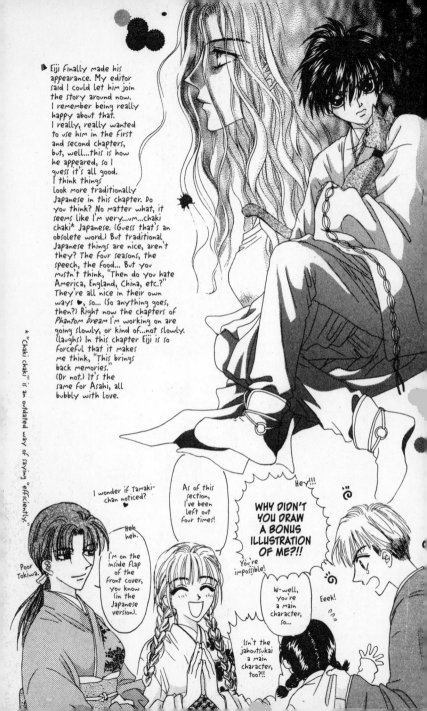

Eiji finally made his appearance. My editor said I could let him join the story around now. I remember being really happy about that. I really, really wanted to use him in the first and second chapters, but, well...this is how he appeared, so I guess it's all good. I think things look more traditionally Japanese in this chapter. Do you think? No matter what, it seems like I'm very...um...chaki chaki* Japanese. (Guess that's an obsolete word.) But traditional Japanese things are nice, aren't they? The four seasons, the speech, the food... But you mustn't think, "Then do you hate America, England, China, etc.?" They're all nice in their own ways ♥, so... (So anything goes, then?) Right now the chapters of *Phantom Dream* I'm working on are going slowly, or kind of...not slowly. (laughs) In this chapter Eiji is so forceful that it makes me think, "This brings back memories." (Or not.) It's the same for Asahi, all bubbly with love.

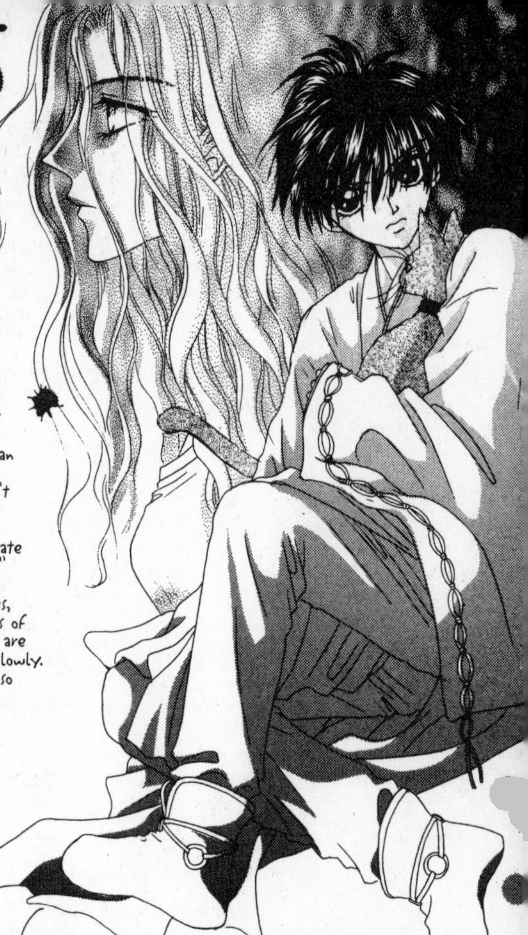

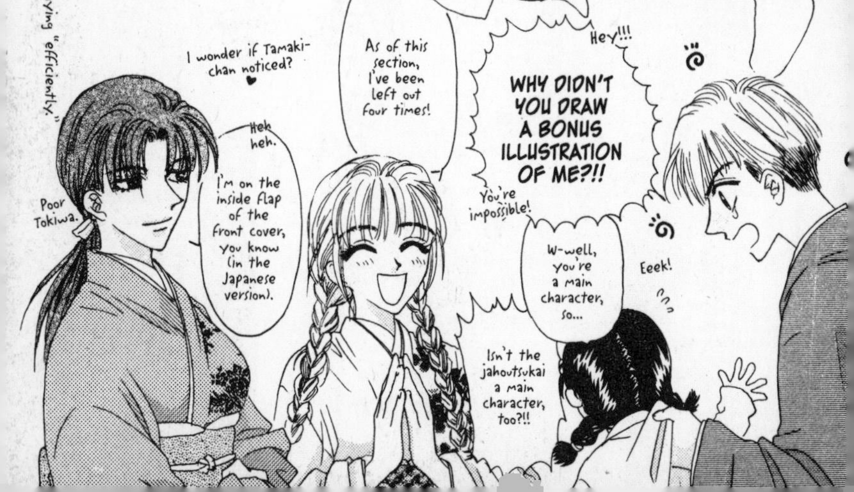
Hey!!!
WHY DIDN'T YOU DRAW A BONUS ILLUSTRATION OF ME?!!
You're impossible!
Eeek!
W-well, you're a main character, so...
Isn't the jahoutsukai a main character, too?!!
As of this section, I've been left out four times!
I wonder if Tamaki-chan noticed? ♥
Heh heh.
I'm on the inside flap of the front cover, you know (in the Japanese version).
Poor Tokiwa.

* "Chaki chaki" is an outdated way of saying "efficiently."

I'm so grateful to everyone!

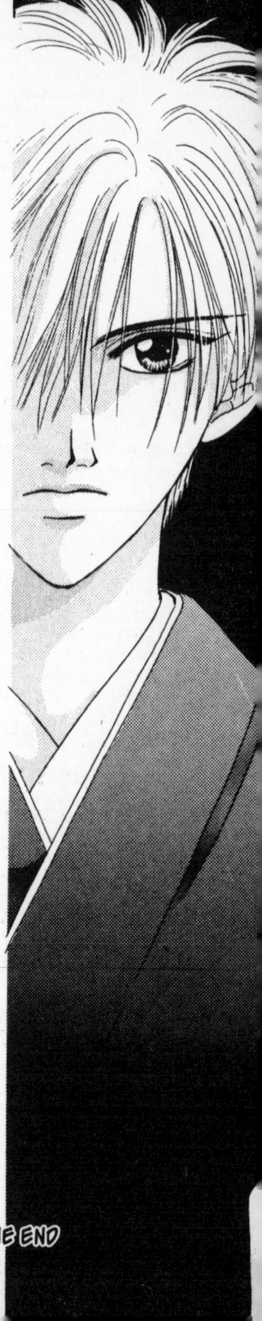

And at the very end, shouldn't I make sure to tell everyone how thankful I am, and name everyone who's supported me? Of course! And so...

My father and mother never once opposed my dream to create manga. In fact, they cheered me on.

My sister let me borrow her name, and gave me the chance to become a manga creator.

My first editor, Tanaka-sama, made me suffer a little because I'm slow to catch on; she probably wanted to give me a hard time to get me on the right path.

Takada-sama, my current editor, helps with the crucial lines of this manga series. (laughs)

My friends, Akitoshi-sama, Mai-sama and Fujisaki-sama, still like me even though I talk and act pretty strangely--just for starters, there's my "_pi_ta Would Be Okay In Outer Space, Too" theory.

And then there's Hotoda-sama, Ogawa-sama and Murase-sama.

I'm sorry I couldn't answer all of your letters.
And Tama-chan, I'm sorry I didn't send you a manga.

And then, of course...

The people who read *Phantom Dream*. ♥
The people who always read my work. ♥
The people who take the time to send me letters. ♥
Everyone, thank you so much! Mwah! ♥

Please treat me kindly in the future, too! (bows) I created this story slowly, complaining non-stop, but I hope you liked it at least a little! Was it totally no good? I hope not--I don't want that to happen. (laughs) Well, then, I'll bid you farewell. See you another time!

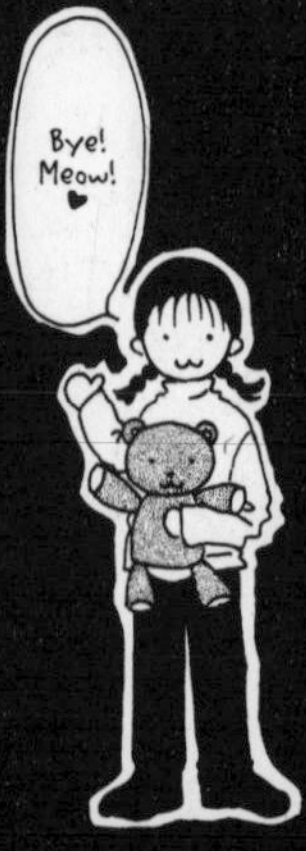
Bye! Meow! ♥

This was Natsuki Takaya.

NATSUKI TAKAYA'S "JUST BETWEEN US" / THE END

IN THE NEXT VOLUME OF

Phantom Dream

THE JAHOUTSUKAI RETURNS TO COLLECT THE
SUIGEKKA--THE DEMON SWORD TAMAKI'S
FAMILY STOLE FROM THE GEKKA FAMILY
TO PREVENT THEM FROM ACQUIRING MORE
POWER. HE ALSO REVEALS SOME DEVASTATING
FAMILY SECRETS TO TAMAKI, WHICH LEAVES
THE YOUNG MONSHU IN SUCH SHOCK THAT HE
DOESN'T EVEN NOTICE ASAHI SLIPPING AWAY
AND HEADING TOWARD THE GEKKA MANSION...

TOKYOPOP MANGA PREVIEW

Fruits Basket

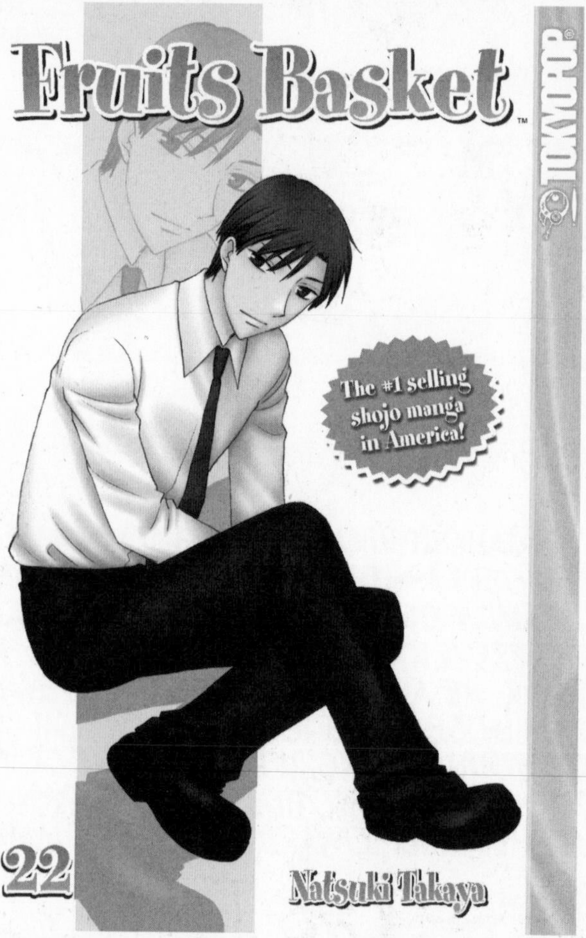
Fruits Basket™
TOKYOPOP®
The #1 selling shojo manga in America!
22
Natsuki Takaya

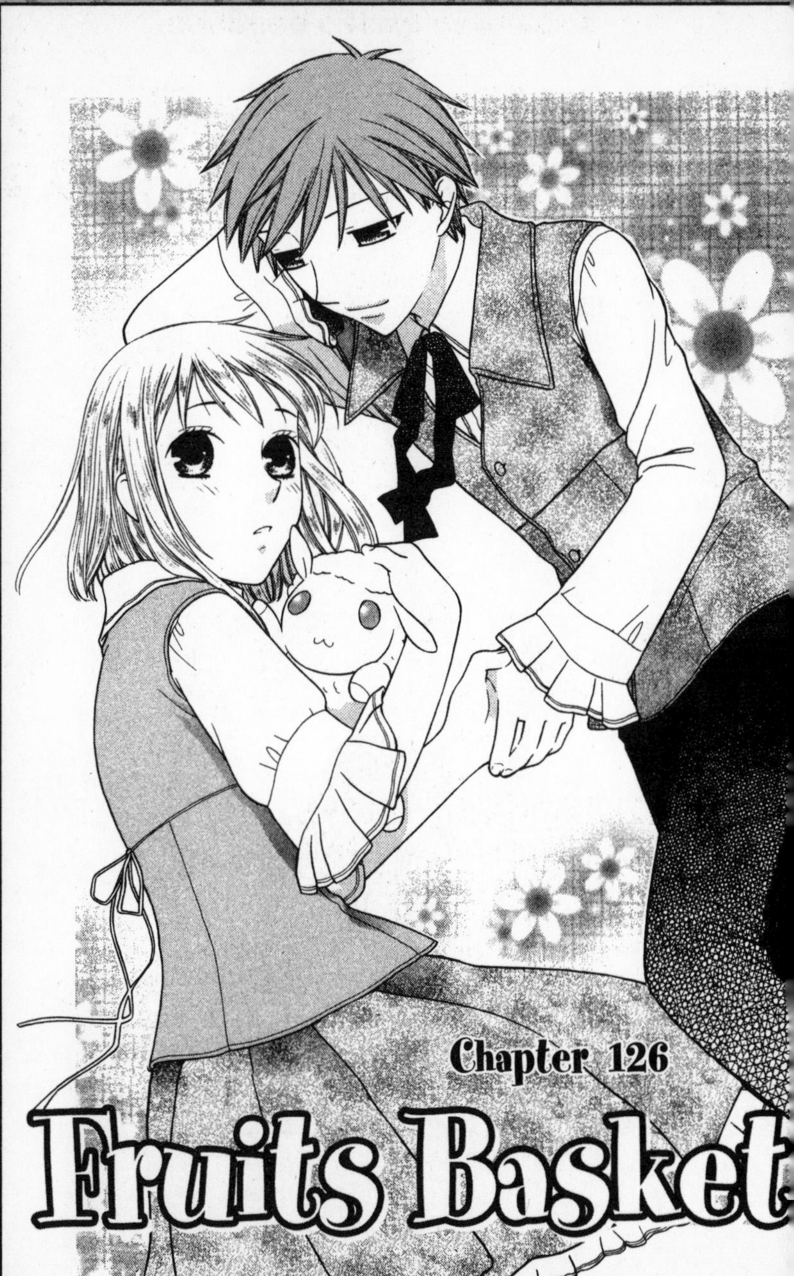
Chapter 126
Fruits Basket

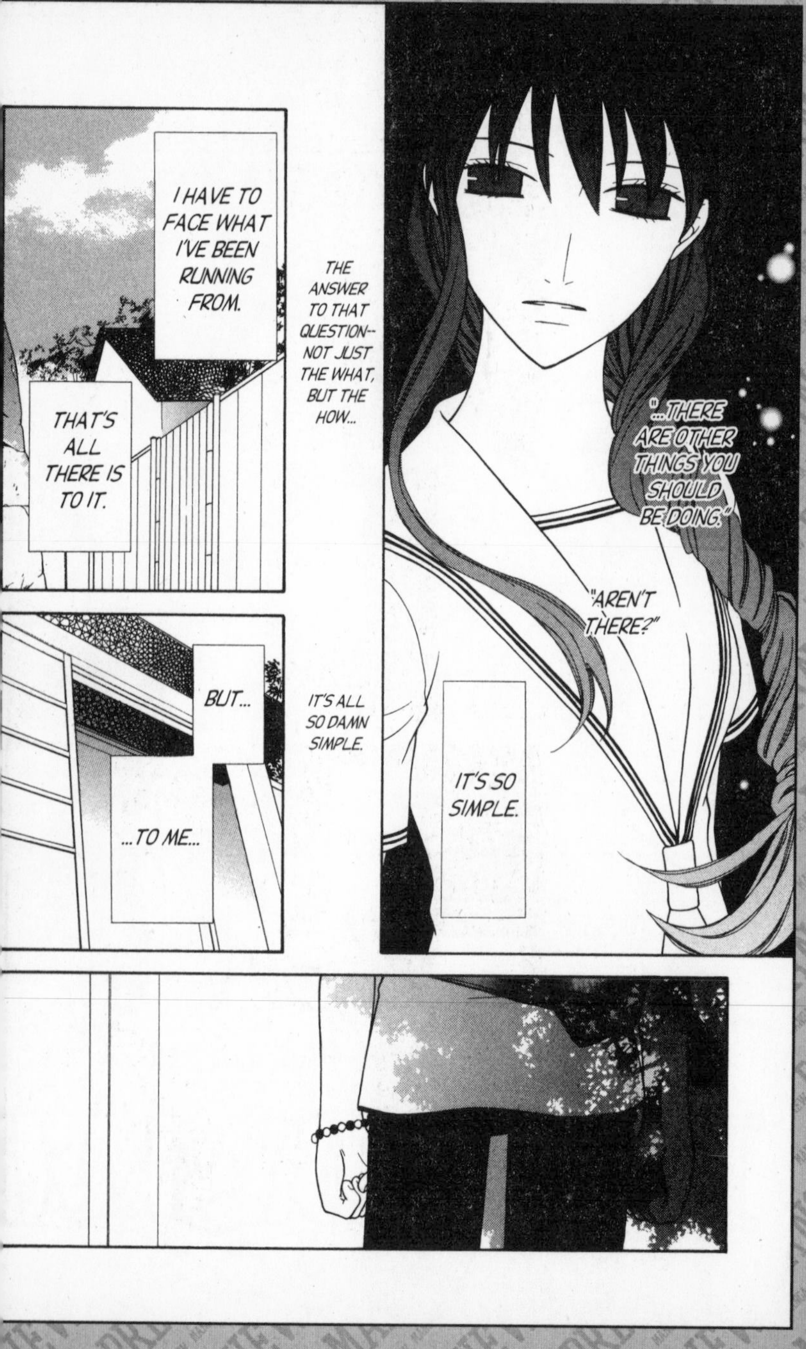
"...THERE ARE OTHER THINGS YOU SHOULD BE DOING."
"AREN'T THERE?"
IT'S SO SIMPLE.
THE ANSWER TO THAT QUESTION-- NOT JUST THE WHAT, BUT THE HOW...
I HAVE TO FACE WHAT I'VE BEEN RUNNING FROM.
THAT'S ALL THERE IS TO IT.
IT'S ALL SO DAMN SIMPLE.
BUT...
...TO ME...

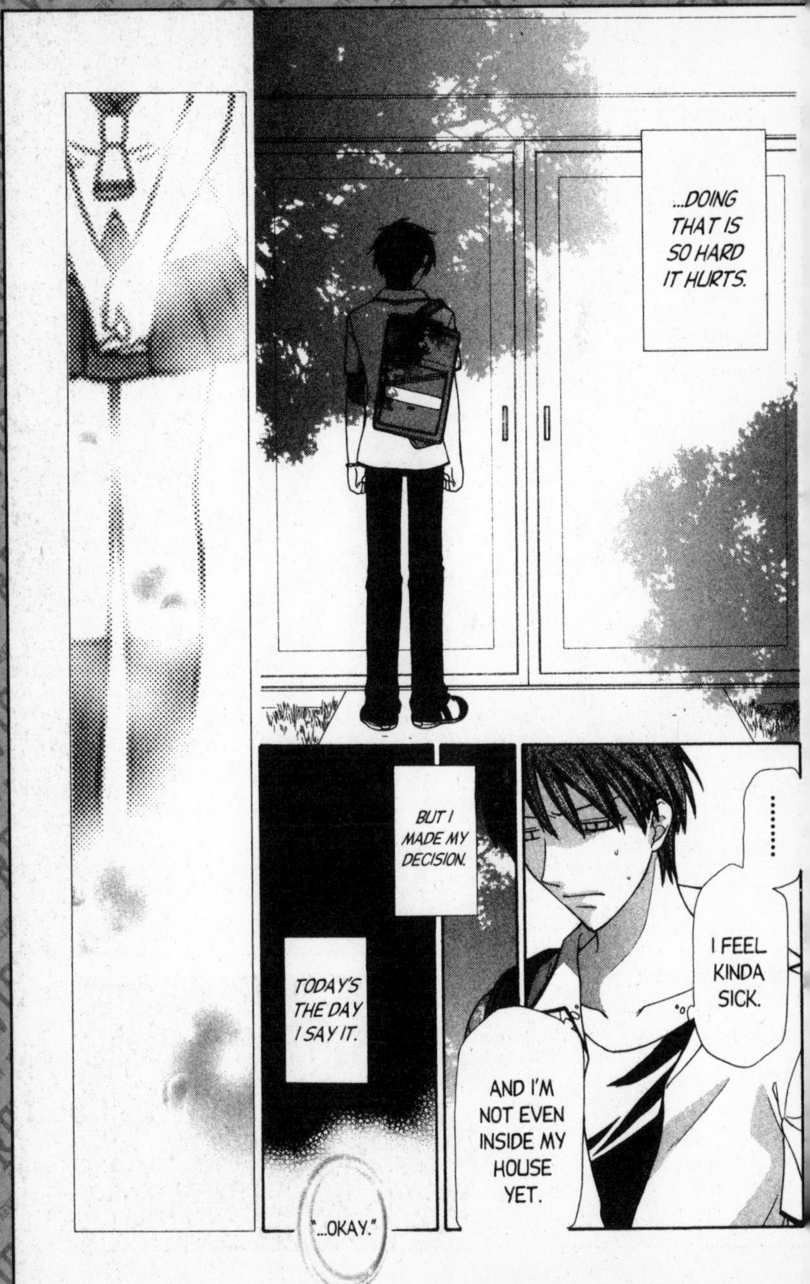
...DOING THAT IS SO HARD IT HURTS.
......
I FEEL KINDA SICK.
AND I'M NOT EVEN INSIDE MY HOUSE YET.
BUT I MADE MY DECISION.
TODAY'S THE DAY I SAY IT.
"...OKAY."

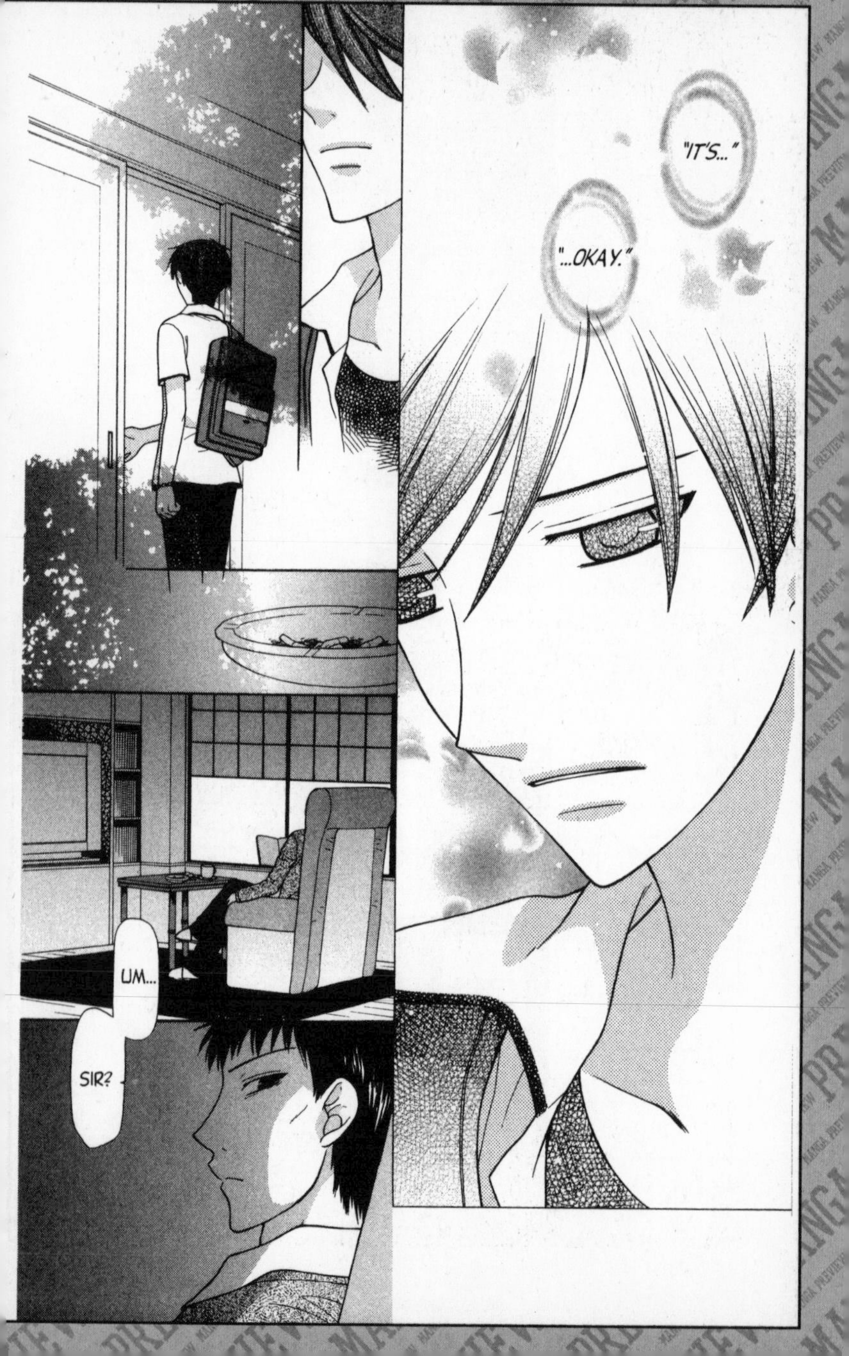
"IT'S..."
"...OKAY."
UM...
SIR?

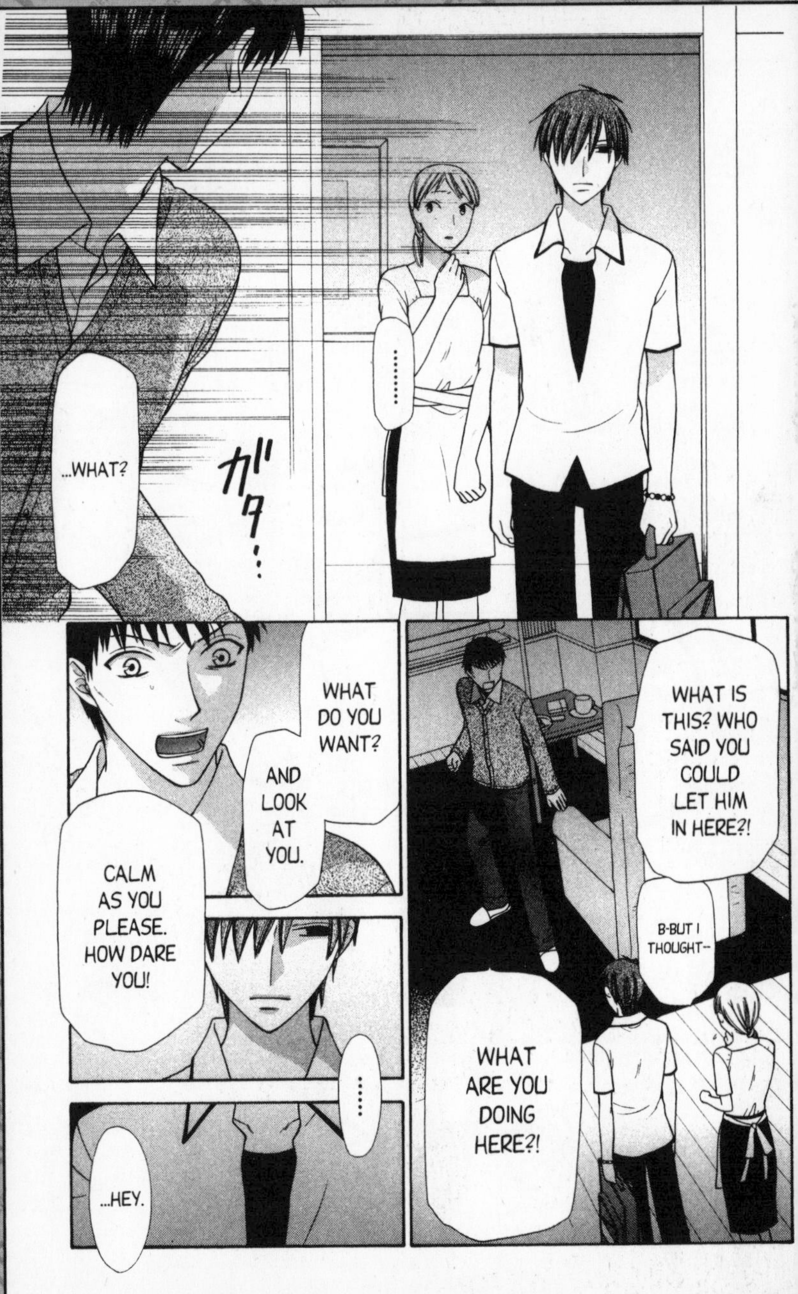
......
ガタ
...WHAT?
WHAT IS THIS? WHO SAID YOU COULD LET HIM IN HERE?!
B-BUT I THOUGHT--
WHAT ARE YOU DOING HERE?!
WHAT DO YOU WANT?
AND LOOK AT YOU.
CALM AS YOU PLEASE. HOW DARE YOU!
......
...HEY.

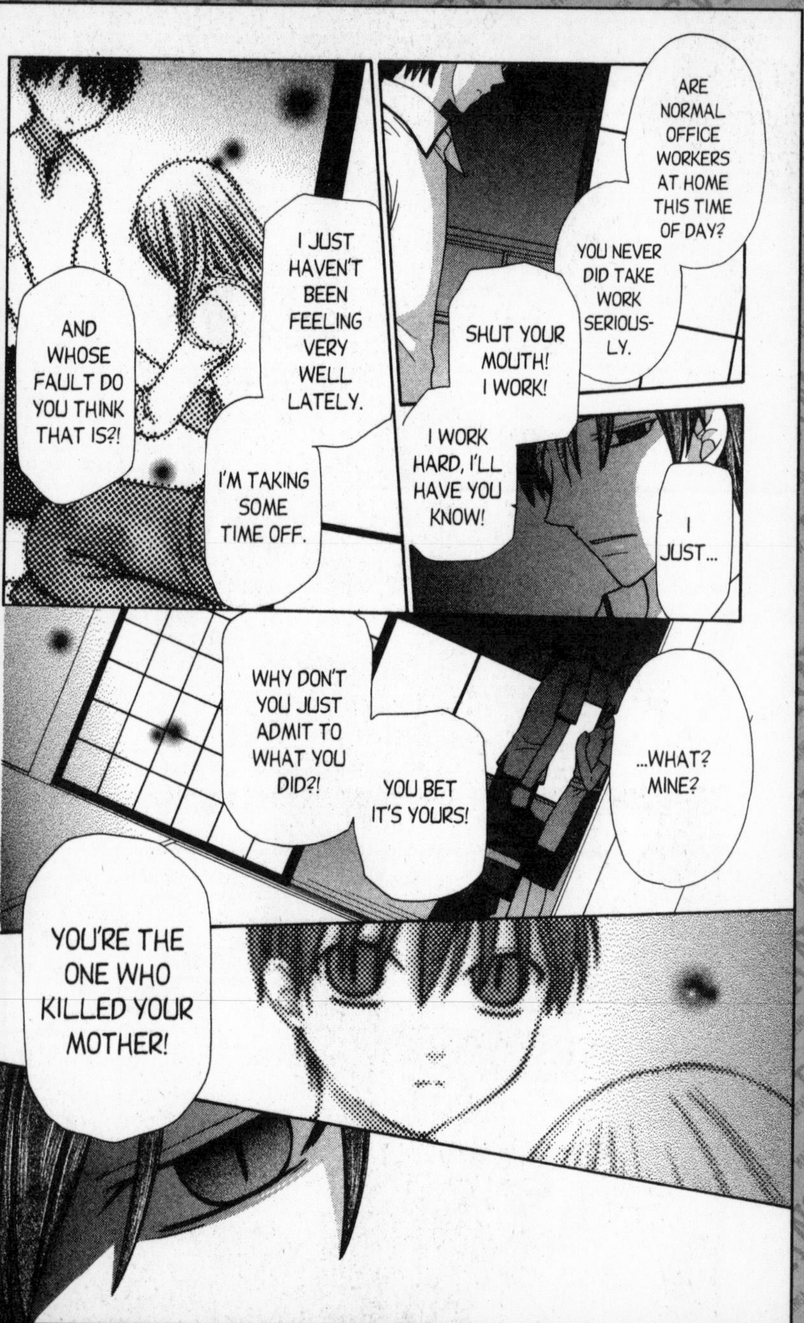
ARE NORMAL OFFICE WORKERS AT HOME THIS TIME OF DAY?
YOU NEVER DID TAKE WORK SERIOUS-LY.
SHUT YOUR MOUTH! I WORK!
I WORK HARD, I'LL HAVE YOU KNOW!
I JUST...
I JUST HAVEN'T BEEN FEELING VERY WELL LATELY.
I'M TAKING SOME TIME OFF.
AND WHOSE FAULT DO YOU THINK THAT IS?!
...WHAT? MINE?
YOU BET IT'S YOURS!
WHY DON'T YOU JUST ADMIT TO WHAT YOU DID?!
YOU'RE THE ONE WHO KILLED YOUR MOTHER!

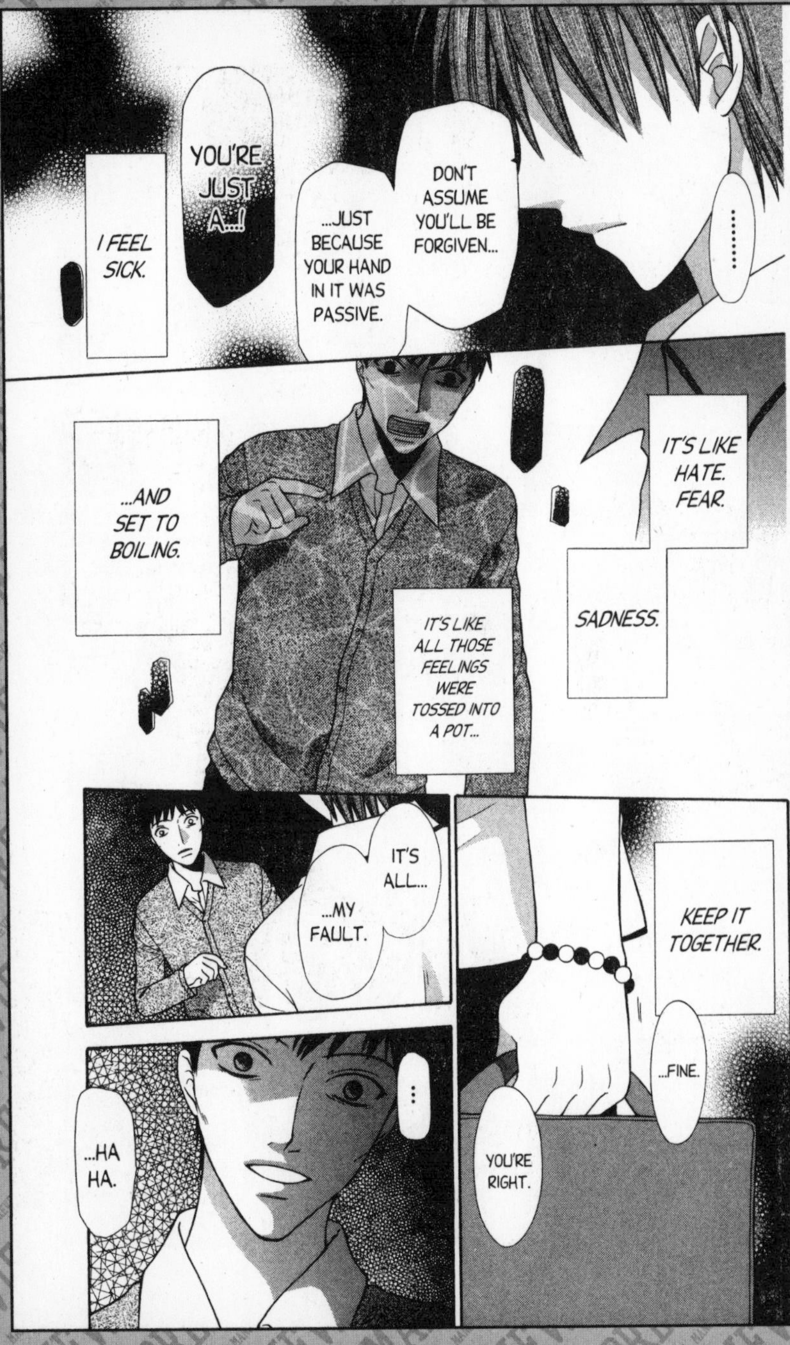
....
DON'T ASSUME YOU'LL BE FORGIVEN...
...JUST BECAUSE YOUR HAND IN IT WAS PASSIVE.
YOU'RE JUST A...!
I FEEL SICK.
IT'S LIKE HATE. FEAR.
SADNESS.
IT'S LIKE ALL THOSE FEELINGS WERE TOSSED INTO A POT...
...AND SET TO BOILING.
KEEP IT TOGETHER.
...FINE.
YOU'RE RIGHT.
IT'S ALL...
...MY FAULT.
...
...HA HA.

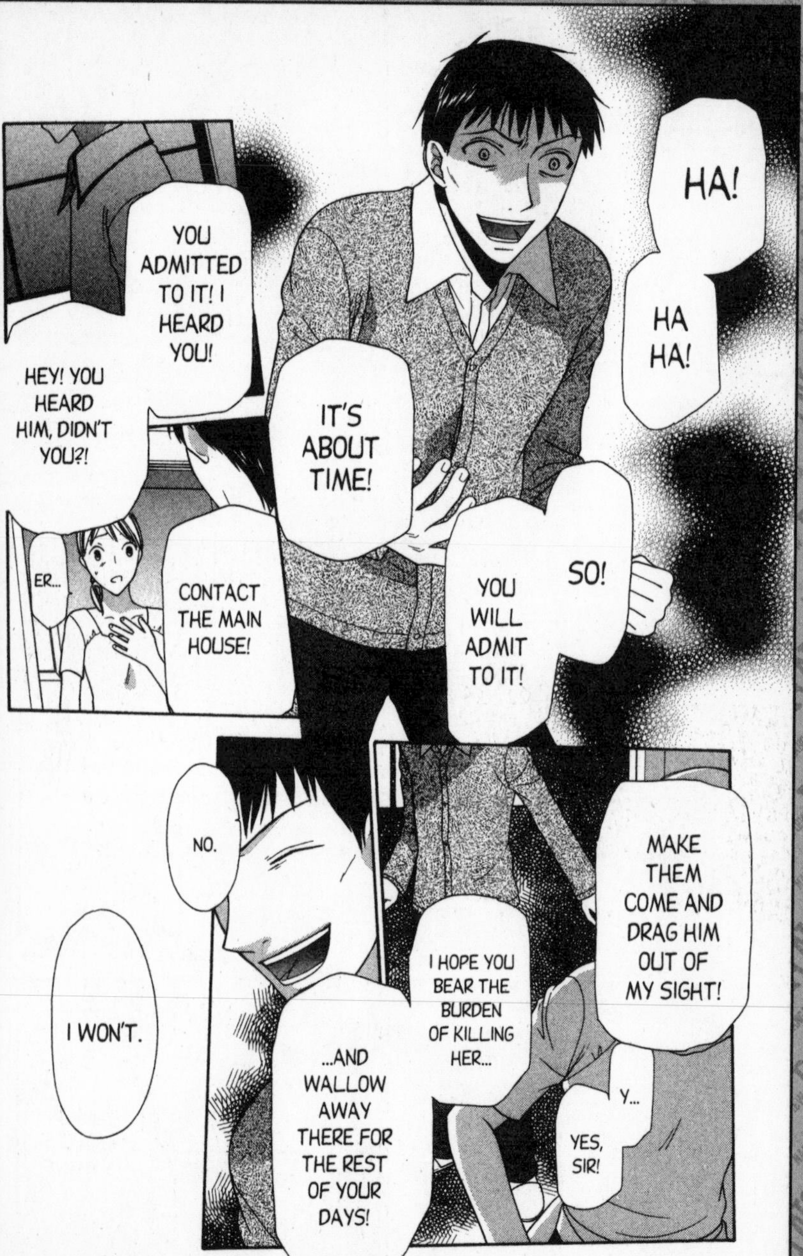
HA!
HA HA!
IT'S ABOUT TIME!
SO!
YOU WILL ADMIT TO IT!
YOU ADMITTED TO IT! I HEARD YOU!
HEY! YOU HEARD HIM, DIDN'T YOU?!
CONTACT THE MAIN HOUSE!
ER...
MAKE THEM COME AND DRAG HIM OUT OF MY SIGHT!
Y...
YES, SIR!
NO.
I WON'T.
I HOPE YOU BEAR THE BURDEN OF KILLING HER...
...AND WALLOW AWAY THERE FOR THE REST OF YOUR DAYS!

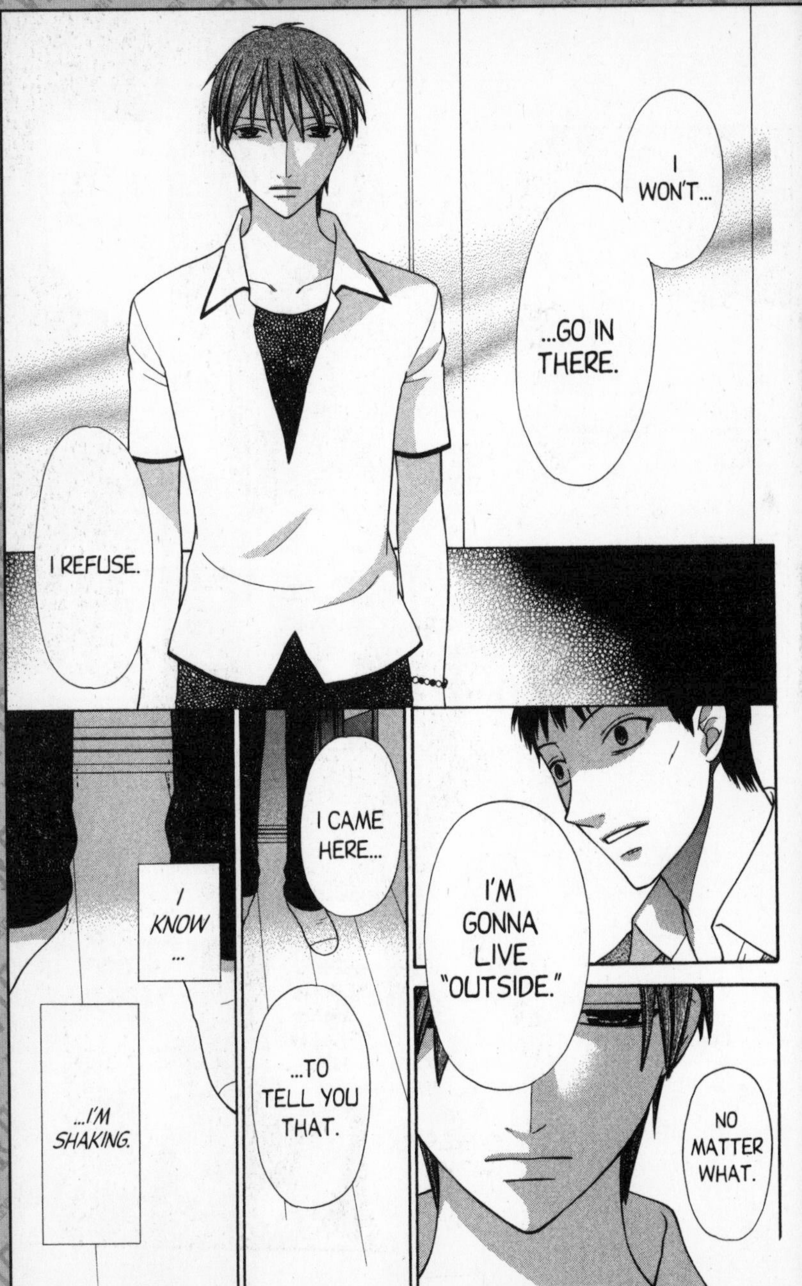
I WON'T...
...GO IN THERE.
I REFUSE.
I'M GONNA LIVE "OUTSIDE."
NO MATTER WHAT.
I CAME HERE...
...TO TELL YOU THAT.
I KNOW ...
...I'M SHAKING.

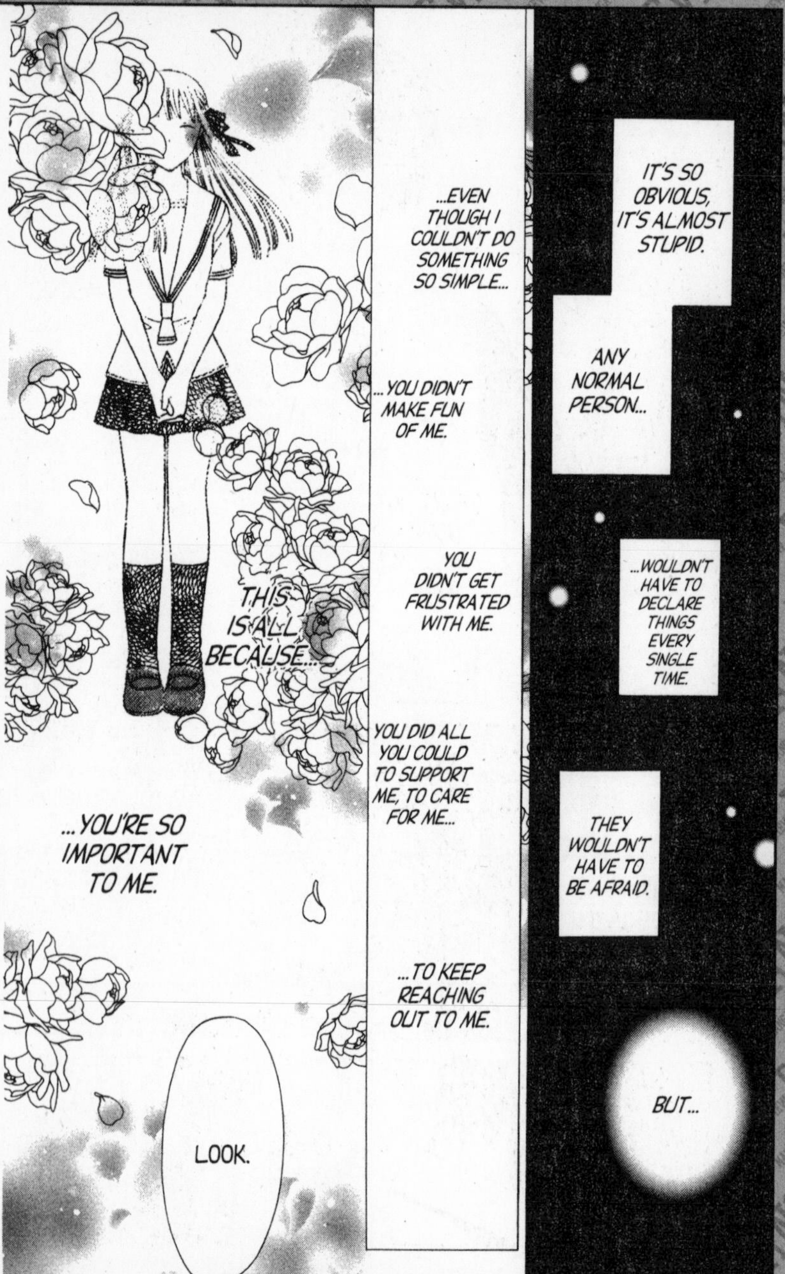
IT'S SO OBVIOUS, IT'S ALMOST STUPID.
ANY NORMAL PERSON...
...WOULDN'T HAVE TO DECLARE THINGS EVERY SINGLE TIME.
THEY WOULDN'T HAVE TO BE AFRAID.
BUT...
...EVEN THOUGH I COULDN'T DO SOMETHING SO SIMPLE...
...YOU DIDN'T MAKE FUN OF ME.
YOU DIDN'T GET FRUSTRATED WITH ME.
YOU DID ALL YOU COULD TO SUPPORT ME, TO CARE FOR ME...
...TO KEEP REACHING OUT TO ME.
THIS IS ALL BECAUSE...
...YOU'RE SO IMPORTANT TO ME.
LOOK.

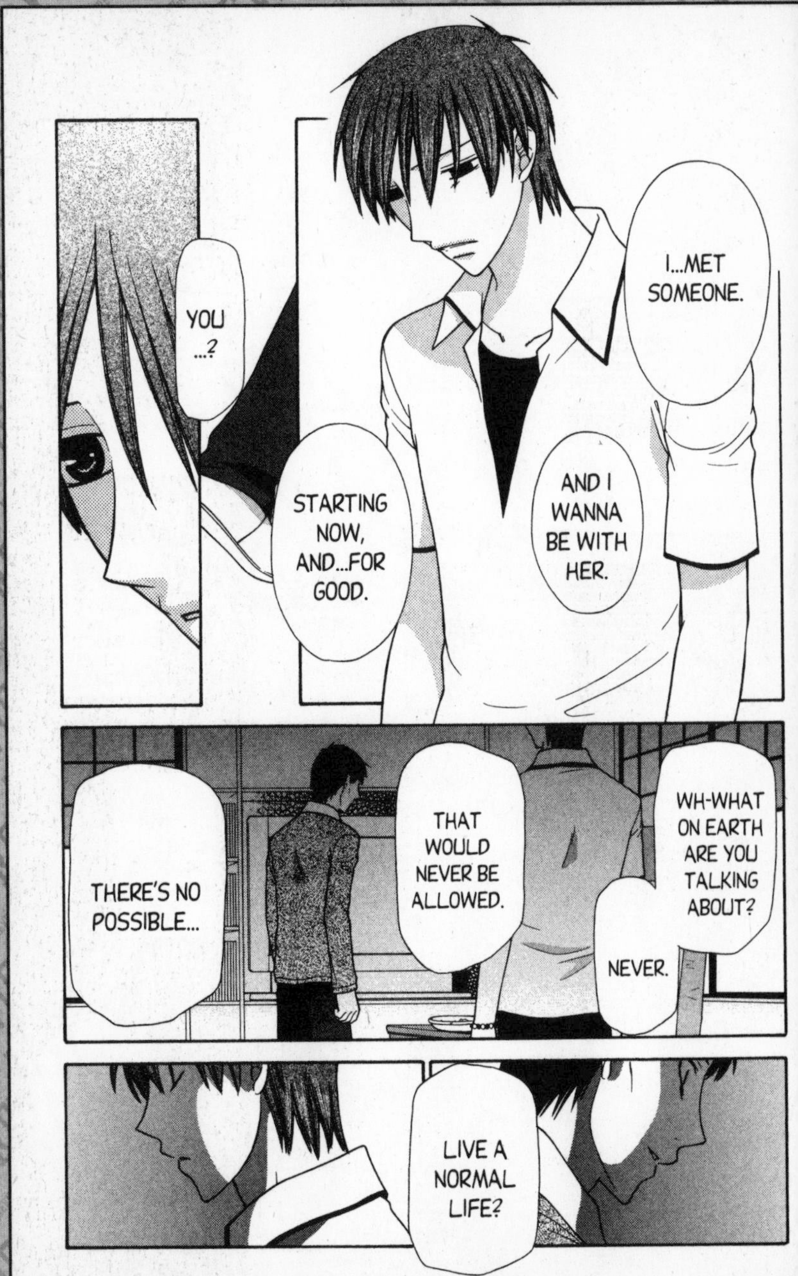
I...MET SOMEONE.
AND I WANNA BE WITH HER.
STARTING NOW, AND...FOR GOOD.
YOU ...?
WH-WHAT ON EARTH ARE YOU TALKING ABOUT?
NEVER.
THAT WOULD NEVER BE ALLOWED.
THERE'S NO POSSIBLE...
LIVE A NORMAL LIFE?

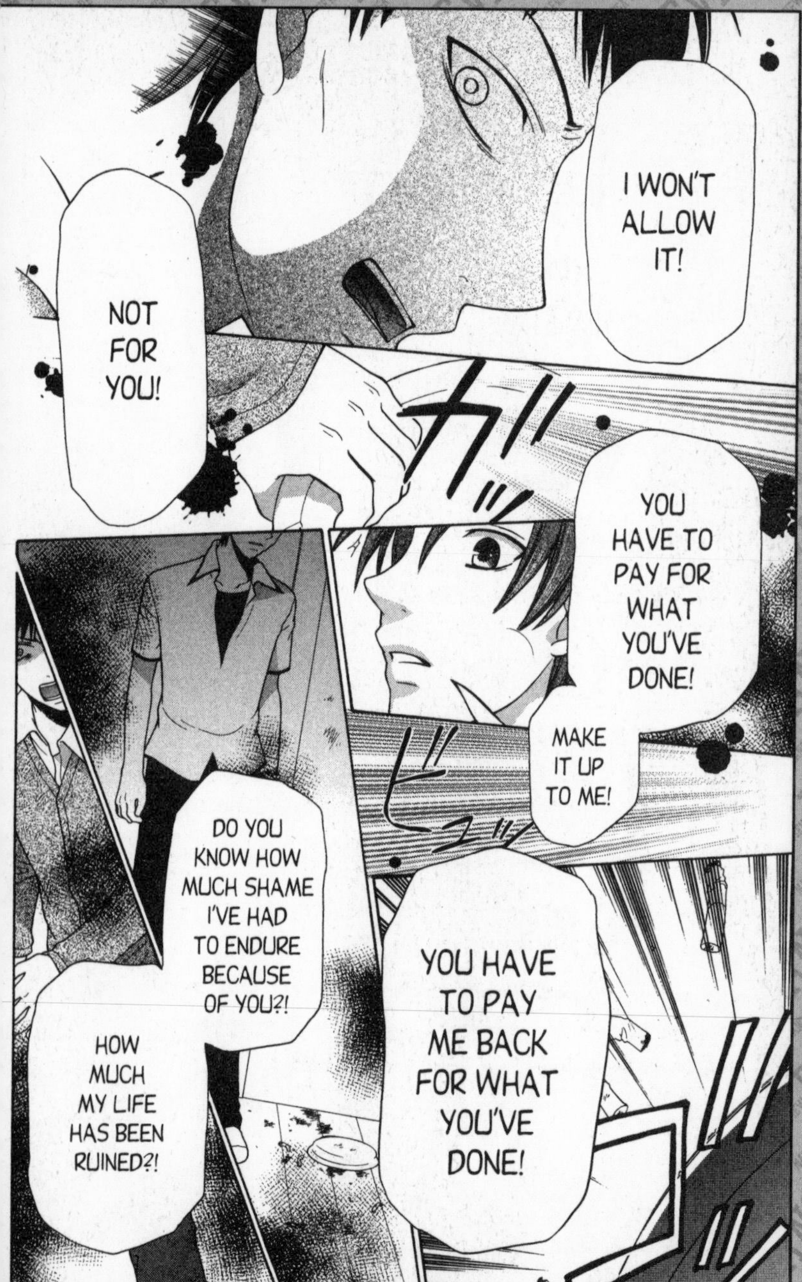
I WON'T ALLOW IT!
NOT FOR YOU!
ガッ
YOU HAVE TO PAY FOR WHAT YOU'VE DONE!
ビュッ
MAKE IT UP TO ME!
YOU HAVE TO PAY ME BACK FOR WHAT YOU'VE DONE!
DO YOU KNOW HOW MUCH SHAME I'VE HAD TO ENDURE BECAUSE OF YOU?!
HOW MUCH MY LIFE HAS BEEN RUINED?!

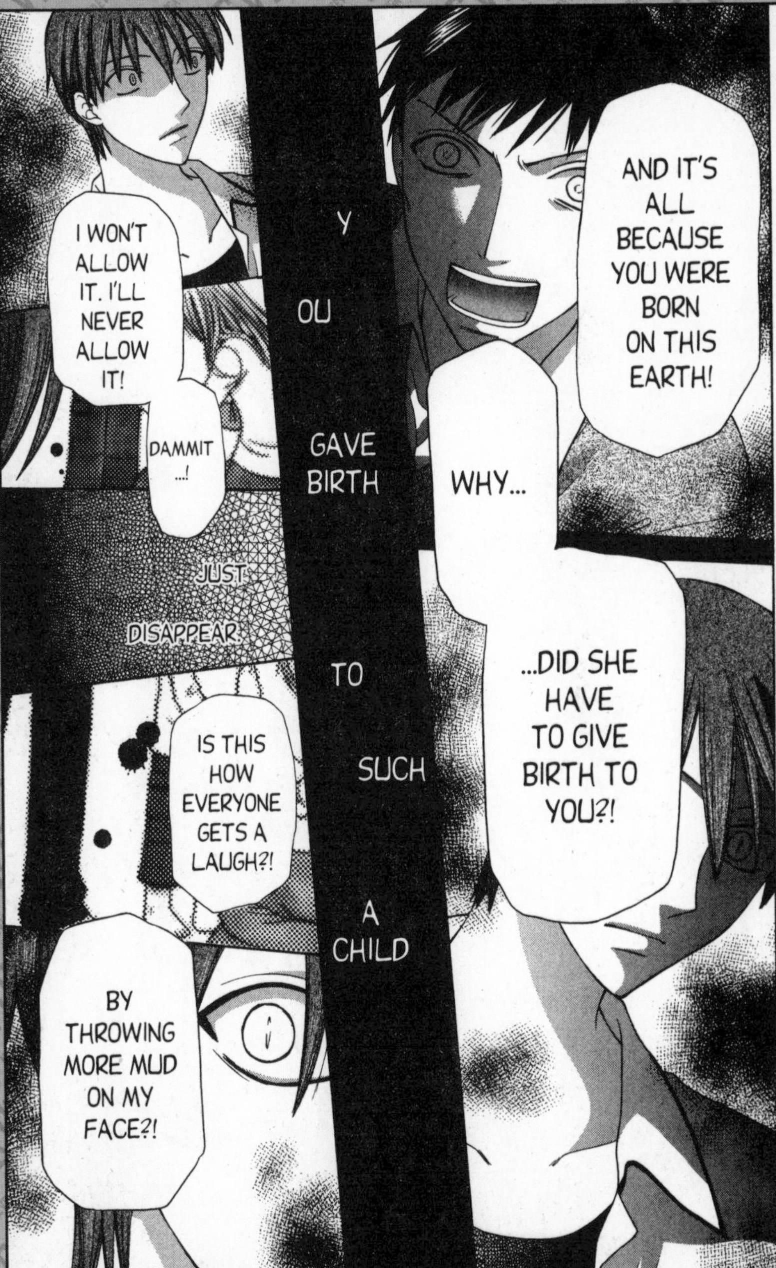
AND IT'S ALL BECAUSE YOU WERE BORN ON THIS EARTH!
I WON'T ALLOW IT. I'LL NEVER ALLOW IT!
DAMMIT ...!
Y OU GAVE BIRTH TO SUCH A CHILD
WHY...
...DID SHE HAVE TO GIVE BIRTH TO YOU?!
JUST DISAPPEAR.
IS THIS HOW EVERYONE GETS A LAUGH?!
BY THROWING MORE MUD ON MY FACE?!

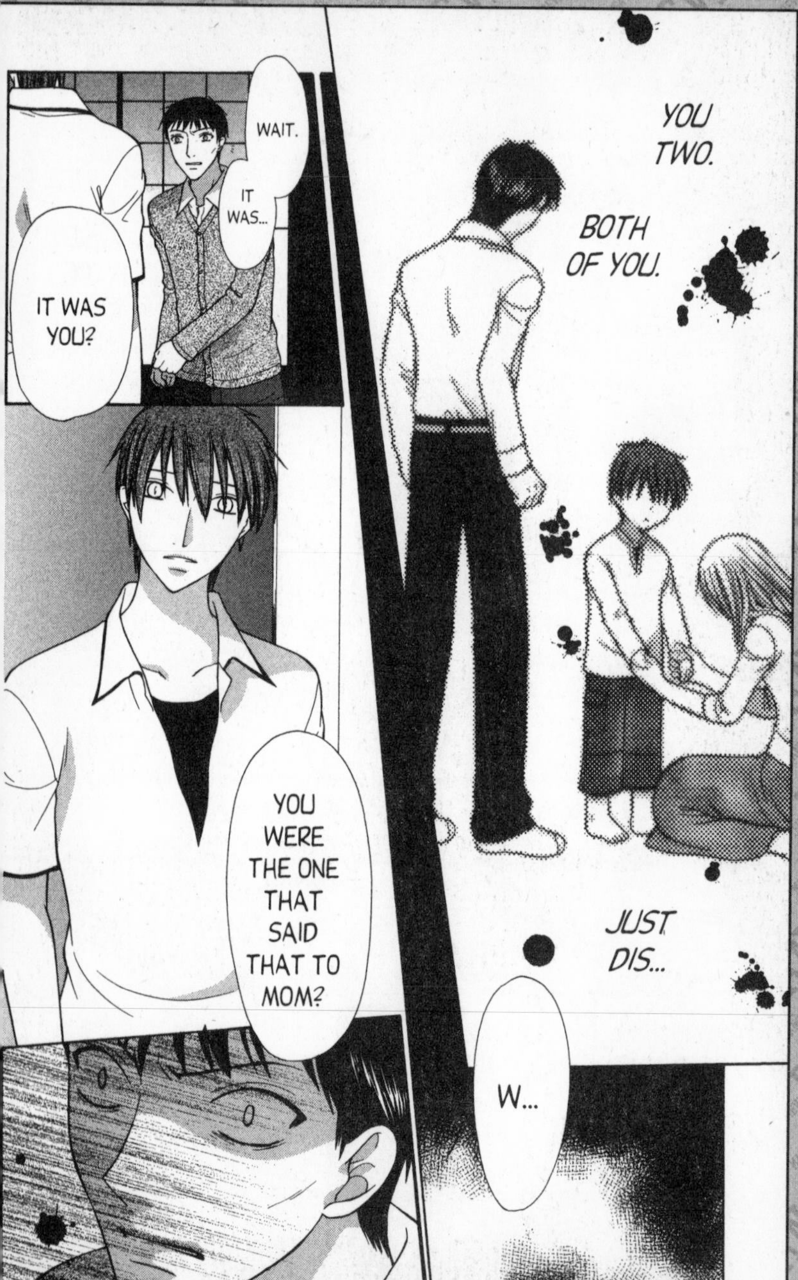
YOU TWO.
BOTH OF YOU.
JUST DIS...
WAIT.
IT WAS...
IT WAS YOU?
YOU WERE THE ONE THAT SAID THAT TO MOM?
W...

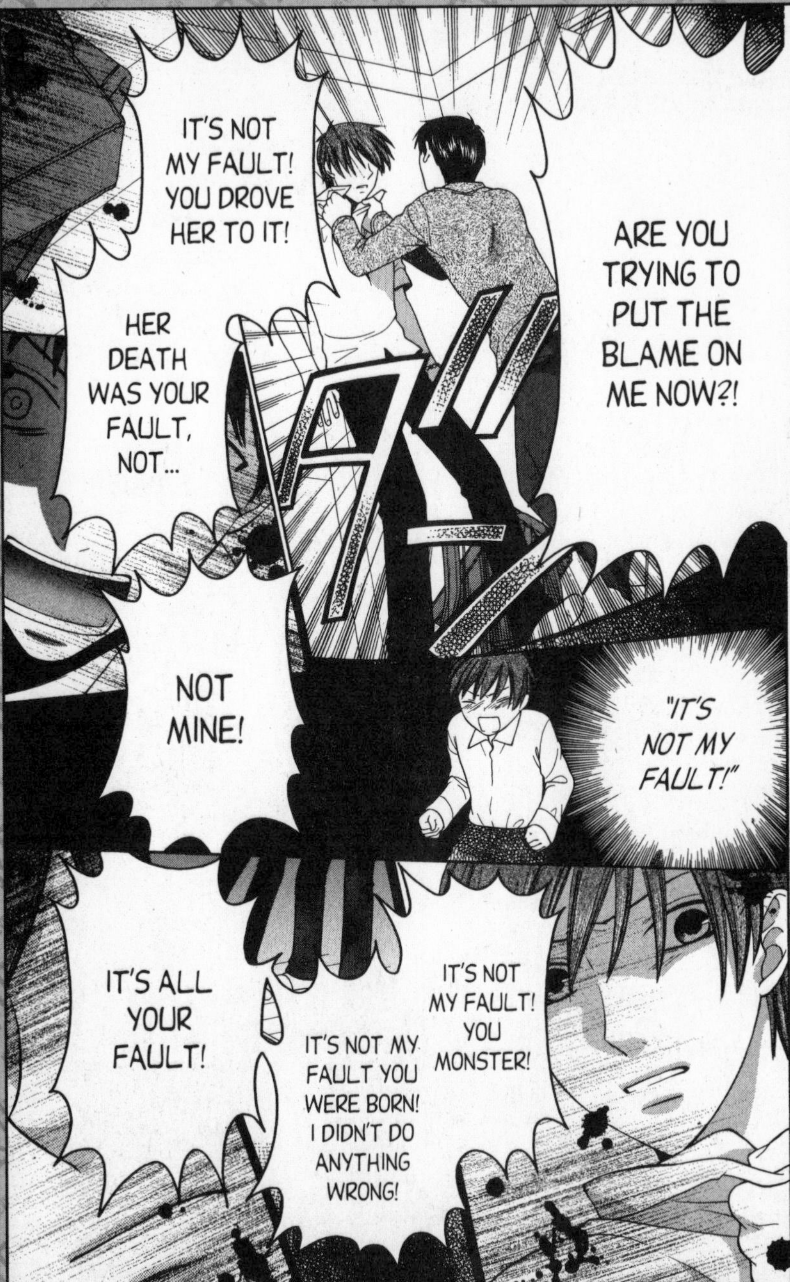
ARE YOU TRYING TO PUT THE BLAME ON ME NOW?!
IT'S NOT MY FAULT! YOU DROVE HER TO IT!
HER DEATH WAS YOUR FAULT, NOT...
"IT'S NOT MY FAULT!"
NOT MINE!
IT'S NOT MY FAULT! YOU MONSTER!
IT'S NOT MY FAULT YOU WERE BORN! I DIDN'T DO ANYTHING WRONG!
IT'S ALL YOUR FAULT!

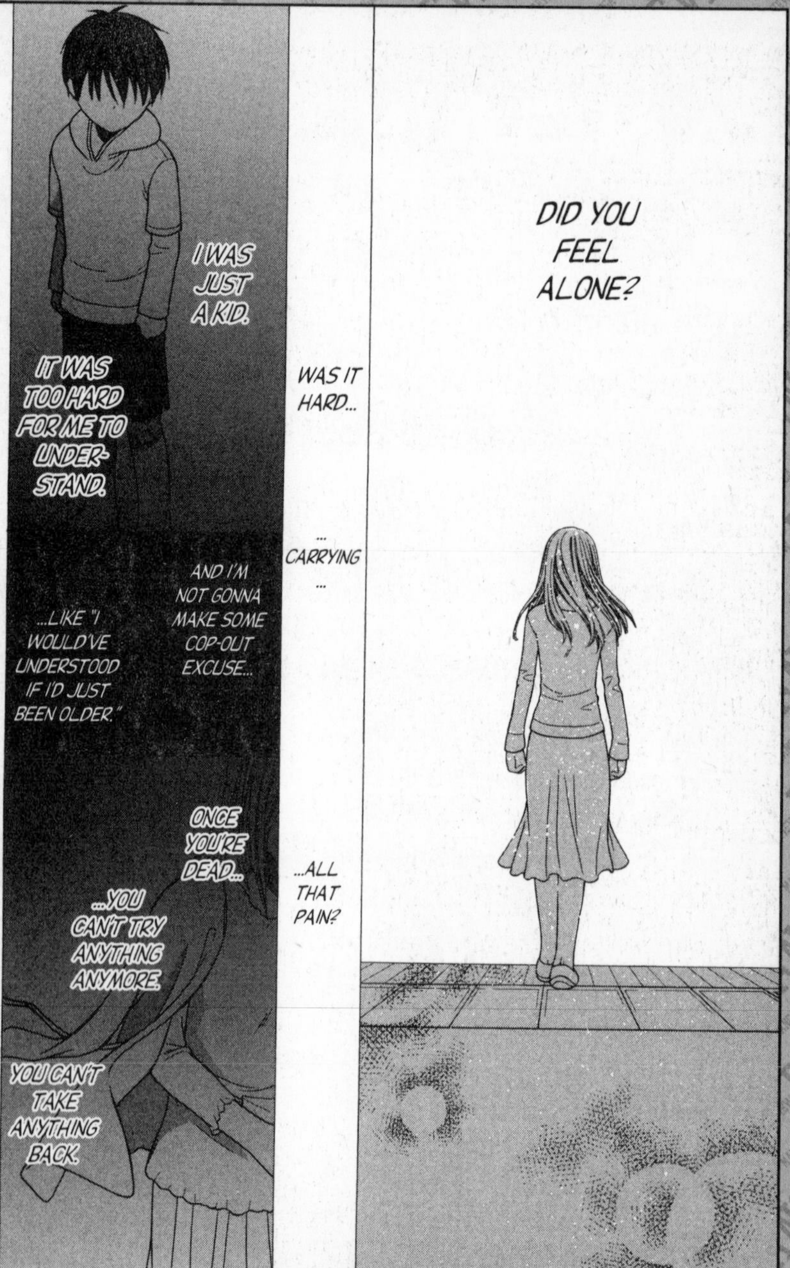
DID YOU FEEL ALONE?
WAS IT HARD...
... CARRYING ...
...ALL THAT PAIN?
I WAS JUST A KID.
IT WAS TOO HARD FOR ME TO UNDER-STAND.
AND I'M NOT GONNA MAKE SOME COP-OUT EXCUSE...
...LIKE "I WOULD'VE UNDERSTOOD IF I'D JUST BEEN OLDER."
ONCE YOU'RE DEAD...
...YOU CAN'T TRY ANYTHING ANYMORE.
YOU CAN'T TAKE ANYTHING BACK.

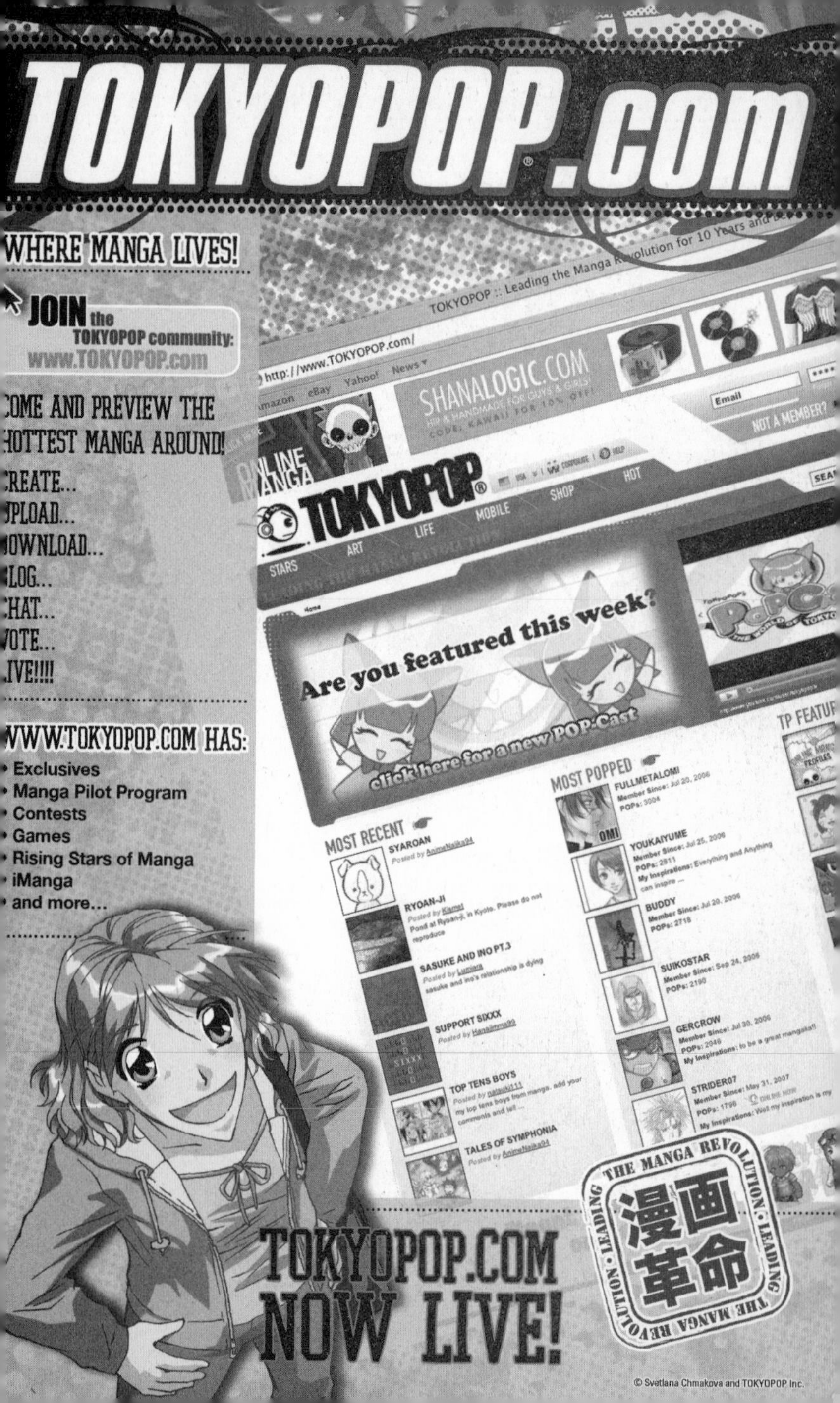
TOKYOPOP.com
WHERE MANGA LIVES!
JOIN the TOKYOPOP community:
www.TOKYOPOP.com
COME AND PREVIEW THE HOTTEST MANGA AROUND!
CREATE...
UPLOAD...
DOWNLOAD...
BLOG...
CHAT...
VOTE...
LIVE!!!!
WWW.TOKYOPOP.COM HAS:
• Exclusives
• Manga Pilot Program
• Contests
• Games
• Rising Stars of Manga
• iManga
• and more...
TOKYOPOP :: Leading the Manga Revolution for 10 Years and
http://www.TOKYOPOP.com/
SHANALOGIC.COM
TOKYOPOP
STARS
ART
LIFE
MOBILE
SHOP
HOT
Are you featured this week?
click here for a new POP-Cast
MOST RECENT
MOST POPPED
TP FEATU
TOKYOPOP.COM NOW LIVE!
THE MANGA REVOLUTION • LEADING THE MANGA REVOLUTION • LEADING
漫画革命
© Svetlana Chmakova and TOKYOPOP Inc.

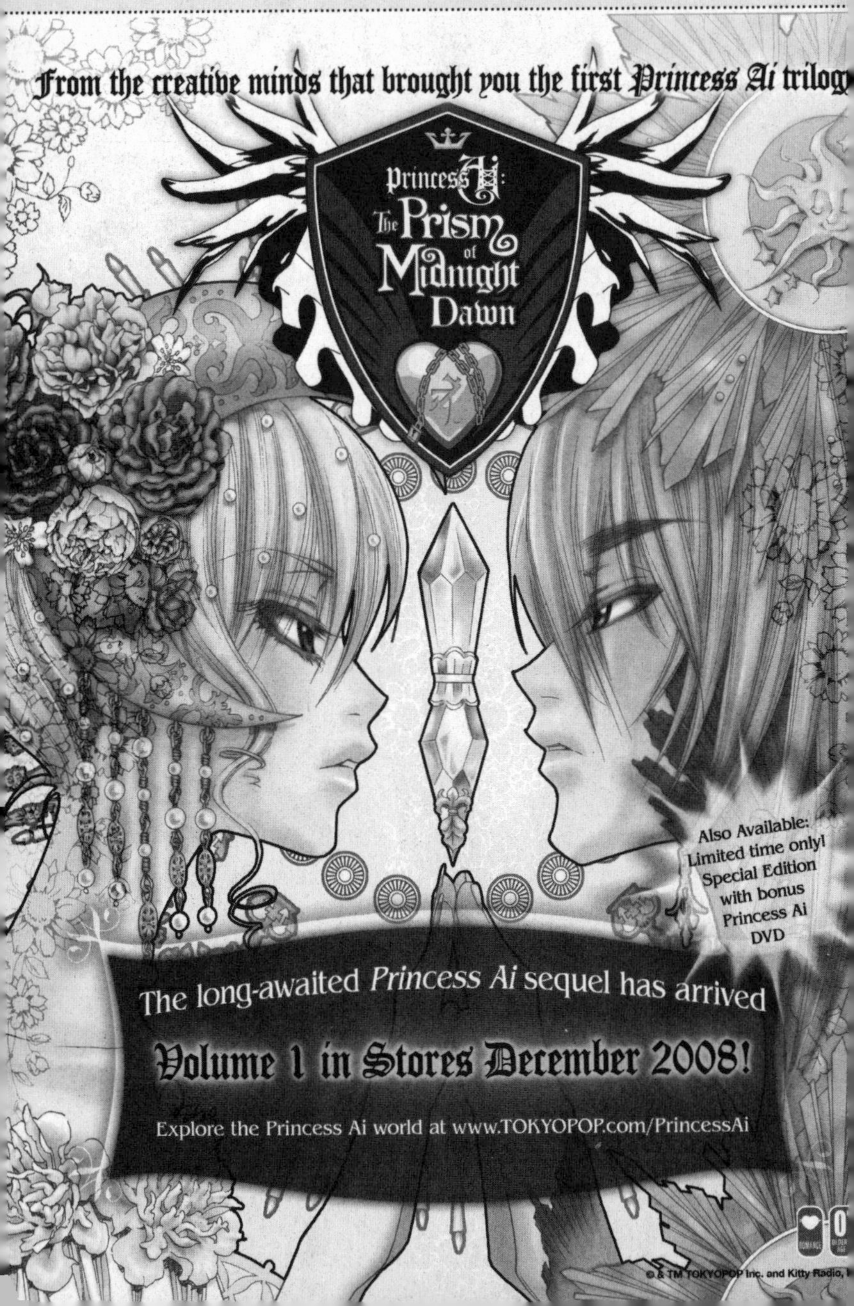
From the creative minds that brought you the first Princess Ai trilog
Princess Ai: The Prism of Midnight Dawn
Also Available: Limited time only! Special Edition with bonus Princess Ai DVD
The long-awaited *Princess Ai* sequel has arrived
Volume 1 in Stores December 2008!
Explore the Princess Ai world at www.TOKYOPOP.com/PrincessAi
© & TM TOKYOPOP Inc. and Kitty Radio,

STORY

This is
You wouldn't

This book is printed "manga-style," in the authentic Japanese right-to-left format. Since none of the artwork has been flipped or altered, readers get to experience the story just as the creator intended. You've been asking for it, so TOKYOPOP® delivered: authentic, hot-off-the-press, and far more fun!

DIRECTIONS

If this is your first time reading manga-style, here's a quick guide to help you understand how it works.

It's easy... just start in the top right panel and follow the numbers. Have fun, and look for more 100% authentic manga from TOKYOPOP®!